Cambridge Studies in Early Modern British History

THE BLIND DEVOTION OF THE PEOPLE

Cambridge Studies in Early Modern British History

Series editors

ANTHONY FLETCHER
Professor of Modern History, University of Durham

JOHN GUY
Reader in British History, University of Bristol

and JOHN MORRILL
*Lecturer in History, University of Cambridge, and
Fellow and Tutor of Selwyn College*

This is a series of monographs and studies covering many aspects of the history of the British Isles between the late fifteenth century and the early eighteenth century. It includes the work of established scholars and pioneering work by a new generation of scholars. It includes both reviews and revisions of major topics and books which open up new historical terrain or which reveal startling new perspectives on familiar subjects. All the volumes set detailed research into broader perspectives and the books are intended for the use of students as well as of their teachers.

Titles in the series

The Common Peace: Participation and the Criminal Law in Seventeenth-Century England
   CYNTHIA B. HERRUP
Politics, Society and Civil War in Warwickshire, 1620–1660
   ANN HUGHES
London Crowds in the Reign of Charles II: Propaganda and Politics from the Restoration to the Exclusion Crisis
   TIM HARRIS
Criticism and Compliment: The Politics of Literature in the England of Charles I
   KEVIN SHARPE
Central Government and the Localities: Hampshire, 1649–1689
   ANDREW COLEBY
John Skelton and the Politics of the 1520s
   GREG WALKER
Algernon Sidney and the English Republic, 1623–1677
   JONATHAN SCOTT
Thomas Starkey and the Commonweal: Humanist Politics and Religion in the Reign of Henry VIII
   THOMAS F. MAYER
The Blind Devotion of the People: Popular Religion and the English Reformation
   ROBERT WHITING
The Cavalier Parliament and the Reconstruction of the Old Regime, 1661–1667
   PAUL SEAWARD

THE BLIND DEVOTION OF THE PEOPLE

Popular religion and the English Reformation

ROBERT WHITING

Senior Lecturer in History, the College of Ripon and York St John

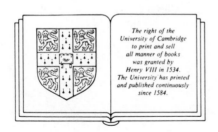

The right of the
University of Cambridge
to print and sell
all manner of books
was granted by
Henry VIII in 1534.
The University has printed
and published continuously
since 1584.

CAMBRIDGE UNIVERSITY PRESS

Cambridge
New York   Port Chester
Melbourne   Sydney

Published by the Press Syndicate of the University of Cambridge
The Pitt Building, Trumpington Street, Cambridge CB2 1RP
40 West 20th Street, New York, NY 10011–4211, USA
10 Stamford Road, Oakleigh, Melbourne 3166, Australia

First published 1989
First paperback edition 1991

Printed in Great Britain at The Bath Press, Avon

British Library cataloguing in publication data
Whiting, Robert
The blind devotion of the people: popular religion
and the English Reformation.
1. England. Christian Church. Reformation   I. Title
274.2

Library of Congress cataloguing in publication data
Whiting, Robert, 1949–
The blind devotion of the people: popular religion
and the English Reformation / Robert Whiting.
p.   cm. – (Cambridge studies in early modern British history)
Bibliography: p.
Includes index.
ISBN 0 521 35606 7
1. Reformation – England.   2. England – Religious life and
customs.   3. England – Church history – 16th century.   I. Title.
II. Series. BR377.W48   1989
274.2'06 – dc 19   88-29233 CIP

ISBN 0 521 35606 7 hardback
ISBN 0 521 42439 9 paperback

BS

For the ladies in my life:
Rowena, Victoria and Alexandra

CONTENTS

ILLUSTRATIONS

PREFACE

Over the sixteen years in which this book has been in preparation, I have accumulated debts of gratitude to an ever-increasing number of individuals and institutions.

For their tireless and invariably courteous assistance in the location, procurement and use of source material, I am indebted to the archivists, librarians and staff of the British Library; Cambridge University Library; the College of Ripon and York St John Library; the Cornwall Record Office; the Dean and Chapter Library, Exeter; the Devon and Cornwall Record Society Library; Devon County Library; the Devon Record Office; Exeter City Library; the Exeter Record Office; Exeter University Library; the Public Record Office; the library of Trinity College, Cambridge; and the York Minster Library. I am grateful also to Mr F. L. Harris for kindly loaning his transcript of the Antony churchwardens' accounts.

Amongst the many constructive suggestions and comments received from fellow-labourers in the field of Reformation studies, I have particularly appreciated those from Dr C. S. L. Davies, Dr J. Guy, Dr A. Kreider, Dr N. Orme and Dr W. J. Shiels. I wish especially to record my thanks to Professor J. A. Youings, who supervised the doctoral research on which this book is based and who has consistently encouraged me to secure its publication; her advice and support I have greatly valued. I am most grateful to Mr R. F. Whiting, Mrs C. I. Whiting and Mr D. Batten for the photographs in this book, and to Mr J. Lindley for his assistance with the maps. I wish also to record my thanks to Richard Fisher and John Guy for their invaluable help with the text. For their encouragement and patience during my seemingly endless research and writing, I am most grateful also to my mother and father; to my friends Julian Fraser and John and Elizabeth Lower; to my colleagues in the history department at the College of Ripon and York St John; and, above all, to my wife Rowena. Their suffering is now over – at least until the next book.

NOTE

In all quotations from primary sources, spelling and punctuation have been modernized and standardized. All dates in the text are new style.

Unless otherwise indicated, the following reference conventions have been employed:

(a) References to individual churchwardens' accounts and corporation accounts are to compilation date. Thus 'CWA Woodbury, 1546' refers to the account compiled by the Woodbury wardens in 1546, and 'CWA Woodbury, 1548–9' to the accounts compiled by them in 1548 and 1549. A query preceding the reference (e.g. '? CWA Exeter SP, 1570') indicates an uncertain interpretation; a query following the date (e.g. 'CWA S. Tawton, 1566?') indicates an uncertain date.

(b) References to *Ancient Cornish Drama* and *Beunans Meriasek* are to line numbers.

(c) References to *LP* are to document numbers.

1

Introduction

In the sixteenth century, the religion of the mass of the English people was subjected by their governments to a series of unprecedented and increasingly destructive assaults.

In the 1520s official attitudes towards the activities and institutions of traditional Catholicism were still essentially supportive. The seven sacraments and a wide range of additional ceremonies, as well as prayers and masses on behalf of the dead, the invocation of saints, and the veneration of images and relics, all continued to enjoy official approbation. So, in most respects, did the papacy, the secular clergy, the monastic orders, the parish churches and the religious guilds. In 1521 Henry VIII indeed received from the pope the title of Defender of the Faith.

From 1529, however, a complex of financial, political and personal factors combined with the influence of Cromwell and Cranmer to substantially modify this official support. An increasingly hostile attitude to the papacy, which in 1532–3 produced Acts against its revenue and jurisdiction, culminated in the Act declaring royal supremacy over the national Church in 1534. This was followed in 1536–9 by the governmental suppression of all monastic houses. Meanwhile the privileges of the secular clergy were eroded, particularly by the limitation of probate and mortuary fees in 1529, and its status as the prime provider of religious knowledge was implicitly undermined by the legitimization of the English Bible in 1538. Important practices were also attacked. The founding of chantries was restricted in 1529, and the confiscation of their property threatened by a statute of 1545. Saints' days were reduced in 1536. The royal injunctions of 1536 and 1538 prohibited pilgrimage, relic veneration, and offering to images. Despite the theologically conservative Six Articles of 1539, and the intermittent persecution of Lollards and Protestants, the reign of Henry VIII thus witnessed an unmistakable change in governmental attitudes towards vital components of the traditional religion.

Between 1547 and 1553 – under the boy king Edward VI, councillors like Somerset and Northumberland, and Archbishop Cranmer – official anta-

1

gonism was increasingly explicit. It was again impelled by economics and politics as much as by theology. The clergy were further reduced in number, particularly by the chantry dissolutions, and in status, especially by the legalization of clerical marriage, the new ordinal and the new services. The wealth of parish churches was attacked, plate, vestments and other treasures suffering official confiscation. The local religious guilds were suppressed. Traditional practices were prohibited by the royal injunctions of 1547 and by subsequent legislation; they included the display of roods and other images, prayers and masses on behalf of the dead, Easter vigils, and the use of holy bread, holy water, palms and ashes. The Latin mass was ousted by the English Prayerbook of 1549, and altars were banned in 1550. The Prayerbook of 1552 was even more overtly anti-Catholic.

Between 1553 and 1558 the reign of Mary Tudor brought a temporary reversal of governmental policies. Papal authority was restored, monasteries legitimized, and married clerics deprived. The confiscation of church goods ceased, and religious guilds were again permitted. Amongst the activities now legal or obligatory were the Catholic sacraments, intercessions, saint invocation, relic veneration and image veneration, and the use of objects like holy bread and water. In 1555 the heresy laws were revived, and an extensive persecution of Protestants commenced.

Official hostility was renewed by the accession of Elizabeth I in 1558. Another wave of decrees, including in 1559 more royal injunctions and the Acts of Supremacy and Uniformity, again banished papal authority, monasteries and religious guilds, initiated a further confiscation of church goods, and prohibited Catholic sacraments and ceremonies as well as intercessions, relics, images and roods. Henceforth Catholicism was the consistent target of governmental disapproval, which would only be intensified by the papal excommunication of the queen in 1570. Within a generation, official attitudes towards the traditional religion had thus been transformed: support had been replaced by enmity.[1]

Changes in government policy are not difficult to chart; it is their impact upon the average man that remains so controversial and obscure. Precisely how did he respond to the assaults launched against the traditional activities and institutions? Did he acquiesce, or did he resist? By what internal motivations were his responses impelled? And by what types of external influence were these shaped? Such problems are patently crucial to an understanding of the English Reformation, yet the solutions proffered by historians have been far from wholly satisfactory. Even the recent and valuable series of local Reformation studies have to a large extent concentrated upon the

---

[1] For surveys as regards changing official attitudes, see, for example, Dickens 1967A; and Hughes 1950–4.

clergy and the gentry, the two best-documented social groups; the mass of the population has suffered relative neglect.[2]

For this reason the present study will focus primarily upon the laity below the level of the gentry. It will commence on the eve of the Reformation, traverse the Henrician, Edwardian, Marian and Elizabethan upheavals, and end with the papal excommunication of 1570. And it will concentrate its attention upon a specific region: the south-western peninsula, which in the sixteenth century consisted of two counties (Devon and Cornwall) and constituted one diocese (Exeter). Several factors make this a particularly suitable region for investigation. Firstly, it contained a substantial portion – probably more than 5% – of Tudor England's total population. Secondly, it has almost invariably been depicted as a classic example of the alleged relationship between remoteness from London and resistance to religious change. This interpretation has usually been supported by reference to the 'Prayerbook rebellion' of 1549. Thirdly, its experience of the Reformation has not until now been comprehensively researched. Selected aspects of the topic have been studied by scholars like W. T. MacCaffrey, A. L. Rowse and J. A. Youings,[3] but no full-scale analysis has yet been essayed. The fourth factor is the most important. The South-West offers the historian a comparative wealth of primary evidence from which to reconstruct the impact of the Reformation at an authentically popular level.

Among the potential sources of evidence most frequently underutilized in conventional histories are the extant art and architecture of parish churches. For example, the importance of intercessory masses for individuals or guilds on the eve of the Reformation is clearly attested by the number of chapels still visible within the region's churches. Pier-niches demonstrate the popularity of image-cults. The proliferation of pulpits and benches suggests an increasing emphasis upon the sermon. Sculptures, wood-carvings, screen-paintings, wall-paintings and stained glass provide insights into devotional idioms before the Reformation; they may also betray the iconoclastic impact of the Reformation itself.[4]

Nevertheless it is upon the documentary sources that historians must primarily rely. Of these a number may be categorized as unofficial. Pre-Reforma-

---

[2] See below, pp. 262–8.
[3] MacCaffrey 1958; Rowse 1941; Youings 1979. See also Cornwall 1977; Rose-Troup 1913; Whiting 1982; and Whiting 1983.
[4] References to art and architecture are based largely upon an extensively personal examination of south-western churches. The pre-eminent authorities are Pevsner 1952A; 1952B; and Pevsner and Radcliffe 1970. Also valuable are Anderson 1955; Bond 1908; 1910; Bond and Camm 1909; Caiger-Smith 1963; Cave 1948; Cook 1954; Cox 1915; 1916; Cox and Ford 1943–4; Crabbe 1854; Dunkin 1882; Ellacombe 1872; Henderson 1923–4; 1925; Hoskins 1954; Nelson 1913; Rogers 1877; Rushforth 1927A; 1927B; Slader 1968; Smith 1969; and Stabb 1909–16.

tion examples include a Cornish miracle play, written in 1504, and an early-Tudor legend concerning one of Cornwall's celebrated relics. Among works from the Reformation period itself are John Leland's record of his travels through Devon and Cornwall between 1535 and 1543, with its information on local cults; three tracts on contemporary religious issues by Philip Nichols, a Devonian who probably lived at Totnes, between 1547 and 1549; the predominantly religious 'articles' devised by the leaders of the south-western rebellion in 1549; and the epistle of a minister, William Ramsey, to his former congregation at South Molton in 1562. Later works include Nicholas Roscarrock's 'Lives of the Saints', with its emphasis on the cults of his native Cornwall; the *Survey of Cornwall* compiled by another Cornishman, Richard Carew; the *Acts and Monuments* of John Foxe, who records the region's two Protestant martyrdoms; and, of pre-eminent importance, the writings of Exeter's John Hooker. Events in Tudor Exeter are chronicled by Hooker in his Commonplace Book, while his 'Description of the City of Exeter' contains the fullest early narrative of the south-western rebellion. Also useful are his 'Synopsis Chorographical' of Devon and his 'Life' of the Devonian Sir Peter Carew.[5] Although writing mainly in Elizabeth's reign, Roscarrock, Carew, Foxe and Hooker drew upon earlier records and upon consultation with witnesses. Roscarrock gathered information on the ancient cults from local men and women, who still spoke 'by tradition of their predecessors'. Foxe's accounts of the local martyrs were based upon the testimony of a minister at Exeter in 1531 and of eyewitnesses in the same city in 1558. Hooker's description of the preaching of Hugh Latimer at Exeter in 1534 must have been based upon the memories of his own father, who had attended it. Personal recollections were also included. Hooker, when about 24, had seen the revolt of 1549 from within Exeter itself, and Roscarrock remembered, from his childhood, the Marian reaction.[6]

The value of these unofficial sources is further enhanced by the diversity of their religious orientations. The author of the Cornish miracle play, the composers of the rebel articles and Nicholas Roscarrock were all committed

---

[5] For Nichols' authorship of 'An Answer to the Articles' (Royal 18 B XI), see Scheurweghs 1933–4. For his Totnes connection, note (a) his presence at sermons in the neighbouring parishes of Marldon and Harberton (*Copy of a Letter*, pp. 10, 32); and (b) the early existence of a Protestant group at Totnes (see below, pp. 152, 155–6, 165). For Roscarrock, see Rowse 1955. For Foxe, see Mozley 1940, esp. pp. 118–203.

[6] For records, see, for example, 'Lives of Saints', fols. 131, 296v, 393v. For witnesses, see *Survey of Cornwall*, p. 289; 'Lives of Saints', fols. 109v, 114v, 202v, 262, 296v, 312v, 323v; *Acts and Monuments*, II, pp. 1038, 2050–1; and Hooker, Commonplace Book, fol. 342. Foxe's 'minister' may have been William Kethe, who was (a) a preacher; (b) a 'native of Exeter'; (c) a Marian exile; and possibly (d) a sojourner with Foxe at Basle in Mary's reign (Garrett 1966, pp. 204–5). For recollections, see 'Description of Exeter', pp. 25–6; and 'Lives of Saints', fols. 312v, 360v.

to traditional Catholicism. Nichols, Ramsey, Carew, Foxe and Hooker, by contrast, were all resolutely hostile.

Sources of this type are supplemented by an even wider range of official records. Those compiled for the various organs of central government include state papers, proceedings of the Privy Council, bills of complaint from the Courts of Chancery and Star Chamber, and chantry certificates and church inventories for the use of the exchequer. Those compiled for institutions at the regional level include registers, act-books, deposition-books and wills for the Bishop of Exeter and his officials as well as the records of the dean and chapter. Of those produced for urban or parochial bodies, the most valuable are financial accounts; these were the work of appointed receivers or of elected churchwardens. Each type of record possesses both merits and limitations as a historical source. Legal depositions, for example, are often one-sided and prone to exaggeration. Two types, nevertheless, can provide particularly significant insights into the development of popular religion: the warden's account and the will.

Churchwardens' accounts appear to survive in greater number for the South-West than for most other regions of mid-Tudor England. Though varying considerably in completeness, significant sequences exist for the Exeter churches of Holy Trinity, St John's Bow, St Mary Steps and St Petrock; for the towns of Ashburton, Camborne, Chagford, Chudleigh, Crediton, Dartmouth, Modbury, North Molton, St Thomas-by-Launceston, Stratton and Tavistock; and for the more rural communities of Antony, Braunton, Broadhempston, Coldridge, Dartington, Iddesleigh, Kilmington, Molland, Morebath, North Petherwin, St Breock, South Tawton, Winkleigh, Woodbury and Woodland. The accounts thus detail the annual revenue and expenditure of parish churches in a variety of settlement types and in widely separated localities. They reveal, for example, the extent to which images were venerated before the Reformation, Bibles purchased in the reign of Henry VIII, altars removed in the time of Edward VI, and masses restored under Mary and suppressed under Elizabeth. The essential veracity of such accounts was ensured by their annual recitation before an assembly of parishioners, as occurred at Throwleigh in 1556. Since wardens were usually elected by the parishioners, their religious policies must generally have reflected the prevailing local attitudes. At St Gennys in 1558, the unpopularity of one warden's attitude to the restored Catholic rites in fact resulted in his dismissal from office by the Eight Men.[7]

Similarly revealing are the wills. Some, including those of Thomas Bond at Exeter in 1501 and of John Bougin at Totnes in 1548, were written

---

[7] CCB 855, fols. 43v, 409.

by the testator himself;[8] most were probably dictated to a clerical amanuensis.[9] Despite the wartime destruction of the diocese's probate records, abstracts and transcripts remain: some 221 relevant examples have been analysed in the preparation of this study. So have some 177 wills which, having been proved in the Prerogative Court of Canterbury, survive intact. Of the 398 testators thus represented, all composed their wills between 1520 and 1569. All were lay people from below the level of the gentry, and all owned property of some sort in the South-West, where all but a handful were evidently resident. The sample includes women – usually widows – as well as men, and inhabitants of towns as well as of rural communities. It consists of 30 wills from 1520 to 1529, 41 from 1530 to 1539, 146 from 1540 to 1549, 91 from 1550 to 1559 and 90 from 1560 to 1569.

Such numbers, while representing only a small percentage of the regional population, nevertheless permit a broad evaluation of religious trends. The opening formula of a will may reflect the testator's attitude to the saints; even if written by an amanuensis it can rarely have diverged drastically from the views of his client. In 1557, for example, Richard Friend of Ermington bequeathed his soul to God, Our Lady and the saints; he then confirmed the conservative nature of his faith by making bequests to intercessions and to images of saints. Formulae, nevertheless, may mislead: in 1528 Joan Tackle of Honiton made bequests to figures of the saints, but in her formula failed to invoke them.[10] More consistently valuable to the historian are the bequests themselves. These can indicate the changing levels of popular investment in intercessory prayers and masses, in images and shrines, in monasteries, friaries, guilds and parish churches, and in various associated components of religious life.

The present study commences with a broad survey of the Tudor South-West, outlining the geographical, economic, social, political and ecclesiastical contexts within which the Reformation occurred. Part One then attempts to assess the nature of popular responses to this revolution. It examines the reactions of men and women to the official attacks directed against the activities and institutions of traditional Catholicism. The aim of Part Two is to explain these reactions by evaluating the causal factors behind them. It investigates firstly the internal motivations by which they were impelled, and secondly the various forms of external influence by which they were shaped.

[8] PROB 11 13, fol. 198v; Murray, 3, John Bougin, 1548.
[9] In most cases this was probably the testator's parish priest. For example, one witness to the will made by Robert Potter of Christow in 1539 was his vicar (PROB 11 26, fol. 106).
[10] CCB 855A, fol. 311v; PROB 11 23, fol. 71.

2

Survey

A narrow neck of land, some 35 miles in width, constituted the sole physical connection between the south-western peninsula and the mainland of Tudor England. Since even this was largely blocked by the Blackdown and Brendon hills, access was normally restricted to the Blackdown–Brendon gap and to the Axe Valley. From this neck the peninsula thrust westwards for some 130 miles: it first broadened to a width of more than 70 miles in Devon, and then narrowed rapidly towards Cornwall's western tip. A ride of at least four days separated east Devon from London. Cornwall was even more remote: it retained its Celtic place names and, particularly in its western districts, its Celtic tongue.[1]

The northern coast of the peninsula was bounded by the Bristol Channel and the Atlantic, and its southern coast by the English Channel. From the lowlands arose extensive areas of hill country and three expanses of highland – Exmoor, Bodmin Moor and the central granite mass of Dartmoor. Streams, rivers and estuaries were abundant. The Taw, Torridge and Camel flowed to the northern coast, but most of the important rivers – including the Exe, Teign, Dart, Plym, Tamar, Fowey, Fal and Helford – ran south. Several originated on Dartmoor, the height of which combined with the maritime environment to ensure a heavy fall of rain.

Patterns of economic activity were largely determined by this physical matrix. Arable farming, producing grain, fruit and vegetables, prospered on the fertile lowland soils, as in the Vale of Exeter or between the Teign and the Dart. The main areas of cattle-raising – for leather, beef, milk, butter, cheese and cream – were the poorly soiled highlands like the fringes of Dartmoor. Sheep-farming, both for meat and for wool, was particularly important; it was strongest in districts with abundant grazing and with arable land requiring manure. Practised mainly in enclosed fields behind high, weather-protective hedges, agrarian activities of this nature remained

---

[1] The following survey is based primarily upon Hoskins 1954; MacCaffrey 1958; and Rowse 1941. Only material from other sources is separately referenced.

fundamental to the region's economy. Yet other enterprises were also important. Tin was extracted from the rich deposits, particularly in Cornwall but
also on Dartmoor. An extensive fishing industry was sustained by the numerous rivers, estuaries and harbours; by 1570 this had expanded to include
the fisheries of Newfoundland. Estuaries accommodated shipbuilding, while
local stone and timber provided material for the construction and furnishing
of houses, farms and churches. Among the most profitable of non-agrarian
activities were the spinning, weaving, fulling and dyeing of cloth. Concentrated in particular localities with access to sheep and to markets, as around
Exeter, this industry produced the celebrated 'kersey'.

When not appropriated by their producers, the products of these various
activities were usually marketed within the South-West. Yet there was valuable trade also with other areas of England, especially with London, as
well as with Wales, Ireland, France, Portugal, Spain and elsewhere. Tin,
fish and cloth constituted the chief exports; imports included wool, salt
and wine.

The sixteenth century witnessed a general though uneven expansion of
this regional economy. Arable and pastoral farming extended further into
the waste, cultivation intensified, sheep multiplied in number. The tin, fish
and cloth industries grew in size, and the volume of trade must have
increased: under Henry VIII the cloth customs of the Devon ports averaged
almost £1,500 per annum. Devon in fact ranked among the wealthiest counties of Tudor England. This expansion is attributable in part to technical
innovations, like the introduction of shaft-mining to supplement the traditional 'streaming' of tin; but the primary stimulus was provided by a significant
growth of population. The number of able-bodied men to be mustered in
Devon rose from 11,720 in 1524 to some 17,000 in 1569–70 – by which
date the region's population had probably passed the 250,000 mark.[2] The
causes of this demographic upsurge included immigration from other counties, and from across the Irish and English Channels, as well as a reduction
in epidemics. (Though still terrifying, as at Exeter in 1570, plague was
increasingly localized.) The consequences included not only an expanding
pool of labour but also a rising consumer demand for food, clothing and
other commodities.

Most of this population still lived in rural settlements, ranging from isolated farmsteads or hamlets to larger nucleated villages. A few dozen towns
could each number their inhabitants in hundreds, while Exeter, Plymouth,
Barnstaple, Totnes, Liskeard, Bodmin and probably others could boast more
than a thousand. Exeter, the largest, contained some 8,000; it ranked fifth
or sixth among England's provincial cities. The population of a settlement

[2] Hughes 1950–4, I, p. 34; Cornwall 1977, p. 95.

might be boosted by its administrative functions, as at Exeter, or by its monastic associations, as at Tavistock, but the determinants of size were primarily economic. Single farmsteads or hamlets were most common in districts like the Dartmoor borderlands, where farming was predominantly pastoral; nucleation was better suited to highly cultivable areas like the Vale of Exeter. Towns generally owed their size to industry or commerce. Many contained forges and workshops, and most organized weekly markets and annual fairs in addition to the daily trading of their shops and stalls. Farm produce was marketed in most towns, but other commodities had more specific outlets. Fish was particularly traded at Plymouth, tin at Ashburton, and cloth at Exeter, Tiverton, Cullompton, Crediton, Totnes, South Molton and elsewhere. Many of the largest towns were ports: Exeter, Plymouth, Barnstaple and several others were enriched primarily by maritime trade.

Communication between settlements was still hindered by extensive areas of moor, marsh and woodland. The region's topography and climate also ensured that roads were seldom straight, smooth or dry. Nevertheless the major towns were linked by main roads, and a network of secondary roads, lanes and trackways traversed most of the region. These were supplemented by bridges – like the stone structures surviving at Staverton and Holne – and by ferries across the chief estuaries. Such routes carried men and women on foot or on horseback, as well as livestock, pack-horses and horse- or ox-drawn wagons. The extant itineraries show that travel could be relatively rapid. It was fastest by boat or ship, either along the numerous navigable rivers of the South-West or along its extensive coastlines.

Most inhabitants of the peninsula earned their livelihood in economy-related occupations. These included the direct exploitation of natural resources, particularly by farming but also by fishing, quarrying and mining; the processing of raw materials, in the form of carpentry, masoncraft, smithing, leather-working, baking, brewing, butchering, or the manufacture and tailoring of cloth; and the distribution of finished products, by shopkeeping, commercial activity and related enterprises. The occupations of a smaller number were not directly economic: these ranged from the Church and the law to domestic service. Participation in more than one activity remained frequent, many tinners and cloth-workers, for example, doubling as small farmers. Distinct from all occupational groups stood the leisured and the unemployed. The former, consisting mainly of the nobility and gentry, depended primarily upon the receipt of rent. The latter, consisting largely of the sick, the old and the very young, depended upon public charity or familial support.

Between and within these groups the distribution of wealth remained conspicuously unequal. In 1530 the nobility and gentry, for example, ranged from a few great proprietors with extensive estates, and a select number of families with several manors each, down to the hundreds of minor gentlemen whose acres were comparatively few. The Courtenays received some £1,500 per annum, and the Bassetts, Carews and Fortescues several hundreds, whereas lesser families might live on £50–100. Ecclesiastical incomes were similarly diverse. The Bishop of Exeter enjoyed some £1,600, mainly from property in Devon and Cornwall. The Dean and Chapter of Exeter Cathedral received more than £1,000, and the incomes of a few well-beneficed clerics were substantial: in 1522 the goods of the vicar of Wendron were valued at £120. Most of the several hundred parish priests, by contrast, earned wages in the region of £10–20 per annum; chantry priests and other unbeneficed clerics invariably received less. The incomes of religious houses ranged from £986 at Tavistock Abbey to less than £29 at Kerswell Priory.

Other social groups were equally diverse. The distributive sector extended from a few great merchants like John Giles of Totnes, who was worth £520 in 1523, through to the multiplicity of lesser merchants and shopkeepers, and finally to their apprentices and employees. The tin and cloth industries, while enriching some entrepreneurs, brought but meagre reward to their labour force. A wide range was spanned also by the all-important agrarian sector. It extended from yeomen with substantial landholdings, usually freehold, down through a mass of husbandmen with smaller tenancies, leased from a landowner, and finally to the landless who laboured for others; these last received wages, and sometimes food or accommodation.

This pattern of acute differentiation – whereby at Exeter, for example, 50% of the property in 1524–5 was owned by 3% of the population – was never substantially altered by the major redistributions of property that characterized the mid-Tudor decades. The revenues of the Bishop of Exeter were drastically reduced, and those of the religious houses were totally removed, but the beneficiaries of these upheavals were primarily members of the already dominant social groups. The Russells, Rolles, Dennises, Grenvilles, Arundells and other established families made spectacular gains. Many more, like the Fulfords and the Drakes, significantly enlarged their estates. Relatively rarely were the beneficiaries merchants or clothiers.

Social differentiation appears indeed to have been increased rather than diminished by the economic trends of these years. Demographic expansion tended to raise both prices and rents, as the demand for essential commodities and for tenancies of land began to exceed the available supply. These processes were observed, for example, by a gentleman of Devon in 1549.[3] It tended also to depress wage levels, as the pool of potential labour widened.

---

[3] Rose-Troup 1913, p. 491.

The prime beneficiaries appear usually to have been gentlemen, substantial farmers and merchants. By raising the rents and entry-fines due from their customary tenants, most of the gentry could probably match or exceed the rate of price inflation. Some, like the Champernownes and Godolphins, profited also from the boom in tin and shipping, and a few enjoyed the rewards of public office. The fortunate minority of farmers with freeholds or with long leases were secure from rack-renting, and they could profitably sell their produce on a rising market. Rising prices must similarly have tended to favour the mercantile community. In addition, gentlemen, farmers and merchants all benefited from the inability of their servants, labourers and other employees to demand a realistic increase in wages.

The general prosperity of the Tudor gentry is attested by its extensive rebuilding and modernization of country houses. Patrons included the Bluetts at Holcombe Rogus in about 1530 and the Haydons at Cadhay after 1545.[4] Similarly suggestive is the reconstruction of farmhouses. This development became widespread after 1560, but for most farmers it must have been the culmination of a generation or two of capital accumulation. Examples in the parishes of Washfield, North Tawton and Highampton bear the dates 1564, 1567 and 1569.[5] The material success of merchants like John Greenway and John Lane is equally evident in their lavish additions to the parish churches at Tiverton and Cullompton.[6]

The most conspicuous victims of economic change were customary tenants and the wage-dependent. The former constituted the bulk of the rural tenantry: at Stokenham in 1548, for example, they numbered 158, as against 10 leaseholders. Holding land by manorial custom, and generally by copy of the manorial court-roll, they were vulnerable to raised rents and fines: resistance carried the risk of eviction. The wage-dependent included agricultural labourers, tinners, spinners and weavers. By 1524 the proportion of the regional population assessed as being on wages already approached one-third in rural parishes, and as much as one-half in large towns like Exeter and Plymouth. The income received by these employees invariably failed to keep pace with the rising cost of their food, clothing and other necessities. Similar difficulties were encountered by the lower clergy, particularly by vicars dependent on the small tithes and by curates whose stipends were static. The widening pool of labour served also to increase the wage earner's chances of unemployment. In 1549 the Devonian Philip Nichols observed that there were now 'more persons, by many hundreds, than do well know how and where honestly to get their livings'.[7]

---

[4] Pevsner 1952A, pp. 100–1; Pevsner 1952B, p. 74.
[5] Pevsner 1952A, pp. 65, 78–9, 159.
[6] See below, pp. 87, 89.
[7] Royal 18 B XI, fol. 33.

The wealth of an individual was invariably a major determinant of his status — the degree of respect, deference and obedience granted to him by his contemporaries. Additional considerations were nevertheless important. These included his parentage, title and education; his pattern of consumption, particularly his expenditure on food, clothes and housing; and, crucially, the extent of his detachment from personal labour. For these reasons the gentleman, whose rent-roll sustained his non-productive life-style, was accorded a markedly higher status than the merchant or the yeoman, who were tainted by commercial or agrarian activity. On account of their relative freedom from manual labour and their greater financial independence, the merchant and yeoman were in turn more highly esteemed than the ploughman, the weaver or the tinner.

Within this hierarchical framework a measure of mobility was always possible. Successful yeomen, like the Quickes at Newton St Cyres, adopted the life-style of gentlemen and were eventually accepted as such. Lawyers, like the Pollards at King's Nympton, or merchants, like Giles and Savery at Bowden and Shilston, bought landed estates and married into established families. Downward mobility was equally frequent. The younger sons of landed families, barred by primogeniture from the inheritance of substantial estates, often descended the status scale by entering commerce or the law. The merchants at Totnes in 1523, for example, included a scion of the Gilberts.

The disposition of power within the region inevitably reflected its social and economic realities. Its temporal and ecclesiastical magnates sat in the House of Lords. The representation of its boroughs in the Commons was provided either by substantial townsmen, especially merchants and lawyers, or by gentlemen, like Sir Arthur Champernowne and Richard Edgcumbe Esquire at Totnes in 1563. Outsiders were chosen as well as local men. By 1570 borough representation was falling under the influence of great patrons, notably the Russells at Tavistock, Dartmouth and possibly Plymouth. County representation was dominated totally by the gentry. Members came from most of the leading families, none of which ever established an exclusive monopoly. The franchise, both in town and in county, was generally limited to freeholders.

Local government remained similarly in the control of the dominant minorities. Commissions of the peace were filled by the relatively few magnates resident in the South-West, notably the Courtenays and the Bishops of Exeter, and by an increasing number of gentry, like the Bassetts, Dennises, Arundells and Godolphins. The total of justices in Devon rose from 32 in 1514 to 51 in 1547. In the absence of a professional civil service, these constituted the indispensable instruments of Tudor authority within the region: they effectively governed the two counties through the Courts of

Quarter Sessions, regulating the economic, social, moral and even spiritual life of the population and striving to translate the decrees of central government into local reality. The same social group also provided the sheriffs of each county – Sir Thomas Dennis, for example, frequently served Devon in this capacity between 1508 and 1556 – as well as most members of the Council of the West, a body instituted by the government in 1539 to supervise this distant region. The Council was headed by Lord Russell, and it was his son Francis, Earl of Bedford, who in 1559 became the most powerful individual in the region as Lieutenant of Devon and Cornwall. Constables and bailiffs of the hundreds, and constables of the parishes, were generally recruited from less exalted levels of the social scale. Nevertheless they seem usually to have been men of some substance.

By 1530 several of the major towns were already incorporated as municipal boroughs. Others achieved incorporation during the subsequent decades of urban growth: they included Exeter, as a distinct county with its own sheriff, in 1537, as well as Torrington in 1554 and Barnstaple in 1557. Such towns enjoyed official acknowledgement of their independence from county sheriffs and other external authorities, and of their right to appoint their own mayor and corporation. The virtual self-government thus achieved was invariably monopolized by small, self-perpetuating oligarchies, in which great merchants predominated; Exeter and Bodmin were typical. In the towns, as in the country, the mass of the population was excluded from power.

The highest levels of ecclesiastical authority, in the persons of popes, cardinals, or even archbishops, were seldom seen within the region. The diocesan level was represented by the bishop, whose seat lay in the magnificent fourteenth-century cathedral at Exeter. From 1504 to 1519 its incumbent was a religious conservative, Hugh Oldham. His successor, whose rule from 1519 to 1551 spanned the era of Henrician and early-Edwardian change, was the aged and often absent John Veysey. Though generally acquiescent in the anti-traditionalist policies of successive regimes, he manifested a conspicuous lack of enthusiasm for the Protestant faith; in consequence he was eventually compelled by the Edwardian government to resign, and was replaced by the resolutely Protestant Miles Coverdale. Veysey was restored by Mary Tudor in 1553 but died in the following year, being succeeded by another moderate conservative, James Turberville. He, in turn, was deprived of office by Elizabeth I in 1559. His replacement, William Alley, was another committed Protestant; he was to retain the see until his death in 1570.

Throughout the Reformation period the authority of the bishop over his diocese was maintained by his suffragans, by his four archdeacons, who were responsible for the archdeaconries of Exeter, Totnes, Barnstaple and

Cornwall, and by a corps of subsidiary officials.[8] Employing injunctions, visitations, and proceedings in Church courts, these supervised not only the cathedral and (until their suppression) the monastic and collegiate establishments, but also the more than 600 parochial communities of which the diocese consisted. Totalling approximately 160 in Cornwall and 450 in Devon, parishes ranged in size from the very small, as in densely populated Exeter, to the extensive, as on and around the sparsely inhabited moorlands. Their religious life was primarily the responsibility of the parish priest, but laymen too were important as members of parish councils and as churchwardens. Parishes constituted the primary religious milieux of ordinary men and women, and thus provided the essential institutional contexts within which they experienced the impact of the Reformation.

[8] For details of the diocesan administrative structure, see Pill 1963.

Part One

ASSESSMENT

3

Dependent activities: sacraments, ceremonies and intercessions

In the parish church at Doddiscombsleigh, fifteenth-century stained glass portrays the key rites of the pre-Reformation Church. Each of the seven panels is linked by a crimson line to the wounds of a central figure of Christ. The message is unmistakable. Through the rites of his Church, as administered by his priests, the Lord conveys his life to the believing community.[1]

Among the most crucial of these were the rites of passage, performed at the principal crisis points of human existence. The birth of a child was followed within days or even hours by its presentation for baptism. The glass at Doddiscombsleigh shows priest and infant at the font; an acolyte holds the service-book, and parishioners assemble to witness. According to a Cornish play of 1504, the waters of baptism removed original sin; they thus procured admission to the believing community.[2] This belief explains the anxiety of parents to secure the rapid baptism of their new-born, as, for example, at Wembury in about 1535.[3] Within a few years, moreover, the child would receive the sacrament of confirmation – usually, as is depicted at Doddiscombsleigh, from the bishop himself. Progressing to adulthood, he usually experienced the sacrament of marriage. At Doddiscombsleigh the hands of bride and groom are ritually linked by the officiating priest. Inevitably there was provision also for the ultimate crisis of human life. At Doddiscombsleigh a dying man receives the last rites from his priest; the latter holds a paten and is accompanied by acolytes. Burial itself was similarly dependent upon clerical ministration. Often, as at Ashburton, corpses travelled to the grave in a procession headed by the cross and illuminated by torches; sometimes the bells would toll.[4]

Rites of passage, experienced but once in each man's life, were accompanied by an impressive multiplicity of annual observances. Among the festivals ritually celebrated in the parish church at Dartmouth, for example, were

---

[1] Anderson 1955, pp. 55–7.
[2] *Beunans Meriasek*, 1841.
[3] *LP*, IX, 1147.
[4] CWA Ashburton.

17

Christmas, Palm Sunday, Easter, Ascension and Whit Sunday; Holy Rood Day, All-Relic Sunday and May Day; the conception, nativity, visitation, purification and assumption of Our Lady; and the feasts of various saints.[5] Candles were distributed at Candlemas, ashes on Ash Wednesday, palms on Palm Sunday. Processions were organized at the feast of Corpus Christi. On Easter Friday, in commemoration of Christ's death, a crucifix was placed within a structure representing his tomb; there it was honoured by vigil, until its triumphant restoration to the high altar on Easter Day.[6] Some rites were peculiar to their locality. The 'measuring' of Ashburton church in 1523–4 was probably a procession to mark its dedication day.[7] At Padstow the parishioners processed on New Year's Day, marching in order of social rank.[8]

Rites performed on a more frequent basis included penance and the mass. At Doddiscombsleigh a penitent kneels before a seated priest to receive his absolution. It was as penance that John Rich, for example, paid 3s 4d to Ashburton church in 1517–18.[9] The window at Doddiscombsleigh also depicts the mass. The priest stands before his altar, on which is a chalice; he dramatically elevates the consecrated host. Transubstantiation was still generally accepted. Popular art, as on bench-ends at Mullion or in glass at Ashton, juxtaposed chalice and host with emblems of the Passion; and the conversion of the host into the physical body of Christ was portrayed by representations of St Gregory's Mass, as on the screen sculpted at Paignton in about 1526.[10] Communion bread was regarded as 'Our Lord's body', and the communicant as one who 'receiveth his Maker'.

Death itself did not release the layman from his dependence upon the Church. Its continuing ministrations supposedly speeded his soul through the purgatorial fires and into the eternal felicity of Heaven.

The essential component of this intercessory activity was prayer. At Exeter Cathedral, prayers were bidden 'for all the souls [that] bideth the mercy of God in the bitter pains of Purgatory; that God, of his mercy, the sooner deliver them through your devoted prayers'. The process began before burial. At Down St Mary, until the 1530s, parsons visited the corpse of each newly deceased parishioner in his or her house; there 'they were wont to say *dirige* and other prayers, with the neighbours of the dead man, for the souls of all such corpses'. Further prayers accompanied the interment: 'hic roget sacerdos orare pro anima defuncti', instructs a manuscript copy of the service

[5] CWA Dartmouth.
[6] E.g. CWA Exeter HT, 1526.
[7] CWA Ashburton, 1524.
[8] STAC 2/8/39, 45–6.
[9] CWA Ashburton, 1518.
[10] Rushforth 1927A, pp. 21–9; Hoskins 1954, p. 450.

1 St Michael's, Doddiscombsleigh. Late-fifteenth-century glass portraying the performance of mass in a parish church. Note the altar and its covering, the chalice, the priest elevating the host, and the kneeling assistants and observers.

discovered at Coldridge. These were merely the initial stages of a process which might continue for years. Many layfolk, like John Hugh of Branscombe in his will of 1521, had endowed a priest to 'pray for my soul', and many more, by making gifts to churches or to guilds, had secured the addition of their names to local bede-rolls. In 1529, for example, John Lane of Cullompton donated money to 100 neighbouring churches, requiring that they enter him on their rolls 'to pray for me in their pulpits'. Donations of this nature are frequent in wardens' accounts before the Reformation – as at Dartmouth, where in 1529–30 Alice Philip and Joan Long both paid 6s 8d for the enrolment of their husbands. Similarly frequent are payments to priests for the recitation of rolls. At Ashburton, for instance, the vicar was paid 'for le bede-roll of all the benefactors of the said church, naming them from the pulpit and praying for them'.[11]

Intercessions were considered to be particularly effectual when incorporated in the performance of mass. 'There is no day', Thomas Bennett reportedly complained to the clergy at Exeter in 1531, 'but ye say divers masses for souls in feigned Purgatory', and the extant wills, accounts and chantry certificates confirm that such rites were still celebrated in overwhelming number throughout the South-West. Some laymen, like John Bridgeman of Exeter in 1523, entrusted their performance to friars; others, like Gilbert Rugge of Widecombe in 1529, to monks. Most, however, endowed parish priests, chantry priests or the chaplains of guilds. In 1524, for example, William Sellick arranged a trental of 30 masses for himself in Tiverton church, as well as 5 masses known as the *Scala Coeli*, while John Simon instructed his wife to pay a priest £5 per annum in return for four years of masses in Exeter St Petrock's – 'for the wealth of my soul and hers, and for such friends as she and I be bound to pray for'. In 1526 Thomas Leigh of South Molton required a year of masses, for himself and for his friends, from a priest in the chapel of St George. In 1529, at Tiverton, John Greenway endowed a priest to pray and sing masses for his soul in the recently erected Greenway chapel, and in the same year another merchant, John Lane, arranged a priest to perform in the new chapel of Our Lady at Cullompton.[12]

Intercessions thus constituted a crucial element of lay piety on the eve of the Reformation. Of the 30 wills from 1520 to 1529, indeed, prayers or masses of this type were endowed in as many as 21, or 70%.

The multiplicity of rites performed in parish churches inevitably necessitated the accumulation of ritual equipment in impressive quantities. Baptism, for example, required appropriate fonts. Many parishes, including Altarnun, Luppitt and Stoke Canon, retained archaic Norman structures, presumably as visible evidence of an ancient right to baptize. Others, such as Chittlehampton, Kingsteignton and Woodbury, acquired new fonts in the late fifteenth or early sixteenth centuries. These latter were usually octagonal in form, and decorated with quatrefoil or other Perpendicular motifs; bowls were relatively small and raised upon pedestals, since baptism was conferred now upon the new-born alone. In order to prevent the removal of their consecrated water for magical purposes, most were protected by a lockable wooden cover; Perpendicular examples survive at Plymstock and Shaugh

---

[11] EDCL 2864; C 1 900/34–5; DRO 745C; PROB 11 20, fol. 229; 23, fol. 29; CWA Dartmouth, 1530; CWA Ashburton, 1510, etc.

[12] *Acts and Monuments*, II, p. 1039; *Certificates, Cornwall*; *Certificates, Devon*; PROB 11 21, fols. 128, 202v; 22, fols. 8, 191v, 302; 23, fol. 29; 24, fol. 10.

Prior. Each font was positioned close to the entrance porch of its church, symbolizing the initiatory significance of the baptismal rite.[13]

The last rites similarly necessitated specific equipment. In 1533–4 the parish of Ashburton possessed a silver box 'to bear the sacrament at the sick folk', and a wooden receptacle for this purpose, painted with Perpendicular motifs, survives in the church at Warkleigh.[14] Processions, again, required appropriate banners. Two, depicting St Clement and St Katherine, were donated to Ashburton church by John Forde in 1517–18, and another, portraying St Sidwell and St George, was given to the church at Morebath in 1528.[15] Probably used also in processions was the silver and gilt cross purchased in the early sixteenth century by the parishioners of Tavistock; this cost a spectacular £62.[16] 'Sepulchres', of wood or of stone, were needed for the Easter celebrations. Stone examples remain, that at Woodleigh being dated by inscription to about 1527. Such structures were covered by cloths, like that bought for 66s at Ashburton in 1511–12, and illuminated by candles; in 1530 Stratton possessed a frame 'to set tapers in, afore the sepulchre'.[17]

Predictably it was the mass and its associated ceremonies that required the most elaborate equipment. Pre-Reformation stone altars occasionally survive, as at Probus and Tawstock; the former retains its consecration crosses, symbolic of Christ's five wounds. A few reredoses also remain, as at St Michael Penkevil. Wooden altars, like the two commissioned by Stratton in 1531, have invariably perished.[18] In addition, wardens' accounts reveal a persistent and often lavish expenditure upon vestments, altar cloths, chalices, pyxes, censers, holy-water sprinklers, crosses, candlesticks and related accoutrements. By 1533 Exeter St Mary Major owned 12 pairs of vestments, 7 copes and a suit of black 'for obits', as well as 5 chalices and a wealth of vessels, cloths, frontals and candlesticks for its altars.[19] Vestments, like the cassock, cope, surplice and stole worn by the priest on a brass of about 1520 at St Just-in-Roseland, could be particularly expensive. In 1528–9 the parishioners of Ashburton spent £32 13s 4d on a cope and three vestments; and South Tawton paid some £27 for vestments in 1531–2. The decorative splendour of such apparel is demonstrated by the

---

[13] Bond 1908; Pevsner 1952B, pp. 17–18, 27. See also Additional 32243, HCWA Stratton, 1517 ('a key to the font').
[14] CWA Ashburton, 1534; Pevsner 1952A, pp. 158–9.
[15] CWA Ashburton, 1518; CWA Morebath, 1531.
[16] REQ 2 9/76.
[17] Pevsner 1952B, p. 313; CWA Ashburton, 1512; Additional 32243, HCWA Stratton, 1530.
[18] Pevsner 1952A, p. 152; Pevsner and Radcliffe 1970, pp. 147, 193; Henderson 1923–4, p. 12; *Blanchminster's Charity*, pp. 91–4.
[19] CWA Exeter SMM, fol. 11.

pre-Reformation copes that survive at Brixham and Culmstock. The latter is made of gold velvet, and is adorned with fleurs-de-lis, pomegranates, angels and an assumption of Our Lady.[20] Pieces of altar plate, particularly chalices and patens, have also occasionally survived – as at West Hill, where an early-sixteenth-century chalice is inscribed with a crucifixion, or at Morval, where a paten is datable to 1528–9.[21]

A variety of service-books was similarly required. At Ashburton, for example, two books of the feast of the Name of Jesus were acquired in 1520–1, while a manual, two processionals and other books were purchased at Chagford in 1526–9. Christopher Stephen donated a missal to the church at Highbray in 1524. By 1533 Exeter St Mary Major could boast numerous mass-books, psalters, legends, portises, hymnals and processionals; a manual, gradual, ordinal and 'sene'; a book of services for the new feasts of Our Lady and Jesus; and two copies of the *Pupilla Oculi*, 'whereof one is chained in the body of the church'.[22] Books, moreover, required lecterns. Pre-Reformation examples remain at Bigbury, Bovey Tracey, Salcombe Regis and Wolborough; the first-named, shaped like an eagle, is datable to 1504–19.[23]

The final requisites were dramatic lighting and emotive sound. The former was provided by candles – which at Dartmouth in 1529–30, for example, cost as much as 21s.[24] The latter was sometimes provided by choirs, as at Stratton,[25] and more often by organs, as at Exeter St Petrock's, Ashburton, Chagford and elsewhere; Ashburton paid £4 6s 8d for new organs in 1519–20.[26] Most parishes, in addition, invested substantially in bells. In about 1508 the inhabitants of Golant contributed £10 towards the bells of Tywardreath church, while at Ashburton the great bell was recast in 1509–10. Pre-Reformation examples still hang in many churches, as at Brushford, Butterleigh and Loxbeare. Ringing preceded services, marked the eve of All Souls, and proclaimed funerals and intercessions. In 1528 Joan Tackle of Honiton bequeathed 6s 8d to eight local churches, 'to have my knell rung in every of those churches immediately after my decease'. Bells, indeed, were popularly believed to possess spiritual power. In Devon they were often inscribed with the text 'Voce mea viva depello cunta nociva',

---

[20] Dunkin 1882, p. 10; CWA Ashburton, 1529; CWA S. Tawton, 1532; Pevsner 1952B, pp. 64, 98.

[21] Pevsner 1952B, pp. 28, 307; Pevsner and Radcliffe 1970, p. 122.

[22] CWA Ashburton, 1521; CWA Chagford, 1526–9; PROB 11 23, fol. 54; CWA Exeter SMM, fol. 11. See also *Bodmin Register*, pp. 38–42.

[23] Pevsner 1952B, p. 52.

[24] CWA Dartmouth, 1530.

[25] Additional 32243, HCWA Stratton, 1531.

[26] CWA Exeter SP; CWA Ashburton, 1520, etc.; CWA Chagford.

and on occasion, as at Ashburton in 1509–10, they were rung during storms for protection against the forces of evil.[27]

On the eve of the Henrician Reformation, the continuing commitment of the region's population to its traditional rites was thus beyond question: levels of participation and investment remained conspicuously high. Inevitably there were exceptions. At Dartmouth in 1501 John Chevilstone played games instead of attending mass and vespers, while at Bratton between 1500 and 1515, 'against all right and good conscience', Thomas Alcott and Alan Morris stole a chalice, mass-book, vestments and other goods from the parish church.[28] Yet such acts of contempt for the ritual system would appear from the surviving evidence to have been rare, and verbal expressions of disbelief were even more uncommon. In 1505–6 John Atwill of Walkhampton questioned indulgences, asserted that public penances should be imposed for serious sins alone, and declared that his servant possessed as much power as his curate to hear confessions and to absolve. He also dismissed bede-rolls as more effective in enriching clerics than in saving souls. Similarly contemptuous of intercessions was Otto Corbin at Exeter in 1515. 'I care not for my soul', he declared, 'so I may have an honest living in this world; and when ye see my soul hang on the hedge, cast ye stones thereto.'[29] Between 1500 and 1530, nevertheless, these were the only two such cases recorded for the entire diocese. Of organized Lollardy there is no trace.[30]

To what extent did this support for traditional rites survive the assaults directed against them in the Reformation decades? The developing state of popular attitudes may be illuminated by evidence of three interrelated types: the verbal, the financial and the behavioural.

The verbal evidence – the words written or (more usually) spoken by south-western people – would seem to suggest the beginnings of a shift in public opinion. Individuals continued to speak in favour of the ancient practices, as, for example, at Axminster in 1535–6.[31] Their utterances, however, were now countered by some explicitly hostile writings – particularly the tracts of Philip Nichols, a young Devonian of relatively modest social origin, written between 1547 and 1549[32] – and by spoken attacks from people like Thomas Bennett, an Exeter schoolmaster, in 1531;[33] Philip

---

[27] CCB 854, sub 28 February 1507/8; CWA Ashburton, 1510, etc.; Hoskins 1954, pp. 354, 359; Pevsner 1952A, p. 115; PROB 11 23, fol. 71; Ellacombe 1872, pp. 240, 242.
[28] *Dartmouth*, p. 213; C 1 246/48.
[29] ER XIII, fols. 144v–5, 179v–81; Mumford 1936, pp. 95–6.
[30] Thomson 1965A, esp. pp. 20–1.
[31] STAC 2/2/267.
[32] Royal 18 B XI, esp. fols. 9v–10, 12–13v, 19v–20, 23, 25–6. For his social origin, see *Copy of a Letter*, p. 5.
[33] *Acts and Monuments*, II, pp. 1037–40.

Gammon, an Axminster shoemaker, in 1535–6;[34] and Agnes Priest, a 'poor woman' from Boyton, in 1558.[35]

Their targets included Catholic baptism. Philip Gammon allegedly proclaimed that 'a child born between a Christian man and a Christian woman [need] have no christsdom – because their father and mother were christened'. The shoemaker was said also to dismiss the sacrament of marriage, maintaining that 'if a man and a woman did live well together, they need not to marry'. Auricular confession was denounced not only by Gammon but also by Philip Nichols and Agnes Priest. Gammon declared that 'if he were in article of death, and saw a priest standing at his window, he would never require him to hear his confession; for he had as lief to be confessed to a post or a stone as to any priest'. Nichols, with equal vehemence, rejected this sacrament as the invention of a corrupt priesthood. He saw it as a device for 'moving men's wives to folly', and for 'enticing men's daughters to lewdness and vice'.

Scorn was also poured upon the traditional intercessions. Thomas Bennett accused the clergy of selling masses for the souls in 'feigned Purgatory'. Agnes Priest denied Purgatory and denounced trentals, *diriges*, soul-masses, purchased prayers and pardons: these, she asserted, were 'foolish inventions'. Philip Nichols agreed that Purgatory was a myth. He claimed that prayers and masses for the dead were further devices of the priesthood; they were designed to increase its wealth and to maintain its ascendancy over 'simple consciences here, in this world'.

Nichols also condemned the traditional liturgy as both incomprehensible and unedifying. The use of holy bread and holy water, and the distribution of palms and ashes, he rejected as 'men's traditions'; he thought them 'fondly [i.e. foolishly] instituted, and much more fondly used among the people'. Agnes Priest similarly dismissed holy bread and holy water as 'abominations'. But it was the mass itself that attracted the most vigorous hostility. Thomas Bennett condemned the Catholic eucharist for its 'superstition' and 'idolatry'. Philip Gammon announced bluntly that 'the sacrament of the altar is not the very body of Christ, but it is a figure and, in itself, a very piece of bread'. Were it truly Christ's body, he argued, 'it was not possible that it could be in so many places in one time'; moreover, 'the bones would crush in his teeth'. Philip Nichols opposed, as superstitious, the reservation and veneration of the consecrated host. Agnes Priest was even more outspoken in Mary's reign. 'I will rather die', she reportedly told the Bishop of Exeter, 'than I will do any worship to that foul idol which, with your mass, you make a god.' 'There was never such an idol as your sacrament

[34] STAC 2/2/267–72, 287; 23/273; 29/111.
[35] *Acts and Monuments*, II, pp. 2049–52.

is, made of your priests and commanded to be worshipped of all men, with many fond fantasies'; it was a 'bready god'. She flatly denied 'that a piece of bread should be turned by a man into the natural body of Christ; which bread doth vinow, and mice oftentimes do eat it, and it doth mould and is burned'.

By mid-century, anti-Catholic declarations were thus no longer virtually unknown. In 1549, indeed, the rebels of Devon and Cornwall protested that '*many* [laymen], rudely presuming unworthily to receive [the communion], put no difference between the Lord's body and other kind of meat; some saying that it is bread before and after, some saying that it is profitable to no man except he receive it, with *many other abused terms*'.[36]

Verbal evidence would thus appear to suggest a measure of decline in popular support for the traditional rites as the official Reformation progressed. Is this suggestion substantiated or repudiated by the evidence of financial activity?

Until the death of Henry VIII, both parishes and individuals continued to invest in the equipment required for traditional rites. Between 1530 and 1547 fonts, for example, were acquired at Antony and Iddesleigh, banners or streamers at Iddesleigh and Morebath, altars at Chagford and Morebath, chalices at Camborne, Morebath and Winkleigh, and vestments at Antony, Ashburton, Chagford, Exeter St Petrock's, Iddesleigh, Morebath, Stratton and Woodbury. Iddesleigh bought a new mass-book, and Woodbury a new canopy 'to hang over the sacrament at the high altar'. Organs were purchased at Ashburton and Woodbury, and bells at Chagford.[37] Bequests, moreover, included altar cloths from John Brown at Uffculme, sacrament lights from John Tanner at Colyton and John Andrew at Torrington, and vestments from John Thomas at Barnstaple, Tristram Hooper at Musbury and John Sherman at Ottery St Mary.[38]

Nevertheless there were already signs of change. With some exceptions, most notably the £55 spent on bells at Chagford between 1538 and 1540, large-scale expenditure was apparently becoming more rare. Vestments, for example, had cost approximately £33 and £27 respectively at Ashburton in 1528–9 and South Tawton in 1531–2; yet only £12 was spent at Exeter St Petrock's in 1540–1, only £7 at Antony and at Stratton in 1545–6, and only £6 at Morebath in 1546–7. Projected investment was sometimes withdrawn. In 1532–3, at Silverton, the executors of Alexander Richard refused

---

[36] *Acts and Monuments*, II, p. 1305.

[37] CWA Antony, c. 1545, 1546; CWA Ashburton, 1539; CWA Camborne, 1538; CWA Chagford, 1532, 1536, 1539–40; CWA Exeter SP, 1541; CWA Iddesleigh, 1536, 1538–9, 1542; CWA Morebath, 1535, 1537, 1539, 1542, 1547; CWA Winkleigh, 1547?; CWA Woodbury, 1539, 1543; Additional 32244, SWA Stratton, 1546.

[38] PROB 11 25, fol. 227v; 29, fol. 151; 30, fol. 333; 31, fols. 15v, 36, 151v.

to honour his pledge to buy vestments for the parish church, and in 1539, at Morebath, a parishioner's 'promise to the side altar' was described as 'all lost and gone'.[39] In 1547, moreover, the decline became absolute. Wills, accounts and other sources unanimously indicate a virtual cessation of expenditure upon equipment for specifically Catholic rites. This cessation was to endure for more than six years.

Only after Mary's accession did investment revive. The accounts for 1553–9 record innumerable payments for vestments, altar cloths, canopies, tabernacles, chalices, pyxes, censers, sprinklers, holy-water buckets, service-books, banners, sepulchres, organs, bells and related accoutrements. Yet by pre-Reformation standards the expenditure was seldom impressive. The £23 devoted to new bells at Woodbury was exceptional: more typical were the £6 spent on a vestment at Exeter St John's Bow, the £4 on a cope at Coldridge, or even the 30s on a cope and vestments at Molland. Some equipment was donated by individuals, like William Hurst at Exeter St Petrock's, or by groups, like the 'wives' at Morebath: the former presented an alb, the latter a manual. Several of the 60 testators from 1553 to 1559 bequeathed sacrament lights, but only one donation of equipment – the altar towel given by Thomas Vawter of Tiverton – was financially significant.[40] After 1559, moreover, expenditure of a traditionalist nature again totally ceased. Only furnishings still acceptable to the Protestant government – like the bell bought for £6 at Stratton in 1565[41] – were now purchased by individuals, groups, or parochial communities.

A downward trend is also suggested by such equipment as survives. With possible exceptions like the font at East Down or the font cover at Swimbridge – both of which display early-Renaissance elements – few of the extant examples are datable to 1530–70. The chalice at Braddock, which is Marian, appears to be the sole surviving piece of Catholic church plate from this period in the entire South-West.[42] All sources would thus seem to agree that after *circa* 1530 – for whatever reason – expenditure upon apparatus for the traditional rites at first declined and eventually ceased.

The sources also agree that the deliberate disposal of such apparatus by parochial communities, usually in return for cash, was an increasingly frequent phenomenon of the Reformation decades. In as early as 1543–4 the townsmen of Plymouth, whose leaders included the merchant William Hawkins, sold chalices and other church treasures worth more than £41. In

---

[39] C 1 712/8; CWA Morebath, 1539.
[40] CWA Woodbury, 1558–9; CWA Exeter SJB, 1559; CWA Coldridge, 1559; CWA Molland, 1557; CWA Exeter SP, 1558; CWA Morebath, 1554; PROB 11 37, fol. 268.
[41] Additional 32244, SWA Stratton, 1565.
[42] Pevsner 1952A, pp. 83, 149; Pevsner and Radcliffe 1970, p. 46.

1544–5 the parishioners of Dartmouth disposed of two chalices and other sacramental equipment to the value of some £16. In 1545–6 the sales at Stratton included plate worth more than £6. But it was the accession of Edward VI that opened the flood gates. By 1549 ritual apparatus had been sold or pawned in several of the Exeter parishes, including Allhallows, St George's, St John's Bow, St Kerrian's, St Mary Arches, St Olave's and St Pancras', as well as in towns like Liskeard, Looe and Stratton and in rural communities like Boconnoc, East Newlyn, Lanteglos and Polruan, Modbury, Morebath, Morval, Morwenstow, North Molton, St Cleer, St Gluvias, St Neot, St Veep, Warleggan and Woodbury. Liskeard, for example, sold chalices and other goods; Morval, a chalice; Warleggan, a cross. At Morebath, where 'the church goods was sold away without commission' in 1548, sales included banners, candlesticks and cloths for the altars of St Sidwell and St George. At Woodbury the sales in 1547 alone included three albs, four sepulchre cloths, a cloth for St Margaret's altar, a surplice, a pyx, a pax, a canopy for the Corpus Christi procession, and another to hang over the sacrament; and there were further sales in 1547–8 and 1548–9. That alienations of this nature had become frequent is confirmed by the sparseness of the inventories compiled by Cornish churches in 1549. Few retained more than three bells, one or two chalices, and occasional crosses, paxes, vestments or other equipment.[43]

Selling continued in the years 1550–3, as at Ashburton, Barnstaple, Crediton, Exeter Holy Trinity, Exeter St Petrock's, Morebath, Stratton, Tavistock and Woodbury. Barnstaple, for example, lost a pyx, vestments, cloths, crosses and no less than six chalices, while Woodbury sold torches, cloths, a frontlet, part of a pyx, and a canopy 'that did hang over the pyx at the high altar'; purchasers included Robert Eliot, Richard Lendale and John Pearce. At Exeter St Petrock's the sales in 1550–1 alone realized more than £63, and in the years 1551–3 a vestment was sold for a further £8 10s.[44] The extent of such alienation is confirmed by the official inventories of 1553, which recorded the recent sale of ritual equipment by some 56 parishes in Devon alone. Proceeds ranged from a mere 15s for two cruets at Ide to £20–5 for apparatus at Dartmouth, Honiton, Kingswear, Portlemouth

[43] *Plymouth Records*, p. 113; CWA Dartmouth, 1545; CWA Exeter SJB, 1549; CWA Modbury, 1548; CWA Morebath, 1548, 1558; CWA N. Molton, 1549; CWA Woodbury, 1547–9; E 117 1/48, 52; *Inventories, Cornwall*, p. xii; *Inventories, Exeter*; Additional 32243, HCWA Stratton, 1545, 1548; SP 10/6/25; 15/3/29; Additional 32244, SWA Stratton, 1546.

[44] *Tavistock Records*, p. 22; CWA Ashburton, 1552–3; CWA Crediton, 1551; CWA Exeter HT, 1551–2; CWA Exeter SP, 1551, 1553; CWA Morebath, 1553; CWA Woodbury, 1551, 1553; Additional 32243, HCWA Stratton, 1551, 1553; *Barnstaple Records*, I, pp. 198–9.

and Torrington, £33 at Staverton, more than £40 at Tavistock and £45 at East Budleigh. Torrington, for example, lost a cross, pax, ship and censers, as well as three suits of vestments and eight copes. Eight of the Exeter churches together disposed of plate worth more than £200 in 1551 alone.[45]

Though temporarily halted in Mary's reign, the destructive trend resumed after Elizabeth's accession. Exeter St Mary Major sold cloths from its altars and sepulchre in about 1559, and Camborne cloths in 1560–1. Molland lost a sepulchre and other apparatus in 1561–2; Plymouth, copes, vestments and equipment in 1563; Kilmington, 'certain stuff' in 1565–6; St Breock, copes, vestments, a banner, a streamer and other goods in about 1566. By 1566 Bodmin had lost most of the plate and vestments recorded in its inventory of 1539. Shortly after 1567 Exeter St Mary disposed of numerous goods, including copes, vestments, chalices, bells, plate, and cloths for altar, font and sepulchre. Between 1568 and 1570 Ashburton sold vestments, copes, cloths, a canopy and a chalice; by 1569 Antony had lost much of its Marian equipment, including a pax, a sacring bell, a chalice, cruets and three copes; and 1569–70 saw the sale of 'certain ornaments' at Exeter St John's Bow and of a chalice at Stratton.[46] Some essentially Catholic apparatus, it is true, remained in churches in 1570, but even this seems usually to have been sold in the subsequent decade.[47]

Even more strongly suggestive of a decline in support for the ancient rites was the increasing incidence of despoliation and theft. In as early as 1534 a thief broke into Morebath church and stole, *inter alia*, a chalice. In about 1545 the constable of Davidstow, John Jelly, persuaded the parishioners to sell their best chalice, but the £6 thus raised he then kept for himself. In addition he ordered the removal of bells from local chapels 'and bestowed them, in like manner, at his pleasure'. Parts of the bells at Davidstow were similarly stolen by John Pearce. In 1546 two chalices and other plate were removed from the church at Halberton by Christopher Sampford. Sampford, bailiff of the hundred, claimed to possess a commission to raise money for the war against France. In reality 'he had no such authority nor commission; and the same jewels shortly after sold, and the money therefore received converted to his own use'. With the assistance of a husbandman, John Warren, he also stole the church's service-books, vestments, chalices and ornaments, to the value of some £40. In the opinion of their

[45] E 117 2/7; *Inventories, Exeter*, p. xiii, etc.
[46] *Plymouth Records*, pp. 232–3; CWA Antony, p. 9; CWA Ashburton, 1569–70; CWA Camborne, 1561; CWA Exeter SJB, 1570; CWA Exeter SMM, fol. 16; CWA Kilmington, 1566; CWA Molland, 1562; CWA St Breock, fols. 16, 21, 23; *Inventories, Cornwall*, p. 32; Additional 32243, HCWA Stratton, 1570.
[47] E.g. CWA Chudleigh, 1574; CWA Crediton, 1571, 1577; CWA Dartington, 1574; CWA Exeter SJB, 1575; CWA Woodbury, 1576; Additional 32244, SWA Stratton, 1571.

fellow-parishioners, Sampford and Warren thus revealed their 'devilish minds against God and Our Blessed Lady'.[48]

In 1547 Woodbury was robbed of two chalices, several cruets, altar towels, housling towels, altar cloths and sepulchre cloths, a cross, pax, censer, ship and pall, and 'a fine white canopy cloth to hang over the sacrament'. In 1548 a pyx was stolen at Duloe, and a pyx and two chalices at Warleggan. In 1548–9 Christopher Sampford removed the bells from Halberton church; he also pillaged marble from its tombs. A cross, pyx, cruets, censers and other equipment – together worth some £100 – were stolen by John Ellis and other parishioners from the church at Broadhembury in 1549. A surplice and rochet disappeared at Morebath in the same year. At about this time treasures worth no less than £200 were sold at Torrington without the parishioners' assent. Among the losses were chalices, a cross, and a monstrance to bear the sacrament at Corpus Christi and on Palm Sunday. The offenders, who included Roger Visick and Richard Davie, were said to have thus ensured the 'utter empoverishing' of Torrington church.

Despoliation reached its climax at Exeter in 1549. A cross, chalice, ship, censer, pax, cruets and other plate were plundered from St Edmund's; a chalice, pyx and pax from St Pancras'; a chalice from St Stephen's. St David's was thoroughly pillaged, and St Sidwell's was 'spoiled of all things movable': it lost all its vestments as well as bells, a cross, a chalice and a large quantity of plate. The culprits were mainly loyalists, seizing the opportunities for plunder afforded by the south-western rebellion. Some were Welsh soldiers but others were local men: they included John Buller, Thomas Chapel, Nicholas Cove, Bernard Duffield, Richard Lake, Edward Senbarbe, William Slocombe, John Stowell, Richard Wallis and Thomas Westcote. Nor was this all. The official inventories of 1553 reported recent thefts of ritual apparatus at Bradninch, Braunton, Christow, Clyst St George, Dawlish, Heavitree, Parkham, Sidmouth, Townstall and Wolborough. At Clyst St George, for example, a pyx was stolen; at Dawlish a cross, censer, ship, cruets and cope; at Wolborough a chalice. Again the offenders seem usually to have been local: they included Duffield and Stowell of Exeter as well as Nicholas Adams, formerly of Townstall.[49]

By 1553, when unofficial sales and official confiscations had together decimated parochial accumulations of equipment, opportunities for such pillage had greatly diminished. In 1554, nevertheless, a thief broke into the church at Morebath; he escaped with vestments, altar cloths, and even 'the pyx

---

[48] CWA Morebath, 1535; STAC 3/2/20; 4/8/47; C 1 1138/93–4. Sampford would not be described as a 'gentleman' until the 1550s.

[49] C 1 1217/3; CWA Morebath, 1549; CWA Woodbury, 1547; E 117 1/52; 2/7; *Inventories, Exeter*, esp. pp. 20–4, 66–70, 75–84; REQ 2 5/335; STAC 4/8/47. See also *Exeter Records*, pp. 363–4.

with the sacrament'. In as late as 1570–1 there was a robbery at Woodbury church, and at about this time Richard Crane detained a cross from the church at Camborne – 'by deceitful mean', it was alleged, 'practising to defraud the parishioners . . . of their right to the same'.[50]

Financial evidence of these types would thus seem to confirm that the Reformation decades witnessed a relatively rapid erosion of devotion to the traditional rites. Expenditure upon their apparatus fell and eventually ceased; sales and despoliations multiplied. Whatever the possible causal factors behind it, the phenomenon is unmistakable.

A further type of essentially financial evidence relates to intercessions. Until the death of Henry VIII, many individuals undoubtedly continued to invest in prayers and masses on behalf of the dead. In 1536, for example, Joan Bidwell of Shobrooke arranged her registration on a local bede-roll, 'to be continually prayed for forever'. She also ordered a trental, and required a priest 'to sing and pray for my soul, my friends' souls, and for all the souls departed, abiding the mercy of God; and that to be done in Shobrooke church'. In 1540 Robert Hone of Ottery St Mary required a number of masses for his soul, 'after the old customable usage', as well as the registration of his name upon fraternity bede-rolls at Cullompton and South Molton – 'there to be prayed for, amongst the brothers'. In 1546 Thomasine Godsland of Barnstaple arranged a priest to sing and pray for herself, her family, and 'all such as I am bounden to pray for'. She also required trentals at her month's mind and year's mind, and monthly masses of Our Lady and of Requiem. Again, however, there were already signs of change. Intercessions had been endowed in 70% of the wills made between 1520 and 1529. Of the 41 wills made between 1530 and 1539, they were arranged in only 21, or 51%; and of the 69 wills made between 1540 and 1546, in no more than 23, or 33%. The sample, though small, would thus suggest a substantial abatement of intercessory investment from the onset of the Henrician Reformation. Wardens' accounts, it is true, show that men and women still paid for the addition of names to bede-rolls, but the particularly comprehensive accounts of the guild of the High Cross at Stratton reveal a decline in enrolments from 1540. Whereas several had been recorded in every account from 1530 to 1539, the number dropped to one only in 1541, 1542, 1544 and 1546, and to nil in 1540, 1543 and 1545.[51]

Equally significant was the increasing expropriation by laymen of chantry properties and endowments. In as early as 1530 the south chapel of Cullompton church, erected four years previously by John Lane, was seized by the Mores and other local men. Lane had intended a chantry priest to perform

---

[50] CWA Morebath, 1555; CWA Woodbury, 1571; C 3 3/60.
[51] PROB 11 27, fol. 69v; 29, fol. 201; 31, fol. 115v; Additional 32243, HCWA Stratton, 1540–6.

within it; the intruders, to the outrage of his widow, used it for burials instead. Similar impieties occurred between 1533 and 1538 at Exeter, Sheepwash and Shillingford. At Exeter, in order to maintain intercessions, property had been bequeathed to the churches of St Kerrian and St Martin. Richard Drewe, however, now appropriated its revenues and thus prevented their performance. An inhabitant of Sheepwash, Edward Thorn, deliberately obstructed the collection of a rent which had maintained intercessions in the church at Silverton. At Shillingford land had been granted to the Dean and Chapter of Exeter Cathedral in return for an obit and prayers on the donor's behalf. In 1537–8 this land was appropriated by an Exeter merchant, John Blackaller; to the deteriment of the intercessions he then refused the clerics their rent. The years 1538–44 saw further disruption at Holsworthy, Marwood, Pilton and South Petherwin. Thomas Newcourt had donated land to maintain a priest in the church at Holsworthy; he was to serve the guild and altar of St Katherine. Thomas' heir, John Newcourt, now detained its deeds and prevented its use for such purposes. Richard Frear claimed land at Clayhanger which, according to a local priest, belonged by right to a chantry at Marwood. Chantry lands were similarly in dispute at Pilton, while land used by a guild of Jesus at South Petherwin – enabling a priest to sing masses of Jesus in the church – was now claimed by John Blackmore. By 1544–7 this predatory attitude was no longer uncommon. At Halberton Christopher Sampford and John Warren reportedly dismissed a stipendiary priest from his post, 'commanding him to depart, saying to him that he should serve there no longer'. At Davidstow the parishioners were persuaded by their constable, John Jelly, to sell their chantry oxen; by hiring these out they had maintained a priest 'to the laud and praise of Almighty God'. Jelly then kept the proceeds for himself. And at Aveton Giffard in about 1547 John Bastard claimed land which, according to other parishioners, belonged in reality to the chantry at Leveton.[52]

The frequency of such attempts at expropriation is confirmed by the chantry certificates of the Henrician and Edwardian commissioners. At Creed, land donated for the maintenance of a priest was found to have been 'conveyed from the churchwardens of long time', but most of the secularization appears to have been recent. The culprits included members of the non-gentle laity. At Bampton, for example, a chantry was dissolved in about 1543 by Michael Mallett: he discharged the incumbent and assumed the property. At Looe, in about 1544, land granted for the maintenance of obits was employed by the townsmen to finance the repair of their bridge. At Morwenstow John Broad failed to provide the intercessions required

---

[52] C 1 781/26; 786/54; 930/1; 959/35–7; 976/32–3; 986/44; 1042/7–9; 1068/15–16; 1200/10–11; STAC 2/25/80, 142; 3/2/20; 7/45.

by a will of which he was executor; instead he kept the money for himself. Occurrences of this nature were discovered elsewhere, as at Helston, Kingsteignton, St Winnow and Truro, though here the offenders' identities remain uncertain.[53]

Commitment to the traditional intercessions had thus been in decline for several years before the accession of Edward VI. Thereafter its collapse was rapid. At Stratton – after a final, panic-induced spate of registrations in 1547 – names ceased to be added to the bede-roll in 1548. Of the 30 testators in 1547, moreover, only 6 still sought to invest in intercession. In 1548 the number dropped to a mere 3 of the 27; and in 1549 to just 1 of the 20. In this last year the sole investor was John Southwood of Hemyock, who on 10 March left 12d to a priest in return for his prayers. Of the 31 wills composed between January 1550 and July 1553, not one attempted to arrange prayers or masses for the dead. Typical of this abandonment of the traditional forms was the will of Richard Lock, husbandman of Yarcombe, in 1550.[54]

To what extent were these forms revived after Mary's accession? The accounts of the High Cross guild at Stratton are again suggestive: for the whole of Mary's reign they fail to record a single registration upon its formerly popular bede-roll. Even more striking is the level of testatorial investment. Of the 60 wills made between 1553 and 1559, prayers or masses for the dead were endowed in 11 – a mere 18%. Richard Friend of Ermington might in 1557 endow a priest 'to sing for my soul and all my friends', and William Foscombe of Launceston might in 1558 arrange obits at Abbotsham, Buckland Brewer and Parkham, but such confidence in the traditional rites was now in patent decline. Markedly more representative of prevailing attitudes were John Waite of Sennen in 1554, John Thawdy, merchant-draper of Bodmin, in 1557, or William Stretch of Brampford Speke in the same year – none of whom arranged a single prayer or mass for the health of his soul.[55]

Elizabeth's early years in power completed the trend. Some testators, like William Spiring of Bradninch in 1560, still vaguely required the disposal of their property 'for the wealth of my soul and all Christian souls', and a few, including the Broadhembury husbandman Thomas Potter in 1567, continued to request commemorative knells after their decease.[56] Yet not one of the 90 testators from 1560 to 1569 still hoped for intercessory prayers

---

[53] *Certificates, Cornwall*, pp. 21, 27, 34, 42, 48, 50, 53; *Certificates, Devon*, pp. xxi–ii, 23–4, 41.

[54] Additional 32243, HCWA Stratton; Moger, 39, John Southwood, 1549; PROB 11 33, fol. 116.

[55] Additional 32243, HCWA Stratton, 1553–9; CCB 855A, fol. 311v; PROB 11 37, fol. 78; 39, fols. 128, 391; 40, fol. 154v.

[56] PROB 11 49, fol. 55v; 50, fol. 152v.

or masses from the clerical estate. Investment in these once vital components of the popular religion had now totally ceased.

The financial evidence, even more than the verbal, thus indicates a drastic and comparatively rapid reduction of commitment to the traditional rites in the Reformation decades. The third and final type of evidence requiring examination is the behavioural – the evidence afforded by men's actions rather than by their words or their investments. To what extent did individuals and communities continue actively to organize and participate in the ancient modes of piety? And to what extent did they attempt – either violently or non-violently – to resist the assaults to which these were subjected?

Until 1547 most parishes continued to organize the accustomed weekly, annual and occasional rites. Easter vigils were still mounted at the sepulchre, as at Exeter St Petrock's in 1542. The reserved sacrament was still carried in procession on Palm Sunday and at the feast of Corpus Christi, as at Woodbury in 1543. Funerals with knells, crosses and tapers were still performed, together with prayers and masses for the dead. Woodbury, for example, regularly rang knells for deceased parishioners, like Richard Westcote in 1538–9, paid its parish priest to celebrate its 'brethren *diriges*', and bought bread and wine for its 'soul priest', 'to sing withal'.[57]

Some practices, on the other hand, were apparently ceasing. At Ashburton the 'measuring' of the church may have been terminated after 1535–6, and payments to the vicar for reciting the bede-roll here were ended after 1536–7.[58] At the same time, the behaviour of some individuals would suggest the beginnings of a decline in lay devotion. At Down St Mary in 1532 Thomas Stone was barred from the Easter communion because of his alleged absences from auricular confession. His parson warned him that 'if he would not be confessed of him or of some other priest, that he might be known as a Christian man, he would not give him his Maker'. In 1533 Hugh Fountain of Ugborough failed to attend services in his parish church, 'as a Christian man should do'. Fountain claimed that Thomas Fowle, John Manadon and others had deliberately deterred him from attendance by using violence. In about 1533, at Denbury, Richard Whiteway ceased to contribute his annual quota of holy bread to the parish church. 'By the reason whereof', complained his churchwardens in 1540, 'the said parish hath been destitute of holy bread for that Sunday for the space of this seven or eight year, contrary to the good and laudable custom of the same parish'. In 1535, at Lawhitton, several parishioners deliberately prevented their priest from performing mass by removing the chalice, mass-book and other requisites. Most of the offenders, including their leader Richard Clotworthy, were hus-

---

[57] CWA Exeter SP, 1542; CWA Woodbury, 1537–47.
[58] CWA Ashburton.

bandmen.[59] But the most striking development was an apparent outburst of sacrilege against the consecrated host itself. In September 1536 it was reported from Penryn that, in Cornwall, 'the sacrament of the altar' had been 'irreverently handled'.[60]

Evidence of this nature would seem to confirm the impression that, from the time of the Henrician Reformation, the commitment of south-western men and women to the traditional rites was already beginning to diminish. With what vigour did they subsequently resist the onslaught launched against these rites by the government of Edward VI?

Throughout the first two years of the new reign, as the official attack upon intercessions and other practices progressed, physical resistance remained a conspicuously unusual local response. A near exception occurred in the hundred of Penwith, where, in 1547, a 'tumultuous assembly' was provoked by the insensitivity of the commissioner William Body; he had created the impression that a seizure of church goods was imminent.[61] Not until June 1549, with the eruption of the so-called 'Prayerbook rebellion', did the regime encounter large-scale and violent opposition within the region. Nor should the significance of even this dramatic event be unduly inflated. It has conventionally been interpreted as conclusive evidence that the south-western people were still resolutely determined to preserve the ancient rites. This interpretation, however, is open to a number of serious objections.[62]

That religious conservatism provided the rebellion with its most important single stimulus can scarcely be denied. Its outbreak at Sampford Courtenay, on the fringes of Dartmoor, was ignited primarily by the parishioners' resolution to restore the abrogated Latin mass, and to 'keep the old and ancient religion as their forefathers before them had done'. Rebels restored the mass in other parishes, and reportedly marched with the reserved sacrament under a canopy as well as with crosses, banners, candles, and holy bread and water. In their 'articles', moreover, the insurgents explicitly demanded the retention of baptism on weekdays as well as on Sundays, asserting that 'the gates of Heaven be not opened without this blessed sacrament of baptism'; the confirmation of children upon resort to their bishop; and the restoration of Latin services, together with holy bread, holy water, palms, ashes and 'all other ancient old ceremonies used heretofore by our mother the holy Church'. 'Every preacher in his sermon', and 'every priest at his mass', was to 'pray specially by name for the souls in Purgatory, as our

[59] C 1 900/34–5; STAC 2/7/93; 15/233–7; CCB 854A, II, sub 24 November 1540.
[60] SP 1/106/135.
[61] Harleian 352, fols. 65v–6v.
[62] For the fullest account of the 1549 rebellion, see Rose-Troup 1913. For more recent evaluations, see Rowse 1941; Fletcher 1973; Cornwall 1977; and Youings 1979.

forefathers did.' Above all, mass was to be celebrated 'as it hath been in times past'. Since the consecrated elements were 'very really the body and blood of our saviour Jesu Christ', the bread was to be displayed over the high altar as an object of worship. Only once in the year, at Easter, were laymen to receive it; of the wine they were never to partake.[63]

Nevertheless it is certain that the motives of the insurgents were by no means exclusively religious. Some, indeed, would seem to have been recruited less by ideological persuasion than by physical intimidation. It was said of Nicholas Bowyer of Bodmin 'that he was forced thereunto; and that if he had not consented to them, they would have destroyed him and his house'. The loyalist 'gentleman of Devon' observed that 'very many' had been recruited 'by force, against their will'.[64] In addition it is evident that there existed powerful material inducements to revolt. The rebel leaders reportedly attracted support by disseminating rumours about the new tax on sheep, claiming that 'after the payment for sheep they should pay for their geese and pigs and suchlike'. The government believed that clothiers' resentment of the sheep tax helped to turn a 'spark of rebellion' into 'so great a flame', and one version of the rebel articles certainly demanded a remission of the taxes on sheep and cloth. Grievances of this nature, particularly strong in a sheep-rearing and cloth-producing region like the South-West, can only have been exacerbated by the acute economic problems of 1548–9. These included the 'death of cattle', and the 'dearth of victuals and other things', of which the rebels in fact complained to the Protector.[65]

Nor, in this period of distress, should the attractions of plunder be disregarded. Philip Nichols claimed that one of the rebels' real objectives was 'an open and common spoil'. 'Their own country they have so spoiled and so disordered that it is miserable to hear', reported the gentleman of Devon. 'Buying and selling ceaseth amongst them, in place whereof is come robbing and reiving.' John Hooker – an eyewitness – noted that they brought horses and panniers to the siege of Exeter, hoping to steal velvets and silks and to carry home plate, money and other riches. William Webber, one of the Devon captains, stole goods and deeds from the house of Richard Pomeroy; John and Thomas Harris of Crediton were 'spoiled' by the rebels; and in Cornwall the insurgents plundered the gentry on St Michael's Mount and stripped the ladies at Trematon of their clothes and rings. According to a contemporary ballad, 'they did rob and spoil all the king's friends'.[66]

---

[63] 'Life of Carew', p. lxxxvi; 'Description of Exeter', pp. 26–9; *Acts and Monuments*, II, pp. 1305, 1308; Royal 18 B XI, fols. 11–12, 14, 19–19v, 22, 25.

[64] Rose-Troup 1913, pp. 307, 489. Cf. the claim of Thomas Holmes (Rose-Troup 1913, p. 346).

[65] *Prayerbook of 1549*, pp. 16, 41, 67; Rose-Troup 1913, pp. 436, 439.

[66] Royal 18 B XI, fols. 3–5; 'Description of Exeter', p. 38; *Survey of Cornwall*, p. 380; Rose-Troup 1913, pp. 337, 381n, 487; Rowse 1941, p. 284.

By no means all of the rebels, therefore, can plausibly be portrayed as pious defenders of the ancient rites. But even more dubious is the assumption – to be found in most of the standard accounts – that the insurgents were necessarily representative of regional opinion. Even Holinshed's claim that they totalled 10,000 is an exaggeration. According to Hooker, a muster of rebels 'out of every quarter' produced at Clyst St Mary a total of 6,000. According to the government estimate – made at the height of the insurrection, and based on reports from 'some that hath viewed them' – the rebels in Devon and Cornwall together numbered no more than 7,000. This figure constitutes a relatively unimpressive percentage of the two counties' approximately 200,000 inhabitants; it can scarcely have equalled the population of Exeter alone.[67] Particular localities, including the parishes around Bodmin, Sampford Courtenay and Clyst St Mary, appear to have supplied a high proportion of the non-gentle lay recruits; others came from Blisland, Crediton, Exeter St Thomas, Poundstock, St Columb Major, St Germans, St Ives, Torrington, Week St Mary, Woodbury and elsewhere. The movement attracted some yeomen, like Blisland's Thomas Holmes, and a few substantial townsmen, including Henry Bray and Henry Lee, mayors of Bodmin and Torrington. Cloth-workers and tinners also seem to have been involved, together with artisans like the tailor Underhill and the shoemaker Maunder. The rank and file must nevertheless have consisted primarily of husbandmen and agricultural labourers, like Sampford Courtenay's William Seager.[68]

While no more than a comparatively modest proportion of the southwestern population thus rose against the anti-Catholic regime, a significant number of individuals and communities proved actively loyal to it. In Exeter – crucially – the rebel summons was firmly rejected by the mayor, John Blackaller, and by his aldermen; these included John Britnall, John Buller, William Hurst and William Periam. They raised soldiers, appointed captains, warders and watchmen, and fortified their walled city with ramparts and artillery, as a result of which it successfully withstood a dangerous and destructive six-week siege. A number of the inhabitants, including the merchant John Wolcott, the clothier Richard Taylor, and two men named Vincent and Shark, attempted persistently to betray the provincial capital to the besiegers. On the other hand, some 100 of the citizens pledged themselves to 'stand firmly and faithfully to the defence and keeping of the city', and several – including the merchant John Drake, the cook John Simmonds, and a Fleming also named John – risked capture, wounding and death by

[67] Cornwall 1977, pp. 95–7; 'Description of Exeter', p. 58; *Prayerbook of 1549*, p. 44.
[68] Rose-Troup 1913, esp. pp. 497–501; 'Description of Exeter', pp. 36–7; Royal 18 B XI, fol. 37. For Bodmin, see *Survey of Cornwall*, p. 292; for Sampford Courtenay, see 'Description of Exeter', pp. 26–9; and for Clyst St Mary, see 'Description of Exeter', pp. 31–2, and CWA Woodbury, 1549. For Underhill and Seager, see Cornwall 1977, p. 66.

participation in sallies. Several city parishes sold plate to pay soldiers' wages, and the merchants John Budleigh, John Periam and Thomas Prestwood together raised a substantial sum of money to finance Lord Russell's army as it marched to Exeter's relief. Albeit with varying degrees of enthusiasm, most of the approximately 8,000 Exonians would seem to have followed the oligarchy's commands and to have 'continued dutiful and obedient' throughout the siege.

Nor was active loyalism confined to Exeter. Although the town of Plymouth was captured, its castle was 'valiantly defended and kept from the rebels'; the defenders were led by William Hawkins. The townsmen of Totnes, headed by William Bougin, raised £693 6s 8d for Lord Russell. The inhabitants of Ashburton sold two chalices and a pyx for £10, 'with the which money they served the king's majesty against the rebels, for the preservation of the towns of Totnes and Plymouth, by the commandment of the lord of Bedford'. The parishioners of Tavistock, by selling plate and vestments, similarly provided 20 men 'to serve the king's majesty in the commotion time'. At Crediton the loyalists included John and Thomas Harris, and at Launceston, towards the end of the insurrection, the inhabitants appear to have turned against the rebels. Other loyalists came from the smaller towns. Thomas Colyford of Cullompton was imprisoned by rebels. A tinner from Teignmouth, John Newcombe, foiled the rebels' attempt to undermine the walls of Exeter by flooding their tunnel. Another tinner, one Kingwell of Chagford, not only carried messages to Lord Russell but also denounced the insurgents – to their faces – as rebels and traitors. Hooker describes him as 'an enemy of the popish state'. An anti-Catholic gentleman, Walter Raleigh Esquire, was rescued from the fury of the rebels by 'mariners' from the port of Exmouth.

Loyalists were also to be found outside the towns. In Cornwall, 'divers dutiful subjects' fled from the rebels to St Nicholas' Island in Cawsand Bay, and in both counties many servants of the rural gentry – like Foxe, a servant of Sir Hugh Pollard – were actively opposed to the rebel cause. It is also to be noted that when Lord Russell first arrived with his government forces in east Devon, numbers of 'the common people . . . served and offered their service unto him'. Many, finding themselves unpaid, subsequently deserted, but after receiving 'a mass of money' from the Exeter merchants, he was again able to recruit 'a great number of men'. Russell himself estimated his local levies to consist of 600–700 horse and 1,000 foot.[69]

It was largely the existence of such loyalism within the South-West itself that eventually permitted the government forces to slaughter the insurgents

[69] For the preceding three paragraphs, see 'Description of Exeter', esp. pp. 31–3, 37–55, 65–6; *Plymouth Records*, pp. 16–17; E 117 2/7, fols. 2v, 11; *Survey of Cornwall*, p. 239; *Prayerbook of 1549*, esp. pp. 33, 35; and Rose-Troup 1913, esp. pp. 202, 243, 301, 381n, 503–9.

at Fenny Bridges, Clyst St Mary, Sampford Courtenay and elsewhere, to relieve Exeter, and to re-establish the effective authority of the Edwardian regime. By 1 September the Protector could rejoice that 'not only the counties remain permanently in good order, but also the multitude so repent their former detestable and naughty doings as they abhor to hear them spoken of'. Certainly the continuing official assault upon Catholic rites in the years 1550–3 appears to have encountered no significant physical resistance. Opposition was expressed now in nothing more potent than words, like the 'lewd and seditious' utterances of the Devonian Thomas Beer, or the prophecy of King Edward's death by an unnamed inhabitant of Cornwall.[70]

That popular responses to the Edwardian Reformation were in reality predominantly acquiescent rather than resistant is confirmed by the obedience with which parishes generally abandoned the prohibited rites. The liturgical use of candles and tapers, for example, was substantially curtailed. At Morebath the purchase of paschal tapers ended after 1548, while at Woodbury in 1548–9 the expenditure on lights dwindled to a mere 5d. Easter vigils were discontinued, the provision of sepulchre lights at Morebath ending in 1547. Funerals with knells, crosses and tapers were suppressed at Woodbury after 1547, at Ashburton after 1548, and at Stratton after 1549. Most important, the accounts indicate that the public recitation of bede-rolls generally ended in 1548, and that masses and other intercessions for the departed were everywhere terminated at about the same time. Woodbury, for instance, made annual payments to its priest 'for saying of four brethren *diriges*, and the ringing to the same', until 1547–8; thereafter these ceased. Amongst the last of such was a *dirige* at Morebath in 1548–9.[71] Most parishes, moreover, would seem to have submitted without overt dissent to the destructive proceedings of the chantry commissioners. Thus Morebath in 1547 sent its Three Men and wardens to Tiverton, 'to make an answer for chantry ground', while three chalices belonging to a chantry chapel at Liskeard were dutifully surrendered to the commissioners in 1548.[72]

Compliance seems also to have been the predominant reaction to official assaults upon the traditional ritual apparatus. The accounts for 1547–9 show that most parishes obediently compiled inventories, sent representatives to appear before the commissioners, and even began to deliver their apparatus into confiscation. Antony, for example, dispatched equipment to Plymouth; and Woodbury, after sending representatives to Exeter, surren-

[70] *APC*, IV, p. 220; Hooker, Commonplace Book, fol. 349.
[71] E.g. CWA Ashburton; CWA Morebath; CWA Woodbury; Additional 32243, HCWA Stratton; Additional 32244, SWA Stratton.
[72] CWA Morebath, 1547; E 117 1/52. This does not mean that there were no attempts to conceal lands formerly used for chantry purposes; see, for example, E 178 518, 659.

dered three copes, ten vestments and other treasures. Morebath was apparently exceptional in delivering vestments, copes, banners, a chalice and other goods into the safekeeping of individual parishioners like John Atcourt, Nicholas Athayne and Thomas Rumbelow. Nor do the confiscations of 1550–3 seem ever to have provoked substantial resistance. 'In the execution of this commission', reported the commissioners for Devon in June 1553, 'we have found the people very quiet and conformable.' Camborne delivered its apparatus to Truro; Stratton, to Lostwithiel; Woodbury, to Exeter. Barnstaple delivered chalices, copes and vestments, including a suit of vestments worth £60. Even Morebath surrendered two copes, two tunicles, a pax and a paten.[73]

Ritual plate and vestments were not the only targets of the government campaign. The removal of church bells, ordered in 1549, appears to have been executed in some parishes; elsewhere it was averted only by the payment of fines.[74] Extensive compliance with another decree of 1549 – which ordered the destruction of Catholic service-books – is suggested by the very frequent expenditure upon such books in Mary's reign. Certainly the inhabitants of Woodbury in 1549–50 loaded their 'Latin books' onto horses and dispatched them to Exeter, 'according to the commandment'. Traditionalist books owned by St Mary Major at Exeter in 1533 had similarly disappeared from its inventories by 1553. Dartington and Morebath seem to have been untypical in delivering mass-books into the safekeeping of parishioners.[75] That baptismal fonts and Easter sepulchres were often either deliberately damaged or (more probably) simply neglected in these years is also implied by their frequent repair in Mary's reign.[76]

Of paramount significance, however, was the co-operation of parishes in the assault upon altars. Marian expenditure on the re-erection of these sacred structures leaves no doubt that their deposition had been very exten-

---

[73] CWA Antony, pp. 36–7; CWA Camborne, 1553; CWA Coldridge, 1552; CWA Morebath, 1548, 1552; CWA Woodbury, 1547, 1549, 1553; *Inventories, Cornwall*, p. ix, etc; Additional 32243, HCWA Stratton, 1551, 1553; *Barnstaple Records*, I, pp. 198–9; Stowe 141, fol. 67.

[74] For the order, see *Prayerbook of 1549*, p. 73; and CWA Woodbury, 1549. For its execution, see CWA Exeter HT, 1549; and CWA N. Molton, 1549. For fines, see CWA Crediton, 1551; CWA Morebath, 1551; CWA Woodbury, 1551; and Additional 32243, HCWA Stratton, 1552. These fines explain the survival of medieval bells in the inventories of 1553 (E 117 2/7) and in many south-western churches today. See also Rose-Troup 1913, pp. 372–7; and Ellacombe 1872, pp. 225, 288–9.

[75] *Prayerbook of 1549*, pp. 49, 127–9; CWA Woodbury, 1550; CWA Exeter SMM, fol. 12; CWA Morebath, 1555; CWA Dartington, 1554. For Marian expenditure, see above, p. 26.

[76] For fonts, see, for example, CWA Coldridge, 1556; and CWA Exeter SMS, 1554. For sepulchres, see, for example, CWA Ashburton, 1556; CWA Crediton, 1554; CWA Dartmouth, 1554; CWA Exeter SJB, 1554; CWA Exeter SMS, 1554; CWA Morebath, 1554; CWA S. Tawton, 1559; CWA Woodbury, 1554; and Additional 32243, HCWA Stratton, 1558.

sive; and in 1549–51 such deposition was recorded in virtually all parishes for which accounts survive. These included Holy Trinity, St John's Bow and St Petrock's at Exeter; the urban parishes of Ashburton, Camborne, Crediton, Dartmouth and Stratton; and the rural parishes of Morebath, North Petherwin, Woodbury and possibly Antony. In at least 7 of these 12 parishes the structures were subsequently sold. St John's Bow, for example, in 1549–50 paid men 'to take down the altars' and sold the stones to John May. Woodbury, after paying 'for the taking down of the altars' in 1549–50, rewarded James Croft 'for carrying out of the rubble of the altars', and sold 'stones of the altars' as well as 'three broad stones that lay upon the altars'. Stratton, after paying for 'drawing down of the altars' in 1551, sold 'stones of the altars' for 4s 4d. At Dartmouth, by 1552, altar stones had been ejected into the churchyard. Two altar frontals belonging to Dartmouth church had been thrown into a vault, and two of its coffers were now 'full of the pieces of the altar work of the reredos'. Even less respectful was the behaviour of Christopher Sampford at Halberton. Impelled (according to the parishioners) by his 'cankered mind toward God's service', Sampford 'did spoil and take away the high altar, and laid the altar stone, sanctified, in his kitchen'. 'Where', they added in horror, 'he keepeth the same to convey his kitchen and filthy waters upon'.[77]

The behavioural evidence thus indicates that official assaults upon the traditional rites were never in fact resisted by more than a limited minority of individuals and communities within the South-West. To what extent does it suggest that these rites were restored after Mary's accession?

Much of the confiscated ritual apparatus was now retrieved by parish churches. Service-books, for example, were returned to Woodbury; plate, including a cross, chalice and holy-water bucket, to Camborne; and vestments to Ashburton, Dartmouth, South Tawton and Woodbury.[78] On the other hand, Marian expenditure on such apparatus[79] suggests frequent non-retrieval. Some of the Cornish plate had been defaced and delivered to the Mint, and equipment from the Exeter churches was detained by the mayor and aldermen until as late as 1555.[80] High altars were re-erected in 1553–4 by most parishes with extant accounts, as at Exeter St Mary Steps, in the

---

[77] For the order, see ER XV, fols. 119v–20 (23 November 1550). For Marian re-erections, see below, pp. 40–1. For depositions, see CWA Antony, 1549; CWA Ashburton, 1550–1; CWA Camborne, 1550; CWA Crediton, 1551–2; CWA Dartmouth, 1552; CWA Exeter HT, 1550; CWA Exeter SJB, 1550; CWA Exeter SP, 1550–1; CWA Morebath, 1551; CWA N. Petherwin, fol. 32v; CWA Woodbury, 1550; and Additional 32243, HCWA Stratton, 1551. For Sampford, see STAC 4/8/47.

[78] E 117 13/105; CWA Ashburton, 1554; CWA Camborne, 1554; CWA Dartmouth, 1554–5; CWA S. Tawton, 1555; CWA Woodbury, 1554, 1558.

[79] See above, p. 26.

[80] E 117 13/105; APC, V, pp. 112–13.

towns of Ashburton, Camborne, Chagford, Crediton, Dartmouth and Stratton, and in the rural communities of Antony, Coldridge, Morebath, South Tawton and Woodbury. At Woodbury, for instance, the restoration was executed by a mason and his apprentice in three days, with John Hoppin transporting the requisite stones in his cart. Some of the new structures, nevertheless, were evidently makeshift: permanent high altars seem not to have been acquired by Exeter St Petrock's, Stratton or Tavistock until 1555–6.[81] Subsidiary altars, like St Margaret's at Woodbury, were frequently restored in 1553–4. Restoration, however, was delayed until 1554–5 at Chagford and Braunton and until 1555–6 at Morebath, while in some parishes, including Exeter St Petrock's, it may never have occurred.[82]

Many of the traditional rites were undoubtedly revived. In 1554, for example, the inhabitants of Hatherland at Washfield persuaded their parson to restore regular masses in their chapel, together with holy bread and holy water, bedes, processions, churchings, Easter communions, candles at Candlemas and palms on Palm Sunday. Most of the parishes with extant accounts began again to burn lights at the major festivals: Crediton, for instance, spent 39s 9d in 1558. Vigils were again mounted at Easter sepulchres, candles distributed at Candlemas, and bells tolled at All Souls. Catholic funerals were once more performed for the region's dead.[83]

On the other hand, a number of the customary rites – including the 'measuring' at Ashburton and the celebration of 'Revel Sunday' at Morebath – seem never to have been restored. At Halberton, where mass had customarily been celebrated in a chapel at Christmas, Candlemas and Easter, the lessee John Warren refused to countenance its restoration. The inhabitants protested by withholding their dues, 'because they had not their service as it was accustomate to be used'. At Menheniot the Twelve Men deliberately prevented their vicar from distributing holy water to local households each Sunday, and limited its distribution to 'but once a quarter'. They also forbade the clerk to unlock the tabernacle, thus presumably preventing the vicar's ministration of communion to the sick. At St Gennys the churchwarden John French not only failed to collect the church bread from local households,

---

[81] *Tavistock Records*, p. 24; CWA Antony, 1554; CWA Ashburton, 1554; CWA Camborne, 1554; CWA Chagford, 1554; CWA Coldridge, 1554; CWA Crediton, 1554; CWA Dartmouth, 1553; CWA Exeter SMS, 1554; CWA Exeter SP, 1556; CWA Morebath, 1554; CWA S. Tawton, 1554; CWA Woodbury, 1554; Additional 32243, HCWA Stratton, 1553, 1556; Additional 32244, SWA Stratton, 1557.

[82] *Tavistock Records*, p. 24; CWA Ashburton, 1554; CWA Coldridge, 1553; CWA Crediton, 1554: CWA Exeter SJB, 1554; CWA S. Tawton, 1555; CWA Woodbury, 1554. For delay, see CWA Braunton, 1555; CWA Chagford, 1555; and CWA Morebath, 1556. For non-restoration, see CWA Exeter SP.

[83] For Washfield, see ER XVII, fols. 24v–5v. For lights, see, for example, CWA Crediton, 1558. For vigils, see, for example, CWA Crediton, 1554. For Candlemas, see, for example, CWA Antony, 1555. For bells and funerals, see, for example, CWA Ashburton, 1554–9.

'as the custom of the parish was', but also neglected to distribute candles at Candlemas. 'On Candlemas day last past', reported a parishioner, 'the parish of St Gennys had no candles made according to the old custom, by reason of the negligence of the said John French, being warden. For this deponent was present there the same day, when that the warden should [have] delivered his candles after mass to every parishioner at the church door: and the said French delivered none.' 'All which', he lamented, 'was contrary to the old order and custom.'[84]

Particularly significant is the evidence concerning intercession. Of the 22 parishes with accounts for 1553–9, the revival of this once indispensable practice is recorded for certain in only 13. Morebath, for instance, recommenced its general *diriges* on behalf of all its benefactors in 1553–4 – though even in this parish the customary masses for individuals seem not to have been restored. The revival of intercessory rites was apparently delayed until 1555–6 at Exeter St Petrock's and Woodbury, until 1557 at Chagford, and until as late as 1558–9 at Exeter St John's Bow, while in 9 of the accounted parishes it may never have occurred.[85] Especially conspicuous is the absence from all the accounts – with the sole exception of those for Dartington – of payments to priests for the recitation of bede-rolls. Despite occasional requests by donors 'to be prayed for', and the existence of an apparently Marian bede-roll among the Camborne accounts, it therefore appears probable that a majority of parishes never revived these formerly ubiquitous prayers.[86]

Even such rites as were restored were no longer universally supported. Individuals, it is true, remained enthusiastic. John Combe of Linkinhorne, at Christmas 1553, thanked God that after an interval of four years he had again 'heard mass and received holy bread and holy water'. Also favourable to the revived practices were William Smith and Walter Staplehead, Mayors of Exeter in 1553 and 1556, and the Exeter aldermen John Blackaller and William Hurst, who in 1554 were described as 'of a good Catholic faith'. 'Much addicted to the superstitious sect of popery' was Foxe's descrip-

---

[84] CWA Ashburton, 1553–9; CWA Morebath, 1553–9; CCB 855, fols. 127v–8v; 371v–3; 381v–3v, 409–9v, 415–15v.

[85] For revival, see CWA Antony; CWA Braunton; CWA Chagford; CWA Crediton; CWA Dartington; CWA Exeter HT; CWA Exeter SJB; CWA Exeter SP; CWA Launceston; CWA Morebath; CWA N. Petherwin; CWA Woodbury; and *Barnstaple Records*, I, pp. 212–13. For non-revival, see CWA Ashburton; CWA Camborne; CWA Coldridge; CWA Dartmouth; CWA Exeter SMS; CWA Kilmington; CWA Molland; CWA S. Tawton; and Additional 32243, HCWA Stratton.

[86] CWA Dartington, 1554–9; PROB 11 41, fol. 253v; 42B, John Phipayne, 1558; Moger, 3, John Belfield, 1558; CWA Coldridge, 1559; CWA Morebath, 1559; CWA Camborne, 1558. See also references to bede-men in CWA Ashburton, 1559; and Additional 32243, HCWA Stratton, 1556.

tion of the husband and children of Agnes Priest at Boyton in 1558; they compelled her to participate in the restored services, confessions and processions.[87] Many of their contemporaries, however, conspicuously failed to exhibit a similar devotion to the ancient rites.

At Linkinhorne in December 1553, for example, John Combe's enthusiasm for the revived practices was openly derided by Sampson Jackman and John Cowlyn of Stoke Climsland. When Combe protested that 'the queen's grace hath granted it', Jackman and Cowlyn allegedly cursed her and declared that 'if a woman bear the sword, my lady Elizabeth ought to bear it first'. The hostility of Exeter's John Midwinter was equally overt. On seeing the parson of St Petrock's dressed in his mass-vestments, Midwinter dramatically 'pointed unto him with his finger' – thus 'remembering, as it were, his old protestations that he would never say mass again'.[88] The attitude of others was expressed in non-participation. Among those suspected of neglecting the communion were William Thorning, apparently of Powderham, Thomas Langmead of Exminster, and William Gooding of Whitchurch. Thorning admitted in 1557 that he had not received communion for three years; no one, he claimed, had called him to do so, 'and therefore he hath abstained'. The reception of holy bread was allegedly neglected by Martin Alley of Kenton, while Thorning, Langmead, Gooding and Alley, as well as William Budd of Swimbridge, were all suspected of refraining from auricular confession. This was admitted by Thorning and Alley, the former explaining that in three years 'he was never confessed', because 'no man called him unto confession'. Alley, in addition, was thought to have shown contempt for the communion of the sick, which his parish priest had brought to him in his illness, and his wife Joan was suspected of a similar impiety.[89]

Several absented themselves from the restored services. In 1556–7, during mass and matins on a Sunday and on two holy days, John Smith of Landkey failed to attend church and to abstain from labour. In 1557 Martin Alley of Kenton allegedly broke the Sabbath and avoided processions. In 1558 at least one evensong was missed by Alice Watts of Ottery St Mary, while in 1559 the services at St Gennys were avoided by John French at 'divers times'. Some offences were flagrant. In 1556 Thomas Perry of Axminster admitted that for nine months he 'doth not remember when he went in procession'. In the same year Roger Gill – another inhabitant of Axminster, who was suspected also of disbelief in transubstantiation – admitted that he had absented himself from services for a month, and from most of the processions for a year. At Upottery, in 1557, it was reported that Joan

[87] SP 11/2/2, 15; Hooker, Commonplace Book, fols. 350–1; *Acts and Monuments*, II, p. 2050.
[88] SP 11/2/2; Hooker, Commonplace Book, fol. 350.
[89] CCB 855, fols. 111v, 113–13v, 115v–16, 150v, 151v, 174v–5, 210v, 361v.

Sweetland 'never came to her parish church'. Another non-attender, predictably, was Agnes Priest of Boyton. 'As oft as I could', she explained in 1558, 'upon Sundays and holy days I made excuses not to go to the popish church'.[90]

The incidence of non-restoration and non-participation must again indicate a substantial decline of popular devotion to the traditional rites. This conclusion is confirmed by the acquiescent and even co-operative reaction of most south-western people to the assault launched against such rites by the early-Elizabethan regime.

When, as John Hooker recalled, the royal commissioners reached Exeter in September 1559, they peremptorily 'forbade any more masses or popish services to be used'. Once more the predominant local response to official instructions was a dutiful conformity. 'We found everywhere the people sufficiently well disposed towards religion', reported the Devon-born commissioner John Jewel, 'and even in those quarters where we expected most difficulty.' The churchwardens' accounts indeed record in 1559–60 a virtually universal cessation of the newly prohibited rites. Elaborate lighting at the festivals was again curtailed: by 1561 Chagford, for instance, devoted a mere 9d to candles. Easter vigils at the sepulchre were everywhere suppressed. Funerals with crosses and tapers appear to have ended, though knells might still be rung. Of paramount importance, however, was the end of intercessions. In every parish with extant accounts, the performance of prayers and masses on behalf of the dead would seem by 1560 to have totally ceased. The general *diriges* at Morebath, for instance, disappeared after 1558, and the recitations of the bede-roll at Dartington after 1559.[91]

Simultaneously the parishes of the South-West submitted with general passivity to the renewed inventorying, confiscation and destruction of their ritual apparatus. At Exeter St Mary Steps, by order of the royal commissioners, the pyx, censer, altar box and Easter sepulchre were all burned in 1559. At Exeter St Mary Major, at about the same time, candlesticks, a censer and a cross were burned, a pax was 'taken away', a canopy, oil box, holy-water bucket and several small bells disappeared, and a 'great candlestick' was melted down and used in the casting of a bell. At Crediton, again in 1559, the sepulchre and the paschal candle were 'cut in pieces', a tabernacle, censer and four candlesticks 'broken', and two holy-water

---

[90] CCB 855, fols. 49, 63, 111v, 174v–5, 191–1v, 214v, 377v, 409–9v, 415–15v; *Acts and Monuments*, II, pp. 2050–2.

[91] Hooker, Commonplace Book, fol. 352; *Zurich Letters*, pp. 44–5; CWA Chagford, 1561; CWA Morebath; CWA Dartington. For knells, see, for example, CWA Exeter SP, 1567. For candles, see CWA Exeter SJB, 1563 (4d); and CWA Woodbury, 1568 (5d). Woodbury ceased to buy lights on St Swithun's day after 1558 (CWA Woodbury).

pots and a cross 'broken in pieces'.[92] Although equipment seems sometimes to have been concealed – at Morebath a chasuble, altar cloth and banner were entrusted to individual parishioners, and a similar device was suspected at Callington[93] – there is little doubt that the loss of plate and cloth was very extensive; indeed it is to the alienation, confiscation and destruction of these early-Elizabethan years that the present-day scarcity of Catholic altar vessels and vestments in the region's churches must be primarily due. And although Morebath in 1559–60 entrusted its mass-book to a parishioner, most parishes appear to have surrendered their Catholic service-books to confiscation. An act-book of the Exeter Chamber which commences in 1560 seems to have been bound from a mutilated service-book. St Breock lost a psalter, processional and manual in 1560, and a mass-book, portis, manual and processional by 1565. Traditionalist books inventoried at Exeter St Mary Major in 1558 had similarly disappeared by 1567; they included two mass-books, two half-processionals, a processional, a manual and 'a parchment book of Our Lady service'. 'Two pieces of old books', evidently already mutilated, were sold by Stratton in 1570.[94]

Altars, moreover, were again destroyed. At Exeter in September 1559, according to Hooker, the royal commissioners 'did deface all the altars and monuments of idolatry'. The churchwardens' accounts confirm that 1559–60 saw the demolition of such structures not only by Exeter churches like St John's Bow and St Petrock's but also by towns like Ashburton, Barnstaple and Crediton and even by rural parishes like Antony, Coldridge, Kilmington, Molland, Morebath, South Tawton, Winkleigh and Woodbury. The wardens of St John's Bow, for example, paid for 'pulling down of the altar and making clean of the same'. The parishioners of Coldridge, after sending representatives to meet the visitors at Barnstaple, paid for 'ridding of the altars of the church'. At Woodbury, following the wardens' appearance before the visitors at Exeter, three men were paid for pulling down the high altar and St Margaret's altar and for carrying away the stones.[95] Further removals occurred at South Tawton in 1560–1, St Mary Steps and St Petrock's at Exeter in 1561–2, St John's Bow at Exeter in 1564–5, Winkleigh in 1565–6 and Chudleigh in 1568. At Chudleigh the Four Men had to pay for 'taking down of the altar stones', but elsewhere

---

92 CWA Exeter SMS, 1559; CWA Exeter SMM, fol. 16; DRO 1660 A 12.
93 CWA Morebath, 1560, 1568; E 178 517. For survivals today, see above, pp. 21–2.
94 CWA Morebath, 1560; *Exeter Records*, p. 308; CWA St Breock, fols. 4v, 16; CWA Exeter SMM, fol. 16; Additional 32243, HCWA Stratton, 1570.
95 Hooker, Commonplace Book, fol. 352; CWA Exeter SP, 1560; CWA Exeter SJB, 1559; CWA Ashburton, 1560; *Barnstaple Records*, I, p. 213; CWA Crediton, 1559; CWA Antony, 1559; CWA Coldridge, 1560; CWA Kilmington, 1560; CWA Molland, 1559–60; CWA Morebath, 1559; CWA S. Tawton, 1560; CWA Winkleigh, 1560; CWA Woodbury, 1559.

it seems that already demolished structures were being removed from the church.[96] Although in some parishes the fate of altars is obscure,[97] only exceptionally – as at Morebath – do they appear to have remained *in situ* in as late as 1570.[98] The rarity of altar stones in the region's churches today must be attributed primarily to this extensive parochial compliance with the official campaign.[99]

Throughout the 1560s, active popular support for the suppressed rites appears to have been restricted to a relatively small number of individuals. In 1564 Bishop Alley's list of the principal Catholics in his diocese included two apparently non-gentle inhabitants of Exeter itself, namely Robert Winter and Hart, the town clerk. Another 'zealous man in the Romish religion' was John Wolcott, merchant and Mayor of Exeter in 1565. And at Alphington until 1567, Thomas Stephens and his wife continued to commend the virtues of holy bread and holy water to their fellow-parishioners, allegedly asserting that these were 'necessary for salvation'. On the other hand, the willingness of five neighbours of the Stephenses – namely John Alderhead, Simon Hamlyn, Mary Harris, Michael Midwinter and William Parr – to testify against them in the Consistory Court would suggest that local support for their activities was limited.[100] It is also significant that with only a few dubious exceptions – including the case of John Clogg, thatcher of Morchard Bishop, in 1569[101] – the South-West appears to afford no evidence whatsoever of Catholic recusancy at the popular level before the 1570s. Even Thomas Stephens of Alphington attended his parish church.

If non-violent resistance to the early-Elizabethan campaign against traditional rites was never extensive, violent resistance was altogether unknown. The destruction of 1559 encountered no opposition remotely comparable to the rebellion of 1549, and the attempt of the Northern Earls to restore the ancient practices by force in 1569 evoked no support from the South-West. The justices of Cornwall, subscribing to the Act of Uniformity in December 1569, in fact assured the Council that 'we find the people of this shire in such conformable order and quietness (thanks be unto God) as neither the queen's majesty nor your highnesses shall need any wary

---

[96] CWA S. Tawton, 1561; CWA Exeter SMS, 1562; CWA Exeter SP, 1562; CWA Exeter SJB, 1565: CWA Winkleigh, 1566; CWA Chudleigh, 1568. Witness to this early-Elizabethan assault is probably borne by the fragments of an alabaster altar at Mabe (Pevsner and Radcliffe 1970, p. 110).

[97] E.g. CWA Braunton; CWA Dartington.

[98] CWA Morebath, 1566, 1572.

[99] See above, p. 21.

[100] *Original Letters*, pp. 67–70; Hooker, Commonplace Book, fol. 355; CCB 856, fols. 143v–6.

[101] CCB 856, fols. 311–11v; see also below, pp. 166–7.

(we hope) to be doubtful of them'. 'This country', agreed the justices of Devon at the same time, 'hath and doth remain in very good and dutiful obedience, peace and quiet; and so, by the help of God, we have no doubt of the continuance thereof'.[102]

[102] SP 12/60/27, 39.

4

Independent activities: prayers, images and cult objects

NB
People seeking personal
access

The dependent activities of the pre-Reformation layman remained reliant upon the clergy and its ministrations. His independent activities, in contrast, were essentially autonomous. A variety of religious practices enabled him in effect to bypass the priests, monks and friars, and thus to attain contact of a more direct and personal nature with the heavenly powers.

The most fundamental of these practices was prayer, which he might perform as an individual or in a group. The inmates of the almshouse founded by John Trotte at Cullompton in 1523, for example, were specifically required to pray for his and certain other souls. Joan Tackle, at Honiton in 1528, bequeathed 4d to each householder in the town to pray for her, and John Greenway, arranging his burial at Tiverton in 1529, ensured similar prayers for his soul by providing the local poor with a dinner and a dole of £20. Prayers on behalf of their deceased 'brothers' and 'sisters' were also recited by the lay members of religious guilds, such as the guild of the Holy Trinity at Helston in 1517.[1] Prayers of these types might be facilitated by fasting, particularly on the specified fast days, and by the employment of rosaries, through which God and Our Lady might be formally invoked. Amongst the offerings to the rood at Crediton in 1524 was 'a pair of beads, all silver, with 53 *Ave Marias* and 6 *Pater Nosters*', and such rosaries were frequently depicted on early-Tudor memorials, like that of Joan Easton at Morchard Bishop.[2]

A more tangible contact with the spiritual world was provided by the three-dimensional image of wood or stone. This was accessible to laymen in the cathedral and in several religious houses as well as in parochial chapels and parish churches. Though sometimes displayed externally, as at St Mawes,[3] it was usually to be found within – upon the rood-loft, over an altar, or in a pier-niche of the type still visible at Frithelstock, Sandford,

[1] PROB 11 21, fol. 18v; 23, fol. 71; 24, fol. 10; Henderson 1935, pp. 75–9.
[2] ER XV, fol. 30v; Hoskins 1954, photograph 16. See, for example, the Kirkham monument, Paignton.
[3] Hooker, Commonplace book, fol. 344.

Tiverton and elsewhere. It was painted, gilded, and even clothed – 'Our Lady of Halberton', for example, boasted mantles, beads and silver rings[4] – while particular emblems facilitated its identification by devotees. At Exeter St John's Bow in 1517, for instance, St James was furnished with his distinctive pilgrim's staff.[5]

The Trinity itself might be depicted, as at St Day.[6] Probably a patriarch was combined with a crucified Jesus and a dove, a representation still to be seen on the screen of *circa* 1500 at Kenn. More frequent, however, was a solitary Christ. As in murals, screen-paintings and sculptures, emphasis was usually placed upon his pain-laden humanity: one figure at Colyton in 1520 was known as 'the pity of Our Lord',[7] and the visually dominant image in most churches, sited high over the chancel screen, was the crucifix or rood. Cullompton retains not only its rood-beam but also a carved representation of Golgotha with rocks, skulls, and sockets for the three crosses. Several churches retain a special window in the south chancel wall to illuminate the rood, as at Swimbridge, or a painted ceilure to emphasize its former position, as at Hennock and Lapford.

Images of the deity were nevertheless outnumbered heavily by representations of the saints. These ranged from celebrities with international reputations to individuals whose cult was merely local and whose historicity was often dubious. By 1530 the exhibits at Ashburton, for example, included Our Lady, the apostles Andrew and John, the widely venerated Christopher, Erasmus, George and Roche, the Englishmen Thomas Becket and King Henry VI, and the Celtic Nectan of Hartland.[8] The popular appeal of Our Lady is attested by numerous pre-Reformation depictions in the region's churches of her childhood, angelic salutation, motherhood, sorrow, assumption and celestial coronation. Examples remain in glass of 1523 at St Neot and of the same date at Broadwood Kelly, and in sculpture of 1517, *circa* 1526 and *circa* 1527 at Tiverton, Paignton and Woodleigh respectively. On the screen at Holne, where she appears beside God himself as Queen of Heaven, a quasi-divine status seems implied. George, with his dragon, appeared frequently in south-western iconography, as in glass of *circa* 1500 at St Neot; Christopher was commonly portrayed in murals, as at Breage, Poughill and St Keverne; Erasmus and Roche were painted on the screens at Hennock and Plymtree, the former displaying his entrails and the latter his plague

[4] STAC 4/8/47.
[5] CWA Exeter SJB, 1517.
[6] See below, p. 54. See also *Bodmin Register*, pp. 38–42; and CWA Dartmouth, 1542.
[7] PROB 11 20, fol. 124v. See also *Bodmin Register*, pp. 38–42.
[8] CWA Ashburton.

sores. Becket is depicted on a screen at Ashton and in a mural at Breage, while the uncanonized but popularly venerated Henry VI is to be seen on a screen at Whimple.

Nor was the array at Ashburton unusual. Amongst the images at Chagford by the 1530s were Our Lady, Eligius, Katherine, Michael and Nicholas. As patron of metalworkers – he is shown forging a horseshoe on a boss at Ugborough – Eligius was particularly appropriate to this stannary town. He was also imaged at Morebath, together with Our Lady, Our Lady of Pity, Anne, Antony, George, Sidwell and Sunday. Sidwell of Exeter was believed to have been a Celtic virgin and martyr; she appears, with the scythe of her martyrdom, on screens at Ashton, Hennock, Holne, Plymtree, Wolborough and elsewhere.[9]

On the eve of the Reformation such images were still constructed, clothed and ornamented with considerable enthusiasm. Figures of Christ, for example, were painted at Ashburton in 1527–8 and at Morebath in 1528–9; the latter work was financed in part by individual gifts, including 20d each from John Taylor and Walter More and 4d from John Hurley. An elaborate crucifix, flanked by figures of Our Lady and St John, was commissioned by the inhabitants of Stratton in 1531; it was to be modelled upon the evidently impressive example at Liskeard. Another rood, accompanied by Mary and John and patterned on that at Brushford, was constructed at Morebath in as late as 1535–6. Its carver, William Popple, received £7, and it was subsequently gilded for at least 26s 8d; 40s was contributed by the parish's 'young men'.[10]

Further expenditure was devoted to saints. In some parishes, like Exeter St John's Bow, South Tawton or Chagford, this was relatively modest – though the first refurbished its St James in 1517, the second spent money on a St Peter in 1525–6, and the third paid 15s for St Eligius' tabernacle in 1531–2. At Ashburton, on the other hand, the parishioners painted Our Lady in 1516–17, bought a new foot for Erasmus in 1520–1, mended Henry VI in 1521–2, painted Roche in 1522–3, and erected a tabernacle for John in 1523–4. In 1525–6 they set up George, and paid a substantial £8 to Antony the painter for painting the tabernacle of John in the south aisle. There was expenditure on a tunic for Andrew in 1527–8, while almost £4 was devoted to George in 1529–30 – in which year a new image of Thomas Becket was also erected. At Stratton in 1531 the parishioners ordered two new figures in tabernacles, one depicting the visitation of Our

[9]　CWA Chagford; CWA Morebath.
[10]　CWA Ashburton, 1528; CWA Morebath, 1529, 1535–8; *Blanchminster's Charity*, pp. 91–4.

Lady and the other St Armil – a Breton hero still visible, with his chained dragon, on the screen at Torbryan.[11]

Particularly impressive was the expenditure of a small and relatively poor community like Morebath. Gifts towards the ornamentation of its St Sidwell in the years 1529–31 included a wedding-ring from Eleanor Nichol and a girdle and beads from Alison Sayer, these latter being intended to provide the image with shoes. There were contributions also to its gilding, like the 5s from Margaret Holcombe. The tabernacle of St Sunday was erected in 1530, St Eligius gilded in 1531, and some 22s spent on gilding Our Lady of Pity in 1533. A new figure, representing 'the nativity of Our Lady' and furnished with a tabernacle, was completed by Thomas Glass in about 1531 and then gilded by John Creche. Its total cost was about £9. William Atpole bequeathed 6s 8d towards this in 1528; in 1529 Walter More gave 20d, Christina Timewell a gown worth 4s, and the widow Joan Rumbelow goods and money worth 19s; and in 1531 Christina Norman and Joan Trychay added a kerchief and 4d, while John Taylor, John Hurley and Joan Lewis each donated 8d. 'A new George, and a new horse to our dragon', were also constructed by Glass in 1530–1 and tabernacled by Creche in 1534. Glass received at least £3 16s 4d, and the tabernacle cost as much as £6 6s 8d. Contributions ranged from the 4d given by Christopher Morse in 1534, and the 20d given by Christina Atwood in 1530, to the generous 20s bequeathed 'to our new St George' by both Margaret Holcombe in 1529 and Margaret at Borston in 1530.[12]

The cult of images necessitated further expenditure not only on special clothes for their ritual veiling during Lent – Exeter St Mary Major, for example, possessed in 1533 'a kerchief for to be laid over the cross in the Lent time'[13] – but also on the erection of elaborate rood-lofts for their prominent display. The ubiquity of such structures is indicated by the region's numerous surviving rood-screens, which seem usually to have been designed to support them, and by its many remaining rood-stairs, which originally provided them with access from below.[14] The stairs at Bridford bear the initials of a rector instituted in 1508, while an inscription at Marwood dates the surviving remnants of the rood-loft, with their Perpendicular motifs, to approximately 1520.[15] The material evidence is confirmed by the documentary. The construction of lofts is recorded at Tywardreath in about 1508 and at Winkleigh between 1513 and 1520; the latter, produced

---

[11] CWA Exeter SJB, 1517; CWA S. Tawton, 1526; CWA Chagford, 1532; CWA Ashburton, 1517–30; *Blanchminster's Charity*, pp. 91–4.
[12] CWA Morebath, 1529–35.
[13] CWA Exeter SMM, fol. 11.
[14] Bond and Camm 1909, I, p. 82; Pevsner 1952B, pp. 24–5.
[15] Hoskins 1954, pp. 349, 433. See also Pevsner 1952A, p. 121.

by John Clement and John Kelly, cost the parishioners the very substantial sum of about £48. 'Costs done about the church, for making of the rood-loft', are similarly detailed by the accounts for *circa* 1520 at North Petherwin. Beginning with an expedition by three parishioners to buy timber at Hatherleigh, the venture continued with the employment of craftsmen from Brittany as well as from the locality, and eventually concluded with the triumphant 'setting up of the rood-loft'. A loft reportedly magnificent in its ornamentation was completed at St Columb Minor in 1521. The structure at Ashburton, produced by Peter Rowalling and his assistants between 1522 and 1526, cost at least £43 – approximately a year's income for the church. Timber was donated by the Abbot of Buckfast, but John Forde gave £10 and the remainder was apparently borne by the parish. At Tiverton, in 1524, William Sellick bequeathed no less than £36 'to the making of the rood-loft'. In 1528 Joan Tackle left £3 6s 8d 'to the making of the rood-loft' at Honiton. It was also in 1528 that William Coxhead bestowed £20 upon the church at Chulmleigh, 'to make there a rood-loft'. In 1531 the inhabitants of Stratton commissioned an elaborate new loft from the craftsmen John Dawe of Lawhitton and John Pares of North Lew. This was to replace the existing structure and to be modelled on the superior example at St Kew. Up to 1537, as the work progressed, Dawe received payments totalling £48.[16]

Opposition to such expenditure was not totally unknown. In 1508 three inhabitants of Golant withheld their contributions to the loft construction in Tywardreath church, arguing that they had already donated to its fabric, glass and bells.[17] There is nevertheless no doubt that on the eve of the Reformation, roods, saint figures and image-bearing lofts continued to be the objects of a considerable financial investment by communities and individuals throughout the South-West.

Similarly impressive is the range of religious functions that the image continued to fulfil. According to the clerical theorists whose views were reported by Philip Nichols, it merely constituted a visual aid for the illiterate – a 'layman's book'. In popular practice, however, its status was unquestionably more exalted. 'By the which "books"', protested Nichols, 'or rather, abominable idols, it is open and manifest that much idolatry hath been committed'.[18]

Certainly it was common for laymen to invoke God, or to solicit the patronage of saints, by burning candles or tapers before their images. Lights

---

[16] CCB 854, sub 28 February 1507/8; CWA Winkleigh, 1513–20; Hoskins 1954, p. 272; CWA N. Petherwin, fols. 36v, 43, 49v; Bond and Camm 1909, II, p. 384; CWA Ashburton, 1523–6; PROB 11 21, fol. 202v; 23, fols. 22, 71; *Blanchminster's Charity*, pp. 91–4; Additional 32244, SWA Stratton, 1534–7.
[17] CCB 854, sub 28 February 1507/8.
[18] *Copy of a Letter*, pp. 49–51.

of this type were maintained not only by the parishes, through their regular collections of 'wax-silver', but also by fraternities – like the guild of the High Cross at Stratton – and by devoted individuals. Morebath provides examples. In 1525 William Donne furnished a taper worth 12d 'to stand afore Our Lady', while in 1527 John Timewell gave three sheep to maintain lights before Jesus. In 1528 William Atpole donated bees to finance lights before Jesus and Sidwell at the principal feasts, 'to burn from the first even-song until high mass be done the morrow', and Joan Hillier provided a candlestick, 'upon the which candlestick she doth maintain a taper before St Sidwell, trimmed with flowers, to burn there every high and principal feast'. 'This', recorded her vicar, 'she doth intend to maintain while she liveth.' Candlesticks or lights for Jesus, Sidwell and Our Lady were similarly bestowed by Thomas Trychay in 1529, Christina Atwood in 1530, Christina Norman and Joan Hucley in 1531, Joan Trychay in 1532 and Harry Hurley in 1534. Nor was Morebath unique. At Honiton in 1528 Joan Tackle bequeathed two great candlesticks to an image of Mary in the chapel of All Saints; they were to stand on the altar 'to the honour of God and Our Blessed Lady and Allhallowen'. Lights before the images at Cullompton – including Our Lady, John, Nicholas and Jesus as well as the rood – were also endowed by the merchant John Lane in 1529 and by John Calloway in 1531.[19]

An alternative to the light was the oblation. Images attracted offerings from the laity not only in great ecclesiastical establishments like Exeter Cathedral but also in the chapels and parish churches of towns – including Camborne, Colyton, Crediton, Honiton, Plymouth and Truro – and even in smaller rural communities like Awliscombe, Morebath, Rewe and Widecombe. Some oblations were monetary. At Colyton in 1520, for example, the wool merchant John Bagwell left 12d to 'the cross with the three hands', 8d each to the Trinity, Nicholas and Katherine, and 4d each to Michael, Clement and the Christ of Pity. The rood at Widecombe received 20d from Gilbert Rugge in 1529, 'St Sekeke of Poole' 20d from Robert Wakeham of Sherford in 1530, and Colyton rood 40d from John Strawbridge in 1531. Other offerings were bestowed in kind. At Crediton in 1524 the rood was inundated not only by coins but also by coats of different colours, 93 rings, and a substantial collection of plate, girdles, buckles, pendants, brooches, crucifixes and beads. Joan Tackle, at Honiton in 1528, left a silver cross to an image of Our Lady and All Saints, her best blue girdle to Our Lady, and a red girdle to 'the image of Our Lady of Awliscombe'. At Morebath in 1529 John Morse donated wax and honey from his bees to Jesus and

---

[19] Additional 32243, HCWA Stratton, 1512–30; CWA Morebath, 1529–32; PROB 11 23, fols. 29, 71; 24, fol. 19.

Sidwell, while Eleanor Nichol bequeathed a little silver cross to Jesus. In
1530 Christina Atwood gave a kerchief to Sidwell, and Thomas Timewell
a sheep to St Sunday. In 1531 Katherine Robins bequeathed beads of coral
and amber, set with silver *Pater Nosters* – 'the which beads must hang
upon the new image of Our Lady every high day, by her mind'.[20]

Offerings were considered particularly meritorious when accompanied
by pilgrimage. For this reason the layman might journey to a religious house
like the cell of Sion Abbey on St Michael's Mount, which boasted an elaborately clothed and ornamented image in silver-gilt of the archangel Michael
himself. Amongst the gifts that it had attracted from pilgrims by 1536 were
plate, coins, cloths, silver ships, tokens, miniature images and 43 silver
rings.[21] Many objects of pilgrimage were nevertheless to be found in local
chapels, as at Liskeard, Looe, Pilton and St Day,[22] or in parish churches,
as at Chittlehampton, Iddesleigh, Pilton and Sidbury.[23] A celebrated representation of the Trinity at St Day not only appealed to testators – like
Marion Lelley of Ruan Lanihorne, who gave 2d in 1525 – but also drew
visitors in such numbers that the hamlet was transformed into a minor
town. 'Men and women came (in times past) from far in pilgrimage', it
was later recalled. Crowds also flocked to the chapel of St George at Looe.
'To the which chapel', recorded William Kendal on the eve of the Henrician
upheavals, 'in the feast of the said St George, there is great resort of all
the country thereabout, for their pilgrimage to an image in the said chapel
of St George.' On one feast day the pilgrims were said to number about
100; they included Kendal himself, who had come two miles from his home
with his wife and a servant.

Pilton attracted pilgrims not only to 'Our Lady of Lorell', who was to
be seen in a chapel, but also to 'Our Lady of Pilton', who was displayed
in the parish church. In the years 1530–3 the offerings to Our Lady of
Pilton alone totalled £10 per annum, in addition to silver rings, beads, girdles
and other gifts worth more than £2. Such sums – which were collected
by a servant of the Prior of Pilton, appropriator of the benefice – would
again suggest a considerable local cult. Other figures of the Virgin drew
her devotees to the parish churches at Iddesleigh and Sidbury. But the most
venerated of parochial images in the South-West was probably that of St

[20] EDCL 2920; ER XV, fol. 30v; Henderson 1923–4, p. 76; CWA Morebath, 1529–31; PROB
      11 20, fol. 124v; 22, fol. 302; 23, fol. 71; 28, fols. 17v, 126; see also below, p. 67.
[21] E 117 10/59; *Worcestre*, p. 99; 'Lives of Saints', fols. 314–14v; *Survey of Cornwall*, p. 378;
      Henderson 1923–4, pp. 222–3.
[22] *Leland*, I, p. 208; STAC 2/26/257; E 315 126/16–17; Henderson 1923–4, pp. 195–7;
      PROB 11 22, fol. 254v.
[23] Glastonbury Commonplace Book, fol. 86; Risdon 1811, pp. 319–24; Chanter 1914,
      pp. 290–308; Hoskins 1954, pp. 364–5; CWA Iddesleigh, 1536–7; E 315 126/16–17; Rad-
      ford 1949, p. 165.

Urith in the village church at Chittlehampton. Supposedly a local maiden martyred by heathens in the sixth century, Urith is depicted on the pulpit of *circa* 1500: she bears a palm to symbolize her martyrdom and a stone to represent her church. Her image was doubtless exhibited in the elaborate pier-niche still visible on the northern side of the nave. Offerings here must have helped to finance the church's magnificent late-Perpendicular tower, and in as late as the 1530s still totalled approximately £50 per annum – another impressive index of continuing devotion.

Men and women venerated images because, as Philip Nichols observed, 'they would have a god that they might sensibly see with their bodily and carnal eyes'.[24] A similarly material and visible form of contact with the spiritual world was provided by the sacred sites, wells and relics with which the pre-Reformation South-West – and Celtic Cornwall in particular – was so richly endowed.

Certain trees, for example, were reverenced on account of their supposed association with local saints. One, at St Breward, was believed to date from Breward's death; another, at St Endellion, was linked with St Illick. Local people 'used to say by tradition that [Illick] came miraculously out of Ireland on a harrow or hurdle, and that she lived there in the time of St Endellion'. A hill near St Minver was honoured as the site of Minver's encounter with the Devil himself.[25] Veneration was accorded also to the stone chairs in the churchyards at Germoe and St Mawes and on St Michael's Mount. These were associated with Germoc, a companion of Breage in the early-medieval evangelization of Cornwall; Mawes, a bishop in Brittany; and Michael, who had allegedly visited the Mount in 'about the year of the Lord 710', and who appears frequently (as on an early-sixteenth-century bench-end at Altarnun) in the region's iconography.[26] But more numerous than such trees, hills and chairs were the celebrated holy wells. Enclosed within small granite buildings, of which a good example survives at Laneast, these were invariably connected with saints. Two at St Endellion, for instance, were thought to have been frequented by Endellion herself, while the well at St Columb Major reputedly marked the place of Columb's martyrdom.[27]

Smaller material objects attracted a similar veneration. Until 1539 a piece of the Crown of Thorns was preserved at Bodmin, while portions of the Holy Cross were exhibited on St Michael's Mount and at Grade, St Buryan and Tavistock. According to the legend retailed in early-Tudor days, the

---

[24] Royal 18 B XI, fols. 21–2.
[25] 'Lives of Saints', fols. 109v, 262, 312v.
[26] 'Lives of Saints', fols. 308, 314–14v; *Worcestre*, pp. 29, 99; *Leland*, I, pp. 188, 200; *Survey of Cornwall*, p. 378.
[27] Pevsner and Radcliffe 1970, p. 89; 'Lives of Saints', fols. 202v–3, 131–1v.

portions at Grade and St Buryan had been miraculously translated from the Holy Land by a Cornishman, Sir Roger Wallisborough. 'And at this day', the legend concludes, 'the said Sir Roger is remembered; and shall be, while this world lasts.' St Michael's Mount boasted also the sword and spurs of the saintly Henry VI. Equally precious was the horn of St Neot in the priory at Bodmin. According to local legend, Neot had 'wrought many miracles; and namely one at a well, in which he used to say the whole Psalter. And being once in that devotion, a hind pursued by hounds fled to him for succour; who willing her to depart, she immediately did so. And the dogs did fly so strangely from her, as the hunt-man seeing it was therewith so astonished as he fell down at St Neot's feet, and became a monk of his order. And his horn was reserved in St Petrock's monastery, in memory of that miracle.'[28]

Of all relics, however, the most effectual in securing contact with the spiritual world were inevitably the corporeal remains of Christ and of his saints. Some such treasures were accessible to laymen in the great ecclesiastical establishments. Exeter Cathedral retains, in its northern chancel aisle, the once venerated tomb of Bishop Edmund Lacey – who, after his death in 1455, had acquired a local reputation for miracle-producing sanctity which endured until the Reformation. In the retroquire of Tavistock Abbey lay the body of St Rumon, 'richly enshrined and by all shows a bishop', while the relics of Nectan the hermit-saint were preserved in the abbey at Hartland. The head of Genesius the Martyr could be seen in the canons' church at Launceston, as could St Sirus in the priory church of St Carrock near Fowey, and the celebrated St Petrock – evangelist of Cornwall and alleged cousin of Constantine the Great – in the priory of his foundation at Bodmin. On St Michael's Mount, enshrined in silver and gilt, was the jaw bone of St Apollonia. On several rood-screens, as at Ashton, this saint is depicted with her tooth between pincers: she had supposedly been tortured by dental extraction.[29]

Most such remains were nevertheless to be found in the local chapels and parish churches. Sidwell the virgin-martyr, for example, lay in the parish church dedicated to her in the suburbs of Exeter. Among those who bestowed her name upon their daughters was Robert Hooker, mayor of the city in 1529. Brandwellan, king's son and confessor, allegedly lay at Branscombe, while Brannoc the hermit was to be found in the church of his foundation at Braunton. A window there formerly showed him arriving in north Devon,

---

[28] *Bodmin Register*, pp. 38–42; *Tavistock Records*, p. 18; E 117 10/59; Harleian 2252, fols. 50v–1v; 'Lives of Saints', fols. 323v–4.

[29] Hooker, Commonplace Book, fol. 311v; Radford 1949, pp. 164–8; CAB 3551, fol. 49v; *Worcestre*, pp. 85, 87, 107, 115; 'Lives of Saints', fols. 322v–3, 357v, 388; *Leland*, I, p. 180; E 117 10/59.

building his church, teaching the people to manure their land by yoking harts, and performing miracles – including the resurrection of a cow. Chittle-hampton boasted the shrine of St Urith: it stood in a narrow chamber still visible to the north of the chancel. Tavistock church claimed to possess hair from the heads of St Katherine, Mary Magdalene, and even Our Lady.[30] But it was in Cornwall that parochial shrines were most prolific. Barnic, for example, was to be found at Fowey, Breage at Breage, Endellion at St Endellion, Ia at St Ives, Juncus at Pelynt, Meubred at Cardinham, Mor-wenna at Morwenstow and Piran at Perranzabuloe. Piran, patron of tinners, was believed to have raised the dead, taught a stork to sing, walked on water, procured fire by prayer and turned water into wine. Endellion, god-daughter of King Arthur, was said locally to have lived at St Endellion in heroic austerity, fed only by the milk of her cow; her miracles included a resurrection. Local tradition was equally certain about the origin of her church and tomb: 'When she perceived the day of her death draw nigh, she entreated her friends after her death to lay her dead body on a sled, and to bury her there where certain young stoats, bullocks or calves of a year old should of their own accord draw her. Which being done, they brought her to a place which at that time was a miry waste ground and a great quagmire on the top of an hill; where in time after there was a church builded on her and dedicated to her, bearing her name.' Her tomb, which appeared to be 'very ancient' and which was enhanced by a table of polished black stone, remained within the church until the 1530s.[31]

When not entombed, the relic might be preserved within a reredos: late-medieval examples with appropriate recesses have been found at Breage, St Allen and St Keverne.[32] Alternatively a reliquary might be provided for its display. The twelfth-century casket of ivory that survives at Bodmin was a repository for relics of St Petrock. Dartmouth church retained, in 1529–30, 'a box of relics'; St Michael's Mount, in 1536, a box 'with divers relics in it of saints'; and Bodmin church, in 1539, 'a little box with relics'. Other types of reliquary included monstrances, as on St Michael's Mount; paxes, as at Bodmin; and crosses, as at Crediton and Tavistock — Crediton, for example, in 1524 boasted a cross 'with a crucifix in the midst for relics'.[33] At certain times such treasures might be paraded for public veneration. The relics of Piran, stationed usually at Perranzabuloe, were 'wont to be

[30] *Worcestre*, pp. 115, 125; PROB 11 26, fol. 76; 'Lives of Saints', fols. 101v–2; Westcote 1845, pp. 308–9; Hoskins 1954, pp. 364–5; Chanter 1914, pp. 290–308; Pevsner 1952A, p. 70; *Tavistock Records*, p. 18.

[31] *Worcestre*, pp. 23, 29, 97, 107, 115; 'Lives of Saints', fols. 202v–3, 359v–60v; C 1 305/78; PROB 11 22, fol. 254v.

[32] Henderson 1923–4, p. 37.

[33] Pevsner and Radcliffe 1970, p. 43; CWA Dartmouth, 1530; E 117 10/59; *Bodmin Register*, pp. 38–42; ER XV, fol. 31.

carried up and down in the country upon occasion', and in Rogation Week were displayed in the daughter church at St Agnes. In the same week a chapel at East Newlyn was visited not only by the local inhabitants but also by the parishioners of Crantock, Cubert and Perranzabuloe. These brought with them the crosses and relics of their patron saints, which were then exhibited in the chapel yard upon four raised stones. At Crantock, similarly, the people of seven parishes would assemble each year, and would display their relics upon seven specially erected stones.[34]

The veneration of sacred sites, wells and relics assumed a variety of forms. Oblations were again frequent. The relic centre on St Michael's Mount, for example, attracted 6s 8d from William Cox of Paul in 1522, 4d from Marion Lelley of Ruan Lanihorne in 1525, and 12d from Stephen Lelley in 1526. Offerings were also made to the head and image of Piran at Perranzabuloe, especially on his feast day, 5 March. These constituted an important part of the incumbent's revenue in 1504 – when a priest who had resigned the benefice nevertheless continued to receive them – and were supplemented by bequests from testators, like the 16d from John Mowla in 1503, the 6d from John Ennis in 1510 and the 4d from Marion Lelley in 1525.[35]

Offering, again, was frequently combined with pilgrimage. Inhabitants of the South-West occasionally visited shrines elsewhere in England: the tomb of Thomas Becket at Canterbury, for example, was thus honoured in Henry VII's reign by Robert Forde of St Michael's Mount. There was also a route to the shrine of St James at Compostella in northern Spain, a cult centre of which 'a staff and a scrip of St James' inventoried by the church at Crediton in 1524 were possibly pilgrims' souvenirs. Similarly attractive was Brittany. In as late as 1537 a ship named the *Magdalene* sailed from Truro to Lantregar on a 'pope-holy pilgrimage'. The pilgrims aboard were 50 in number; they included a local merchant, Richard Barrett.[36]

The cost and slowness of transportation nevertheless ensured that the great majority of shrines visited by south-western people were located within their own peninsula. St Michael's Mount, with its chair and its relics, was predictably 'frequented as a great pilgrimage', and was 'greatly haunted ... by far travelling'. At Tavistock the shrine of St Rumon had long received offerings, and may have been the destination of the 'pilgrim' who passed through Ashburton in 1507–8. The shrine of St Urith, in association with her image, drew numerous travellers to Chittlehampton; the stone post at Brightley Cross was possibly erected for their direction. Crowds were similarly lured to the cathedral at Exeter by the shrine of Bishop Lacey. 'Upon

[34] 'Lives of Saints', fols. 114v, 323v, 359v–60v; Henderson 1925, p. 163.
[35] PROB 11 21, fol. 32v; 22, fol. 254v; Henderson 1923–4, pp. 222–3, 401–2; C 1 305/78.
[36] C 1 80/35; CAB 3551, fol. 57v; ER XV, fol. 30v; *LP*, XII (2), 301, 1325.

the report of many feigned miracles', says Hooker, 'great pilgrimages were made to his tomb', and the extent of his cult has been confirmed by the discovery at Exeter of a medieval mould, the purpose of which was the manufacture of badges for the pilgrims. In 1528 the cathedral chapter still paid a man to tend the pyx over Lacey's tomb, to usher the pilgrims, and to collect their offerings; his wage was doubled when these exceeded £7 13s 4d per annum. In as late as 1534 the tomb remained an object of pilgrimage.[37] Similar devotion, albeit on a localized scale, was paid to the holy wells at Altarnun, Camborne, Madron, Padstow and elsewhere. The well of St Madern at Madron, for example, attracted annual pilgrimage from its many devotees.[38]

Whether achieved by means of rosary, image, relic or well, the layman's contact with the powers of Heaven was regularly maintained by his observance of annual feast days in their honour. The parishioners of Braunton, for instance, organized a feast on Easter Monday to commemorate St Brannoc. At St Endellion there was a day not only for Endellion herself, on 29 April, but also for Illick, on the Saturday after Epiphany. The inhabitants of Halberton, whose church was dedicated to Our Lady, arranged revels and sports as well as special services on the day of her assumption and on the following Sunday.[39] Celebrations of this nature were accompanied by the public reading of books known as 'legends'. Compiled in the fourteenth century and preserved by parish churches until the Reformation, the legends recited in the diocese of Exeter included national saints like William of York and Thomas Cantelupe but appear to have concentrated upon local figures like Boniface, Breage, Budoc, Buryan, Carantoc, Ia, Mylor, Piran and Sidwell. The legend of Sidwell, for instance, related her birth at Exeter, her martyrdom, and the origin of her well and church. That of Breage described her birth in 'Lagonia', her arrival in Cornwall with Sinwin, Germoc, Elwen, Crewern, Helen and other saints, her coming to Pencair, and her foundation of churches at Trenwith and Talmeneth. The legend of Ia, preserved at St Ives, explained that she had been the daughter of an Irish nobleman and a disciple of St Barricus. After landing at Pendinas she had supposedly persuaded Dinan, a great lord of Cornwall, to build her a church in that location.[40]

---

[37] 'Lives of Saints', fols. 314–14v, 388; *Survey of Cornwall*, p. 378; *Worcestre*, p. 115; CWA Ashburton, 1508; Risdon 1811, pp. 319–24; Westcote 1845, p. 287; Hoskins 1954, pp. 364–5; Chanter 1914, pp. 290–308; Glastonbury Commonplace Book, fol. 86; James 1901–2, pp. 230–4; Hooker, Commonplace Book, fol. 311v; Radford 1949, pp. 164–8; CAB 3551, fol. 49v.

[38] *Survey of Cornwall*, p. 289; 'Lives of Saints', fols. 111v, 298v, 304, 327v–8; Henderson 1923–4, p. 318.

[39] 'Lives of Saints', fols. 101v–2, 202v–3, 262; STAC 4/8/47.

[40] *Leland*, I, pp. 187, 189, 192, 196, 228, 230, 232–5, 237.

Whatever the practices employed by laymen to make contact with the
heavenly powers, it would seem to have been the saints rather than the
persons of the Trinity who were the more frequently invoked. Church bells
were commonly dedicated to a saint, and their inscriptions included prayers
like 'Ora pro nobis', or as at Plymtree, 'Protege virgo pia quos convoco
sancta Maria'. Inscriptions like 'S. Johannes, ora pro nobis' and 'S. Stephane,
ora pro nobis', similarly appear in the early-sixteenth-century glass at St
Neot: here a number of the donors are indeed depicted in prayer to particular
saints. Patronage of this nature was considered to be especially effectual
in obtaining protection from the divine wrath at the time of death and
at the final judgement. In a mural of the Weighing of Souls in the church
at Bovey Tracey, a rosary – representing prayers to Our Lady – was in
fact depicted as tipping the scales of judgement in the favour of her devotees;
these were shown nestling in the security of her mantle. Similarly revealing
of contemporary attitudes was the formula 'Jesus, mercy; Lady, help'; it
appeared on memorials, as at Bigbury, and on bells, as at Marldon and
Townstall. Wills could be equally explicit. The will composed in 1501 by
an Exeter merchant, Thomas Bond, asserted his belief in the Catholic faith
and the Trinity but also admitted his dread of death, 'the which no manner
of person living in this world cannot escape'. After commending his soul
to its Creator, Bond turned to Mary: 'I ask for charity, Our Lady, St Mary
the Virgin: with [the] saints, all the Company of Heaven, be mine advocate
in the hour of my death and at the day of the great judgement.' Of the
30 wills with recorded formulae from 1520 to 1529, a comparable appeal
to the Virgin or the saints occurred in 17. In 1523, for instance, Gregory
Colvercock of Brixham bequeathed his soul 'to Almighty God, my Maker
and Redeemer; and to the most blessed Virgin, Our Lady, St Mary, his
mother; and to all the Holy Company of Heaven'.[41]

Yet the benefits of saintly patronage were never exclusively other-worldly.
A Cornish play of 1504 showed its audiences the miraculous rescue of a
young man as the result of his mother's prayers to Our Lady, and it assured
them that 'whoever worships [Mary] shall be eased'.[42] There is no doubt
that, in an age of widespread disease and rudimentary medical science, the
attractiveness of saints' images, relics and wells lay very largely in their
reputed ability to procure either physical or mental healing.

In 1535–6 an Axminster man was shot by a crossbow but escaped with
his life. This survival he subsequently ascribed to the miraculous intervention

---

[41] Ellacombe 1872, pp. 239–48; Rushforth 1927B, pp. 150–90; PROB 11 13, fol. 198v; 21,
     fol. 19. A sketch of the (lost) Bovey Tracey mural is displayed in the parish church. A
     rosary and small figure from a similar mural survive at Linkinhorne.
[42] *Beunans Meriasek*, 3170 *et seq*. The text describes this episode as deriving from a Life,
     the *Miracula de Beato Mereadoco*.

of St Leonard, before whose image he seems to have prayed.[43] At Ashburton the image of Roche was doubtless the medium of prayers against plague: at Paignton a sculpted figure of this saint, still visible on the monument of *circa* 1526, retains a scroll on which such a supplication was probably inscribed.[44] Similarly curative were the 'feigned miracles' performed at Exeter by Bishop Lacey. Waxen representations of human and animal limbs and heads, and of a complete female figure, have been discovered over his tomb; the attached strings indicate that they were originally suspended above the bishop's body, mutely invoking his blessing upon the depicted individuals and their beasts.[45] Healing was also sought at the Exeter shrine of St Sidwell, where 'it pleased God, in testimony of her virtue and innocency, to show many miracles in curing diseases'. Similar wonders appear to have been worked by St Urith at Chittlehampton, while the healing of insanity was attributed to the shrine of St Merteriana the Virgin in the parish church at Minster.[46]

Equally potent were the holy wells. 'Sundry miracles' were reported from the well of St Madern at Madron, 'and especially on the feasts of Corpus Christi'. No less efficacious was the well near Padstow which, it was said, had been miraculously created by St Cadoc. 'Such as came to that well should, by drinking of it, find help for their infirmities – and especially for expelling venomous diseases and worms out of their bellies'. The wells of St Meriasek at Camborne and of St Nun at Altarnun, in contrast, were famous particularly for their treatment of the insane. At Altarnun – according to eyewitness reports transmitted to Richard Carew – the patient would be repeatedly immersed in the healing waters until, 'by foregoing his strength, [he] had somewhat forgot his fury'. Then he was carried to the parish church, where prayers were said for him and mass was performed. 'If his right wits returned', sneered Carew, 'St Nun had the thanks; but if there appeared small amendment, he was "bowsened" again and again ... for recovery.' Some patients, according to Nicholas Roscarrock, were thus 'dispossessed', and others 'cured of their frenzy'.[47]

On the eve of the Reformation a variety of devotional practices thus continued to flourish, enabling laymen to use prayers, fasts, rosaries, images, relics and wells and to avoid exclusive dependence upon clerically controlled

---

[43] See below, p. 62.
[44] CWA Ashburton, 1523; Rushforth 1927A, pp. 10–11.
[45] Hooker, Commonplace Book, fol. 311v; Radford 1949, pp. 164–8. The images are now displayed in the Dean and Chapter Library, Exeter.
[46] 'Lives of Saints', fol. 393v; Risdon 1811, pp. 319–24; Westcote 1845, p. 287; *Worcestre*, pp. 29, 31.
[47] 'Lives of Saints', fols. 111v, 298v, 327v–8; *Survey of Cornwall*, p. 289; Henderson 1923–4, p. 318. For Camborne, see below, p. 201.

rites. To what extent did these practices survive the assaults directed against them in the Reformation decades?

Again the verbal evidence is suggestive.[48] Fasts, for example, were denounced by Axminster's Philip Gammon in 1535–6. He considered them 'vain', and 'nothing in value for [the] health of man's soul'. Rosaries too were condemned, as by Agnes Priest of Boyton in 1558. Particular scorn was heaped on images. When, at Axminster in 1535–6, the survival of a wounded man was attributed to prayers before an image of St Leonard, Philip Gammon asked a neighbour whether someone reprieved from execution after praying before the gallows ought to worship the gallows in gratitude for his life. 'Whereby he meant', concluded the neighbour, 'that the prayer to St Leonard did no more prevail him than the prayer to the gallows would have done.' Images were denounced as 'Mahomet's puppets' and 'very idols' by Philip Nichols of Totnes between 1547 and 1549. He thought them liable to lead men into idolatry, 'so long as there is one left standing in the temples', and compared their devotees to the Israelite wor-shippers of the golden calf. Agnes Priest condemned images as 'idols', 'stocks and stones', even 'whores'; their worship, she asserted, could only 'damn souls'. When, in 1558, she discovered a craftsman repairing images in Exeter Cathedral, she reviled him as 'mad', 'accursed' and a 'whore-hunter'. Simi-larly contemptuous was William Budd of Swimbridge. In 1557 he reportedly declared that the rood in his parish church 'looked like the knave that made it'.

Hostility was also expressed to the cult of saints. 'We ought to worship God only', declared the schoolmaster Thomas Bennett at Exeter in 1531, 'and no saints.' At his death in 1532, Bennett ignored the urging of tradition-alists and flatly refused to invoke either Our Lady or the saints. Philip Nichols expressed his contempt for the 'false, feigned Lives and Miracles' associated with the saint cults, and rejected pilgrimages as 'abuses'. Agnes Priest con-demned prayers to the saints and all belief in saintly intercession. But the most vehement antagonism was voiced by Philip Gammon. The Axminster shoemaker not only proclaimed that he would never pray to Our Lady, he also denied her sanctity and her intercessory power. He reportedly doubted even her virginity, maintaining that 'Christ was never conceived of Our Lady without actual deed of man', and openly likened her to a mere bag: 'As long as Christ was within her, she was good and precious; and when Christ was born, she was but like to any other woman.' Instead of being assumed into Heaven, she was 'buried as any other woman was,

---

[48] For Gammon, see STAC 2/2/267–72, 287; 23/273; 29/111. For Priest, see *Acts and Monuments*, II, pp. 2049–52. For Nichols, see *Copy of a Letter*, pp. 49–51; Royal 18 B XI, fols. 13v, 21–4. For Budd, see CCB 855, fol. 210v. For Bennett, see *Acts and Monuments*, II, pp. 1037–40.

and lieth in the ground'. Instead of being divinely crowned as the Queen of Heaven, she was 'no better than a queen that was painted upon the cards'.

Substantially more representative of public opinion than such individual outbursts was the phraseology employed in wills. Throughout the Henrician years a considerable number of testators continued to bequeath their souls not only to God but also to the Virgin and the saints. Joan Greenway of Tiverton, for example, committed herself in 1539 'to Almighty God, to his blessed mother St Mary, and to all the saints in Heaven', while in 1545 Tristram Hooper of Musbury commended himself to 'Almighty God, the Father, the Son and the Holy Ghost; and holy Virgin Mary, mother of God our Saviour Jesus Christ; with all the blessed Company of Heaven, to pray for me'. Nevertheless it may be significant that whereas commendations of this type had appeared in 17 of the 30 wills with recorded formulae in the years 1520–9, or 57%, they were included in only 21 of the 51 in the years 1530–46, or 41%. Of the 16 in the years 1547–9, moreover, they occurred in no more than 3, or 19%, and in the 18 in the years 1550–3 they were totally absent. Nor was their restoration under Mary more than partial. Conservatives like the Tiverton clothier John Ap Price in 1558 might still bequeath their souls to 'Almighty God, my Maker and Saviour and the Redeemer of all the world, and to Our Blessed Lady St Mary the Virgin, his most glorious mother, and to all the holy Company of Heaven', but commendations of this type appeared in only 9 of the 32 formulae in the years 1553–9, or 28%. More typical now were John Waite of Sennen in 1554 or John Williams of Huxham in 1558, both of whom simply commended themselves to God. After 1559, moreover, the traditional phraseology again declined: in the 30 formulae in the years 1560–9 it was totally omitted.[49]

The wills, though relatively few, would therefore suggest a devastating erosion of prayer to the saints. A similar conclusion is indicated by the extant inscriptions on bells, memorials and glass: by the 1560s, saint invocations would seem to have been everywhere omitted. The traditional formulae were absent, for example, from a bell erected at Molland in 1562.[50] Public expressions of faith in Our Lady or in the 'holy Company of Heaven' would thus appear to have been generally suppressed.

The verbal evidence must again be supplemented by the financial. To what extent were pre-Reformation levels of expenditure upon the independent practices in fact sustained by individuals and communities in the Reformation decades?

[49] PROB 11 27, fol. 226v; 30, fol. 333; 37, fol. 78; 41, fol. 253v; 42A, John Williams, 1558.
[50] Ellacombe 1872, pp. 226, 255.

In some areas, particularly the important area of relic veneration, patterns of investment are not easy to trace. Wills, accounts and other sources would nevertheless suggest that throughout the period 1538–53, when the practice was officially disapproved of, offering to the region's multitudinous saint shrines and relic collections was in fact generally suppressed. Mary's reign, moreover, affords no evidence of its widespread revival, despite a few possible exceptions like the 6d and 8d donated by Thomas Payne and Jenkin Jack respectively to 'St Piran's foot' at Perranzabuloe in 1558.[51] There is apparently no record of Marian oblations at formerly popular shrines like those on St Michael's Mount, in Exeter Cathedral, and in the many parish churches. After 1558, finally, the cessation was absolute.

Much more comprehensively documented is the level of expenditure upon images and their veneration. Wills, accounts and other sources together indicate, for example, that investment in image-bearing rood-lofts – which until *circa* 1531 had been substantial – in fact experienced a marked decline in the years 1532–47. The loft at Atherington, carved in *circa* 1545 and surviving in part today, was one of the relatively few new structures to be certainly commissioned in these years. The craftsmen responsible were Roger Down and John Hill of Chittlehampton and John Pares of North Lew; but the work of Down and Hill together cost only £14 7s 7d, and the refusal of the parishioners to pay them more than £10 could mean that the original estimate had been lower still.[52] Similarly suggestive of a waning enthusiasm is the fact that, apart from a small sum in 1542–3, payments to John Dawe for carving the rood-loft at Stratton were ended after 1537–9 – when it was fitted with windows and an image, and when Dawe received £26 16s. 8d. Since disbursements to the craftsmen at Stratton fell far short of the £200 specified by their contract, it may be that the ambitious construction projected in 1531 was curtailed by the parishioners in 1539.[53] Major expenditure on the loft at Ashburton, which had included some 50s on its alabaster 'pageants' between 1536 and 1538, also seems to have ended after its painting (for rather less than £16 13s 4d) in 1538–9. By 1540–7 the investment of parishes in rood-lofts was usually limited to their small-scale ornamentation, as at Chagford in 1545–6.[54]

The later-Henrician years also saw a substantial reduction of parochial expenditure upon roods and figures of the saints. By 1540–7 this was generally restricted to the purchase of Lent cloths and to minor renovations,

---

[51] Henderson 1923–4, p. 402.
[52] C 1 1116/49; Hoskins 1954, p. 272.
[53] Additional 32244, SWA Stratton, esp. 1538–9, 1543; *Blanchminster's Charity*, pp. 91–4. This £200 was to cover the loft and certain other furnishings. Additional 32243, HCWA Stratton, 1541, records payment 'for carrying of a image of Our Lady', presumably the figure commissioned in 1531.
[54] CWA Ashburton, 1537–9; CWA Chagford, 1546.

such as the painting of Woodbury's rood (for 20d) in 1545–6 or the regilding of Morebath's in 1546–7.[55] At Morebath, where investment in imagery had been impressive until the early 1530s, it was relatively insignificant by 1540. At Ashburton the last major disbursements occurred in 1536–7, when two images were painted for 6s 4d, and in 1538–9, when Peter Rowalling received 9s 'in part-payment of a greater sum for making the image of St Christopher'; and the absence of further payments from this church's accounts could mean that Rowalling's commission was never completed. After 1538–9, in fact, not one new image appears to have been purchased by any of the parishes with extant accounts. These included Holy Trinity, St John's Bow, St Mary Steps and St Petrock's at Exeter as well as the towns of Ashburton, Camborne, Chagford, Dartmouth and Stratton and the rural parishes of Antony, Iddesleigh, Modbury, Morebath, South Tawton, Winkleigh and Woodbury.[56] In decline also was parochial expenditure upon the traditional image lights. Morebath, for example, had customarily maintained lights not only before its rood but also before Antony, George, Our Lady, Jesus, Sidwell and Sunday. Thus in 1533 the wardens paid 'for oil afore St Sidwell, and for a taper for the whole year'. After 1536, however, lights before these six figures began to disappear, and by 1541 their extinction would seem to have been complete.[57]

The decline of communal investment was accompanied by a reduction of individual donations. At Morebath, on the eve of the Reformation, gifts and bequests to the apparatus of image worship had been frequent. By 1540, however, they seem totally to have ceased. Of the 100 wills in the years 1533–46, 9 contained donations to roods or rood-lights: in 1540, for example, Robert Hone left 3s 4d to the rood-light at Ottery St Mary. Yet bequests to rood-lofts and saint images were now conspicuous by their apparently total absence.[58] But of all the changes in the pattern of expenditure, arguably the most significant was the cessation of the oblations traditionally offered by pilgrims and other devotees to the region's principal cult figures.

The monastic dissolutions of 1536–9 inevitably entailed the elimination of images that had attracted offerings from layfolk. These included the elaborate silver-gilt St Michael at St Michael's Mount, which cannot long have survived its discovery by the official visitors in 1535–6.[59] But substantially

[55] CWA Woodbury, 1546; CWA Morebath, 1547.
[56] CWA Exeter HT; CWA Exeter SJB; CWA Exeter SMS; CWA Exeter SP; CWA Ashburton; CWA Camborne; CWA Chagford; CWA Dartmouth; Additional 32243, HCWA Stratton; Additional 32244, SWA Stratton; CWA Antony; CWA Iddesleigh; CWA Modbury; CWA Morebath; CWA S. Tawton; CWA Winkleigh; CWA Woodbury.
[57] CWA Morebath.
[58] CWA Morebath; PROB 11 29, fol. 201.
[59] E 117 10/59.

greater damage was inflicted by the royal injunctions of 1536, which extended the iconoclasm to the allegedly 'superstitious' cult figures in parochial churches and chapels. At Pilton, for example, the oblations customarily made by pilgrims to the two images of Our Lady were not long permitted to continue. George Rolle, lessee of the priory after its suppression, received £12 in offerings to Our Lady of Pilton in as late as 1536–7, but in August 1537 a royal commission was directed to Bishop Veysey and the gentlemen Hugh and Richard Pollard, as a result of which both Our Lady of Pilton and Our Lady of Lorell were obediently removed from the parish. 'By reason whereof', complained Rolle in 1543, 'the resort of the king's liege people ceased, and is clearly extinct.' Nor was this case unique. Another venerated image was maintained at Camborne by the guild of St Ia, one of the evangelists of early-medieval Cornwall. It still attracted devotion in 1534–5, when the Camborne accounts commence: 1d was then given 'for offering to the saint's foot'. Gifts of this type, however, are conspicuously absent from all the church's subsequent accounts. Similar evidence comes from Iddesleigh. In both 1536 and 1537 – the first years of this parish's accounts – small sums 'ex dono perigrinorum' were received by a guild in the parish church. Dedicated to 'Blessed Mary of Iddesleigh in the chancel', it doubtless maintained an image of the Virgin, but the elimination of this cult in response to the injunctions is again suggested by the absence of such pilgrim gifts from every subsequent account.[60]

An even more drastic decline of investment followed the royal injunctions of 1538, which ordered the removal of all images that had attracted pilgrimage or offering. 'The king this year sent out his commissions throughout this realm', reports Hooker, 'for defacing and pulling down of all such idols and images as whereunto any offerings and pilgrimages had been made; and for this country [i.e. the South-West] Dr Heynes, dean of the cathedral church and chaplain to the king, was a commissioner.' Hooker records that this zealous anti-Catholic duly executed his commission 'throughout this diocese'. In Cornwall, for example, 'he defaced and pulled down an image called St Saviour, which was builded in the outside of the north wall of the chancel of the parish church of St Mawe-in-the-Sand'; and this was but one instance 'among others'. The testimony of Hooker is substantiated by other contemporary sources. The canons of Exeter, for example, lamented in 1541 that Dr Heynes had recently destroyed images within the cathedral itself. Some of the figures there had certainly received offerings from layfolk.

---

[60] *Documents of Church History*, pp. 269–74; E 315 126/16–17; CWA Camborne, 1535 *et seq.*; CWA Iddesleigh, 1536–7 *et seq.* By 1541, silver beads, rings and a crucifix had been committed to the keeping of the Four Men of Iddesleigh (CWA Iddesleigh, 1541); these may well represent the parish's confiscation of the cultic offerings.

Similar iconoclasm at Plymouth is indicated by the delivery to its mayor, in 1539–40, of a crown for Our Lady, a cross from the hand of St Saviour, tapers for the illumination of St Clare and clothes for the Virgin and Child, together with 'offering pence' and other gifts to the sacred figures. The mayor, William Hawkins, was a merchant and a resolute anti-traditionalist in religion. Even more devastating was the financial impact of iconoclasm upon a celebrated cult centre like Chittlehampton. In 1538–9 the profits of its vicarage plummetted from £76 17s 10d to a mere £27 13s 2d. This decline was subsequently attributed by an official enquiry to 'the taking away of the image of St Urith, and the ceasing of offerings that used to be made there by pilgrims'. And in about 1542 the impact upon another local cult was observed by John Leland. 'About half a mile ere I came to Liskeard', he noted, 'I passed in a wood by a chapel of Our Lady, called Our Lady in the Park; where was wont to be great pilgrimage.' Pilgrims had doubtless offered to an image of Mary; they evidently offered no more.[61]

Not only were laymen everywhere ceasing to invest in images; some were now daring to deliberately despoil them. In as early as 1534, at Morebath, a silver shoe belonging to the venerated image of St Sidwell was stolen by a thief. A comparable impiety occurred at St Austell. Its parish church had been donated a tenement by John Cockmathew in order to maintain image lights – 'as well certain tapers, burning yearly in the festival days before the high cross in the said church, in the honour of Almighty God, as before other images there'. At some point between 1533 and 1538, however, Cockmathew's feoffees ceased to provide the lights, 'and the whole profits thereof', complained the churchwardens, 'of their great covetous minds, do convert to their own uses'. But the most blatant expropriation occurred at Rewe. On 6 October 1538 a variety of treasures were removed from its parish church by Walter Bailiff, James Baron, John Collis and John Richards; the spoils included garments of velvet and satin as well as rings, girdles, silver ships, beads and sums of money. These had all been oblations, 'offered there to certain images in the said church'. When subsequently sued in the Court of Chancery by Roger Wallace, lessee of the parsonage, the four parishioners boldly appealed to the royal injunctions – which, they pointed out, by 6 October had been 'sent into all shires': 'Amongst which injunctions it was commanded that all images standing in any church, churchyard or other hallowed place, to which said image any offerings, idolatry or other oblations were made or done unto, should be pulled down and taken away within a convenient time. The said defendants, finding

---

[61] ER XV, fols. 76v–7; Hooker, Commonplace Book, fol. 344; CAB 3552, fol. 14v; *Plymouth Records*, p. 110; Chanter 1914, pp. 290–308; *Leland*, I, p. 208.

the said garments or vestures of velvet or satin called "mantles", having annexed to them divers coins of money with other jewels, set up of long time past at the costs and charges of the parishioners there ... did take, convert and employ [them] and every [one] of them to the use and maintenance of the said church of Rewe, as lawful was for them to do.'[62]

The financial commitment of laymen to the veneration of images was thus in serious decline for several years before the advent of the Edwardian regime. After 1547 its collapse was virtually total. Bequests to roods and to rood-lights now came to a halt and, in all parishes with accounts, the collection of 'wax-silver' for the provision of lights had apparently ceased by 1549. Payments for tapers before the rood at Morebath had ended by 1548, as had payments for the 'making of the beam-light' at Woodbury. Nor do any of the accounts for Edward's reign record the purchase of a single rood, rood-loft or saint figure. At Morebath even the customary expenditure upon 'cleansing of the imagery' ended after 1547.[63]

Equally revealing of local attitudes is the level of expenditure after Mary's accession. For the entire reign, the accounts, wills and other sources record the erection of no more than two new rood-lofts – at Exeter St Petrock's between 1555 and 1557 and at St Breock in 1557. The former was, by pre-Reformation standards, inexpensive. The part-payment to John Hill was only £10, and the parishioners' contributions, which ranged from William Hurst's £1 to Stephen Parker's 8d, totalled only £5 9s 8d. The loft at St Breock, constructed by the 'carver' Christopher William, cost no more than £16. Henrician lofts, as at Ashburton, Stratton or Winkleigh, had cost as much as £40–50.[64] Expenditure on new roods was frequent but seldom lavish. Only 43s 4d was spent at Crediton, 40s at Ashburton, 34s 4d at Tavistock, 33s 4d at South Tawton, 25s at Exeter Holy Trinity, 15s at Coldridge, 12s at Antony and a mere 6s 8d at Exeter St Mary Steps. In 1535–6, by comparison, the rood-figures at Morebath had cost some £7. Coldridge bought its rood in 1553–4, but purchase was delayed until 1554–5 at Antony, Crediton and South Tawton, until 1555–6 at Ashburton, Exeter Holy Trinity and Tavistock, and until 1556–7 at Braunton and Exeter St Mary Steps.[65] There was minor expenditure also on the ornamentation and illumination of roods, Antony, for example, spending 10s on painting and Stratton 2s 6d on tapers. On the other hand, Morebath seems not

[62] CWA Morebath, 1535; C 1 728/23; 924/9–10.
[63] CWA Morebath; CWA Woodbury.
[64] CWA Exeter SP, 1556–7; CWA St Breock, fol. 6. For Ashburton, Stratton, Winkleigh, see above, pp. 51–2.
[65] CWA Crediton, 1554–5; CWA Ashburton, 1556; *Tavistock Records*, p. 25; CWA S. Tawton, 1555; CWA Exeter HT, 1556; CWA Coldridge, 1554; CWA Antony, 1555; CWA Exeter SMS, 1557; CWA Braunton, 1557. For Morebath, see above, p. 50.

to have revived its pre-Edwardian custom of burning 'tapers afore the high cross'.[66]

Investment in saint figures was even less impressive. 4s was spent on 'gold for the tabernacle' at Braunton in 1555–6, and 3s 4d on the repainting of St Andrew at Stratton in 1557–8. At Morebath the gold stripped from the images in Edward's reign seems never to have been replaced. And although Woodbury expended 13s on 'making of the image of St Swithun' in 1556–7, and Coldridge 30s on 'making of the tablement and two images' in 1556–8,[67] not one new saint image is recorded in the accounts for 1553–9 at Holy Trinity, St John's Bow, St Mary Steps and St Petrock's in Exeter, in the towns of Ashburton, Barnstaple, Camborne, Chagford, Crediton, Dartmouth, Stratton and Tavistock, or in the rural parishes of Antony, Braunton, Dartington, Kilmington, Molland, Morebath and South Tawton.[68] Several parishes bought Lent cloths for their imagery,[69] and many, like Kilmington, revived the collection of wax-silver – though again there were apparent exceptions, including St Mary Steps and St Petrock's at Exeter.[70]

No more enthusiastic was the level of individual donation. Oblations to the Trinity figure at St Day may have revived, and offerings of an unspecified nature were made in the chapels of Our Lady and St Derwa at Camborne.[71] On the other hand, there is no evidence of gifts to the once venerated saint figures in parishes like Pilton, Sidbury or Chittlehampton: donations of this type are absent from the wills made, for example, by Katherine Walsh of Pilton, William Clapp of Sidbury and Humphrey Chapel of Chittlehampton.[72] Of the 60 wills in the years 1553–9, in fact, bequests to images appeared in only 4. Three financed rood-lights, and the fourth – 6s 8d from Richard Friend of Ermington in 1557 – was directed 'toward the making of two images of Sts Peter and Paul, patrons of our church'.[73] The Marian evidence thus leaves little doubt that even the return of official approbation generally failed to rekindle the layman's traditional devotion to the sacred figures. After 1559, moreover, expenditure totally ceased. The con-

---

[66] CWA Antony, 1555; Additional 32243, HCWA Stratton, 1559; CWA Morebath.
[67] CWA Braunton, 1556; Additional 32243, HCWA Stratton, 1558; CWA Morebath; CWA Woodbury, 1557; CWA Coldridge, 1558.
[68] CWA Exeter HT; CWA Exeter SJB; CWA Exeter SMS; CWA Exeter SP; CWA Ashburton; *Barnstaple Records*, I, pp. 212–13; CWA Camborne; CWA Chagford; CWA Crediton; CWA Dartmouth; Additional 32243, HCWA Stratton; Additional 32244, SWA Stratton; *Tavistock Records*, p. 25; CWA Antony; CWA Braunton; CWA Dartington; CWA Kilmington; CWA Molland; CWA Morebath; CWA S. Tawton.
[69] E.g. CWA Woodbury, 1554–5.
[70] E.g. CWA Kilmington, 1557–60. See also CWA Exeter SMS; and CWA Exeter SP.
[71] Henderson 1925, p. 54; CWA Camborne, 1557–9, 1561.
[72] PROB 11 37, fol. 191v; Moger, 5, Humphrey Chapel, 1558; 6, William Clapp, 1555.
[73] CCB 855A, fol. 311v.

struction of rood-lofts, roods and saint images seems everywhere to have
ended, and investment by parishes, guilds and individuals in their illumination or ornamentation to have been universally suppressed.

The essentially verbal and financial evidence must again be compared
with the behavioural. Can the people of the South-West be said to have
mounted significant resistance to the campaigns against their traditional
independent practices? Or were they more prone to acquiesce in their suppression?

One practice that laymen seem generally to have abandoned in response
to official pressures was their performance of public prayers on behalf of
the dead. Until 1547 such prayers were still requested by testators. In 1540,
for example, Robert Hone of Ottery St Mary donated 1d to each spectator
at his burial, in return for their prayers; forgave his debtors, on the condition
that they pray for him; and left 12d to each of his god-children 'to say
a *Pater Noster, Ave* and Creed, praying for my soul'. In 1546 Gilbert Kirk
of Exeter bequeathed 4d to each householder in St Mary Arches parish,
'to pray to Our Lord God to have mercy on my soul and all Christian
souls'. During Edward's reign, however, requests of this type vanished from
the wills. Though occasionally revived under Mary – as in 1554, when
the Exeter alderman John Tuckfield left money to his apprentice, servants
and maids, 'to pray for me' – they again disappeared in Elizabeth's reign.
A final, isolated example occurred in January 1561, when William Turner
of Cullompton still hoped for an annual dole to the poor on his burial
day – 'to pray for me, and my father and mother; and my two wives, Thomasine and Joan; and all Christian souls'. By this date, moreover, the performance of such prayers by the inmates of almshouses and by the members
of guilds seems generally to have ceased. At Cullompton, where the inhabitants of John Trotte's almshouse had prayed for his soul since *circa* 1523,
their prayers were cut short when the almshouse was dissolved – by Trotte's
own sons – in *circa* 1544. The organization of lay prayer for the dead
by religious guilds was similarly ended when these institutions were suppressed by Edward and Elizabeth.[74]

The use of rosaries, particularly in private, was probably slower to disappear. Users included an aged woman of Clyst St Mary who, in 1549, was
reproved by the gentleman Walter Raleigh for her continuing reliance on
beads; John Holwell and George Seward, who in Mary's reign bought beads
from Woodbury church; and a widow of Winkleigh, who bequeathed a
set in as late as 1567. By this date, on the other hand, rosaries were usually
omitted from the depictions of individuals on memorials and in church

[74] PROB 11 29, fol. 201; 31, fol. 44; 39, fol. 203; 44, fol. 159v; *Certificates, Devon*, p. xxi.
For guilds, see below, pp. 105–12.

art; and even in Mary's reign their employment had apparently been abandoned by anti-traditionalists like Agnes Priest of Boyton and George Helier of Swimbridge.[75] It is possible also that 'Lady' bells, traditionally rung at the hours when *Aves* were to be said, were deliberately defaced in Edward's reign: one had to be mended at Ashburton in 1553–4.[76] Commitment to the formal Catholic fast seems similarly to have declined. Rejected by Philip Gammon at Axminster in 1535–6, it was abandoned 'in King Edward's time' by a number of persons – including Stephen Tucker of Stoke Climsland – who deliberately ate meat during Lent. Tucker was also accused of fast-breaking in Mary's reign, when Joan Hancock of Exeter was similarly charged with preparing meat in Lent and on Fridays, and a poor man of the same city confessed to eating bacon during Lent.[77]

From 1536, when a royal proclamation decreed their reduction, the observance of feast days in honour of the saints was also subjected to official attack. Local reaction seems generally to have been subdued, the government agent Dr Tregonwell reporting from Penryn in September 1536 that 'the people of the country' were 'marvellously well pleased' that churches were still permitted to retain their patronal feast days. Certainly the only serious attempt to defend the abrogated days by force was limited to the remote Cornish parish of St Keverne, where, in the spring of 1537, two fishermen named Carpisack and Treglosack hoped to emulate the 'Northern men' who had recently mounted the Pilgrimage of Grace. They purchased 200 jerkins to serve as armour, and commissioned a local painter to produce a banner portraying Christ, Our Lady and St John, together with Henry VIII and his queen, 'and all the commonalty kneeling, with scripture above their heads, making their petition to the picture of Christ that it would please the king's grace that they might have their holy days'. 'We will carry this banner with us on Pardon Monday', hoped Carpisack, 'and there it shall be showed among all the people that will be there: who will follow this banner.' His optimism proved ill founded. The painter reported him to Sir William Godolphin, the dissidents were arrested, and Carpisack appears to have been hanged, in chains, at Helston. The 'privy insurrection of Cornishmen' feared by some people at Exeter failed totally to occur. After investigating the conspiracy, Godolphin reported that 'the country is in a marvellous good quiet'; and later, after travelling through Cornwall for the quarter sessions, he declared that 'there is no shire in the realm more conformable to be ordered further'. Far from supporting the Pilgrimage

---

[75] 'Description of Exeter', pp. 31–2; CWA Woodbury, 1554, 1556; *Acts and Monuments*, II, p. 2051; CCB 855, fol. 210v.
[76] CWA Ashburton, 1554.
[77] STAC 2/2/267; CCB 855, fols. 5v, 71–1v; Hooker, Commonplace Book, fol. 351.

of Grace, the South-West sent men to suppress it – some 364 from Cornwall and as many as 968 from Devon.[78]

The only significant resistance to the proclamation was non-violent. In as late as 1539, in the archdeaconry of Exeter, many artificers, husbandmen and labourers still ended their work at noon on Saturdays and holy days. Fishermen would not put to sea on saints' days, while blacksmiths and hay-carriers refused to work on St Eligius' day. 'Some shoesmiths be so fondly and superstitiously set to worship St Loye's day', it was reported, 'that [they] in that day will not shoe any man's horse.'[79] In October 1539, however, Bishop Veysey ordered parish priests to denounce such practices and to warn their congregations that offenders would be punished, and the Council of the West, instituted in the same year, was similarly instructed to suppress holy days and to punish dissidence with severity. To this pressure the populace seems generally to have succumbed. Of subsequent attempts to preserve the prohibited days there is no trace: not even the rebels of 1549 appear to have advocated their restoration. The Edwardian era in fact witnessed further decline. At Morebath, for example, payments for 'cleansing of the churchyard against St George tide' – the feast of this church's patron – were ended after 1547. Only a limited number of saints' days, including the patronal feasts, would seem still to have been celebrated in Elizabeth's reign.[80] By this time the traditional public reading of the 'legends' must also have ceased. Although still 'read in divine services' when Leland visited the region in *circa* 1542, it is improbable that these books remained long in use after 1543 – when the removal of 'feigned legends' from service-books and calendars was commanded, in order to erase 'the names and memories of all saints which be not mentioned in the scripture or authentical doctors'. The Cornishman Nicholas Roscarrock would later lament that many of the traditionally venerated saints had indeed been virtually forgotten, 'the violence of hostility consuming books and records in such sort as there is nothing remaining but bare names'.[81]

But even more striking was the general failure of the south-western people to defend their ancient shrines. In the years 1536–9 the popularly venerated relics in monastic houses – such as the portion of the Holy Cross and the jaw bone of St Apollonia on St Michael's Mount – would seem everywhere to have suffered despoliation by the royal commissioners without resistance from their former devotees. Acquiescence appears also to have been the

[78] *Reformation in England*, pp. 73–4; SP 1/106/134–5; 118/247–8; *LP*, XI, 580; XII (1), 1126–7; XII (2), 182, 557, 595; Rowse 1941, p. 229.

[79] ER XV, fol. 83v.

[80] ER XV, fol. 83v; Titus B 1, fol. 176; CWA Morebath; *Survey of Cornwall*, pp. 187–8.

[81] *Leland*, I, p. 237; *LP*, XVIII (1), 167; 'Lives of Saints', fol. 388. For the fading of memories of the saints, see 'Lives of Saints', fols. 78v, 254v, 291v, 298v, 304, 312v, 323v. For the survival of some traditions, see 'Lives of Saints', fols. 109v, 114v, 202v, 262, 296v.

prevalent response to the injunctions of 1536 and 1538, which carried the campaign against relics into cathedral, chapel and parish church. By about 1542, when Leland inspected the cathedral at Exeter, its formerly celebrated tomb of Bishop Lacey had been 'defaced' by Dr Heynes: an indent still shows where a brass depiction of the bishop was then ripped away. Nor did inhabitants of rural parishes necessarily offer more resistance than the Exeter citizens. At St Endellion, according to parishioners whose testimony was later recorded by Roscarrock, the revered tomb of Endellion herself was similarly 'defaced in King Henry VIII's time'. Subsequently it was removed to the south aisle, where it remains today. At Chittlehampton the veneration of St Urith's tomb appears to have ended with the suppression of her image and pilgrimage in 1539. Not even the Scilly Isles, 30 miles south-west of Land's End, would seem to have resisted the official campaign. Leland, in *circa* 1542, noted the existence of 'St Lide's Isle, where in times past at her sepulchre was great superstition'. The tomb of Elidius – in reality a male saint – had stood on the island now known as St Helen's, but had attracted devotion from as far afield as Cornwall. By 1542 the cult was evidently no more than a matter of 'times past'.[82]

In view of Leland's hagiological interests it is also suggestive that, on this journey through the South-West, he visited several former cult centres – including Hartland, Launceston, Padstow and Fowey – without noting the survival of their medieval shrines.[83] At Bodmin, it is true, he observed that 'the shrine and tomb of St Petrock yet standeth in the east part of the church', while at Germoe he noted that the tomb of Germoc 'is yet seen there', but in neither case is it clear that the mutilation inflicted upon such structures elsewhere had been effectively prevented.[84] Other evidence points in the same direction. A box of relics was inventoried at Dartmouth in 1536–7 but seems to have vanished shortly after; nor did it reappear in this church's Marian accounts. The last extant records of the piece of the Crown of Thorns at Bodmin, and of the portion of Holy Cross and hairs of St Katherine, Mary Magdalene and Our Lady at Tavistock, occur in the inventories compiled by these two parish churches in 1539. By the 1560s, when new inventories were made by both churches, the relics had disappeared. At Liskeard a silver shrine was sold by the church before 1549.[85]

Apart from a few dubious cases – as at Camborne, where a 'relic cloth'

---

[82] E 117 10/59; *Documents of Church History*, pp. 269–74; ER XV, fols. 76v–7; *Leland*, I, pp. 190, 226–7; 'Lives of Saints', fols. 202v–3; Chanter 1914, pp. 290–308; *Worcestre*, p. 113; Henderson 1923–4, p. 63.

[83] *Leland*, I, pp. 172, 174–5, 179, 203–4.

[84] *Leland*, I, pp. 180, 188.

[85] CWA Dartmouth, 1537 *et seq.*; *Inventories, Cornwall*, p. 32; *Tavistock Records*, p. 27; E 117 1/52. See also above, pp. 55, 57.

was made in 1555–6[86] – only in two parishes is there clear evidence that relics survived the Henrician assault. These are Grade, where a piece of Holy Cross was apparently inventoried in as late as 1553,[87] and Perranzabuloe, where the parade of the relics of St Piran was temporarily revived 'in the time of Queen Mary'; the latter were seen by Roscarrock as a child.[88] In both places the treasures must have been hidden by parishioners since *circa* 1536. Mary's reign also saw the restoration of assemblies at East Newlyn, but it is not clear that these still included the traditional display of local relics.[89] Nor is there evidence in accounts, wills or other sources of any attempt to resurrect the former shrines in Exeter Cathedral or in parish churches like those at Braunton, Chittlehampton and St Endellion. At Braunton, for example, the Marian accounts contain no reference to the previously celebrated shrine of St Brannoc.[90]

Such relics as had survived would seem to have been finally destroyed by the royal commissioners in the visitation of 1559.[91] Certainly the assemblies at East Newlyn failed to survive into Elizabeth's reign.[92] In subsequent years even once hallowed trees, like those associated with St Breward and St Illick, would be deliberately attacked; the latter, according to Roscarrock, was cut down 'in our time'.[93] By about 1580 one of the stones formerly used to display relics at East Newlyn had been ignominiously converted into a cheese-press.[94] Stone chairs and holy wells were less easy to demolish, and several, including Germoc's chair at Germoe and the well at Laneast, survive today, but their role in the popular religion was in manifest decline. Elizabethan men and women seem no longer to have sought healing from St Nun at her well in Altarnun. Such practices, sneered Richard Carew, belonged to 'our forefathers' days, when devotion ... exceeded knowledge'.[95] The healing well of St Madern at Madron had similarly waned in popularity. 'As he is coy of his cures', observed Norden in 1584, 'so now are men coy of coming to his conjured well.'[96]

---

[86] CWA Camborne, 1556.

[87] Henderson 1923–4, pp. 187–8, citing E 117 12/42. See also above, pp. 55–6.

[88] 'Lives of Saints', fol. 360v. See also above, pp. 57–8.

[89] 'Lives of Saints', fol. 323v. See also above, p. 58.

[90] CWA Braunton, 1554–9. See also above, pp. 56–7.

[91] *Zurich Letters*, p. 44. This visitation, which covered much of southern England, allegedly uncovered many relics, but there is no evidence that such objects were still common in Devon or Cornwall.

[92] 'Lives of Saints', fol. 323v.

[93] 'Lives of Saints', fols. 109v, 262.

[94] 'Lives of Saints', fol. 323v.

[95] 'Lives of Saints', fols. 327v–8; *Survey of Cornwall*, p. 289.

[96] Henderson 1923–4, p. 318. For date, see Rose-Troup 1913, p. 402. See also Roscarrock's use of the past tense in his references to healings at wells ('Lives of Saints', fols. 111v, 298v, 327v). Some wells nevertheless continued to be visited in the seventeenth century and later (see, for example, Henderson 1923–4, pp. 318–19).

But arguably of greatest importance were the reactions of south-western people to assaults upon images. In Henry VIII's reign the destruction of the region's most venerated figures appears almost always to have been executed without significant popular resistance. Philip Nichols would subsequently rejoice that King Henry had 'commanded and caused such images in all places to be plucked down'.[97] Not only in monastic houses, as on St Michael's Mount, but also in Exeter Cathedral and in parish churches or chapels at Chittlehampton, Pilton, Rewe, St Mawes and elsewhere, cults were effectively smashed without apparent counteraction from their erstwhile devotees.[98] Resentment was undoubtedly created: Dr Heynes, in particular, found himself 'marvellously hated and maligned at' for his iconoclastic zeal.[99] Yet only rarely does resentment appear to have been translated into active resistance. At both Pilton and Rewe the only recorded protests came from the lessees, whose interest in images was financial rather than religious.[100] In fact the sole recorded attempt to halt the Henrician iconoclasm by force was that mounted by a group of traditionalist women at Exeter in 1536. Under the leadership of Elizabeth Glandfield, they physically attacked the two craftsmen who – in obedience to orders from the official visitors – had begun to demolish the rood-loft in St Nicholas' Priory. One of the craftsmen was compelled to jump from a window in fear of his life. The rioters later explained that 'their only intent was to let [i.e. obstruct] two Bretons, carvers; which made their avaunt that they would pull down the crucifix of the said church of St Nicholas, with all the saints there, naming them to be "idols"'. That the women attracted a measure of public sympathy is suggested by the bills in their favour that were subsequently posted around the city. On the other hand it is notable that, despite the government's initial fears, the dissidents included no men, and that the two craftsmen were indeed positive supporters of the iconoclastic campaign. The destruction, moreover, had been actively furthered by the civic authorities. An unsuccessful attempt to quell the riot had been made by an alderman, John Blackaller, and the arrest of the women had been executed by the mayor, William Hurst.[101] Laymen elsewhere were prepared to co-operate with the official campaign: they included William Hawkins, Mayor of Plymouth.[102] In October 1538, at St Germans, a traditionalist friar indeed complained that 'men were too busy pulling down images without special

[97] Royal 18 B XI, fols. 21–2.
[98] See above, pp. 65–8.
[99] Hooker, Commonplace Book, fol. 344.
[100] E 315 126/16–17; C 1 924/9–10.
[101] Hooker, Commonplace Book, fol. 343; SP 1/102/33.
[102] *Plymouth Records*, p. 110.

commandment of the prince'. He was assured by William Dynham that those pulled down had been 'such as idolatry was committed unto'.[103]

Not until Edward's reign, when the total elimination of images was officially decreed,[104] did extensive resistance eventually occur. It appears to have been this intensification of the assault that provoked, in April 1548, a violent reaction from the parishes around Helston. The dissidents came largely from St Keverne, though some joined from Constantine, Grade, Gwennap, Helston, Illogan, Mullion, Parva Ruan, Perranzabuloe and Redruth. Of 26 lay participants whose status is recorded, there were 10 husbandmen and 4 yeomen, 9 mariners, 1 groom, 1 miller and 1 smith. Led by a priest from St Keverne and by a yeoman and a husbandman (namely John and William Kilter) from Constantine, the insurgents murdered the commissioner William Body and demanded a return to the late-Henrician religious situation. Although allegedly numbering some 3,000, they did not win total west-Cornish support. Hugh Mason of Grade, for example, reportedly remained 'a true man to his prince in all points in this broil'; and he was conveyed to the safety of Exeter by another apparent loyalist, William Leigh. Outside western Cornwall, moreover, support for the rising was minimal. In fact it was suppressed by loyalists who came not only from Plymouth – whence a company under Henry Blase rode into Cornwall, 'against the rebels there' – but also from parishes in eastern and northern Cornwall, including Antony, Boconnoc, East Newlyn, Lanteglos and Polruan, Launceston, Morval, St Veep, St Winnow and Stratton. Morval, for instance, provided mounted men 'to resist the last commotion', while St Veep sent forces 'west, to resist the commotion'. In consequence the rising was quelled (in the words of the Black Book of Plymouth) 'with small trouble'.[105]

A potentially more serious challenge to the official religious policy was presented by the rebellion of June–August 1549: its articles required 'images to be set up again in every church'. Yet even this outburst of conservative resistance was never actively supported by more than a relatively small proportion of the regional population. Nor, in practice, does the restoration of deposed images appear to have been a significant feature of rebel activity. The temporary re-erection of the rood at Stratton is the only instance recorded in surviving sources.[106] After 1549, moreover, physical resistance seems totally to have ceased.

The rebel demand that images be restored 'in every church' itself implies

[103] *LP*, XIII (2), 596.
[104] *TRP*, I, p. 394.
[105] Rose-Troup 1913, pp. 74–96, 425n; Rowse 1941, pp. 257–60; *Plymouth Records*, pp. 16, 115; E 117 1/52; CWA Antony, 1549; CWA Launceston, 1548; Additional 32244, SWA Stratton, 1548.
[106] Royal 18 B XI, fol. 19v; Additional 32243, HCWA Stratton, 1548–9. At Stratton the rood was removed in 1548, re-erected in 1549, and again removed in the same year.

that their deposition had been general, and certainly the extant accounts
and other sources would indicate that by 1550 the great majority of parochial
communities had obediently removed their sacred figures from public display. Roods, for example, were taken down in 1547–8, as at Holy Trinity,
St John's Bow and St Petrock's in Exeter and at Ashburton and Stratton.[107]
The assault upon crucifixes was extended even to stone crosses in churchyards, as at Barnstaple in about 1550 and at Woodbury in 1549–50.[108]
Similar treatment was accorded to saints. At Exeter Holy Trinity, St George
apparently came down in 1548, and was followed by image standings in
1549–50. At Exeter St Lawrence, two apostles and a silver figure of St
George on horseback had been 'carried out of the church' by 1549. At
Ashburton, St George and the other saints were removed in 1547–8 and
1549–50. At Stratton, St George, his horse and the standings for two other
figures were taken down in 1547–8; so were the 'pageants in the rood-loft',
possibly Our Lady and St Armil, in 1549. At North Molton, image standings
were removed in 1548–9; and at Whitchurch, images had been deposed
by 1550. At Morebath, similarly, the images were banished from their positions of honour in the parish church: they included Our Lady, St John,
various 'pageants', and figures of a king and queen which had belonged
(as in a window at St Neot) to a tableau depicting St George.[109] Not infrequently the elaborate image-bearing rood-lofts were themselves attacked.
Their defacement or destruction was recorded not only in the Exeter churches
of Holy Trinity, St John's Bow and St Petrock's, all in 1549–50, but also
in the town of Ashburton, in 1550–1, and even in the remote rural parishes
of Morebath, in 1550–1, and St Breock, in about 1550. At St Breock, for
example, the rood-loft was 'drawn down, by commandment'.[110]

In many cases the redundant apparatus of image veneration was consigned
to storage. At St Lawrence's and St Mary Arches in Exeter, clothes for
the sacred figures were thus preserved. Images themselves might sometimes
survive: at Exeter St Lawrence some were removed to the house of a warden,
Richard Hart, while at Morebath the deposed figures were delivered to
parishioners like John Williams at Berry and William Morse at Lawton.
That a significant number of roods and saints evaded both sale and destruction in the Edwardian period is indicated by their subsequent re-erection

---

[107] CWA Exeter HT, 1548; CWA Exeter SJB, 1548; CWA Exeter SP, 1548; CWA Ashburton,
1548; Additional 32243, HCWA Stratton, 1548.
[108] *Barnstaple Records*, I, p. 198; CWA Woodbury, 1550.
[109] CWA Exeter HT, 1548, 1550; *Inventories, Exeter*, p. 39; CWA Ashburton, 1548, 1550;
Additional 32243, HCWA Stratton, 1547–9; CWA N. Molton, 1549; CCB 855, fol. 151v;
CWA Morebath, 1555.
[110] CWA Exeter HT, 1549; CWA Exeter SJB, 1550; CWA Exeter SP, 1550: CWA Ashburton,
1551; CWA Morebath, 1551; CWA St Breock, fol. 6.

in Mary's reign.[111] Sales, nevertheless, were by no means infrequent. At St Breock, for instance, the rood-loft was sold: it fetched a derisory 26s 8d. Part of 'the cross in the churchyard' was sold (for 12d) by the wardens of Woodbury in 1549–50. The years 1549–50 saw also the sale of a tabernacle of St Margaret at Woodbury, of a tabernacle of St George at Whitchurch, and of actual images at Exeter St Petrock's. 'Gold that was upon the images' was sold in 1550–1 at both Crediton and Morebath; at Morebath the figures thus stripped presumably included Sidwell, Eligius and Our Lady, all of which had been gilded in 1529–33. Sales of image cloths included 'one white cloth, for to hang before the rood', at Woodbury in 1547, a cloth 'that served for the high cross' at Morebath in 1548, eight cloths 'that covered images' at Stratton in 1549, and a rood-cloth in the same church in 1550–1. In 1550–1 the wardens at Woodbury sold even the 11 pewter bowls that formerly 'did stand upon the rood-loft, to set tapers on'.[112]

The apparatus thus appropiated by individuals was sometimes treated with conspicuous contempt. In 1548–9 the bailiff of Halberton, Christopher Sampford, removed from the parish church its rood, its figures of Our Lady and St John, its rood-loft, and even its 'great image, of stone, of the Assumption of Our Blessed Lady' – a figure formerly clothed in a mantle of black velvet and adorned with beads and silver rings. 'And [he] hath laid the same image in his oven', the horrified parishioners would lament in Mary's reign; 'and turned the back of the same image upward in the midst of the bottom of the same oven; and doth bake his bread upon the back of the same image'. Its mantles, rings and beads appear to have been removed by John Warren. Equally irreverent was William Gooding of Whitchurch. After buying the tabernacle of St George from his parish church in 1550, he used it – 'contemptuously', it was feared – to seal his 'purlieus'.[113] Numerous images, moreover, were deliberately defaced or destroyed. At Exeter, for example, noses were knocked from the sculpted figures in the cathedral. At Halberton, in 1548–9, an image was allegedly defaced, broken, and ejected into the churchyard. At South Tawton, at about this time, the face of an image of St Peter appears to have been mutilated; and at Ashburton, in 1549–50, it is certain that once venerated images and their tabernacles were deliberately burned. That defacement and destruction of this nature

[111]   *Inventories, Exeter*, pp. 39, 47; CWA Morebath, 1555. For Marian re-erection, see below, p. 79.

[112]   CWA St Breock, fol. 6; CWA Woodbury, 1547, 1550–1; CCB 855, fol. 151v; CWA Exeter SP, 1550; CWA Crediton, 1551; CWA Morebath, 1548, 1551; Additional 32243, HCWA Stratton, 1549, 1551. For the Morebath figures, see above, p. 51.

[113]   STAC 4/8/47; CCB 855, fol. 151v.

had been extensive is suggested by Marian expenditure on the repair of old figures and on the purchase of new roods.[114]

After Mary's accession the surviving imagery could legitimately be restored to public display.[115] Pre-Edwardian roods appear to have been re-erected in 1553–4 at St John's Bow, St Mary Major, Dartmouth, Dartington and Woodbury, by 1554–5 at Chagford and Stratton, by 1555–6 at Camborne and by 1556–7 at Exeter St Petrock's. In as early as 1553–4 the parishioners of Woodbury, for example, bought iron and nails 'for the setting up of the rood', and paid 20d for 'dressing of the rood with Mary and John'.[116] But such spontaneity was not universal – Chagford, for instance, failed to re-erect its rood before 1555 – and the restoration of saints might be even more delayed. Not until 1554–5 did the parishioners of Morebath return the deposed images to their church – 'by the which doings', thought their vicar, 'it showeth that they did like good Catholic men'. Not until 1555–6 does South Tawton appear to have mended its damaged saints, paying 3s for 'carving of the face of the image of St Peter', and 1s 'to carve the image of St Andrew'. Only in 1556–7 does St Brannoc, the patron, appear to have been re-erected at Braunton; and only in 1557–8 were St George and his tabernacle restored at Braunton, and St Andrew, the patron, returned to his position of prominence at Ashburton. At Chagford, where John Gebard received 20s 2d for his labour, the images seem not to have been repaired and reinstated until as late as 1559. In some parishes the restoration of saints may never have occurred.[117] The repair of damaged rood-lofts, moreover, was delayed at Morebath until 1555–6 and at Kilmington until 1557–8.[118]

Nor was the restored imagery necessarily treated with respect. In late 1553 a cross was stolen from the church at Silverton by a local man named Helier. He then publicly 'abused' it, planting it in a wayside hedge and – in an irreverent parody of the rood – hanging pictures of Our Lady and St John from its arms on pieces of thread; there they dangled 'like thieves'. Similarly hostile to the traditional veneration of roods was Kenton's Martin Alley. In 1557 he admitted that 'he did creep the cross when he was a child – and not since'. No more respectful was the attitude of John Williams and George Helier towards the rood at Swimbridge. This image, the rood-

[114] *Acts and Monuments*, II, p. 2051; STAC 4/8/47; CWA S. Tawton, 1556; CWA Ashburton, 1550. For Marian expenditure, see above, p. 68.
[115] *Documents of Church History*, pp. 377–80.
[116] CWA Exeter SJB, 1554; CWA Exeter SMM, fol. 13; CWA Dartmouth, 1554; CWA Dartington, 1554; CWA Woodbury, 1554; CWA Chagford, 1555; Additional 32243, HCWA Stratton, 1556; CWA Camborne, 1555–6; CWA Exeter SP, 1557.
[117] CWA Morebath, 1555; CWA S. Tawton, 1556; CWA Braunton, 1557–8; CWA Ashburton, 1558; CWA Chagford, 1559.
[118] CWA Morebath, 1556; CWA Kilmington, 1558.

beam and ceilure of which survive today, had customarily attracted bequests. Williams, it was alleged in 1557, 'refused to do his penance before the crucifix', 'railed upon his curate', and announced 'that he would not fast [before the rood], but that the curate should fast himself for [him]'. Helier was also said to treat the rood with 'contempt', and to refuse to pray before it.[119]

When, in 1559, the official assault was renewed,[120] conformity again constituted the most usual local response. Physical resistance was now apparently non-existent. In fact, 1559–60 saw the deposition of images by parochial communities throughout the South-West – not only in Exeter, where, for instance, the rood and 'pageants' of St Petrock's came down, but also in towns like Ashburton, Barnstaple, Chagford and Crediton, and in rural areas like Dartington, Winkleigh and Woodbury. Thus at Chagford, after a meeting with the commissioners at Exeter, the wardens paid 'for taking down of the images' and of their standings, while at Dartington, after a meeting with the commissioners at Totnes, the wardens paid 'for taking down of all the images and tabernacles'. Often, significantly, the deposition of imagery under Elizabeth was more prompt than had been its erection under Mary.[121]

Deposition was sometimes followed by sale. Exeter St Petrock's sold two stone images – to William Hurst, for 6d – in 1562–3, and Stratton disposed of its 'cherubins', for 20d, in as late as 1570. Lent cloths for roods or saints were also sold, as at Exeter St Mary Major after 1558 and at Ashburton in 1568–9.[122] Defacement and destruction, moreover, were again frequent. Hooker records that when, in September 1559, the royal commissioners reached Exeter, 'they defaced and pulled down and burned all images and monuments of idolatry'. The burnings, performed publicly in the cathedral close, were accepted by the citizens with apparent passivity; indeed, 'they which in Queen Mary's days were accounted to be most forward in erecting them up, and in maintaining of them, were now made the instruments to make the fire and to burn them'. Nor were the holocausts confined to Exeter. At Barnstaple, in 1558–9, the sacred figures were defaced and burned. At Ashburton, in 1559–60, the images were similarly consigned to the flames. At Crediton an inventory of the parish church, compiled on 4 October 1559, lists the images that had been 'defaced' and 'burned': these included

[119] SP 11/2/15; CCB 855, fols. 175, 210v. For bequests to Swimbridge rood, see Moger, 2, 58, 168; 11, 129–30.
[120] *TRP*, II, pp. 118—19, 123.
[121] CWA Exeter SP, 1560; CWA Ashburton, 1560; *Barnstaple Records*, I, pp. 212–13; CWA Chagford, 1560; DRO 1660 A 12; CWA Dartington, 1559; CWA Winkleigh, 1560; CWA Woodbury, 1559.
[122] CWA Exeter SP, 1563; Additional 32243, HCWA Stratton, 1570; CWA Exeter SMM, fol. 16; CWA Ashburton, 1569.

'the high cross, with Mary and John', as well as St George, St Katherine, St Margaret, and three angels. Even in the rural parish of Woodbury, in 1558–9, men were paid by the wardens 'for taking down of the images and for burning of them'.[123] Although obscure in some of the parishes with extant accounts, including Braunton, Kilmington, Molland, Morebath and South Tawton,[124] reaction to the governmental campaign would therefore appear again to have been predominantly compliant: images were obediently eradicated from the pattern of parochial religion. A silent testimony to this compliance is borne by the empty figure niches to be seen in parish churches throughout the region to this day.[125]

In 1561, moreover, the reduction of rood-lofts was officially decreed. With some possible exceptions like Chagford – where the loft would remain in as late as 1574 – the majority of parishes seem once more to have conformed. At Exeter St Petrock's, for instance, the loft was largely demolished in as early as 1561–2, and its rood-beam carried away. Although it survived in part, its potential for 'superstitious' purposes ceased with the 'stopping up of the rood-loft door' in 1563–4. The years 1561–2 also saw the partial or total destruction of rood-lofts in towns and even in rural parishes: these included Chudleigh, Morebath and Woodbury, and probably North Molton, St Breock and Tavistock. At Chudleigh, for instance, the wardens paid for 'taking down the rood-loft'. At Woodbury the wardens provided drink for 'the workmen which pulled down the rood-loft this year'. At St Breock, in 1562, the 'carver' Christopher William appears to have destroyed the structure which he had himself erected in Mary's reign, and 'a piece of timber that was in the rood-loft' would be sold by this parish in 1565.[126]

Compliance, it is true, was not always immediate. Among the recalcitrants were some parishioners of Cornwood; one of these, William Warren, declared in May 1562 that 'he would see the queen's majesty's broad seal first, for the plucking-down of the [loft], before that he would mell withal'. Other inhabitants of Cornwood, including Robert Hill and Walter Sherwill, nevertheless supported the official policy and reported the recalcitrants to the bishop's chancellor – whereupon the loft was doubtless soon removed. A similar fate probably befell the loft at Rockbeare after a local yeoman, John Holmere, had reported to the Consistory Court in August 1562 that it was 'not down'. More of the once important structures were obediently

---

[123] Hooker, Commonplace Book, fol. 352; *Barnstaple Records*, I, pp. 212–13; CWA Ashburton, 1560; DRO 1660 A 12; CWA Woodbury, 1559.

[124] CWA Braunton; CWA Kilmington; CWA Molland; CWA Morebath; CWA S. Tawton.

[125] See, for example, above, pp. 48–9. At Molland a pier-niche retains the broken image of a saint (Pevsner 1952A, p. 123).

[126] Bond and Camm 1909, I, p. 105; CWA Chagford, 1574; CWA Exeter SP, 1562–4; CWA Chudleigh, 1562; CWA Morebath, 1562; CWA Woodbury, 1562; CWA N. Molton, c. 1562; CWA St Breock, fols. 6v, 13v; *Tavistock Records*, p. 26.

reduced in 1562–3, as at South Tawton and probably at Dartington; in 1563–4, as at Exeter St Mary Steps, Ashburton and Coldridge; and in 1564–5, as at Stratton and probably at Kilmington. At Stratton the ceiling and beam of the loft were demolished in 1564, and two men were paid for 'taking down of the rood-loft' in 1565. Its sale, arranged in 1570, would eventually earn £5 6s 8d – a fraction of its original cost.[127] In many parishes the destruction of lofts would be completed in the 1570s.[128] Although remnants were to survive until as late as the nineteenth century, these had invariably been denuded of images and had often been converted into organ platforms, choir galleries or even pews.[129]

Throughout the Reformation, in short, the responses of south-western people to assaults upon their traditional practices would appear to have been predominantly compliant. Acquiescence and even positive co-operation were almost always more common than effective resistance.

[127] CCB 779, sub 15 May 1562; CCB 855A, fol. 215; CWA S. Tawton, 1563; CWA Dartington, *c*. 1563; CWA Exeter SMS, 1564; CWA Ashburton, 1564; CWA Coldridge, 1564; Additional 32243, HCWA Stratton, 1563–5, 1570; Additional 32244, SWA Stratton, 1564–5, 1572; CWA Kilmington, 1565.
[128] CWA Exeter SP, 1577: CWA Ashburton, 1576, 1580: CWA Chudleigh, 1577; CWA Crediton, 1579; CWA N. Molton, 1576; CWA Dartington, 1577; CWA Woodbury, 1576.
[129] Bond and Camm 1909, I, II, esp. II, p. 275.

5

Inclusive institutions: parish churches, chapels and guilds

Of those Catholic institutions in which the layman was permitted to participate, the most important on the eve of the Reformation were unquestionably the church and chapels of his parochial community.

The parish often maintained chapels and always a church. If the layman dwelled at a distance from his church, he would usually attend services in a parochial chapel; an example remains at Bulkworthy in the parish of Buckland Brewer. If attached to the household of a gentleman or substantial yeoman, he might worship in a private chapel of the type still visible near Lapford at Bury Barton.[1] It was nevertheless the church that accommodated most of the important religious activities of the parochial community. Usually this was located close to the centre of its town or village, though not infrequently it was surrounded only by a hamlet and sometimes it stood at some distance from its maintaining settlement. It undoubtedly performed a number of essentially secular functions, but its primary purpose was always the provision of an architectural environment suitable for the activities of traditional Catholicism.

The typical church of the pre-Reformation South-West was approximately rectangular in plan. Its walls were of local stone and its roofs of timber, generally of wagon-type with bosses at the intersections, though stone vaulting might cover a porch or aisle. Its most spacious component, the nave, housed the parishioners themselves; here, during services, they stood, knelt or sat. The nave might also contain altars, as indicated, for example, by openings in the rood-screen at Swimbridge; tabernacled images, before which men and women prayed, lit candles or left offerings; and gravestones, beneath which they were finally interred. The building's focal point, however, was invariably the chancel at its eastern end. Smaller in area, this was generally reserved for the officiating clergy – by whom indeed it was often entered by a separate door in its south wall. Demarcated from the nave by a rood-screen, and from its aisles by parclose screens, it contained the high altar,

---

[1] Hoskins 1954, p. 227.

2 St Andrew's, Sampford Courtenay. A typical parish church of the late-medieval South-West. Notice the churchyard, the tower, the porch, the nave, the chancel and the aisles. This church witnessed the first Devonian resistance to the Prayerbook of 1549.

at which the central rite of traditional religion was regularly performed. Recessed into its south wall were the piscina, a basin for the ritual ablutions, and possibly sedilia, the seats for the officiating priest and his assistants. Its north wall occasionally contained a permanent 'sepulchre' for the Easter celebrations.

These two indispensable components – the nave and the chancel – would frequently be supplemented by transepts, extending north and south from the main axis; by aisles, located north or south of nave or chancel and separated from them by arcades; or by screen-enclosed chapels, which might be added in a variety of locations. Such areas usually accommodated subsidi-

3 St Mary's, Atherington. A typical church interior. Note the separation of chancel from nave by a rood-screen, and the remnants of the rood-loft, built in about 1540, with its conspicuously empty image niches.

ary altars, particularly for masses on behalf of individuals or guilds; this function is often indicated by surviving piscinae. They might also contain venerated images or even the shrine of a saint. In addition there was usually a porch south-west of the nave. It accommodated legal and commercial transactions as well as parts of processions, baptisms and marriages, for which purposes it was frequently fitted with stone seats; often it contained also a stone stoup for the reservation of the holy water. Sometimes it boasted an upper chamber, for storage, schooling, or a priest's lodging.

Most churches were enhanced by a substantial tower. Though occasionally erected over a transept or over the intersection of chancel and nave, this generally stood to the west of the nave. In addition to its functions as landmark and community status symbol, it housed the ritually important bells and – by virtue of its height – ensured the transmission of their sound throughout the parish. Among the most impressive of the region's late-Perpendicular towers are those at Ashburton, Chittlehampton, Hartland, South Molton and Totnes; they are often elaborately ornamented and pinnacled, and sometimes approach or exceed 100 feet in height. The final major component was the churchyard. Surrounding the church on all sides, this was itself encompassed by a hedge or wall, through which the lich-gate provided entry. It accommodated not only burials but also processions and secular activities like fairs, markets, revels and Ales. In consequence a church house was often erected within the churchyard or nearby; among many surviving examples is that of *circa* 1500 at Widecombe.[2]

The scale, complexity and architectural quality of a church were inevitably determined by the requirements and the resources of its parochial community. The larger and more elaborate were usually situated in densely populated and wealthy districts like the Vale of Exeter or the South Hams, while the smaller and simpler were more frequent where – as on the fringes of Dartmoor or of Bodmin Moor – the settlements were dispersed and the finances more limited. Cullompton represents the former type, and Honeychurch the latter. Throughout the South-West, nevertheless, the fifteenth and early-sixteenth centuries witnessed an upsurge of church construction that can only be described as spectacular. In innumerable parishes the existing structures were modified, enlarged, or almost wholly replaced – a fact which explains the relative scarcity of Saxon, Norman, Early English and Decorated architecture in the region today.[3] That this trend persisted strongly into the decades immediately preceding the Reformation is unquestionably indicated by wills, wardens' accounts and episcopal registers. It

---

[2] This description is based upon personal examination of extant examples. For churches in general, see Cook 1954; and Cox and Ford 1943–4. For south-western churches, see Pevsner 1952A; 1952B; and Pevsner and Radcliffe 1970.

[3] Hoskins 1954, pp. 270–1; Pevsner 1952B, p. 20.

is also confirmed by rebuses, like that of a rector of *circa* 1519 at Silverton; by coats of arms, like those of Bishops Oldham and Veysey at Ottery St Mary; and by inscriptions, like those of 1517 and 1526 at Tiverton and Cullompton.[4] The structures wholly or partly erected in the decade 1520–9 alone in fact included the churches at Maristow, Sandford, Thornbury and Launceston – the last particularly impressive in its dimensions and its profuse ornamentation – as well the towers at Probus, Tiverton, Ugborough and probably Chulmleigh, the porches at Awliscombe and Axminster, and the aisles or chapels at Axminster, Cruwys Morchard, Cullompton, Honiton, Kentisbeare, Littleham, Marldon, Ottery St Mary, St Neot and Tiverton. Some of the most sumptuous church-building in the South-West was thus chronologically coincident with the arrival in England of Protestant ideas.[5]

The outlay of capital was inevitably substantial. The labour force, with its specialized skills in masoncraft, wood-carving, iron-working and glazing, required commensurate payment in wages, and the materials, though generally procured from south-western sources like the quarries at Beer or the granite outcrops of Dartmoor, might still require transportation over a considerable distance.[6] While much of the money was provided by wealthy ecclesiastics[7] or by members of the local nobility and gentry,[8] there can be no doubt that an important contribution was frequently made by the middle and even the lower ranks of lay society. A merchant of Topsham, John Raleigh, in 1501 left £10 towards the erection of an aisle in his parish church. In *circa* 1508 the inhabitants of Golant contributed £4 towards a new aisle for the church at Tywardreath. At Golant itself, where the church was built in *circa* 1509, donors' inscriptions on the roofs include the names of individuals and of guilds; among these are fraternities dedicated to St George, St James, St John the Baptist, St Katherine and All Saints. In 1511 William Bullock gave 10s towards the raising of the fine granite tower at Plympton St Mary. An aisle added to Exeter St Petrock's in 1511–12 was financed by the parishioners. The construction of the church at Truro was similarly supported by local gifts, including 10s from Richard Trewick in 1512. The richly ornamented porch, south aisle and south chapel at Tiverton, with their battlements, sculptures and niches, were all financed in and after 1517 by a local wool merchant, John Greenway; figures of the donor and his wife remain both in sculpture and in brass.

---

4 Pevsner 1952B, pp. 221, 263. For inscriptions, see below, pp. 90–1.
5 Pevsner 1952A, p. 155; Pevsner 1952B, pp. 44, 96–7, 182–3, 188, 196, 203, 221; Pevsner and Radcliffe 1970, pp. 96–7, 147, 197; Hoskins 1954, pp. 324, 381, 412, 418, 432, 448, 472, 509; Bond and Camm 1909, II, p. 334; Slader 1968, p. 62; PROB 11 23, fols. 22, 29, 71; STAC 2/17/209; ER XV, fol. 33.
6 Hoskins 1954, pp. 259–60.
7 E.g. the Prior of Montacute at Awliscombe (Hoskins 1954, p. 324).
8 See below, pp. 219–20.

4 St Peter's, Tiverton. Sculpture of 1517 over the south porch. Notice the kneeling figures of John and Joan Greenway, who financed the porch, south aisle and south chapel, and the Virgin Mary, who is shown experiencing her Assumption. Note also the vacant niches to left and right.

The magnificent tower at Probus – profusely decorated and, at 129 feet, the tallest in Cornwall – was erected by the parishioners in *circa* 1520–3. They not only employed masons and labourers but also worked themselves, carrying stone in their carts from the quarry to the church. The superbly fan-vaulted south aisle at Cullompton was erected in 1526 by another wool merchant, John Lane. Its exterior sculpture depicts sheepshears, ships and other emblems of the donor's trade. In 1528 William Coxhead bequeathed £20 to the church at Chulmleigh, 'toward the making of a new tower there'; the resultant four-staged and pinnacled structure remains today. At Honiton, according to inscriptions on the capitals, the chancel aisles of *circa* 1528 were built by John and Joan Tackle. At Kentisbeare the south aisle was constructed by John Whiting, a merchant who died in 1530; one capital depicts a wool-pack, a ship, and the shield of the Merchant Adventurers.[9]

Furnishings as well as fabrics were the object of substantial investment. Several dozen late-medieval pulpits, often richly carved and sometimes bearing figures of the saints, are still to be seen in the region's churches: that at Holne, for example, is dated by its heraldry to 1504–19. The ends of pre-Reformation benches, mostly with carvings, remain in their hundreds. Those at Altarnun, for example, are dated by an inscription to 1525. Only a fraction of the pre-Reformation glass survives, but three of the magnificent windows at St Neot, for example, are dated by their inscriptions to 1523, 1528 and 1529.[10] Even more elaborate are the rood-screens to be seen in more than 100 churches in Devon alone. Dating mostly from the late-fifteenth and early-sixteenth centuries, these are usually constructed in timber, painted, and enriched with fan-vaults and carved cornices; their traceried windows afforded visibility into the chancel from the nave. Among the most spectacular are those at Ashton, Bovey Tracey, Bradninch, Dartmouth, Hartland, Kentisbeare, Plymtree, Swimbridge and Wolborough; that at Bradninch, for instance, is dated by an inscription to 1528. Rood-screens, moreover, were often supplemented by parclose screens, as at Ashton or Colebrooke.[11]

Again the financial contribution of the non-gentle laity was undoubtedly vital. At Ashburton, for instance, it was the parishioners as a body who apparently financed the seating of their church between 1510 and 1527. A window depicting the patron, St Sampson, was bought for the church at Tywardreath in *circa* 1508 by the people of Golant, and two cases of

---

[9] Murray, 27, John Raleigh, 1501; PROB 11 17, fol. 187; 23, fols. 22, 29, 71; CCB 854, sub 28 February 1507/8; CWA Exeter SP, 1512; STAC 2/17/209; Prince 1701, pp. 324–5; Henderson 1923–4, pp. 179–80, 457; Pevsner 1952B, pp. 182–3, 188; Hoskins 1954, p. 418.

[10] See below, pp. 203–5, 237–9.

[11] Bond and Camm, 1909, I, II, esp. II, p. 281.

glass were contributed to the church at Truro in 1515 by John Harwell. At St Neot, according to the inscriptions, one of the stained-glass windows was donated in 1523 by the wives of the parish, a second in 1528 by the young men, and a third in 1529 by the 'sisters' or young women. The wives and the sisters are depicted in their windows, some 20 appearing in each group. The rood-screen at Tiverton was financed in *circa* 1517 by John Greenway, and the screen at Kentisbeare before 1530 by John Whiting. In 1531 parclose screens and other furnishings were commissioned by the parishioners of Stratton.[12]

An impressively high proportion of their material resources was thus devoted by individuals, groups and parochial communities to the construction and furnishing of their churches. While probably stimulated in part by a desire for status in the eyes of contemporaries or of posterity, there is no doubt that this expenditure reflects primarily the pervasive religiosity of the pre-Reformation South-West. At Probus in *circa* 1520–3, for example, it was reportedly 'of their good minds and devotions' that the parishioners rebuilt their church.[13] Frequently the specific intention was to honour a saint. The completion in *circa* 1500 of the church at St Mabyn, for instance, was celebrated with a hymn in praise of St Mabyn herself. The church at Launceston, rebuilt between 1511 and 1524, retains in a niche at its east end a prominent figure of St Mary Magdalene, to whom it was dedicated. On the screen at East Portlemouth the donor and his wife were shown kneeling on either side of a coronation of Our Lady, and in the sculpture over their porch of 1517 at Tiverton, John and Joan Greenway may still be seen in prayer before an assumption of Our Lady. At Cullompton, according to his wife, John Lane similarly erected his chapel of 1526 'in the honour of God and the assumption of Our Lady'.[14]

Equally compelling was the urge to secure prayers on behalf of the donor's soul. 'Orate pro animabus Katharine Burlas, Nicholai Burlas et Johannis Vyvyan, qui istam fenestram fecerunt fieri' – thus pleads the inscription on an early-Tudor window, which also portrays the donors themselves, in the church at St Neot. At Teignmouth an inscription formerly requested spectators to 'pray for the souls of Thomas Smith and Clement his wife, John Smith and Isabel his wife, all good benefactors'. Another inscription – also, for maximum effect, in English rather than in Latin – remains on the exterior of the church at Cullompton. It reminds spectators that the

---

[12] CWA Ashburton, 1511–27; CCB 854, sub 28 February 1507/8; Henderson 1923–4, p. 457; Rushforth 1927B, pp. 150–90; Prince 1701, pp. 324–5; Pevsner 1952B, p. 188; Hoskins 1954, p. 418; *Blanchminster's Charity*, pp. 91–4.

[13] STAC 2/17/209.

[14] 'Lives of Saints', fol. 296v; Bond and Camm 1909, II, p. 216; STAC 2/25/80, 142. See also *Beunans Meriasek*, 994–6.

south chapel was founded in 1526 by John Lane and his wife, Thomasine, requests these spectators to recite a *Pater Noster* and an *Ave* for them, for their children and for their friends, and expresses the hope that God will have mercy on their souls and will finally bring them to glory. Even more explicit were the texts engraved on a memorial slab, and 'in great letters' on the interior wall, in the chapel erected by the Greenways at Tiverton in 1517: 'O that the Lord may / Grant unto John Greenway / Good fortune and grace / And in Heaven a place'; 'Of your charity, pray for the souls of John and Joan Greenway, his wife ... and for their fathers and mothers, and for their friends and their lovers. On them Jesu have mercy. Amen. Of your charity, say *Pater Noster* and *Ave*.' The less wealthy might similarly be spurred to support church-building by their fear of Purgatory. In 1524, for example, contributors to the rebuilding of the church at Thornbury were rewarded by the grant of an indulgence or pardon from the Bishop of Exeter.[15]

The participation of the layman in his parish church extended beyond its construction and furnishing to its maintenance and supervision. The leading roles were usually played by a small council of parishioners – known as the Four Men, the Five Men, or whatever – and by the two or more churchwardens. At Halberton, for example, there were Six Men, 'elect and chosen by all the parishioners'. These 'had the rule, keeping, and whole governance of the church goods of the said parish, and the laying forth, disbursing and employing of all such sums of money as was disbursed, bestowed or employed about the reparation or amendment of the said church [or] house, jewels, bells and ornaments of the same church'.[16] The churchwardens, who in most cases were similarly elected each year by the parishioners, were recruited mainly from the substantial farmers, tradesmen and craftsmen. They received the various revenues due to the church; maintained its fabric and its furnishings; safeguarded its plate, vestments, and other ritual accoutrements, purchasing additions and replacements when required; and presented detailed accounts of their stewardship each year to their fellow-parishioners.[17] In towns, moreover, a supervisory function was often performed by the ruling oligarchies. At Dartmouth, in the reign of Henry VIII, the oath sworn by each mayor included a pledge to maintain the divine service in St Saviour's church; and similarly active roles were played by the mayors at Bodmin, Launceston and elsewhere.[18]

The layman was also vital to the continuing financial sustenance of the

---

[15] Rushforth 1927B, p. 163; Westcote 1845, p. 444; Prince 1701, pp. 324–5; ER XV, fol. 33.
[16] C 1 1138/88–92.
[17] This description is based upon their extant accounts. See also Cox 1913.
[18] *Dartmouth*, p. 188; CWA Dartmouth; BA Bodmin; Peter 1885, p. 317.

parish church. The incomes of churches showed considerable variation: Exeter Holy Trinity, for example, received £9 19s 7d in 1529, whereas Ashburton could boast an impressive £61 14s 4d. One major source of revenue was usually rent, which was collected annually from the tenants of properties donated by past benefactors. These were generally in the form of land, though Exeter St Mary Steps owned three shops on Stepcote Hill, and Chagford church held shares in the local tin-workings. Also lucrative were the church Ales, which, as at Morebath, might indeed constitute the largest single source of income. At Plymouth the Ale was held in the churchyard at the feast of Corpus Christi 'for the honour of God and for the increasing of the benefits of the church of St Andrew'; no tavern was permitted on that day to sell ale or wine. At Ashburton, as in 1526–7, the Ale was associated with a revel, in which parishioners dressed as Robin Hood and his band. Revenues were further supplemented by surpluses from the church's religious guilds, which at Ashburton in 1525–6, for example, yielded as much as £26; by annual collections, including 'wax-silver', 'housling money', and 'pardon money'; and by fees for the use of pews, for burial, for intercession, and for a variety of other services.[19]

Gifts remained frequent, and were specified in 16 of the 30 wills in the years 1520–9. John Bagwell, for example, left 6s 8d to the church at Budleigh in 1520. In 1522 Nicholas Ennis of Luxulyan donated a cow to the church at Newlyn, and a heifer and a calf to that at St Enoder. In 1523 John Bridgeman of Exeter gave 6s 8d to his own parish church, St Mary Major, as well as 12d to each of the 18 other parish churches within the city. The church at Wolborough was bequeathed 20s by Henry Bartlett in 1526, while John Bowerman of Hemyock left 6s 8d to that at Clayhidon in 1528. The wardens' accounts confirm that, on the eve of the Henrician Reformation, churches continued to attract a stream of donations in money, in goods, in property or in livestock. At Ashburton in 1522–3, for instance, 4d each was donated by Richard Mewcombe and John Redrise, 6d by John Harell, 6s 8d by John Dolbeare, and a girdle mounted with silver by Margaret Forster.[20]

The devotion, inevitably, was never universal. It was not unknown for a parish church to be desecrated by a brawl, as happened at Dartmouth in 1506, at Ashburton (between William South and William Sampson) sometime between 1525 and 1527, and at St Teath in 1527.[21] It might also

[19] This description is based primarily upon the extant churchwardens' accounts. For specific references, see CWA Exeter HT, 1529; CWA Ashburton, esp. 1526–7, 1529; CWA Exeter SMS; CWA Chagford; CWA Morebath; *Plymouth Records*, p. 29. For guilds, see below, pp. 105–8.

[20] PROB 11 20, fols. 124v, 229v; 21, fol. 128; 22, fol. 84v; Moger, 3, John Bowerman, 1528; CWA Ashburton, 1523.

[21] ER XIII, fol. 135v; CWA Ashburton, 1526–7; STAC 2/22/376.

be deprived of its income. At Ashburton in 1519–20 the Fordes disputed various properties with the feoffees of the church, and at Exeter between 1518 and 1529 some property of St Kerrian's church was acquired in doubtful circumstances by the mayor and bailiffs, thus allegedly ensuring 'the great decay of the said church for evermore'.[22] Occasionally a church might be robbed: money and goods were stolen between 1504 and 1519 from the church at Tavistock.[23] Nor was neglect unknown. Before its reconstruction in *circa* 1520–3, the church at Probus 'was in marvellous great ruin and decay, insomuch that God's divine service there conveniently could not be done'.[24] With exceptions of this nature, which appear to have been relatively uncommon, the available evidence would indicate that the devotion of the people to their parish churches remained conspicuously strong.

To what extent was this devotion maintained in the Reformation decades? At Axminster in 1535–6 the shoemaker Philip Gammon declared bluntly that he 'would never go to the church for devotion, or [for the] holiness of the place; but [only] because other men did such, to keep them company'. He added that when he died, 'he had as lief to be buried in a dung-heap as in any church'.[25] Such expressions of hostility to the parish church seem still to have been rare, but the financial and the behavioural evidence would together suggest that attitudes towards this traditional institution were indeed beginning to change significantly.

Investment in the construction of churches did not cease overnight. Among the structures datable by inscription, documentary record or stylistic feature to the period 1530–49 are the church at Woodland, the chancel at Stratton, the aisles at Instow, Mortehoe and Tawstock, and the towers at Cullompton, Exeter Allhallows and Morwenstow. The tower at Cullompton, for example, was bequeathed 12d by John Hill in 1546, while an inscription at Instow attests the erection of the north aisle by Richard Waterman and his wife in 1547.[26] By this date, nevertheless, there were signs that the traditional enthusiasm for church-building had already started to decline. It may be significant, for example, that it was only by pawning some of its church's treasures that Morwenstow financed 'the finishing of the tower and windows'. It is also suggestive that both at Launceston and at Liskeard the townsmen failed to commission late-Perpendicular towers of a height and elaboration commensurate with their wealth and communal status. At Launceston, incongruously adjacent to the parts so impressively rebuilt between

---

22 CWA Ashburton, 1520; C 1 536/62.
23 CCB 854, I, fol. 31.
24 STAC 2/17/209.
25 STAC 2/2/267, 269.
26 Slader 1968, p. 62; Hoskins 1954, pp. 381, 416, 441, 489, 518; Pevsner 1952A, p. 108; Pevsner 1952B, p. 96; Additional 32244, SWA Stratton, 1544–5; Additional 32243, HCWA Stratton, 1545; Moger, 22, John Hill, 1546; *Inventories, Exeter*, p. 11; E 117 1/48.

1511 and 1524, the outmoded fourteenth-century tower was permitted to remain, and at Liskeard the tower never equalled – let alone excelled – the structures erected by its rival communities. In both cases the curtailment, at the time of the Henrician Reformation, of an originally more comprehensive constructional programme would appear to be the most probable explanation. The abandonment of building-projects is indicated elsewhere. At Kea, a licence to rebuild the parish church in a more central location was obtained in 1532, but the project was subsequently abandoned, and was not to be executed until 1802. At Heanton Punchardon, where an aisle was commissioned between 1538 and 1544, it was not completed and the parishioners refused to allow their mason his full payment. At Cury, moreover, an aisle planned in 1543 seems never to have been built. A cow, a calf and a quarter of malt were bequeathed by Henry Hill of Chittlehampton in 1530 towards the 'making of the almotry' at Burrington; 20s by Henry Dotting in 1541 towards the building of an ambulatory at Totnes; and 20s by John Thomas in 1545 towards the erection of a new tower at Fremington. Yet it is not clear that any of these three bequests were in fact fulfilled. At Fremington, certainly, no new tower was built: the pre-Perpendicular structure remains to this day.[27]

John Leland, touring the South-West in *circa* 1542, failed to record the continuing construction of a single parish church. The churches which he noted – and which he frequently described admiringly as 'fair' – were almost invariably the product of earlier generations.[28] And after 1550 – when, according to an inscribed date, the tower at Bradford was raised[29] – the decline of enthusiasm was even more conspicuous. Inscriptions, documents and other sources would indicate that in the following two decades the entire diocese saw no more than one complete rebuilding – at St Budeaux in 1563 – and only occasional major additions – notably the bay of 1564 at Morwenstow and the porch of 1567 at Kilkhampton.[30] By this time, moreover, bequests to church-building had disappeared from the wills. In the early-sixteenth century the region's constructional achievement had attained its zenith; by the 1560s it was plummeting to its nadir.

Investment in church furnishings experienced a similar decline. Pulpits and benches, it is true, were still frequently added in the Reformation decades: bench-ends at Dowland and Lewannick, for example, are dated

---

[27] E 117 1/48; C 1 1074/18; PROB 11 23, fol. 148v; 29, fol. 5; 31, fol. 151v; Henderson 1923–4, pp. 139, 250–1; 1925, pp. 115, 124; Pevsner 1952A, p. 88.

[28] *Leland*, I, pp. 169–244.

[29] Hoskins 1954, p. 342.

[30] Hoskins 1954, p. 460; Pevsner 1952B, p. 231; Pevsner and Radcliffe 1970, p. 123; Henderson 1925, p. 96.

by inscriptions to 1546.[31] On the other hand, major expenditure on stained glass was increasingly rare. At St Neot, significantly, the latest of the inscribed dates is 1529.[32] Of perhaps 150 extant or recorded screens from before 1570, moreover, only about 20 can plausibly be attributed to these last four decades – either by an inscribed or documented date, as at East Allington, Modbury and Throwleigh, or by stylistic features, particularly Renaissance motifs, as at Atherington, Braddock, Gidleigh, East Down, Holbeton, Ilsington, Lapford, Lustleigh, Marwood, Mawnan, Monkleigh, Morchard Bishop, Mullion, Sutcombe, Swimbridge, Tawstock and Ugborough. Most of these, furthermore, were probably constructed in the first half of this period. The dated examples at Throwleigh, Modbury and East Allington were erected in 1544, 1544–5 and 1547, and the structure at Atherington must predate the loft erected upon it in *circa* 1545. Only a few, as at Lustleigh, Mullion and Ugborough, are possibly Marian, and fewer still Edwardian or early-Elizabethan. The screen completed at Morwenstow in 1575 would mark the virtual termination of a formerly glorious south-western tradition.[33] In the earlier years of this period, moreover, projected expenditure was sometimes curtailed. At Awliscombe, where John Searle had undertaken to finance the painting of a ceilure over the rood, he reneged on his promise sometime between 1533 and 1538.[34]

The Reformation decades in fact witnessed an increasing tendency among merchants, yeomen and other substantial members of the non-gentle laity to divert their investment from their churches to their homes. By 1570 their houses had often begun to develop into buildings which were more spacious, better lighted, and beautified with wood-carving, plasterwork and glass. In Devon, indeed, most parishes retain at least two or three such buildings from the Elizabethan and early-Stuart era; notable concentrations occur at Exeter, Plymouth and Dartmouth. They bear visible testimony to a fundamental secularization of the layman's priorities and aspirations.[35]

Closely related to this trend was the decline in the revenues of parish churches. Even before the end of Henry's reign this was sometimes to be discerned. At Exeter St John's Bow, income fell from £8 in 1530–1 to £5 in 1545–6; at Chagford, from £29 in 1530–1 to £22 in 1545–6; at Stratton, from £34 in 1531–2 to £16 in 1545–6; at Broadhempston, from £42 in 1530–1 to £20 in 1538–9; and at Dartington, from £21 in 1530–1 to £11

---

[31] See below, pp. 241–2.
[32] Rushforth 1927B, pp. 150–90.
[33] For dated examples, see Pevsner 1952B, p. 125; CWA Modbury, 1545; and Bond and Camm 1909, II, p. 353. For Atherington loft, see C 1 1116/49; and Hoskins 1954, p. 272. For possibly Marian examples, see Bond and Camm 1909, II, pp. 228, 330, 388, 392. For Morwenstow, see Bond and Camm 1909, II, p. 391.
[34] C 1 819/12.
[35] Hoskins 1954, p. 277.

in 1545–6.[36] In some parishes the levels were maintained or even increased, but after Edward's accession the decline became general and often catastrophic. Exeter Holy Trinity experienced a slump from £14 in 1545–6 to £3 in 1550–1; St John's Bow, from £9 in 1546–7 to £1 in 1551–2; and St Mary Steps, from £8 in 1546–7 to £5 in 1551–2. Ashburton saw its revenue fall from £49 in 1546–7 to £13 in 1552–3; Camborne, from £13 in 1539–40 to £6 in 1551–2; Chagford, from £14 in 1546–7 to £8 in 1550–1; and Stratton, from £16 in 1545–6 to £2 in 1550–1. Antony witnessed a drop from £13 in 1545–6 to £1 in 1550–1; Morebath, from £9 in 1545–6 to £2 in 1548–9; Winkleigh, from £17 in 1541–2 to £6 in 1548–9; Woodbury, from £7 in 1545–6 to £2 in 1551–2; and Woodland, from £5 in 1545–6 to £3 in 1552–3.[37] Some churches, including Morebath, now ran into debt.[38] Only rarely, as at Exeter St Petrock's, were the Henrician levels sustained. Even the Edwardian totals were often boosted artificially by the sale of church goods – which in 1550–1, for instance, earned more than £13 at Woodbury and more than £63 at Exeter St Petrock's.[39]

In most parishes the accession of Mary would appear to have inaugurated a recovery which extended into the reign of Elizabeth. This, nevertheless, was no more than partial. Some Marian or early-Elizabethan parish churches, including St Mary Steps, St Petrock's, Camborne, Morebath, Woodbury and Woodland, could boast an approximate return to the totals of the 1530s; but in others, including Holy Trinity, St John's Bow, Ashburton, Chagford, Stratton and South Tawton, these overall levels were not regained.[40] When, moreover, the diminishing purchasing power of the currency is taken into account, a general long-term decline in the real value of church incomes would seem beyond dispute. The Phelps Brown index of English prices depicts a generally upward movement from its base figure of 100 in 1510 to 169 in 1530 and 158 in 1540, followed by a series of leaps to 248 in 1546, 262 in 1550, 370 in 1556 and 409 in 1557. The figure drops to 265 in 1560 but stands as high as 300 in 1570. Although statistics of this type can suggest no more than an approximate order of magnitude, it appears probable that the incomes of churches would have needed almost to double between 1530 and 1570 in order merely to keep

---

[36] CWA Exeter SJB, 1531, 1546; CWA Chagford, 1531, 1546; Additional 32244, SWA Stratton, 1532, 1546; CWA Broadhempston, 1531, 1539; CWA Dartington, 1531, 1546.

[37] CWA Exeter HT, 1546, 1551; CWA Exeter SJB, 1547, 1552; CWA Exeter SMS, 1547, 1552; CWA Ashburton, 1547, 1553; CWA Camborne, 1540, 1552; CWA Chagford, 1547, 1551; Additional 32244, SWA Stratton, 1546, 1551; CWA Antony, 1546, 1551; CWA Morebath, 1546, 1549; CWA Winkleigh, 1542, 1549; CWA Woodbury, 1546, 1552; CWA Woodland, 1546, 1553.

[38] CWA Morebath, 1551, 1558.

[39] CWA Woodbury, 1551; CWA Exeter SP, 1551.

[40] See graph 2, pp. 279–80.

pace with the rate of inflation. This, by a substantial margin, they invariably failed to do.[41]

How is this downward trend to be explained? One major factor was a diminution of the rents upon which most of the churches had traditionally relied. In many cases, particularly in Edward's reign, these were dutifully surrendered to the chantry commissioners. On 25 February 1549, for example, the government sold a number of local properties that had formerly supported 'superstition': they included property at Exeter that had financed the singing of an antiphon in St Petrock's church.[42] Equally significant, however, was the increasing expropriation of such rents by local people. In as early as 1530–1, when several men were accused by the vicar of Pelynt of seizing the profits arising from a local chapel, five men allegedly expropriated lands which belonged to the church at Marystow, and the Eight Men of Ashburton were involved in lawsuits concerning tenements which belonged to the church. The years 1538–44 saw further disruption at Broadclyst, Kentisbeare and Bradstone. Rent due to the church at Broadclyst was detained by Walter Whitrewe and John Hart; land used to maintain the church at Kentisbeare was claimed by John Godbard; and land employed by the parishioners of Bradstone for the maintenance of their church was allegedly seized by Henry Clobury. Between 1543 and 1545 land devoted to the support of the church at St Giles-in-the-Wood was similarly acquired in dubious circumstances by John Coker.[43]

From *circa* 1550 Anthony Will refused to pay the rent on his land at Callington; it had customarily been used to maintain the church. After four years of non-payment, the church was said to be 'greatly decayed'. At North Lew, between 1556 and 1558, John Cove similarly deprived the parishioners of a rent which had served to maintain their church. His intransigence not only hindered the performance of divine service but also (they claimed) was 'likely to be the utter decay and ruin of their said parish church'. Such cases continued in Elizabeth's reign. In 1568–9 Exeter St Petrock's was engaged in a lawsuit concerning 'the church lands lying in Paul's street'. In *circa* 1570 evidences relating to a house that had helped to maintain the church at Littlehempston were detained by certain men, and a chapel at Coldridge, which had been used by the churchwardens for the maintenance of the church, was dubiously appropriated by John Osmond. Its lands were then dispersed among 'divers and sundry persons'.[44]

A second important reason for the decline of church incomes was the

---

[41] Phelps Brown and Hopkins 1956.
[42] *CPR*, II, p. 259.
[43] STAC 2/21/94; 25/310; CWA Ashburton, 1531; C 1 996/12; 1091/32–5; 1094/22–3; 1378/39.
[44] C 1 1348/86–8; 1482/97; C 3 192/5; 202/65; CWA Exeter SP, 1569.

disappearance of religious guilds, the financial surpluses of which had customarily flowed into the central coffers of their parish churches. Many appear to have been dissolved in the last decade of Henry's reign, and most of the remainder were suppressed in the reign of his son. In some parishes, including Stratton, it was to this factor that the drastic downturn of church income was primarily due. Guilds, moreover, were only partially revived in the Marian years, and experienced further decline after Elizabeth's accession.[45] Other sources of revenue were similarly beginning to fail. Church Ales may sometimes have been in decline under Henry – at Stratton the profitable Robin Hood festivities associated with the Ale seem to have ended in *circa* 1540 – while in the reign of Edward, as at Ashburton, Morebath and Woodbury, they were sometimes suppressed. Ales generally returned under Mary and survived under Elizabeth. Nevertheless the Robin Hood elements sometimes failed to reappear in the years 1553–8, as at Stratton, or disappeared thereafter, as at Antony, Chudleigh and Braunton after 1559, 1561 and 1564 respectively.[46]

Further losses are attributable to the cessation of traditional collections. In Edward's reign the collection of wax-silver, for example, seems everywhere to have ended,[47] and at Woodbury the 'Two-Penny Gathering' finished after 1547.[48] Both of these collections returned under Mary, but the former again ceased after 1559. Moreover, rates levied for the support of churches were sometimes resisted. At Aveton Giffard the parishioners had customarily paid an annual contribution towards the maintenance of their church, each of them providing wheat, barley and oats in a quantity proportionate to the extent of his land. Under Edward VI, however, the custom broke down and the parishioners merely paid money – 'some years more and some years less, as they could agree'. Nor was the traditional system restored fully under Mary, when at least one parishioner – Hugh Harry – refused to contribute. Similarly resistant was Kenton's Martin Alley, who in 1557 confessed that he 'gave no penny to the church these three years, towards the reparation of the church'. And at Fremington, in 1565, John Exeter refused to pay a rate that had been levied to maintain his parish church.[49]

A final and particularly revealing factor behind the decline of church

---

[45] Additional 32244, SWA Stratton; see also below, pp. 109–12.
[46] Additional 32244, SWA Stratton; CWA Ashburton; CWA Morebath; CWA Woodbury. At Morebath they ended after 1548 but were revived in 1551. For Marian Ales, see, for example, CWA Exeter SJB; CWA Exeter SMS: CWA Ashburton; CWA Braunton; CWA Dartington; CWA Kilmington; and CWA Woodbury. For Robin Hood, see Additional 32243, HCWA Stratton; CWA Antony; CWA Chudleigh; and CWA Braunton.
[47] See above, p. 68.
[48] CWA Woodbury.
[49] CCB 855, fols. 174v–5, 203v–4, 206v; CCB 855A, fol. 492.

incomes was the reduction of gifts. The wardens' accounts show that these continued throughout the reign of Henry VIII. Woodbury, for example, still received the customary 'gifts given by them that be departed' – as in 1538–9, when a ewe and a lamb were bequeathed by Richard Westcott and a ewe by Mother Trappnell. At Morebath, in 1542, the parishioners donated labour as well as money to the repair of the church house. 'If they should have done this for money', rejoiced their vicar, 'they would not have done it and given such attendance -- not for an angel and noble apiece of them, and if it had not been to the church.' By 1547 such devotion had sometimes started to wane: payments promised to churches were retracted, as at Chagford in 1545–6.[50] After 1547 the decline was unmistakable. The wardens' accounts record either a substantial diminution of gifts, as in the Exeter churches of Holy Trinity, St John's Bow and St Petrock, or even a virtual cessation, as at Exeter St Mary Steps, Ashburton, Morebath and Woodbury. At Woodbury, for example, gifts from the 'departed' ceased after 1547 and remained absent throughout the reign. At Morebath the vicar was subsequently to record in the accounts that from 1548, when Lucy Scelly served as its high warden, there was 'no gift given to the church, but all [went] from the church. And thus it continued from Lucy's time unto Richard Cruce, and from Cruce unto Richard Hucley, and from Hucley unto Richard Robins, and from Robins unto Robin Atmore. And by all these men's time – the which was by time of King Edward VI – the church ever decayed.'[51]

A partial recovery from this disastrous slump is indicated by the Marian and early-Elizabethan accounts. At Woodbury, for instance, gifts recommenced in 1553–4, and parishioners contributed £6 towards the new bells in 1558–9. At Morebath, according to the vicar, 'the church was restored again' in Mary's reign: it received numerous donations and repaid its debts, the vicar noting 'how gently (for the most part) men have paid of their own devotion, without any taxing or rating'. Donations continued in Elizabeth's reign, William Hurst, for example, giving 20s to Exeter St Petrock's in 1567–8.[52] By this date, however, the real value of gifts had been eroded by decades of inflation, and an examination of the testamentary evidence would indeed suggest that the level of giving was in substantial decline.

After appearing in 16 of the 30 wills in the years 1520–9, or 53%, gifts to parish churches were included in 19 of the 41 in the years 1530–9, or 46%, and in 30 of the 69 in the years 1540–6, or 43%. In 1538, for instance,

[50] CWA Woodbury, esp. 1539; CWA Morebath, 1542; CWA Chagford, 1546.
[51] CWA Exeter HT; CWA Exeter SJB; CWA Exeter SP; CWA Exeter SMS; CWA Ashburton; CWA Morebath; CWA Woodbury. For the vicar of Morebath's comments, see CWA Morebath, 1558.
[52] CWA Woodbury; CWA Morebath, esp. 1558; CWA Exeter SP, 1568.

John Forde of Ashburton left 20s each to five parish churches, 'to the maintenance of God's service and ordinances', while in 1539 the church at Christow was bequeathed 13s 4d and four sheep by Robert Potter. After 1547 this modest decline became drastic. Bequests to parish churches appeared in only 18 of the 77 wills in the years 1547–9, or 23%, and in no more than 3 of the 31 in the years 1550–3, or 10%. Men like William Wheaton of Ide, who in 1549 left 10s to the maintenance of his parish church, were now in a distinct minority. A temporary revival was inaugurated by the accession of Mary: gifts of this type were included in 29 of the 60 wills in the years 1553–9, or 48%. Thus in 1554 the yeoman John Weston bequeathed 6s 8d to the reparation of Colyton church, and 20d to the reparation of 12 other neighbouring churches, while in 1558 Thomas Leigh of Aylesbeare left cows, ewes, lambs and a rent to the churches at Aylesbeare, Farringdon, Sowton and Woodbury. The reign of Elizabeth, nevertheless, saw further decline: bequests of this nature are found in only 26 of the 90 wills in the years 1560–9, or 29%. John Cosowarth of Colan might, in 1568, bestow 33s 4d upon the reparation of six local churches, but more typical now were men like Robert Eliot of Morchard Bishop in 1565 or Robert Pyne of Axminster in 1567, neither of whom, despite their relative wealth, donated a penny to the maintenance of a parish church.[53]

If laymen were increasingly reluctant to invest in churches, they were also willing on occasion to exploit them for the sake of private gain. In as early as 1529–32, at St Michael Penkevil, goods and the profits of a tin-work donated to the maintenance of the church were allegedly misappropriated by Pascoe Carpenter, John Daniel and John Tresamble. The culprits, ironically, were themselves churchwardens. At approximately this date, at Week St Mary, certain parishioners reportedly retained both money and goods which belonged by right to the parish church. In consequence, complained its wardens, it not only lacked several pieces of equipment but also was unrepaired and 'in great decay'. At Antony, in 1537, a number of parishioners failed to repay money to the church, and there were still three or four recalcitrants here in 1544. At Halberton, between 1544 and 1547, it was one of the Six Men who perpetrated 'divers great deceits and wrongs' against the parish church. Abusing his office of 'great confidence and trust', John Weare took advantage of the church's purchase of three new bells to defraud it of more than £40, and with equal dishonesty he claimed double expenses for certain other of the 'church works'. Nor was Weare unique. In 1549, £37 was stolen from the church at Broadhembury; the offenders, who were led by John Ellis, were themselves parishioners. In the 1550s

---

[53] PROB 11 26, fols. 79v, 106; 32, fol. 251v; 37, fol. 110; 40, fol. 211v; 48, fol. 491v; 49, fol. 13v; 51, fol. 51.

debts were owed by several people to the church at Woodbury, though these were eventually repaid. At Antony as many as 16 parishioners owed money to the church in 1557; by 1558 these had increased to two dozen, and the Eight Men were considering legal action. At Spreyton, in 1562, Oliver Bennett utilized his status as one of the Two Men to defraud the church of five nobles. Similarly willing to profit from his office was Thomas Clawin, churchwarden at Ashbury in 1566–7. Clawin, it was alleged, failed to render an account of his stewardship, neglected to transmit the annual balance to his successor, detained the income received from two stores, and owed 11s 6d to the church. Also accused of misappropriating parochial revenue was Edward Sweetland, at Stoke Gabriel in 1567. At Rewe, in 1569, three parishioners and a warden – namely John Richards, Roger Richards, Richard Lovell and Richard Burrage – were suspected of disorderly accounting and of mishandling the church's money. A wooden chest, which was supposed to contain the 'church stock', was found upon examination to be empty.[54]

The financial evidence would thus indicate a substantial decline of commitment to the parish church in the Reformation decades. To what extent is this conclusion confirmed by the evidence of personal and corporate behaviour?

In some parishes there may have been an increasing reluctance to assume positions of responsibility within the church. At North Petherwin, in 1539–40, several of the parishioners 'refused to be the churchwards'; there were further refusals in this parish in 1543, in 1546, and again in 1560. Some wardens, moreover, were manifestly unenthusiastic in the performance of their duties. At St Gennys, in 1559, John French not only absented himself frequently from the church which he had been elected to serve; he also failed to gather corn from the parishioners for their traditional ale-brewing in Procession Week, and neglected to collect the penny customarily paid by each parishioner in whose home the Gospel was recited. The loss to the parishioners, 'towards the maintenance of their church', was £3.[55]

A similarly negligent attitude towards churches and chapels was increasingly demonstrated by parochial communities. A chapel at St Austell, attended by the parishioners since they had grown too numerous for their church, was reported in 1557 to lack both roofing and glass – 'by reason whereof, divine service cannot conveniently be celebrated in the quire'. Other chapels, including those formerly associated with the local saint cults at St Endellion and Tredrizzick, were allowed to fall into decay in Elizabeth's reign. At St Day the chapel which had once housed the famous image of

---

[54] C 1 623/12; 1138/88; 1217/3; STAC 2/29/156; CWA Antony, pp. 1, 33, 54, 56; CWA Woodbury, 1553–8; CCB 855A, fols. 222, 234–4v; CCB 856, fols. 15–15v, 25v–6, 351v–3.
[55] CWA N. Petherwin, fols. 14v, 27v; CCB 855, fols. 409–9v, 415–15v.

the Trinity was in fact sold in 1568.[56] But of primary significance was the increasing neglect of parish churches. The extent of this trend, which was particularly apparent in the two or three generations after *circa* 1550, is attested by the widespread reconstruction of towers, arcades and windows which – as is evident from surviving examples – had become a necessity throughout the South-West by the seventeenth century. An instance is provided by the church at Walkhampton. Churches were reported to be in decay at Week St Mary in as early as *circa* 1530, at Nymet Tracey between 1544 and 1547, at Morebath between 1548 and 1553 and at Callington in 1554, while ruin was said to be imminent at North Lew between 1556 and 1558. At Nymet Tracey in the years 1544–7, for example, both the chancel and the churchyard were described as 'greatly in ruin and decay'. At Exeter St Martin's 'reparation' was said to be 'necessary' in 1554.[57]

Neglect, furthermore, was in places accompanied by deliberate destruction. In some cases this seems to have been executed by government agents and passively permitted by the local people; in others it was actively executed by the people themselves. In 1542, for example, John Leland noted the desecrated condition of chapels at Barnstaple, Launceston and Fenny Bridges; they had all been 'profaned'. Since that at Barnstaple had been dedicated to Thomas Becket, it may have been a victim of the campaign launched against this saint in 1538.[58] Nor were the churches inviolate. In parishes which, like St Anthony-in-Roseland, had been appropriated by monastic houses, the dissolutions of 1536–9 may sometimes have been followed by the pulling-down of the parish churches' chancels.[59] The suppression of religious guilds may also have been followed by attacks upon their chapels in the parish churches. In 1541–2, when a guild at Stratton known as 'Our Lady Holmadons' appears to have ended, a workman was paid 'for drawing down of Our Lady chapel'. In 1549, after the dissolution of the important guild of St George at Lostwithiel, its former chapel in the parish church was deliberately 'defaced'. This action was executed on the orders of the mayor, Richard Hutchings.[60]

Even more violent was the destruction at Halberton, where, in October 1553, the parish church was reportedly vandalized by a mob of husbandmen, labourers and other local men. Their leader, predictably, was Christopher Sampford. 'Bent', it was thought, 'utterly to deface and abolish the honour of God', they removed the church's pews and seats, pulled down the chancel

---

[56] CCB 855, fol. 184v; 'Lives of Saints', fols. 202v–3, 312v; Henderson 1923–4, pp. 196–7.
[57] Hoskins 1954, pp. 272–3, 511; STAC 2/29/156; C 1 1160/75–6; 1348/86–8; 1482/97; CWA Morebath, 1558; PROB 11 39, fol. 203.
[58] *Leland*, I, pp. 169, 175, 240. For the anti-Becket campaign, see below, p. 116.
[59] Henderson 1923–4, pp. 18–20.
[60] Additional 32244, SWA Stratton, 1541–2; E 315 122/15–28.

screen, attacked the walls, stole the glass and the ironwork from the windows, and even attempted to dig up the foundations. The wardens of Halberton subsequently lamented that divine service was no longer possible in their desecrated building. At Exeter, moreover, the mayor and aldermen were ordered by the government in 1555 to 'build up the towers of the churches of St Sidwell's and St Edmund's', which had been 'by them pulled down and defaced'. This demolition had presumably occurred during or after the military operations of 1549. Edwardian damage at Exeter St John's Bow is possibly implied by its payment in 1549–50 'for mending the interclose betwixt the chancel and the church'. Further attacks followed the accession of Elizabeth. At Woodbury, in 1559–60, a man was paid for 'taking down of the holy-water stone'; this must have involved the mutilation of stonework in the porch. At Exeter, in 1560–1, St John's Bow similarly paid for 'mending of the hole where that the holy-water bucket stood'. This church seems also to have ripped out its sedilia, 'the seage that the priest sitteth in' being removed in 1569–70. In addition, an extensive assault upon church glass in the reigns of both Edward and Elizabeth is possibly indicated by the frequent expenditure devoted to its repair. At St Breock, to cite but one example, a glazier received 40s 'for mending the windows' in 1565.[61]

The neglect, destruction and defacement of parish churches and chapels in the Reformation decades seems often to have been accompanied by a deterioration of behaviour within them. Irreverent activities included the refusal of men to remove their headgear, a charge against Martin Alley of Kenton in 1557 and against Sander Sheeptor of Ilsington in 1568–9; the disruption of services by loud talking, of which John Foxe was guilty at Dean Prior in 1566; and even the perambulation of the church in servicetime, an offence committed in Mary's reign by Martin Alley of Kenton, William Gooding of Whitchurch and William Seward of Bradninch. Alley admitted that, in church on Easter Eve, he had 'walked, with another man, before the quire door', while Gooding confessed that 'he walketh [in the church] sundry times, in Matins and Evensong time'. Seward confessed that he 'hath walked upon Sundays and holy days, at the time of divine service, for his ease', and he was suspected of similar behaviour at the sacring, Gospel, *Te Deum* and *Benedictus*. Even more blatant contempt was demonstrated by Martin Alley when he permitted his pigs to stray into the sacred precincts of Kenton church: it was said that 'when the church gates are open, his hogs goeth in'.[62]

---

[61] STAC 4/8/47; *APC*, V, pp. 112–13; CWA Exeter SJB, 1550, 1561, 1570; CWA Woodbury, 1560. For glass, see CWA St Breock, fol. 14; and below, p. 209.

[62] CCB 855, fols. 115v–16, 140v–1, 150v, 151v, 174v–5; CCB 855B, sub 17 December 1566; CCB 856, fols. 320–1.

But the most significant change in men's behaviour in their churches and chapels was the upsurge of 'quarrels, riots, frays and blood-sheddings', which, according to a proclamation of 1552, 'doth daily more and more increase'.[63] Some such disturbances occurred in churchyards, as at Sampford Peverell, where there was violence between William Shepherd and Richard Hussey in 1558, or at Winkleigh, where an Ale was disrupted by an argument and an assault in 1560.[64] Many, however, took place within the actual buildings. At St Cleer, in 1534, a number of men stormed into the church and penetrated 'even to the high altar'. In this most sacred of locations they began to quarrel and to threaten, and physical violence was prevented only by the presence of the parish constable. At Launceston, in 1538, there was an assault in St Stephen's church: some twenty men were involved. In *circa* 1540 the same church witnessed an attack upon William Body by a crowd of local people, headed by John Wise: 'The most part of the people then being within the said church, accompanied with the said Wise to a great number, violently and riotously bore out and carried with force the said Body out of the said church, and did put him in fear and danger of his life.' There were quarrels in the church at St Veep in 1541, when the constable was abused by a parishioner named Dawe, and in a chapel at Marazion in 1544, when angry words and threats were exchanged at Evensong time by John Chenowith and John Hick. In 1548 there was violence in the church at Stoke Climsland, John Collins being dragged from his pew and threatened with murder if he sat there again.[65]

A heated argument between two parishioners of Throwleigh in 1556 was conducted in the chancel of their parish church. First they 'multiplied words, and swore sundry oaths'; then they came to blows, one of them seizing a banner-staff to wield against his opponent. In 1557, at high mass, the church at Landrake was disturbed by a similarly bitter altercation between Agnes Cornish and Margery Cloak. In the same year, and again at 'high mass time', violence appears to have been employed by two bailiffs who executed a legal process against a parishioner in the church at Alviscombe. At about this date, service-time in the church at Poundstock was dramatically disrupted when a man was assaulted and his bride-to-be was forcibly abducted. At Exeter, in 1558, it was Richard Gifford and John Howell who 'undecently, and after an uncomely manner, behaved themselves' in the church of St John's Bow. After they had 'quarrelled, broiled, and chid', Gifford assaulted his opponent. In 1562 and 1568 there was verbal abuse

---

[63] *TRP*, I, pp. 537–8. See also *Documents of Church History*, p. 433; and *TRP*, II, pp. 177–9.

[64] CCB 855, fols. 360v, 470–0v.

[65] STAC 2/10/244–56; 15/316; 23/95; 3/1/58; CCB 854A, I, sub 11 November 1541; Henderson 1923–4, pp. 214–15.

in the churches at Spreyton and Sheepwash, while violence erupted in the chancels at St Cleer in 1568 and North Huish in 1569. At St Cleer the vicar was forcibly dragged from the communion table by two bailiffs. At North Huish, during a 'brawl', Philip Harvey used threatening language, seized the parson's servant, and even brandished a dagger.[66]

Though never total, devotion to the parish churches on the eve of the Reformation had been unquestionably impressive. The available evidence would suggest that in the Reformation decades this devotion experienced a substantial and even drastic decline. Yet another important component of the traditional piety had been profoundly modified.

After the parish, with its church and chapels, the most important of the Catholic institutions open to the layman on the eve of the Reformation was the religious guild. The membership of such an organization was sometimes restricted to the practitioners of a particular trade. At Helston in 1517, for example, a fraternity dedicated to the Holy Trinity consisted of the local cordwainers or shoemakers. Other guilds, like the Young Men and the Young Women at Morebath, recruited from a specific age group or gender group within the parish. Some, moreover, appear to have been dominated by a social or political elite – as at Exeter, where by 1531 every member of the Twenty-Four who governed the city was expected to belong to the fraternity of St George. In most cases, nevertheless, active participation and financial support were attracted from a variety of social groups. Typical was the guild of St Katherine at Chagford, which may have operated from a house that still stands near the church; it received income from parishioners' gifts as well as from the local sale of its sheep and their wool. The guild of the High Cross at Stratton – the accounts of which commence in 1512 – was financed by gifts, by fees for various services, and by its own yearly Ale, while the guilds at North Petherwin drew revenue from the sale of bread and of ale.[67]

Among the religious activities organized by such institutions were the maintenance and illumination of particular images. At Camborne, for example, an image of St Ia appears to have been maintained by the guild that bore her name. At Stratton the guild of the High Cross was associated with the rood, for the lighting of which it bought wax, tapers and candles, as well as with other figures – in 1527 it paid for the painting of the figures' Lent cloths.[68] The primary function of a guild, however, was in most cases

[66] STAC 4/9/38; *Exeter Records*, p. 308; CCB 855, fols. 43v, 188v, 266v; CCB 855A, fols. 222, 234–4v; CCB 856, fols. 297–7v, 307v–8, 449v–53.
[67] Henderson 1935, pp. 75–9; *Exeter Records*, p. 45; CWA Chagford; CWA Morebath; CWA N. Petherwin, esp. fols. 14, 22v, 32v, 38v; Additional 32243, HCWA Stratton.
[68] CWA Camborne, 1535; Additional 32243, HCWA Stratton, esp. 1527.

intercession: it was intended to secure the rapid passage of its departed members through the 'bitter pains of Purgatory'.

Many guilds, including that of the High Cross at Stratton, arranged the burial of their deceased; this might be accompanied by knell, cross and lighted tapers.[69] Many, in addition, maintained a separate bede-roll, which listed their departed for the purpose of prayer. At Stratton, between 1512 and 1530, most years saw local people buying places for their family or friends on the roll of the High Cross guild, which was regularly recited by the vicar. In 1527, for example, Alison Pudner paid 6s 8d 'for her husband's grave, and to set him upon the bede-roll', while Robert Hecket gave a crock worth 10s 'for to set three names upon the bede-roll'. Rolls of this type survive among the early-sixteenth-century accounts for North Petherwin. Folio 38v, for instance, begins with a general exhortation to pray for the deceased brothers and sisters of the guild of St Michael, and then records their particular names. Frequently, moreover, the guild hired its own priest, who would perform intercessory masses at an altar in the parish church. In the church at Helston, for example, masses were celebrated for the departed members of the Holy Trinity guild; during their performance the rosary would be recited by each of the surviving brothers and sisters. At Chagford the guild of St Katherine similarly hired priests and organized obits, including an anniversary for its departed on the morrow of St Katherine, while at Stratton the guild of the High Cross both maintained its own chantry priest and paid the vicar to perform perpetual obits. This guild boasted also a 'bede-man', who presumably announced its obits; his bell was mended in 1529–30. Even in a smaller community like North Petherwin, the guilds arranged *diriges* and masses on behalf of their dead.[70]

The activities sponsored by such institutions could be elaborate. At Lostwithiel, in the reign of Henry VIII, an annual parade along the main street was arranged by the guild of St George. One of its members represented St George himself: he rode on horseback, was attended by mounted followers, and was furnished with armour, a crown, a sceptre and a sword. On arrival at the parish church, he was received by the priest, and then was escorted into the guild's chapel to hear a *dirige* performed. Finally the whole company retired to a house in order to hold their customary feast. On the morrow, moreover, a requiem mass would be celebrated on behalf of the brethren.[71] The organization of such activities explains the substantial collections of ritual apparatus often possessed by the guilds. Stratton's High Cross guild owned vestments, altar cloths and chalices; its

[69] Additional 32243, HCWA Stratton.
[70] Henderson 1935, pp. 75–9; CWA Chagford; CWA N. Petherwin, esp. fol. 38v; Additional 32243, HCWA Stratton, esp. 1527, 1530.
[71] *Survey of Cornwall*, pp. 322–3; E 315 122/15–28.

wardens paid for the 'blessing of five altar cloths' in 1512, and for the blessing of two chalices in 1518.[72]

The popularity of guilds on the eve of the Henrician Reformation is indicated by the numbers in which they were maintained by parochial communities. In the churches of Exeter, it is true, they were relatively few. At Ashburton, by contrast, they numbered at least 16. Each of these boasted its own 'store' of money and goods, and several were associated with particular altars: chapels were dedicated to Our Lady, St John, St Katherine and St Margaret, St Nicholas and St Thomas. At Chagford, in addition to the 'Hogenstore' and the Young Men, guilds were dedicated to Our Lady, St Antony, St George, St Eligius, St Katherine, St Lawrence, St Nicholas, the High Cross and the Name of Jesus. There were approximately 9 guilds at Stratton, and 12 at Camborne; several of the latter were dedicated to local saints, including Ia, Meriasek and Winwaloe, and at least 4 arranged *diriges*. A number of groups were maintained even by relatively small communities. Approximately 5 operated at Broadhempston, 6 at South Tawton, 7 at Morebath, and as many as 11 or 12 at Antony, North Petherwin and Winkleigh. Those at North Petherwin, for example, were dedicated to the Trinity, Our Lady, Allhallows, St Christopher, St George, St John, St Luke, St Michael, St Nicholas, St Patern and St Thomas.[73] Most such guilds were supervised by their own wardens, who included women as well as men. At Chagford, for example, John Wolcott served as warden of St Michael's store in 1535–6, and Joan Langman as warden of the store of Our Lady in 1536–7. Only occasionally do wardenships appear to have been refused, as by Thomas Priest at Stratton in 1519.[74]

The pre-Reformation popularity of guilds is attested also by the level of investment in them. When, between 1501 and 1514, a tower was added to its separate chapel by the guild of the Holy Rood at Bodmin, the project was largely financed by local gifts. One woman, for example, contributed a silver spoon; one man, a silver girdle; another man, the hide of a cow.[75] Of the 30 wills in the years 1520–9, moreover, bequests to guilds appear in 17, or 57%. John Hart, for example, donated 3s 4d to every store in the church at Bovey Tracey in 1520; Andrew Brusard, 33s 4d to five stores in the church at Brixham in 1521; and John Bridgeman, in return for its prayers, 20s to a brotherhood of St John the Baptist at Exeter in 1523. At Totnes, in 1526, Thomas Hamlyn bequeathed money to five guilds in

---

[72] Additional 32243, HCWA Stratton, esp. 1512, 1518.
[73] CWA Antony; CWA Ashburton; CWA Broadhempston; CWA Camborne; CWA Chagford; CWA Exeter HT; CWA Exeter SJB; CWA Exeter SMS; CWA Exeter SP; CWA Morebath; CWA N. Petherwin; CWA S. Tawton; CWA Winkleigh; Additional 32243, HCWA Stratton; Additional 32244, SWA Stratton.
[74] CWA Chagford, 1536–7; Additional 32243, HCWA Stratton, 1519.
[75] BA Bodmin, Accounts of the building of the Berry tower.

the parish church, and to one, which was dedicated to Our Lady of Pity, he also left the income from certain land so that its priest would pray for him and for his family. In the same year a merchant of South Molton, Thomas Leigh, ordered an annual *dirige* and mass from a local guild of the High Cross, gave 12d each to seven guilds in the parish church, and donated money, cloth and timber 'to the building of the chantry house belonging to the guild of the Trinity'.[76]

On the eve of the official Reformation, guilds thus continued to play an important role in the religious lives of individuals and of parochial communities. To what extent was this role maintained in the subsequent decades of the Reformation?

Verbal expressions of hostility to the guilds seem still to have been rare, though criticism of the image cults and intercessions which they promoted was increasingly fierce. Again it is the financial and behavioural evidence that indicates a significant modification of traditional attitudes. Bequests to guilds, for example, after appearing in 57% of the wills in the years 1520–9, were included in 21 of the 41 in the years 1530–9, or 51%, and in only 19 of the 69 in the years 1540–6, or 28%. Although John Brown of Uffculme, for instance, bequeathed a silver chalice, a mass-book, a bell, cruets and vestments to the local fraternity of Our Lady in 1535, and Thomas Smallridge left sheep to three of the stores in the church at Ashton in 1539, it would therefore appear probable that investment in such institutions was in substantial decline in the latter years of Henry VIII. After the accession of Edward the trend was unmistakable. Bequests to guilds featured in no more than 6 of the 77 wills in the years 1547–9, or 8%; Henry Weeks, for example, donated money and a sheep to stores at Honeychurch and Monk Okehampton in 1548. In the 31 wills in the years 1550–3, moreover, bequests of this type are conspicuous by their total absence. Even more notable is the failure of guilds to regain their traditional status after Mary's accession. Robert Easton of Chudleigh – who, in as late as April 1559, bequeathed 6s 8d to the local store of Our Lady – was the sole testator among the 60 from the years 1553–9 to invest in a guild. In the 90 wills in the years 1560–9, furthermore, such guilds as survived were unable to attract a single bequest.[77]

This decline in investment was accompanied at times by financial exploitation. At Zeal Monachorum, in as early as 1534, money belonging to the stores of St John and St Katherine was dishonestly retained by a parishioner. At Holsworthy, between 1538 and 1544, land belonging to the guild of St Katherine was apparently claimed by John Newcourt; and at South Pether-

[76] PROB 11 19, fol. 208; 20, fol. 130v; 21, fol. 128; 22, fol. 191v; Moger, 19, Thomas Hamlyn, 1526.
[77] PROB 11 25, fol. 227v; 26, fol. 117v; 31, fol. 299; Moger, 13, Robert Easton, 1559.

win, also between 1538 and 1544, land belonging to the guild of Jesus was similarly claimed by John Blackmore. At Antony, towards the end of Henry's reign, no less than eight of the stores were owed money by local people. 'St Antony', for example, was owed £1 by Laurence Sergeant and £3 13s 4d by Walter Bruce, while 'Candlemas' had six debtors and 'Our Lady' ten; the culprits were so slow to repay that the Six Men began to threaten legal action. At Yealmpton, in 1544, Nicholas Thorning failed to return rings and more than £16 in money that had been entrusted to his care by the store of Our Lady. The brethren of Our Lady accused him of theft; Thorning claimed that he had himself been robbed of the valuables by 'malicious and ill-disposed persons'. Since the rings and money had originally been collected for 'good and godly purposes' within the parish church, these remained 'yet undone'. Opportunities for exploitation of this nature were soon to be drastically reduced by the suppression of guilds under Edward and Elizabeth, though in as late as 1567 contributions to one of the stores at Ashbury would be withheld by Thomas Clawin.[78]

The behavioural evidence is as suggestive as the financial. The wardenship of guilds was refused at Chagford in 1529, at Crediton in 1534, at Morebath in 1536, and at Chagford and Chudleigh in as late as the 1560s. At Chudleigh in 1561, for example, a parishioner was fined by the store of Our Lady 'for that he refused to do the office of this store'.[79] Equally disruptive were the internal dissensions at Cullompton, where, between 1538 and 1544, the brethren of the guild of St John not only quarrelled with their priest but were also engaged in a bitter conflict amongst themselves: the More family claimed a pre-eminence on account of its benefactions.[80] Most significant of all, however, was the increasing reluctance of parishes to maintain guilds in the numbers that had existed on the eve of the Reformation.

At Exeter St John's Bow, for example, annual payments for 'obits of St Gregory' were recorded in the wardens' accounts until 1535–6; thereafter they ceased. At Ashburton, where a priest had been paid to celebrate masses at the altar of Our Lady, his payment ended after 1536–7. Several other stores made their final appearance in the Ashburton accounts in 1537–9. At Chagford, where the guild of St Antony had organized masses, it disappeared from the accounts after 1536–7 – at which time the Chagford guild of St Nicholas seems also to have ceased. At St Thomas-by-Launceston, where a guild of the Blessed Virgin had maintained its own bede-roll, its accounts ended after 1537. At Broadhempston the stores of Our Lady and

---

[78] CCB 778, sub 17 March 1533/4; CCB 856, fols. 25v–6; C 1 959/35–7; 976/32–3; 1042/7–9; 1162/52; 1185/31; CWA Antony, pp. 69, 71–3, 75–7, 86.
[79] CWA Chagford, 1529, 1560–9; CWA Morebath, 1536; CWA Chudleigh, 1561; CCB 778, sub 12 January 1533/4.
[80] C 1 1029/46–50.

St Christopher apparently ended after 1539, at which time no less than four guilds would seem to have disappeared from the church at Morebath: they had been dedicated to St Antony, St Sidwell, St Sunday and Our Lady. At Chagford the guild of St Eligius seems to have ended after 1539–40, and several of the guilds recorded in the accounts for Camborne up to 1540 – notably 'Ia', 'Winwaloe', 'Nials', '[Se]bastian', and 'Jane and Margaret' – were conspicuously absent thereafter. At Stratton the guild of 'Our Lady Holmadons' seems to have suspended operations after 1541–2, when its chapel was indeed pulled down. Another guild dedicated to Our Lady, at Woodbury, appears to have been dissolved in 1542–3; its goods, which included beads and altar frontals, were transferred to the central churchwardens, and it failed to appear in the subsequent accounts. At North Petherwin, where the guild of St George had organized *diriges*, masses and readings of a bede-roll, its last account is dated 1543, and no accounts from the years after 1540 exist for as many as eight of the guilds previously operative in this parish. The accounts for two stores at Dartmouth ended after 1543–4, and similarly suggestive absences occur in the accounts for the last years of Henry VIII at Ashburton. While allowance must be made for the fact that some account sequences are incomplete, it is difficult to avoid the conclusion that parishes were frequently dissolving their guilds in the decade preceding the accession of Edward.[81]

Equally important was the reaction of local communities to the Edwardian instructions for the suppression of guilds.[82] At Ashburton in 1548 some twenty parishioners – including three yeomen, a pewterer, a baker, a tinner, a mercer and a smith – attempted to resist the confiscation of lands and market-tolls formerly belonging to the guild of St Lawrence; violence was allegedly employed in the market-place against a commissioner's servant.[83] The usual response, nevertheless, would once more appear to have been a dutiful compliance. In every parish for which accounts survive, it is evident that by 1550 the suppression of religious guilds had been to a very large extent completed.

At Stratton, for example, the account of the central stockwardens for 1547 records the continuance of guilds dedicated to the Trinity, Christ, the High Cross, Our Lady, Our Lady and St George, Allhallows, St Andrew, St Armil and St Thomas. The next account, made in November 1548, records only four. By 1549 only the guild of the High Cross remained, and even this seems subsequently to have been dissolved. The pattern recurs. At Mod-

[81] CWA Ashburton; CWA Broadhempston; CWA Camborne; CWA Chagford; CWA Dartmouth; CWA Exeter SJB; CWA Launceston; CWA Morebath; CWA N. Petherwin; CWA Woodbury; Additional 32244, SWA Stratton.
[82] *Documents of Church History*, pp. 328–57.
[83] STAC 3/2/14.

bury the last account for the Young Men was compiled in 1546, and the last accounts for the stores of Our Lady and the High Cross in 1547. The year 1548 saw the last appearances of the guild of All Saints at Launceston and of the Brewers of the Processional Ale – who had organized rites as well as selling bread and ale – at North Petherwin. At approximately this time both the Young Men and the Young Women were disbanded at Morebath. At Woodbury, where the annual fraternity *diriges* ended in 1548, three ewes which had belonged to the store of St Margaret were sold in 1549–50. By 1549, former complexes of eleven or twelve guilds had been reduced to three at Antony and one at Camborne – and even these were soon to end. At Woodland the store of Our Lady apparently ceased after 1550; there was further disruption at Ashburton, where only the store of the Hogners appears to have survived, and at Chagford, where no stores were recorded in 1551.[84]

The few guilds that survived this deluge of destruction were invariably shorn of their intercessory and image-supportive functions. At North Petherwin, for example, the guild of St Christopher had regularly organized a *dirige*, mass, and recitation of its bede-roll. Throughout the reign of Edward this guild continued to exist, but after 1548 'superstitious' activities of this type were entirely absent from its accounts. The religiously traditionalist identity of this local institution had been effectively effaced.[85]

As revealing as the acquiescence of most parishes in the Edwardian campaign against guilds was their reluctance to revive such institutions after Mary's accession. A few, it is true, were hesitantly restored. Thus Morebath, in 1556, saw the 'beginning of the Young Men wardens again, that stayed eight year [i.e. ceased between 1548 and 1556] and had no wardens'. Yet of the 22 parishes with accounts from the years 1553–9, not one could remotely match the nine, ten, eleven, twelve or even more guilds sustained by several communities under Henry VIII. Only 7 of the 22 appear to have revived as many as two, three or four: thus Coldridge, with its 'Hogners', 'Grooms', 'Whitsun wardens' and 'St Antony's wardens', now stood among the best-provided. In another 7 of the 22 parishes, no more than a single guild appears to have been restored, and in the remaining 8 not even one guild seems ever to have been revived. Nor did these few Marian institutions necessarily resume their traditional Catholic functions. At Braunton, it is true, the guild of St Brannoc still bought provisions 'against St Brannoc's obit for the brothers and sisters', hired a priest 'to come to say mass when our Ale was', and paid a man 'for going about the town the brotherhood

---

[84] CWA Antony; CWA Ashburton; CWA Camborne; CWA Chagford; CWA Launceston; CWA Modbury; CWA Morebath; CWA N. Petherwin; CWA Woodbury; CWA Woodland; Additional 32243, HCWA Stratton; Additional 32244, SWA Stratton.
[85] CWA N. Petherwin, fols. 3, 30–2.

day', presumably to proclaim it. Nevertheless in only 5 of the 22 parishes do guild intercessions of this type appear to have been performed in the years 1553–9. A guild, in fact, might now be little more than a fund-raising agency of its parish church. At North Petherwin, for instance, the guild of St Christopher failed to revive the *diriges*, masses and bede-roll recitations that it had organized until 1548, while at Stratton the obits and readings of the bede-roll formerly sponsored by the guild of the High Cross would seem never to have been restored.[86]

If the revival of guilds in Mary's reign was no more than very partial, responses to the early-Elizabethan campaign against them were again predominantly compliant. Many, such as the Hogners and St Antony at Coldridge, were dutifully suppressed in 1559–60, and others, such as St Christopher at North Petherwin and Our Lady at Chudleigh, were apparently dissolved in the subsequent decade.[87] Few parishes in the 1560s retained more than one or two of these once numerous institutions – Chagford, with its St George, St Katherine, Maidens and Young Men, was unusually well provided – and even these had been effectively divested of their traditional religious functions. At Chagford, for example, they seem merely to have raised funds for their parish church. At Braunton the two guilds dedicated to St Brannoc and to St John and St George, though still dispensing food and drink to the poor on 'brotherhood day', no longer arranged their customary intercessions, and at North Petherwin the guild of St Christopher, though surviving until 1566, existed only in a similarly emasculated condition.[88] In many parishes, moreover, including St John's Bow, St Mary Steps and St Petrock's at Exeter as well as Ashburton, Crediton, Antony, Dartington, Kilmington and Woodbury, it is doubtful whether even one of the traditional guilds survived.[89] Again, with no more than minor resistance, a previously important component of the popular religion had been virtually destroyed.

---

[86] CWA Braunton; CWA Coldridge; CWA Morebath, esp. 1556; CWA N. Petherwin, fols. 3v–4; Additional 32243, HCWA Stratton.

[87] CWA Chudleigh; CWA Coldridge; CWA N. Petherwin.

[88] CWA Braunton; CWA Chagford; CWA N. Petherwin, fols. 4–4v.

[89] CWA Antony; CWA Ashburton; CWA Crediton; CWA Dartington; CWA Exeter SJB; CWA Exeter SMS; CWA Exeter SP; CWA Kilmington; CWA Woodbury.

$$\text{⋘ } 6 \text{ ⋙}$$

Exclusive institutions: papacy, religious orders and secular clergy

Of those Catholic institutions in which the layman played no part the most important to him on the eve of the Reformation were the papacy, the religious orders and the secular clergy.

Of these the most remote from him was inevitably the papacy. Nevertheless it would be mistaken to assume that this ancient institution was wholly absent from his religious consciousness. Popes, with their distinctive triple croziers and tiaras, were frequently depicted in his parish church. A window erected at St Neot in as late as 1528 shows the local saint receiving, as his supreme accolade, the blessing of the 'holy father'.[1] Thomas Becket, soon to be denounced by Henry VIII as an enemy of the royal supremacy in the English Church, was similarly honoured by murals, as at Breage, and by screen-paintings, as at Ashton. Parishes, moreover, still contributed their 'Peter's Pence' to the papal coffers. Thus at Morebath, according to the account for 1531, each householder paid ½d per annum, and each cotter ¼d. It was possibly as a receptacle for such payments that the hollow pre-Reformation lectern in Exeter Cathedral was originally employed.[2] And to the anger of occasional critics – most notably of John Atwill of Walkhampton, who, in 1505–6, protested that they made money rather than saved souls – papal indulgences continued to be highly valued by many men and women. A belief in the automatic efficacy of these pardons for sin seems in fact to have been expressed between 1509 and 1529 by the Devonian Walter Langford. Although a notorious perjurer, as well as a fornicator, thug, thief and extortioner, Langford declared openly 'that there is no jeopardy to be forsworn, if he have or may have the pope's pardon'. In 1530, certainly, inhabitants of the South-West were still buying indulgences which they believed to possess the papal authority; these were being sold by the representatives of a guild from York. Among the popular beliefs castigated

---

[1] Rushforth 1927B, p. 182.
[2] CWA Morebath, 1531; Pevsner 1952B, p. 143. See also CWA S. Tawton, 1530.

113

by Thomas Bennett at Exeter in 1531 was the notion 'that we have redemption through pardons and bulls of Rome'.[3]

The reverence thus accorded to the 'holy father' explains the confidence with which the clergy at Exeter, on the very eve of the Henrician schism, could still describe his headship as 'the confession and consent of all the world'. Indeed in 1532, when the anti-papalist Thomas Bennett was burned at the stake outside Exeter, 'such was the devilish rage of the blind people that well was he or she that could catch a stick or furse to cast into the fire'. 'The hate of the people [at] that time, by means of ignorance, was hot against him'. Such sentiments also explain the reluctance of at least some laymen to accept the assumption of ecclesiastical supremacy by Henry VIII. 'There are so many of these papistical persons', the Abbot of Hartland would claim in 1538, 'the which put their mind and trust in that abominable monster of Rome, that they have and do daily infect all these parts.'[4]

By this date, nevertheless, overt expressions of papalism were already beginning to decline. Reports of treason or of sedition had not been infrequent, as at Exeter in 1536–7 and 1538, at Plymouth in 1533, 1535–7 and 1538, and at Dartmouth in 1537; yet in most of these cases it is not clear that the offenders were in fact supportive of the authority of the pope rather than antagonistic to particular religious or matrimonial policies of the king. At Plymouth in 1533, for example, the offence was 'seditious and opprobious speech of the queen's grace'; at Exeter in 1536–7 the overthrow and death of the king was prophesied by William Jordan; and at Dartmouth in 1537 the words 'The devil take the king and his lady both' were uttered by the 'spinster' Emelina Pettifen. Nor is it apparent that Peter Strache – who, at Exeter in 1538, announced that he 'set not a turd by the king, neither by his council' – was necessarily an advocate of the papal claims.[5] By *circa* 1537, certainly, the government could assert in an instruction to the justices of Cornwall that 'privy maintainers of [the] papistical faction' had been reduced to 'muttering in corners as they dare',[6] and after 1539, when the Council of the West was enjoined to punish seditious words and to publicize papal abuses,[7] any public declarations of papalism would appear to have ceased.

By 1540, indeed, parishes like Exeter St Petrock's and Ashburton were beginning, in the phraseology of their accounts and inventories, to explicitly acknowledge the ecclesiastical supremacy of the king. In the account

[3] ER XIII, fol. 145; XV, fol. 61; STAC 2/34/91; *Acts and Monuments*, II, p. 1039.
[4] *Acts and Monuments*, II, pp. 1039–40; SP 1/132/3–4.
[5] LP, VIII, 87, 676; X, 52, 462; XI, 166; XII (1), 152–3, 685; XII (2), 480; XIII (1), 416, 453, 580; SP 1/80/193; C 82 767/4/16; Hooker, Commonplace Book, fol. 344.
[6] Stowe 142, fol. 14.
[7] Titus B 1, fol. 176.

compiled at Ashburton in 1539, for example, Henry VIII is described as
'Defender of the Faith and, on earth, supreme head of the Church of England'. In the subsequent decade a formula of this type was adopted by most
of the parishes with extant accounts, including Holy Trinity, St John's Bow
and St Mary Steps at Exeter as well as Dartmouth, Launceston, Modbury,
Stratton and Woodbury.[8] Individuals, moreover, were increasingly virulent
in their hostility to the claims of Rome. In as early as October 1531, Thomas
Bennett had posted upon the doors of Exeter Cathedral a dramatic declaration that the pope was Antichrist. During his subsequent interrogation by
the ecclesiastical authorities − which eventually brought him to the stake
− he added to 'Antichrist' the titles of 'thief', 'hireling', 'boar from the wood',
and 'whore of Babylon'. The Roman Church he denounced as 'a den of
thieves', 'an aumbry of poison', an institution 'as far wide from the true
universal and apostolic Church as Heaven is distant from the Earth'; it
was 'the Devil's Church'. The outspoken schoolmaster reportedly asserted
also that each of the national Churches should be supervised by its own
bishop − 'under the prince, the supreme governor under God': 'So to say
that all the Churches, with their princes and governors, be subject to one
bishop, is detestable heresy. And the pope, your god, challenging this power
to himself, is the greatest schismatic that ever was in the Church − and
[the] most foul whore, of whom John in the *Revelation* speaketh.'[9]

The anti-papalism of Thomas Bennett appears to have been shared by
his wife, by his young son, and by 'certain of his friends' at Exeter.[10] Similar
views would be expressed by Philip Nichols of Totnes in the safer days
of Edward VI. 'How many godly preachers', he asked, 'with other good
souls, hath the Bishop of Rome put to death ... sith he came to the supremacy
and bearing a rule over kings and emperors?' 'Many writers', explained
this young layman, 'have compared the pope to King Pharaoh of Egypt;
and indeed it may well be. For, as long as he governed the Church, he
made us bond-slaves, he and his ministers. Yea, we were so blindly led
and so tyrannously handled, and that with such villainy, that I am sure
the Israelites were never so shameful intreated of King Pharaoh and his
ministers as we have been of this Pharaoh and his shaven generation.' But
now Henry VIII, a latter-day Moses, had delivered his people: 'Pharaoh's
power is taken from him. His bulls be not regarded; his superstitious sects
of religion be gone; and a great many of his Mohametry and other baggage

[8] CWA Ashburton, 1539; CWA Dartmouth, 1545; CWA Exeter HT, 1546; CWA Exeter
SJB, 1544; CWA Exeter SMS, 1542; CWA Exeter SP, 1540; CWA Launceston, 1548;
CWA Modbury, 1545; CWA Woodbury, 1544; Additional 32243, HCWA Stratton, 1546;
Additional 32244, SWA Stratton, 1545.
[9] *Acts and Monuments*, II, pp. 1037–40.
[10] *Acts and Monuments*, II, pp. 1037–40.

did the worthy King Henry destroy.'[11] Nor was the expression of such views to be silenced by the temporary restoration of papal authority in the reign of Mary. At Linkinhorne, in December 1553, a vigorous hostility to 'the pope's laws' was voiced by Sampson Jackman.[12] At Exeter, in 1558, the pope was openly denounced by Agnes Priest of Boyton as the Antichrist, the Devil and the whore of Babylon. 'I defy him', she declared, 'and all his falsehood!'[13]

Even more significant than such individual verbal outbursts against the formerly venerated 'holy father' was the financial and behavioural acquiescence of the population at large in the destruction of his authority. In as early as 1531, when Bennett posted his anti-papal bill upon the cathedral doors, it was noticeable that the mayor and common council of Exeter were at first 'not so busy to make searches to find this heretic', and subsequently they in fact refused to allow his burning within their city, for which reason it was removed to Livery Dole outside the walls. At the stake, moreover, some of the spectators reportedly 'did pronounce and confess that [Bennett] was God's servant and a good man'.[14] But it was as the hostility of the government towards the pope became increasingly explicit that his local support most markedly declined. Parishes like Morebath now ceased to render to him the traditional 'Peter's Pence';[15] his previously popular indulgences were no longer purchased; and appeals to his arbitration from the Consistory Court were no longer made.[16] By 1534, as John Hooker of Exeter would later record, 'the pope and his usurped authority was utterly exiled and banished out of this land'.[17] Similarly acquiescent was the predominant local response to the official campaign against Thomas Becket – who was denounced as an opponent of the royal supremacy – from 1538. Although some minor depictions of this archbishop were allowed to survive, as on the screen at Ashton, it was probably at this time that the Becket mural at Breage, for example, was obliterated by whitewash; it was not to re-emerge until the nineteenth century. By *circa* 1542, certainly, the parish church at Plympton St Thomas – which, as Leland discovered, had been originally 'so called of Thomas Becket' – was obediently rededicated to the politically innocuous St Maurice. By 1545, moreover, at Ashburton, a chapel in the parish church that had been dedicated to St Thomas the Martyr was similarly rededicated to St Thomas the Apostle.[18]

[11] *Copy of a Letter*, pp. 24–8; *Godly New Story*, pp. 24–6.
[12] SP 11/2/2.
[13] *Acts and Monuments*, II, p. 2051.
[14] *Acts and Monuments*, II, pp. 1037–40; Hooker, Commonplace Book, fol. 341.
[15] CWA Morebath. See also *Documents of Church History*, pp. 209–32.
[16] *Documents of Church History*, pp. 187–95.
[17] Hooker, Commonplace Book, fol. 342.
[18] *TRP*, I, pp. 275–6; *Leland*, I, p. 216; CWA Ashburton, 1538, 1545.

Equally revealing was the frequent willingness of laymen to act as informers against the real or imagined opponents of the king and of his ecclesiastical authority. At Plymouth between 1535 and 1537, for instance, a group of religiously traditionalist townsmen was reported to Thomas Cromwell as allegedly 'seditious'. The accused were Thomas Fowle, Peter Grisling, John Pollard and William Sommaster; their accusers, most or all of whom were merchants, were William Ashridge, John Eliot, William Hawkins and James Horsewell. At Exeter, in 1536–7, John Blackaller and other civic leaders were accused by Richard Lamprey of a failure to punish treason. They were eventually acquitted. In 1538, again, the allegedly seditious utterances of Peter Strache were reported to the Mayor of Exeter by Hugh Arderon, Martin Quiffin and Robert Watson.[19]

Accusations of this type by members of the non-gentle laity were directed not only against individuals of their own status but also against gentlemen and priests. In collusion with the proctor of an ecclesiastical court, Adam Wilcox, the Exonian John Northbrook brought an accusation of treason in 1539 against a local gentleman named Bonefant. This charge followed a discussion by Wilcox, Northbrook and Bonefant of the religio-political 'prophecies' then current: these featured a 'mould-warp' and a 'dun cow', asserted that Henry VIII was 'cursed of God's mouth', and foretold his imminent destruction. The accusation resulted in Bonefant's examination by the Mayor of Exeter and Sir Richard Pollard, and eventually brought him to execution at Southernhay in August 1539.[20] Nor were the clergy safe from such informers. In 1538 the injudicious utterances of a priest at Week St Mary were dutifully reported to the authorities by Robert Consen, John Leigh and John Shame of North Petherwin; their testimony landed him in Launceston gaol. In *circa* 1540, moreover, the portis-book of the parson of Jacobstowe was delivered by two of his own parishioners – John Andrew and Thomas Parrot – to the bishop's chancellor. They accused him of failing to remove from it the recently prohibited 'service of Thomas Becket'.[21]

While co-operation in the imposition of royal authority would thus appear to have been frequent, active resistance was again no more than minimal. 'At my coming into this shire', reported Dr Tregonwell to Cromwell from Penryn in September 1536, 'I found as much conformity amongst men, and as ready to obey the king's authority, injunctions, and other orders declared to them, as ever I saw any men obey the same. Insomuch that I dare affirm to your lordship that this country is as quiet, and true to

[19] *LP*, VIII, 87, 676; X, 52, 462; XI, 166; XII (1), 152–3, 685; XII (2), 480; XIII (1), 453; Hooker, Commonplace Book, fol. 344.
[20] Hooker, Commonplace Book, fol. 344. For prophecies, see *LP*, XI, 790.
[21] *LP*, XIV (1), 87; C 1 973/69–70.

the king our sovereign lord, as any shire within his grace's realm'.[22] Not even the minor disturbances of 1536–7 can plausibly be classified as papalistic. The banner commissioned by Carpisack at St Keverne would suggest that he intended to appeal not to the pope but to 'the king's grace';[23] and the rioters at St Nicholas' Priory explicitly denied any opposition to the Crown, either 'in act [or] in thought'.[24] The same is true of the aristocratic 'Exeter conspiracy' of 1536 – a minor affair which attracted little support from the South-West[25] – and also of the more serious riot around Helston in 1548. At Helston, in fact, the dissidents declared 'that they would have all such laws and ordinances touching Christian religion as was appointed by our late sovereign lord King Henry VIII'.[26]

By several of their enemies, including John Hooker, Philip Nichols and the 'gentleman of Devon', the south-western rebels of 1549 were emotionally denounced as supporters of 'the authority of the Idol of Rome'.[27] In reality, however, the insurgents seem never to have demanded the revival of papal supremacy. Despite their vague appeal to 'the general councils and holy decrees of our forefathers', it was in most respects to the religious conditions of 1547 rather than to those of 1529 that they evidently sought to return. Their written demands required 'the laws of our sovereign lord King Henry VIII, concerning the Six Articles, to be in use again, as in his time they were'. At Sampford Courtenay, moreover, they asked for a return to the religious situation that had obtained at the end of Henry's reign, and at Clyst St Mary, with equal lack of ambiguity, they demanded that religion should 'remain and tarry in the same state as King Henry VIII left it'.[28] By 1549, in brief, even the most militant of religious traditionalists would appear to have accepted the royal supremacy in the Church as an unchallengeable fact.

More immediately relevant than the pope to the average inhabitant of the pre-Reformation South-West were the members of the various religious orders. Numbering several hundred within the peninsula, these consisted of monks, regular canons and nuns, who remained largely separated from the layman in their cloistered communities, and friars, who ventured more freely from their urban bases into society at large.

Between layman and monk the tensions were by no means infrequent. These arose primarily from the role of the monasteries as owners of extensive

---

[22] SP 1/106/134.
[23] See above, p. 71.
[24] SP 1/102/33; see also above, p. 75.
[25] *LP*, XIV (1), 532; Rose-Troup 1913, pp. 20–46; Rowse 1941, pp. 233–44.
[26] Rose-Troup 1913, p. 80n; see also above, p. 76.
[27] 'Description of Exeter', p. 37; Royal 18 B XI, fol. 3; Rose-Troup 1913, p. 489.
[28] Royal 18 B XI, fols. 7v, 9v; 'Description of Exeter', pp. 27, 35.

land. Tavistock Abbey, for example, not only became engaged in a land dispute with a local butcher, Walter Cole, between 1518 and 1529, it also aroused hostility by maintaining a weir on the River Tamar at Gully Hatches. In 1527 the weir was attacked and demolished by a mob of some 300 local men, who allegedly raised a commotion 'like unto an insurrection' with fires and guns. At about this time, moreover, Buckfast Abbey was in dispute with its tenants at Staverton and South Brent, and between 1515 and 1518 the Abbot of Dunkeswell was sued for enclosure by Thomas Brook, who denounced him as 'cruel and covetous'.[29] Further conflict was provoked by monastic tithes. In 1510, for example, a servant of the Prior of Launceston was loading onto his cart the tithe due from land at Penkelly, but it was then seized and carried off by Edward Robert.[30] Nor were laymen necessarily averse to stealing the property of a monastic house. Between 1518 and 1529 the abbey at Newenham was allegedly robbed of deeds, goods, and more than £600 in money: the culprits were its own lay servants, John Baker, John Francis and John Strawbridge.[31]

Complaint was also aroused by the legal and judicial privileges of monastic establishments. In 1519 John Seymour of Launceston protested against the 'great powers, menacing and threatenings' of the Prior of St Germans. The prior, he alleged, had not only stolen his land, money and goods, he had also caused Seymour to be beaten and clapped in the priory stocks. In 1524 the townsmen of Bodmin complained against the power of their prior's courts, and friction over privileges existed in 1527 between the citizens of Exeter and the brethren of St Nicholas' Priory. In 1528 the Abbot of Tavistock was accused by John Whitfield of harbouring a suspected murderer in his abbey, and of conveying him thence into sanctuary at St Keverne.[32]

Yet the pre-Reformation relationship between layman and monk was frequently more harmonious than such cases might suggest. In the 1520s, for example, the parishioners of Exeter St Petrock's borrowed vestments from St Nicholas' Priory, while the inhabitants of Ashburton and Chagford received gifts towards the maintenance or furnishing of their churches from the Abbots of Buckfast and Torre.[33] Nor should the role of monks, nuns and regular canons in the popular religion be dismissed as insubstantial. In spite of their undoubted individual failings – which included simony, malversation, laxity of observance, and occasionally drunkenness or fornication[34] – the essential sanctity of their vocation seems still to have been

---

[29] C 1 382/1; 491/24; STAC 2/18/221; 29/169; 30/115.
[30] CCB 854, I, fol. 257.
[31] C 1 548/16.
[32] STAC 2/22/353; 25/60; *Bodmin Register*, pp. 298–302; *Exeter Records*, p. 269.
[33] CWA Ashburton, 1522; CWA Chagford, 1524; CWA Exeter SP, 1523.
[34] See, for example, Rowse 1941, pp. 162–93.

the predominant popular assumption. In *Beunans Meriasek*, the Cornish drama of 1504, the hero is seen choosing a life of prayer, chastity, asceticism, and detachment from human society;[35] and in the glass erected at St Neot in 1528, Neot himself is depicted as a Benedictine monk.[36] Monastic houses, moreover, were still visited by laymen, not only (as at St Nicholas' Priory in Exeter) in order to receive their charity,[37] but also (as on St Michael's Mount) in order to venerate their precious images and relics.[38] A significant number of men and women, in addition, continued to provide them with bequests, either as gifts, as payments of unrendered tithe, or as fees for intercession.

In 1522, for example, Nicholas Ennis of Luxulyan bequeathed tin-workings to the monks of Tywardreath. St Michael's Mount, a cell of Sion Abbey, received monetary donations from William Cox of Paul in 1522, from Marion Lelley of Ruan Lanihorne in 1525, and from Stephen Lelley in 1526. In 1526 too Thomas Hamlyn bequeathed money for forgotten tithes to the Prior of Totnes. In 1528 John Bowerman of Hemyock gave 6s 8d to the abbot and convent at Muchelney, and Joan Tackle of Honiton entrusted no less than £120 to the Abbot of Forde; this was to maintain a priest, who would sing masses for her soul for 20 years. In 1529 Gilbert Rugge of Widecombe bequeathed, to the brethren of St Nicholas' Priory in Exeter, 'as much money as will please them'. In return they were 'to have a trental to be sung for my soul, and [for] all the souls which I am bounden to pray for'. In 1531 John Strawbridge of Colyton left £5 to the religious at Newenham, and £6 13s 4d to the Cistercians at Quarr, while in 1532 William Webber of Thorncombe donated 12d to each 'priest' in the abbey at Forde, and 40s to its abbot.[39]

Even more important to the average layman were the friars. Their relative lack of landed wealth would seem to have saved them from much of the opposition encountered by the monks, and their activities were in general aimed more directly than those of their cloistered counterparts towards the spiritual welfare of lay society.

Lay gifts to the friars were frequent. In 1526, for example, Thomas Hamlyn of Totnes left 2s to the Franciscans of Guernsey; in 1529 Gilbert Rugge of Widecombe gave 2s to the Franciscans of Exeter; in 1531 John Calloway of Cullompton made bequests to the friars observant at Greenwich and Richmond; and in 1532 3s 4d was donated to the friars at Ilchester by

---

[35] *Beunans Meriasek*, esp. 426–7, 444–9, 1132–6.
[36] Rushforth 1927B, p. 179.
[37] MacCaffrey 1958, p. 101.
[38] See above, pp. 54, 58.
[39] PROB 11 20, fol. 229v; 21, fol. 32v; 22, fols. 254v, 302; 23, fol. 71; 25, fol. 95v; 28, fol. 17v; Moger, 3, John Bowerman, 1528; 19, Thomas Hamlyn, 1526.

William Webber of Thorncombe.[40] In return for financial support of this nature the laity received important services. They were provided, firstly, with instructional sermons. To these – as the anti-Catholic Thomas Bennett complained in 1531 – the local people continued to flock.[41] Many, moreover, still resorted to friars in order to make their confession and to receive shriving or absolution. 'In shrift', the Exeter friars were reportedly told by Bennett, 'ye beguile them.' In 1532 Thomas Stone allegedly travelled some 14 miles from his home at Down St Mary in order to make his confession before the Exeter Dominicans.[42] Laymen, in addition, still paid for the privilege of burial by friars; some, indeed, were buried in the habit of a friar. 'By the merits of your orders', protested Bennett to the friars at Exeter in 1531, 'ye make many brethren and sisters. Ye take yearly money of them; ye bury them in your coats.' In 1515 John Harwell required burial by the friars of Truro, to whom he bequeathed £4. In 1524, at Exeter, John Simon left money to both the Dominicans and the Franciscans; in return they were 'to bring me to church at the day of burying'.[43]

But it was probably as intercessors on behalf of the dead that the friars were most highly esteemed. In 1522 the friaries at Bodmin and Truro were each bequeathed 10s by Nicholas Ennis of Luxulyan; they were to perform trentals for his soul. In 1523 John Bridgeman of Exeter left 53s 4d to the Franciscans for a perpetual obit, and in 1524 William Sellick of Tiverton donated 10s to 'all the houses of friars within Devonshire' in return for trentals on his behalf. In 1526 John Cavel ordered a mass and *dirige* for his and certain other souls from the Dominicans of Truro. In 1529 the Tiverton merchant John Greenway left 40s to the friars preacher at Exeter, 'to the intent that the friars there being shall devoutly say and sing four trentals, for my soul and all Christian souls, immediately after my decease'. He also ordered trentals from the friars minor at Exeter, and from the friars minor and friars preacher at Plymouth. In 1534 Robert Hooker of Exeter arranged for the Dominicans and Franciscans to say trentals for himself, his parents, his late wives and all Christian souls, and in 1535 a trental was commissioned from the Exeter Franciscans, at a cost of 10s, by John Flood of Topsham.[44]

It is therefore apparent that until the 1530s, despite the existence of certain tensions, the religious orders in fact continued to attract a significant degree

[40] PROB 11 22, fol. 302; 24, fol. 19; 25, fol. 95v; Moger, 19, Thomas Hamlyn, 1526.
[41] See below, pp. 239–41.
[42] *Acts and Monuments*, II, p. 1039; C 1 900/34–5.
[43] *Acts and Monuments*, II, p. 1039; PROB 11 22, fol. 8; Henderson 1923–4, p. 260.
[44] PROB 11 20, fol. 229v; 21, fols. 128, 202v; 24, fol. 10; 25, fol. 280v; 26, fol. 76; Henderson 1923–4, p. 260.

of support and even reverence from the south-western people. To what extent was this to be sustained in the subsequent decades?

Verbal evidence would again suggest decline. In as early as 1531, at Exeter, the friars were vigorously denounced by Thomas Bennett. He regarded them not only as irredeemably 'superstitious' but also as deceivers of the people. Similarly antagonistic was James Horsewell of Plymouth, who in 1533 reported to Richard Cromwell the supposedly seditious activities of the 'knave friars'. Philip Nichols, in the reign of Edward VI, was predictably hostile to monks as well as to friars. He rejoiced in the suppression by Henry VIII of the 'superstitious sects of religion', and sweepingly dismissed their former inhabitants as a 'rabblement of cloisterers'. Distaste for the 'houses of religion' was voiced also by Sampson Jackman at Linkinhorne in Mary's reign.[45]

But again more accurately indicative of popular attitudes is evidence essentially financial and behavioural in form. One possibly suggestive financial development was the apparent reduction of investment in religious houses during the years immediately preceding their suppression. Bequests to monks disappeared totally from the analysed wills after 1532, and bequests to friars occurred only twice after 1535. In April 1538 John Forde of Ashburton left 20s for trentals in the friaries at Exeter and Plymouth, and in September 1539 – by which time they had been dispossessed – Henry Hendy of St Mabyn still hoped to leave 10s to the friars of Bodmin. Equally significant is the fact that Mary's reign witnessed no revival of the traditional investment. Although a few religious communities were temporarily restored in other regions of the realm, these failed to attract a single bequest from the 60 south-western testators of 1553–9.[46]

Members of the non-gentle laity indeed proved willing to profit from the dissolution – and, in effect, to ensure its permanence – by purchasing at favourable rates the property of suppressed houses. The monastic manor of Canonteign was purchased in 1542 by a Crediton merchant, Robert Davie. The manor of Trenant, formerly a possession of Tywardreath Priory, was bought in 1545 by the mercantile Rashleighs of Fowey; and the Buckfast manor of Engleborne was acquired in 1546 by William and John Wotton, respectively a clothier of Harberton and a merchant of Totnes. At Exeter the ex-monastic lands were bought in 1549 by the Chamber and 32 of the wealthier citizens, including Maurice Levermore. Equally few scruples against the despoliation of religious houses were exhibited by parochial communities. Morebath acquired in 1536–7 a window from the priory at Barlinch. The bells of Bodmin Priory were purchased in 1538 by the

---

[45] *Acts and Monuments*, II, p. 1039; *LP*, VI, 394; *Godly New Story*, pp. 24–6, 60; SP 11/2/2.
[46] PROB 11 26, fol. 79v; 32, fol. 106v.

parishioners of Lanivet. Tabernacles, paving-stones, desks, organs and a cope that had belonged to the abbey at Tavistock were bought in 1539 by the neighbouring parish church. Panels from the abbey at Buckland appear to have been incorporated into the pulpit of the parish church at Yarcombe. Sometimes the monastic buildings were themselves dismantled. When, in 1539, the citizens of Exeter repaired their ancient bridge, the requisite stone was unashamedly pillaged from the fabric of St Nicholas' Priory. And when, in 1553, the townsmen of Totnes rebuilt their guildhall, the site employed was that recently vacated as a result of the demolition of their priory.[47]

Nor were these the only indications of a change in popular attitudes as the Reformation advanced. In some areas the years following the opening of the Reformation Parliament witnessed outbursts of violence against religious houses. In 1531 the abbey at Hartland was invaded by a group of local men. They broke open the doors of the abbot's chamber, threatened him, and 'put [him] in such fear that he was in danger of his life'. Sometime between 1533 and 1538 a servant of the Prior of Bodmin, while attempting to collect the fish tithes for his master, was brutally attacked by a number of men at Padstow. They escaped with the prior's fish. In 1536, moreover, the prior complained that the inhabitants of Bodmin itself were making common the woods and waters belonging to his house, and were even barring him from fishing in his own water. Nine or ten of the hostile townsmen had not only seized fish from his servants but had also threatened their lives. Despairing of redress at the sessions, the prior now appealed to Thomas Cromwell to have the culprits punished; otherwise, he protested, he could no longer remain in the county.[48]

But an even more significant trend in the years after 1529 was the upsurge of anti-monastic litigation. Between 1529 and 1532 there were lawsuits by laymen against the houses at Frithelstock, Tywardreath and St Germans. William Shilston, engaged in a land dispute with Frithelstock Priory, complained to the Court of Star Chamber. In the same court John Tregodick charged the Prior of Tywardreath with an illegal entry into land at Fowey, while Richard White took the Prior of St Germans before the Court of Chancery; there he sued him for alleged assaults. In 1532–3 the Prior of Launceston was similarly brought before Chancery, where Robert Arthur alleged that he had failed to repay a loan. The prior was again before this court in the years 1533–8, when Joan Escott accused him of retaining tithes which the priory had leased to her late husband and herself. At approximately the same time, Thomas Archpole of Alphington charged the Abbot of Tavis-

---

[47] CWA Morebath, 1537; *Tavistock Records*, pp. 16–19; Hooker, Commonplace Book, fol. 345; Hoskins 1954, pp. 84, 507; MacCaffrey 1958, pp. 184–5; Pevsner 1952B, p. 314; Rowse 1941, pp. 203, 205.
[48] STAC 2/29/55; 31/38; *LP*, XI, 133.

tock with the illegal expropriation of woodland. In *circa* 1537 the Prior
of Launceston appeared once more before Chancery, accused by Thomas
Ashridge of claiming an excessive mortuary after the death of the latter's
servant. Ashridge asserted that the servant's goods had been worth less
than two marks; in consequence, he protested, the prior 'ought to have
no mortuary, by the statute thereof lately made'.[49]

Litigation of this type was instigated not only by individuals but also
by urban and parochial communities. In 1533–4 the townsmen of Plymouth
were in dispute with the priory at Plympton, and the inhabitants of Fowey
appealed to Thomas Cromwell to uphold their liberties against the Prior
of Tywardreath. In *circa* 1535, moreover, the parishioners of Wembury
petitioned the government against the Prior of Plympton. They complained
that although the benefice was worth £50 per annum to the prior, he refused
to provide a regular priest; in consequence the inhabitants had sometimes
died without shriving, housling, christening, burying or 'nailing'. The priest
sent by the prior on Sundays allegedly performed mass, matins and evensong
all in the morning, and then returned to Plympton in time for dinner. When
a priest was summoned to baptize a sick child, he took eight hours to arrive
and found the child dead, and when the wives came to church on Easter
Monday for their purification, there was no priest to perform the rite. The
parishioners of Wembury protested also that redress was difficult to gain,
because half of them were tenants of the prior: these he had threatened
to evict if they hired their own priest.

At approximately this date the inhabitants of Bodmin complained that
their town was greatly decayed and desolate because of the constant trouble
and vexation produced by the prior. In particular they resented his powers
as lord of the leet, and his failure to provide services in the two local chapels
from which he drew income. In 1537 an agreement was reached between
townsmen and prior: it extended the privileges of the former. But the most
vehemently hostile of such suits was that directed against the Abbot of
Torre by his 'poor neighbours'. In a petition presented to the Court of
Star Chamber after the official visitation of his house, the laymen denounced
the abbot's 'evil disposition' and condemned his 'vicious and abominable
living towards God'. They accused him of 'vexing' and 'troubling' his 'poor
neighbours', and in particular of retaining knights, esquires, gentlemen and
lawyers – 'whereby', they protested, 'the said abbot oppresseth your said
poor and faithful subjects, menacing and threatening them in such wise
that they dare not complain unto your highness'. Abbot Read, they claimed,
'hath divers and sundry times made his open avaunt and boasted himself,
saying that whosoever attempteth the law with him shall have no remedy

[49] STAC 2/18/77; 29/11; C 1 686/45; 695/2; 714/39; 719/25; 785/1–5.

in seven years, whether his matter be just or wrong'. The laymen alleged that he had interfered in a court case concerning one of his female friends. Even more seriously, they claimed that when the royal visitors had arrived to inspect Torre Abbey, the abbot had surreptitiously removed a large part of its valuable plate. His intention, they added, was 'to deceive and utterly defraud your grace thereof'.[50]

If laymen's support for religious houses was declining as the dissolutions approached, their attitudes towards the actual processes of suppression in the years 1536–9 would seem once more to have been predominantly acquiescent or even positively co-operative. At Exeter, for example, the dissolution of the Franciscan and Dominican houses was assisted by the mayor, Thomas Hunt. At Plymouth the suppression of the Carmelite and Franciscan communities and the confiscation of their goods was executed with the co-operation of the mayor, Thomas Clotting, and the mayor-elect, William Hawkins, as well as of James Horsewell and other townsmen.[51] The people of the South-West in fact failed totally to mount significant resistance to the Henrician dissolutions: the region witnessed nothing remotely comparable to the northern Pilgrimage of Grace. Even the small-scale disturbance in the Exeter priory of St Nicholas in 1536 was, as the participants themselves insisted, directed against the incidental acts of iconoclasm rather than against the suppression itself.[52]

In 1549, it is true, the minority of south-western people who rose in rebellion demanded the restoration of establishments 'for devout persons, which shall pray for the king and the commonwealth'. These were to be financed by a confiscation of 'the half-part of the abbey lands and chantry lands in every man's possession', and by a diversion of the alms collected in church boxes. The rebel scheme, nevertheless, was restricted to 'two places, where two of the chief abbeys was, in every county'. In the entire diocese it would have revived only four houses, presumably at Bodmin, Launceston, Plympton and Tavistock; it made no mention of the other great foundations, nor of the smaller monasteries and nunneries, nor of the houses of the friars.[53] Even the most extreme traditionalists were now demanding no more than a token restoration of these formerly important institutions.

While a significant role in the religious life of the pre-Reformation layman might certainly be played by monks, nuns, regular canons and friars, it was almost invariably secondary to that performed by the members of the secular clergy. These included the bishop, who stood at the apex of the

---

[50] *Plymouth Records*, p. 108; *LP*, VIII, 743; IX, 1147; *Bodmin Register*, pp. 293–4, 304–5; STAC 2/21/96; Rowse 1941, pp. 89, 178.
[51] *LP*, XIII (2), 354, 381, 389.
[52] See above, p. 75.
[53] Royal 18 B XI, fol. 33v.

diocesan pyramid; the archdeacons, deans and cathedral canons, who constituted its middle tiers; and finally – and in closest proximity to the average
layman – the parish priests, chantry priests and other unbeneficed clerics,
of whom its lower strata consisted. During the Reformation decades this
corps of men was subjected to a number of significant alterations. Not only
did it diminish markedly in numerical strength, especially after the suppression of chantries by Edward VI. Its legal and financial privileges were reduced
by the Reformation Parliament, and its spiritual status was unmistakably
eroded – particularly when, under Edward and Elizabeth, its sacramental
and mediatorial roles were substantially reduced. At the same time, the
commitment of its members to traditional Catholicism was progressively
weakened, and in some cases replaced by Protestant conviction.[54] The
changes experienced by the clerical estate were undoubtedly major. Were
they accompanied by any perceptible change in popular attitudes towards
it?

The verbal evidence is again suggestive. Until the 1530s, it appears to
have been unusual for south-western laypeople to denigrate or deride the
priesthood as an institution. One of the few exceptions was provided by
John Atwill of Walkhampton, who in 1505–6 not only criticized the cupidity
of the clergy but also denied its exclusive authority to absolve.[55] Markedly
more representative of customary attitudes were the words of Axminister's
Thomas Crabbe in 1535–6. Every man, asserted Crabbe, 'must needs have
a priest at his coming into the world, and a priest at his departing'.[56]

By this date, however, expressions of disrespect and even of contempt
for the clerical body were already beginning to increase. In 1531, at Exeter,
the solemn ceremonies of excommunication performed by the cathedral
clergy had been laughingly derided by Thomas Bennett. He thought them
'merry conceits'; they were 'interludes, played of the priests'.[57] Even more
outspoken was Philip Gammon at Axminster in 1535–6. 'Priests', he
announced sweepingly, were 'all nought.' 'Priests', he added, 'did put Christ
to death: whose names were Anan[ias] and Caiaphas.' Bishops he regarded
with similar contempt. He informed Margery Hoare 'that the blessing of
a bishop was as good as the blessing of his old horse', and when she protested
'that it could not be true, for the bishop was anointed with holy oil', the
shoemaker merely retorted 'that there was as much virtue in the oil of a
beast['s] foot as was in the oil that the bishop was anointed withal'.[58]

Equally strident in their anti-clericalism were the writings of Philip Nichols

[54] See below, pp. 229–32.
[55] ER XIII, fols. 144v–5; Mumford 1936, pp. 95–6.
[56] STAC 2/2/267.
[57] *Acts and Monuments*, II, p. 1038.
[58] STAC 2/2/267.

of Totnes in the years 1547–9. Before the Reformation, he assured his readers, the higher clergy had been proud, envious and malicious, had lived in luxury, and had indulged in sexual misdemeanours: 'whether they were whore-mongers, adulterers, and worse, let all the world be judge'. They had persecuted good men, and they had failed to instruct the people in Christian faith and practice. 'Alas, few of them could teach anything at all; for they were (for the most part) great men's sons, brought up in hawking and hunting.' Nor were the lower clergy spared. The priests, declared Nichols, had committed both adultery and fornication, 'as it cannot be denied but that they commonly did'; and in the pursuit of their selfish and lustful ends they had exercised a tyrannical domination over the exploited laity: 'For the days hath been that, if a man had found a priest...in the bed with his wife, he durst not to have laid his hands upon him; whereas if it had been another man, although he had slain him it had been accounted no fault at all. No man might have sued them at the common law. Yea, these Egyptians were waxed so proud that they had divided themselves from the poor Israelites, insomuch that they must be called "spiritual fathers", and we, "the lewd people". And if any poor Israelite had grudged at any time to bear their heavy and intolerable burdens, there was no remedy but cruel death without mercy.' No greater was Nichols' respect for the traditionalist priests of his own day. These he denounced as 'caterpillars, which do all for lucre'.[59]

Contempt for the clergy continued to be voiced in the reigns of both Mary and Elizabeth. 'I would all priests were hanged!', declared Sampson Jackman at Linkinhorne in 1553. In 1557, at Kenton, William Luscombe allegedly boasted of his adultery and dismissed as inconsequential the penances imposed in such cases by the ecclesiastical courts. It was 'but a sheet matter'. And in 1568, at Plympton St Mary, Christopher Lowman refused flatly to acknowledge the authority of his vicar. 'He is no master of mine!', he proclaimed; and when Ralph Black protested that the vicar was a minister, 'and therefore we must all obey him', Lowman replied: 'No, I will not take him for my master: for he is not able to teach me.' He then sneered that 'they which can say one verse, two and three verse, are made ministers now'. 'I will be a minister also', joked another parishioner, William Robins; 'for I can say one verse, two verse, and three verse.' Thereupon Lowman declared that he could become a minister upon payment of a mark or ten shillings.[60]

Statements of this nature, which would suggest a significant decline in respect for the clergy as a body, were moreover accompanied by an appar-

---

[59] *Godly New Story*, pp. 24–5, 59–62, 72; Royal 18 B XI, fol. 10.
[60] SP 11/2/2; CCB 855, fol. 257v; CCB 856, fol. 470.

ently increasing volume of criticism, complaint and accusation against its individual members. Before the Reformation, it is true, these phenomena were by no means unknown. Between 1504 and 1519 the vicar of Tavistock, for example, was publicly accused by a parishioner of involvement in theft. In *circa* 1510, at Michaelstow, a priest was openly charged by a layman with sexual misconduct. Richard Broad of Minster claimed that women had been smuggled into the priest's lodgings at night, and that they had been dressed in male clothing for disguise. Between 1518 and 1529 the parson of Throwleigh was denounced in the Court of Chancery by several of his own parishioners, including Richard Brown, John Jale, John Sholbeare and William Wyatt; they particularly deprecated his 'crafty means'.[61] In the Reformation decades, nevertheless, the level of accusations would seem to have risen markedly. The supposed inadequacies of clerics now attracted a veritable barrage of criticism from an increasingly censorious laity.

Clerical 'covetousness' was one possible item of complaint. 'Covetous' and 'extortionous' were among the terms employed by a number of husband-men from Awliscombe to describe a local chantry priest. Under the leadership of William Hussey, in 1545 they presented to the Court of Requests a list of his alleged transgressions. It was also in 1545 that the parson of Uplyme was accused in public, by a parishioner, of practising 'unthriftiness' and of receiving a stolen horse. Malice might also be alleged. In 1557 Martin Alley of Kenton declared that his vicar – who had threatened him with discipline for his irreverent behaviour – now 'went about to suck [his] blood'. Other accusations against clerics included drunkenness, as at St Michael Penkevil in 1565, and swearing, as at Ilsington in 1569. The vicar of Ilsington, claimed Richard Downing, was 'as great a swearer as is in the world'. Even the recreational activities of the clergy might be denounced. In *circa* 1540 the Provost of Glasney College was accused by William Carvanyon of indulging in hawking and hunting, and hunting constituted one of the charges laid against his vicar by William Martin at Sheepwash in 1569.[62]

But the most frequent type of accusation was inevitably the sexual. In several cases it was the alleged concubine of a cleric at whom the charge was flung. In 1541–2, for example, Joan Clement was denounced by Cicily Vallance of Exeter as a 'priest's whore'. In 1560 it was claimed by John Prout of Calstock that Thomasine Bligh was similarly a priest's whore: 'she had a child by a priest', he asserted, 'before that she was married'. 'Priest's whore' was also the phrase hurled at Mary Tucker by John Stephens of Exeter in the same year. 'Thou art a whore and a priest whore', a woman was told by Edmund Butcher at Winkleigh in 1561; 'for a priest had to-doing

---

[61] CCB 854, I, fols. 31, 212; C 1 582/71.
[62] REQ 2 8/324; C 1 1144/28–30; STAC 2/9/63; CCB 855, fols. 174v–5; CCB 855B, sub 4 July 1565; CCB 856, fols. 307v–9v, 318v–22.

with thee at home, in the midst of thine own floor.' In 1565, at North Tamerton, another woman was reviled by a man as a 'whore and priest's whore'.[63]

More often it was the supposedly guilty cleric who was himself denounced. When, in 1541, a number of Exeter people met to play at tables in the house of one Lake, they rapidly turned to 'jesting upon priests', and their main jest was the alleged propensity of priests to 'live incontinently with men's wives'. One of the company announced that a priest had been found with the sister of John Blackaller. Lake, the host, then claimed that another priest had been discovered with a baker's wife, and Lake's wife added that attempts had been made to conceal this offence by bribery. This damaging story was subsequently repeated by Lake to a shopkeeper of St Petrock's. The same year witnessed similar outbursts at Brampford Speke and Yealmpton. At Brampford, Alice Palmer assured her neighbours that she had seen a married woman entering the vicarage at nine o'clock in the evening, and that this woman 'came not out again that night'. At Yealmpton, Walter Kine composed a highly offensive ballad to celebrate the supposed liaison between the parson and his kinswoman. Kine not only sang it in public places, including the village street; he even taught it to the young people of the parish. 'Now it is a common song', reported a local man, 'and sung abroad in the country.'[64]

In 1542 the constable of St Breock, George Wolcock, 'did speak against the misliving and unchastity of one Sir Matthew Poldon, priest'. 'The which priest', proclaimed Wolcock, 'ordered his life and living contrary to the laws of Almighty God'. Between 1544 and 1547 several citizens of Exeter, led by the vintner Robert Stirbirch, secured the indictment of a priest under the statutes relating to clerical incontinence. This, he complained, effectively destroyed his 'good name and fame'. In 1545, at Honiton, the parson of Uplyme was denounced by Ralph Merrick 'in the common street, before a great multitude'. Merrick accused him of exercising an 'evil rule', and added 'divers other opprobrious words': there were rumours concerning a pregnant woman in the parsonage. On a separate occasion, moreover, an angry deputation of his parishioners marched to the parsonage at Uplyme and there assailed him with 'bragging and brigous words' – treating him, he protested, 'as though he had been a man of the worst sort in the world'. And in *circa* 1546, after complaints from several of his parishioners, the vicar of Paul was charged with incontinence at the sessions in Truro; in consequence he suffered 'infamy, slander and rebuke'. The supposed liaisons

---

[63] CCB 854A, I, sub 10 January 1541/2; CCB 855, fols. 498v–9, 505; CCB 855A, fol. 22v; CCB 855B, sub 26 July 1565.

[64] CCB 854A, I, sub 8 December 1541, 23 December 1541; II, sub 30 June 1541.

Clerical behaviour did matter

of the vicar with two of the local wives were said by the parish constable to be 'the common fame and report . . . in all the said parish'.[65]

The 1550s brought no relief. 'Whore-monger' was one of the epithets applied to the vicar of Alvington by one Fairweather, an inhabitant of Malborough; others included 'flea-carrier', 'maggot-carrier' and 'knave'. Other people in the neighbourhood allegedly regarded the vicar as 'vicious', and 'called him by worse names'. At Whitchurch, William Gooding reviled the vicar as a 'vagabond'. He accused the priest of relations with the wife of the parish clerk, and declared that 'the vicar lay in her house all the last Christmas'. Equally abusive was the crowd that gathered outside the parish church at St Austell in 1557. It had been drawn by a rumour that the vicar had taken a woman into the church – ostensibly in order to hear her confession – and had then locked the doors from inside. Two of the crowd began to hammer upon the doors, and John Woolridge hurled abuse at the cleric within. 'Art thou weary of my company?', he shouted; 'I defy thee, knave!' Pascoe Cornwall denounced the priest as a whore-master, and declared that he was even now ravishing his victim: 'Hark, do not you hear her cry? *I* hear her cry!'[66]

In 1562 there were cases reported from Honiton Clyst, Week St Mary, Rockbeare and Spreyton. At Honiton Clyst it was claimed by a man and a woman that 'the vicar of Chudleigh hath kept Mistress Yarde'; at Week St Mary the vicar's relationship with Magdalene Wale was the subject of gossip among 'divers persons'; and at Rockbeare a woman at the vicarage was similarly discussed by the suspicious parishioners. At Spreyton, in the parish church at service-time, the vicar was openly reviled by Oliver Bennett as a 'pilled priest', 'whoreson priest', and 'whore-monger and bawdy priest'. The vicar was so shaken that he removed his surplice and cancelled the service, but Bennett was unrepentant and, when subsequently rebuked by the cleric, boldly called him 'pilled priest' and 'naughty priest' to his face. In 1565, at St Michael Penkevil, the rector was accused by George Carminow of committing fornication. Even more lurid were the accusations hurled by laymen against the vicar of Dawlish in 1566. 'If the vicar's faults were known as well as mine', proclaimed Edward Ward, 'he was as well worthy for to ride in the cart as I.' 'Bear ye with him as much as ye may', he told his companions; 'for at the last you will bear with him so long that he will jape your wives and maidens, all them that be in your parish.' When Robert Helwill declared that the vicar would jape no wife of his, Ward 'swore, by God's blood, that the vicar would', and other parishioners accused him of attempted rape. Similarly outspoken were Richard Berry of Coldridge

---

[65] STAC 2/31/11, 178; C 1 1139/23–4; 1144/28–30.
[66] CCB 855, fols. 49v–50, 70v, 150v–1v, 184v–5v, 235.

in 1567 and William Martin of Sheepwash in 1568–9. Berry denounced his vicar as a 'bawdy knave priest'. Martin reviled his vicar – while he stood in the pulpit – as a 'naughty knave', 'rascal knave' and 'varlet knave'. Martin also accused him of dancing with women, of 'lying' and 'playing' with women in the church house during Ales, and of sexually misbehaving with the daughter of one Blackmore as well as with the daughters of Martin himself.[67]

That accusations of this type by no means always represented an objective evaluation of clerical morals is suggested by the frequency with which they resulted in denials and in actions for slander. Thus the parson of Uplyme, publicly denounced by laymen in 1545, insisted that in reality he had for 16 years 'endeavoured himself to teach and instruct his parishioners there in the laws of God', and had maintained an 'honest conversation and behaviour, as is meet and convenient in this behalf'. At Exeter, between 1544 and 1547, a priest charged with incontinence angrily attributed the accusation to a conspiracy among the citizens; he described them as 'evil-disposed'. In *circa* 1546 the vicar of Paul similarly protested that his accusers were 'malicious' and 'evil-disposed'. Indeed he was able to produce witnesses to establish his good character, and was duly acquitted.[68] Even more dubious was the accusation levelled against Dr Gammon, a canon of Exeter, in 1568. It was announced by Thomasine Tucker of Honiton Clyst that Gammon was the father of her illegitimate child. Subsequently, however, she confessed that he was in fact innocent – and revealed that she had been pressurized into implicating him by a number of local people, including John Leach and Dewens Rooks. She had been offered money, and had even been threatened with expulsion from the parish if she refused to co-operate. Here, evidently, a charge against a cleric had been deliberately fabricated.[69]

The trend was far from universal. In 1558, for example, it was said that the vicar of Hatherleigh was regarded throughout his parish as an honest man.[70] Nevertheless the verbal evidence in its various forms would certainly imply a substantial erosion of popular respect for the clergy in the Reformation decades. Is this impression confirmed by the evidence of financial activity?

Bequests to members of the secular clergy were specified in as many as 21 of the 30 wills in the years 1520–9, or 70%. Some, such as the 20d left by Henry Bartlett to the parish priest at Wolborough in 1526, were made for 'tithing and offerings negligently paid'; others, including the £16

[67] CCB 855A, fols. 181, 215–17, 222–3, 234–4v; CCB 855B, sub 4 July 1565, 19 December 1566; CCB 856, fols. 210v–11v, 307v–9v.
[68] C 1 1139/23–4; 1144/28–30; STAC 2/31/178.
[69] CCB 856, fols. 271–3v. For Gammon, see also below, p. 244.
[70] CCB 855, fol. 375v.

bequeathed by Andrew Brusard at Brixham in 1521, were fees for prayers or masses on behalf of the dead. Several were outright gifts, William Sellick of Tiverton, for example, leaving gowns to two priests in 1524, and Joan Tackle of Honiton donating a featherbed to the vicar of Yarcombe in 1528. Bequests of these types, however, appeared in only 23 of the 41 wills in the years 1530–9, or 56%, and in only 25 of the 69 in the years 1540–6, or 36%. In the reign of Edward, moreover, they featured in no more than 17 of the 77 wills in the years 1547–9, or 22%, and in only 8 of the 31 in the years 1550–3, or 26%. Richard Lock of Yarcombe, who bequeathed 20d to his parish priest in 1550, was now markedly less typical than John Deyman of Widworthy, who left nothing to clerics in 1551. Nor was the trend reversed thereafter. Bequests to the secular clergy were specified in only 11 of the 60 wills in the years 1553–9, or 18%, and in a mere 3 of the 90 in the years 1560–9, or 3%. William Mules of Mortehoe bequeathed a sheep to his vicar in 1567, and in 1568–9 John Cosowarth of Colan and Henry Stidston of Tamerton Foliot left money for forgotten tithes.[71]

Again the trend should not be exaggerated. At Blisland, in 1547, the salary of a priest was augmented with 'certain money given him by the devotion of the parishioners there';[72] and at South Molton in *circa* 1560 the stipend of the minister was increased by voluntary contributions from the members of his congregation.[73] Nevertheless the testamentary statistics would unquestionably indicate a drastic diminution of financial support for the clergy as the Reformation progressed.

This trend was accompanied, moreover, by an apparent increase in lay resistance to the payment of clerical dues. Some, such as mortuaries, had long been disputed – as at St Teath, where Robert Battin came into conflict with the vicar in 1510, or at Bodmin, where in 1526 the townsmen denied the right of their vicar to claim hearse cloths from the corpses of dead parishioners. From *circa* 1529, however, resistance appears to have intensified. In 1529 itself the inhabitants of one parish in north Devon reportedly objected as a body, and prevented their priest from taking as his mortuary the cow of a deceased parishioner. In the autumn of this year, at South Hill, several of the parishioners withheld mortuaries from their parson; the ringleaders were Sampson Mannington and Robert Tarrent. Shortly after these incidents, moreover, laymen began to exploit the legislation of the Reformation Parliament as a weapon against clerical demands. At Dittisham, according to a parishioner several years later, the standard mortuary before

---

[71] PROB 11 20, fol. 130v; 21, fol. 202v; 22, fol. 84v; 23, fol. 71; 33, fol. 116; 34, fol. 86v; 51, fol. 51; Moger, 29, William Mules, 1566/7; 40, Henry Stidston, 1569.
[72] PRO E 301 9/30.
[73] Lansdowne 377, fol. 10v.

the Statute of Mortuaries was a wether sheep. 'But sithens the making of
the said Statute', reports the parishioner, 'the inhabitants of the same parish
have paid money according to the value of their goods – as is appointed
in the same Statute.' At Harberton, according to a local woman, any person
dying in possession of six oxen had customarily forfeited one as his mortuary.
Since the Statute, however, 'she believeth that no vicar of Harberton hath
been possessed of any such mortuary'. Thus when John Sweet, the owner
of six oxen, died at Harberton in 1535–6, his son paid only a fee of 10s.
Equally quick to utilize the new legislation were the parishioners of Down
St Mary. Indeed their parson was so aggrieved by their attitude that between
1533 and 1538 he withdrew their customary funeral services 'because he
cannot have the best beast in the name of a mortuary, as he (before the
Statute) was used to have'. Even the restricted fees would encounter resistance. Mortuary disputes appeared in the Consistory Court in 1533–4, and
were still provoking trouble in 1558, 1565 and 1569. At Crediton in 1565,
for instance, payment of the mortuary for her deceased husband was refused
by Sibley Maunder.[74]

As is attested by the records of the Consistory Court, conflict over tithes
had been by no means infrequent before the Reformation. A disagreement
concerning the tithe payable on local woodland brought the parson and
the parishioners of St Mawgan-in-Kerrier before the Court of Chancery
between 1518 and 1529, and in 1526 the townsmen of Bodmin challenged
the claim of their vicar to a tithe of their butter and cheese. On the other
hand, the townsmen acknowledged his customary right to a tithe of their
calves, milk, flax, hemp, leeks, onions, beans, peas, apples, pears and hay;
and at about the same time it was customary for the inhabitants of Lawhitton
to carry their tithes of butter and cheese to their parish church, and to
leave them for their priest before an image of St Michael.[75] Again it appears
to have been in the Reformation decades that the conflicts most markedly
increased. In 1535 a royal proclamation ordered the payment of tithe 'without further denial, contradiction, molestation or trouble', and subsequent
proclamations in 1547 and 1559 would imply a rising tide of lay resistance.[76]
The trend is confirmed by south-western evidence.

Between November 1533 and November 1534, for example, the Consistory Court at Exeter heard no less than 18 disputes concerning tithes. In
the years 1538–44, when the Dean of Crediton attempted to collect tithes
from John Howe and John Walsh, they responded by suing him in the

[74] CCB 778; CCB 854, I, fol. 202; CCB 855, fols. 304, 331–2; CCB 856, fol. 434v; *Bodmin Register*, pp. 36–8; Prince 1701, pp. 181–2; C 1 666/8; 900/34–5; CWA Crediton, 1565.
[75] CCB 775; CCB 776; CCB 854, I, II; CCB 854A, I, sub 18 January 1541/2; C 1 581/88; *Bodmin Register*, pp. 36–8.
[76] TRP, I, pp. 224–5, 398; II, p. 121.

Court of Chancery. Between 1544 and 1547 Jose Penrose and Ralph Bosis-
towe refused tithe to the Deanery of St Buryan, and in 1546 the parson
of Silverton was deprived of his corn tithes by Thomas Vowlford and Edward
Bustard. The 1550s saw no abatement. Gregory Goodridge, for instance,
disputed corn tithes with the parson of Littlehempston; the rector of Bick-
leigh complained that Richard Richards, who owned land in his parish,
'refuseth to pay the tithe thereof'; and at Manaton a farmer rendered no
tithes from his land for a year and a half. At Hatherleigh, William Morecombe not only persisted in withholding tithe from the vicar but also
absented himself from the parish in order to evade the retribution of the
law. In the 1560s, at St Just, the rector was refused tithe from a local wood
by William Williams, while at Heavitree near Exeter, where the rector or
his lessee had customarily received tithe from Heavitree and Polsloe, this
was 'now of late... denied by Mr Blackaller'. Even more overtly hostile
to such clerical dues was Philip Harvey of North Huish. In 1569 a servant
of his parson attempted to collect a tithe of his corn. 'Get thee out of the
ground', exploded Harvey, 'or else I will send thee packing!'[77]
    Individual defaulting – examples of which could be multiplied – was
accompanied by group resistance. In 1532 the vicar of St Keverne complained
that his parishioners were refusing to pay tithe; he believed that they had
been incited by his enemies. Similar problems were encountered by the vicar
of Morebath in 1537. At Down St Mary it was in the years 1533–8 that
the conflict erupted. Its parson claimed a tithe of his parishioners' bullocks,
pigs, bees, honey, butter, cheese and other produce, as well as of the Ale,
goods and stores of the parish church. Thomas Stone, however, now protested that these were 'exactions' and 'unreasonable demands'; he alleged
that they were contrary to parochial custom, and flatly refused to pay. In
this he was subsequently followed by most of his fellow-parishioners. Indeed
the unpopular parson – who maintained that he was demanding no more
than the dues traditionally rendered by inhabitants of Down St Mary –
now openly lamented that in the entire parish there were 'not above five
or six honest men and women'. Equally antagonistic were the townsmen
of Helston. Led by their mayor, John Pearce, in *circa* 1540 they ceased
to pay tithe for their corn-mills to the vicar of Wendron. The vicar, insisting
that this payment had been rendered 'by all the time whereof no man's
remembrance is to the contrary', denounced the townsmen as 'perverse'
and 'froward'. Revealingly, he also expressed his fear that their action would
provide a 'perilous example [to] the whole country next adjoining'. Nor
were such fears unjustified. At Sidmouth, in 1557, a number of fishermen

[77] CCB 778; CCB 855, fols. 45v, 238, 375, 376v, 451–2; CCB 855A, fol. 489; CCB 856,
    fols. 449v–53; C 1 1011/50–2; 1117/16; 1170/43; 1300/41–4; Pill 1968, p. 48.

disputed the tithe on fish with their rector, and at Brixham, in 1565, fish tithes were similarly denied to the vicar by local fishermen. Extensive resistance is also recorded in the accounts for Crediton. A list of the tithes unpaid by the townspeople in 1565 included a number of local properties, and between 1566 and 1568 the summoner was still attempting to deal with the recalcitrants. In as late as 1571 'divers' of the Creditonians would be found refusing 'to pay their tithes and other duties belonging to the church'.[78]

Similarly under attack in the Reformation decades were the annual 'offerings' traditionally collected by the clergy. At Bodmin in 1526 the townsmen had recognized the right of their vicar to four such collections – at All Saints, Christmas, Easter and the Nativity of St Petrock – and four collections per annum were also customarily contributed by the parishioners of Lamerton to their vicar. At Lamerton, however, in 1551 the inhabitants reduced their collections to three. 'And some of the parish', records John Hatherleigh, 'was glad thereof, and contented to pay but a little, as this deponent was one; and paid none, by the space of four years.' Not until 1555 was the fourth offering revived, and even then Hatherleigh was reluctant to contribute. 'Master Vicar', he told the cleric to his face, 'I trust and if it be not my duty, you will pay me back again!' Another parishioner of Lamerton, one Bowden, simply refused to pay. And at St Issey, in 1566, an inhabitant withheld the offering customarily rendered to the vicar or his lessee by each communicant at Easter.[79] Some dues, moreover, were totally suppressed. At Hatherleigh, as in other parishes, a 'chrisom' had traditionally been paid to the vicar by each mother who brought a new-born baby to the church. In 1564 it was reported that such payments had ended 'of late', and after 1565 chrisoms also disappeared from the accounts at Crediton.[80]

The decline of the layman's traditional investment in the clergy is epitomized by the transformation that occurred at Exeter. John Hooker observed that before the Reformation, each of the 19 parish churches in the city had been endowed sufficiently to maintain its own mass-priests. 'Such', remarked Hooker, 'was the blind devotion of the people in that Romish religion.' By the reign of Elizabeth, in contrast, few of the 19 could maintain even a clerk or a scholar: most had no incumbent.[81]

Over this same period the financial exploitation and even outright robbery of clerics by laymen would seem to have become an increasingly frequent phenomenon. On the eve of the Reformation such impieties had certainly

---

[78] CCB 855, fol. 193v; CCB 855B, sub 7 June 1565; C 1 900/34–5; 1020/4–9; CWA Crediton, 1565–71; CWA Morebath, 1537; Henderson 1923–4, p. 267.
[79] *Bodmin Register*, pp. 36–8; CCB 855, fols. 50v–1v, 53; CCB 855B, sub 24 July 1566.
[80] CCB 855A, fol. 422v; CWA Crediton.
[81] 'Description of Exeter', p. 9.

on occasions been committed. At St Giles-in-the-Wood, in 1517, the curate's clothes and books were pillaged by John Sendale, William Sendal and Robert Panston, and in 1527 the goods of another cleric were allegedly stolen at St Teath.[82] Once again, however, it was in the Reformation decades that the most marked proliferation of such incidents would appear to have occurred.

Rents, for example, were deliberately withheld. In 1533 the parson of Clayhidon leased his parsonage to Richard Buckland in return for £30 per annum, but when subsequently he lost his copy of the lease Buckland simply refused to render the stipulated amount. To the 'great loss and hindrance' of the parson, he failed also to maintain the parsonage houses and 'suffereth them utterly to decay'. Buckland, concluded the priest, possessed 'but a small conscience'. Between 1538 and 1544, at Branscombe, the vicar was engaged in a dispute with John Sherman concerning a lease of the vicarage, and at approximately the same time, at Rewe, Roger Wallace not only failed to pay his rent for the parsonage but also contrived a fraudulent insertion in his lease which – to the chagrin of the parson – rendered it renewable every five years. Rent was allegedly withheld from the vicarage at Egloshayle by John Vyvyan between 1544 and 1547. In the 1550s rent was detained from their vicar by inhabitants of Stokenham, while at Brixham John Plumley and Edward Harris refused to pay the vicar the dues agreed for their lease of his benefice.[83]

Other revenues of the clergy might be appropriated. Between 1529 and 1532 some £30, paid by the parishioners of Plymouth as oblations, tithes and other dues, was detained from the vicar by James Horsewell. In 1540 the parson of Plymtree was defrauded of the tithe corn sold on his behalf by Richard Coe. In the same year the parson of Shillingford made a verbal contract with two of his parishioners, Richard Clace and German Pike: in return for a small fee they were to collect tithes, oblations and other dues on his behalf. Subsequently, however, the two laymen refused to deliver the collected revenues, and the priest, defrauded of some 20 marks, found himself 'without remedy' in common law. He now realized that Clace and Pike were 'men of untruth, and of crafty imagination'. In 1547 Nicholas Nichols and others, seizing the opportunity presented by a vacancy, acquired glebe lands belonging to the vicarage of St Austell and St Blazey; they then collected the tithes and other revenues for their own profit. Even when a new vicar arrived they continued to refuse him his dues. At St Teath, in 1554, the tithes and oblations due to the parson were seized by a yeoman, John Chapel. At approximately this date a number of laymen, including

---

[82] STAC 2/22/376; 35/74.
[83] C 1 721/36; 1002/1; 1073/1–2; 1170/48; 1466/76–80; 1467/41.

Christopher Berry, were sued by the vicar of Northam for allegedly expropriating the revenues of his vicarage and the profits of his glebe, while the income of the vicarage at St Kew was reportedly purloined by Matthew Lapp. And in *circa* 1569 the vicar of Ilsington complained that Hugh Diggow – a man, he thought, 'of an evil disposition' – had acquired the vicarage and its lands 'by subtle and crafty sleights and policies'.[84]

The clergy's land was disputed or seized. At Hawkchurch, land was seized from the parson in 1532; at Okehampton, a land dispute between the husbandman Peter Davy and a chantry priest resulted in a lawsuit against the priest between 1533 and 1538; and at Dittisham, Tristram Cannicle was sued by the parson in a dispute concerning parsonage land between 1538 and 1544.[85] The parsonage or vicarage might itself be attacked. At Lawhitton in 1535 a number of men reportedly forced an entry to the parson's house and expelled his servants. At Awliscombe in 1541 a group of 'pernicious persons' invaded the vicar's house, ejected his servants and declared (to his 'utter infamy and slander') that they would seize all his goods for the sheriff; they also plundered his victuals. At Nymet Tracey between 1544 and 1547 William Wattes angered the parson by removing the tables, doors and windows from his parsonage. In Edward's reign the vicarage at St Stephen's-by-Saltash was forcibly entered by John Debble of Millbrook, Robert Smith of St Germans and Thomas Spore of North Hill. The intruders caused substantial structural damage and stole property worth more than £33 from the vicar – whom they regarded (he lamented) with a 'cruel mind'. In the reign of Mary 'great ruin and spoil' was inflicted upon the vicarage at St Just, to the 'great losses' of the vicar, and the parsonage at Stoke Climsland was allegedly expropriated and then despoiled by Robert Benny. Benny was said not only to have removed tables, doors and gates but also to have pulled down the parsonage chapel, carrying off the timber from its screens.[86]

Other possessions of the clergy were also at risk. In late 1529, at South Hill, timber was stolen from the parson by Sampson Mannington and Robert Tarrent. In 1540 the labourers hired by the vicar of Hartland were forcibly expelled from a wood at Wear Giffard by a group of 10 or 12 men; this caused the vicar 'great hurts and losses'. It was also in 1540 that the parsonage at Bridestow was reportedly raided by laymen, who seized corn and grain from the parson's barn as well as livestock from his glebe. In Edward's reign the corn of the vicar of Townstall was allegedly despoiled by Nicholas Adams, Roger Came, Thomas Stowford and others, while the house of

---

[84] C 1 636/24; 1023/77; 1061/30; 1193/54–7; 1347/16–18; 1366/5–6; 1386/35; C 3 9/41.
[85] *LP*, V, 1217; C 1 778/19; 1004/52.
[86] STAC 2/7/93; 19/341; C 1 1160/5–6; 1273/55–6; 1373/14; 1389/68–71.

the parson of Bittadon was forced open and looted by Edmund Burnet and other men. In 1554 the parson of St Teath was allegedly robbed of personal possessions by the yeoman John Chapel, an individual (he complained) of 'devilish and extort power'. Later in Mary's reign, while at Holsworthy, he was again despoiled: goods and deeds worth no less than £200 were reportedly stolen from him by John Drewe and his son.[87]

The financial evidence, like the verbal, would therefore appear to indicate a substantial erosion of popular respect and support for the secular clergy in the Reformation decades. Both species of evidence must be compared, finally, with the evidence of personal and corporate behaviour.

One possible index of laymen's attitudes towards the clerical estate is the extent to which they sought to enter it. The rite of ordination – depicted, for example, in the glass at Doddiscombsleigh, where a bishop lays hands upon the ordinands who kneel before him – remained a frequent occurrence in the diocese of Exeter on the eve of the Reformation. Between 1504 and 1519 some 66 individuals were ordained priest, and there were a further 21 ordinations at Christmas 1520 alone. Between 1545 and 1551, in contrast, the diocese experienced an apparently total cessation of ordinations. Nor was the subsequent revival more than very partial: only about ten elevations to the priesthood are recorded for the reign of Mary. This decline is by no means wholly attributable to a surplus of priests after the monastic dissolutions, since only a limited number of ex-religious appear to have been instituted to benefices within the region. At the beginning of Elizabeth's reign, in fact, a marked scarcity of priests in the South-West was observed not only by Sir John Chichester but also by the canons of Exeter Cathedral. The canons noted that few or no laymen were now entering the clergy.[88]

But even more important to evaluate is the extent to which laymen were prepared to submit themselves to clerical authority. It is clear that traditional habits of deference and obedience were by no means totally eradicated in the Reformation decades. It was no accident that in 1549 the south-western rebels should choose several priests to be their leaders. They were reportedly dissuaded from burning Exeter by the vicar of St Thomas'.[89] A similar level of submission was accorded to their minister by the early-Elizabethan parishioners of South Molton. In 1562, in reply to their request, they received from him a lengthy and authoritative epistle; its purpose, he declared, was that 'you, and your children also after you, may after my decease remember and perform the things therein written'. He also rejoiced that the people of South Molton had accepted his ministry as divinely inspired, and had

[87] STAC 2/21/163; 32/4; 3/3/81; C 1 666/8; 1347/16–18; 1369/11–20; 1424/5.
[88] ER XIII-XIX; SP 12/6/17; CAB 3552, fol. 134v; Boggis 1922, p. 323; Pill 1963. For institutions of ex-religious, see below, p. 229.
[89] See below, p. 230. For the vicar of St Thomas', see 'Description of Exeter', pp. 65–8.

become followers of his teaching and his personal example.[90] For at least some laymen, the authority of clerics remained high.

For an increasing number, nevertheless, this authority was becoming open to question and even contradiction. In 1531 the Exeter clergy found themselves engaged in vigorous theological argument with Thomas Bennett. In 1547, at Harberton, a cathedral canon was similarly challenged by Philip Nichols. In 1549 even the traditionalist parishioners of Sampford Courtenay were prepared to withstand their priest, telling him bluntly, as he prepared to perform the new service, 'that he should not so do', and 'willing and charging' him to restore the Latin mass. Eventually the cleric 'yielded to their wills'. By Mary's reign such disobedience was no longer uncommon. At Kenton, Martin Alley deliberately ignored his vicar's commands and sat in the quire of the church. When rebuked, the incorrigible Alley 'defied the vicar, saying that he would sit where he list'. At St Tudy the parishioners dared to elect a clerk without obtaining their rector's consent. At Menheniot the vicar's attempts to dismiss a clerk were resisted and eventually defeated by the Twelve Men. And in 1558 Boyton's Agnes Priest was prepared to argue theology not only with clerics but even with the Bishop of Exeter himself. 'Thou art an unlearned person and a woman', the bishop was forced to exclaim in perplexity. 'Wilt thou meddle with such high matters, which all the doctors of the world cannot define?'[91]

Yet the 'unlearned' continued increasingly to disobey. In 1559, at Exeter, the canons were publicly defied by a number of the citizens, who included John Periam and Richard Prestwood as well as several women. These invaded the cathedral quire – which traditionally had been reserved for the canons – and blithely seated themselves in the canons' stalls. The clerics' attempts to dissuade them were unavailing. No more submissive was Oliver Bennett when, in 1562, he was ordered by the vicar of Spreyton to attend church in his own parish at Cheriton Bishop. Bennett retorted flatly that he would remain at Spreyton 'whether that the said vicar would or no'. In 1566, at Dean Prior, John Foxe not only ignored his vicar's repeated commands to desist from disrupting a church service, but also – 'in scorn and derision', it was feared – laughed in the frustrated cleric's face. And in 1567, at Broadclyst, the vicar's attempts to denounce individuals from the pulpit were stoutly challenged by members of his congregation. But even more blatantly resistant to clerical authority was Philip Harvey of North Huish. In 1569, in the chancel of his parish church, he was rebuked by his parson for mistreating the parson's servant. Harvey not only replied in the disrespectful second person singular – 'Wherein have I misused thy man?' – but also remained

---

[90] Lansdowne 377, fols. 8v–11. See also below, p. 253.
[91] *Acts and Monuments*, II, pp. 1038–40, 2050–1; *Copy of a Letter*, esp. pp. 32–3; 'Description of Exeter', p. 27; CCB 855, fols. 127v–8v, 174v–5, 266.

obdurately in his seat while the cleric stood before him. 'What a slave art thou', exclaimed another parishioner, 'to sit upon thy tail when that thou dost talk with thy better.' A brawl ensued, during which Harvey seized the parson's servant by the head and beard and then brandished a dagger; he had to be forcibly disarmed. When the parson again attempted to admonish him, his retort again was insolent: 'Thou, parson, art the occasion thereof!' 'Dost thou "thou" me?', asked the cleric; 'I am thy better.' Harvey retorted that even Christ had been addressed as 'thou'. 'You are in a high mystery', answered the other; 'and because that thou dost misuse me in the chancel, I do require thee to sit out'. '*I*', replied the layman, 'do require *you* to sit out of the church!' Two days previously, Harvey had told the parson's servant that he wished to see 'twenty such parsons hang'; 'and so do you tell your master', he had added, 'when you come home'.[92]

Of particular significance was the layman's changing attitude towards the moral and spiritual discipline imposed upon him by either the individual cleric or the ecclesiastical court. On the eve of the Reformation, penances, excommunications and other clerically imposed punishments would seem still to have been generally regarded with respect and even awe. Attitudes of this type were certainly manifested by the congregation in Exeter Cathedral when, in 1531, a heretic was solemnly cursed by the clergy with bell, book and candle. 'What a shout and noise was there', reports a contemporary witness; 'what terrible fear; what holding up of hands to Heaven: that curse was so terrible.' In the subsequent decades, moreover, many layfolk continued to submit themselves penitently to ecclesiastical discipline. Thus in 1554, in the parish church at Marystow, a public penance for fornication was performed by Elizabeth Hardimead, while in 1561, in the cathedral, a similarly humiliating punishment for slander and sexual misconduct was borne by Alphington's John Norden. Norden consented to stand there bareheaded, bare-footed, and clothed symbolically in a white sheet.[93]

By this date, nevertheless, the submissiveness of the laity would seem to have markedly declined. In 1533, for example, an offender named Rewe appears to have refused to perform the penance imposed upon him. Between 1533 and 1538 – after his excommunication by an ecclesiastical court for marrying without banns, 'contrary to the laws and customs of holy Church' – William Senthill of Moretonhampstead apparently attempted to secure redress by suing his parish priest in the Court of Chancery. Before the end of Henry's reign, moreover, the diocesan official who excommunicated Richard Mayne of Cornwood for adultery was subsequently brought by

---

[92] Hooker, *Commonplace Book*, fol. 352; CAB 3552, fols. 140, 145–8; CCB 855A, fols. 222, 234–4v; CCB 855B, sub 17 December 1566, 28 February 1566/7, 10 March 1566/7; CCB 856, fols. 449v–53.

[93] *Acts and Monuments*, II, p. 1038; CCB 855, fol. 158; CCB 855A, fol. 62.

him before the Court of Star Chamber to be sued for slander. By the 1550s resistance was no longer rare. When John Star of Shute was summoned to appear before a Church court for committing fornication, he angrily 'gave the summoner one blow, with his fist'. At Hatherleigh a similar summons was persistently evaded by William Morecombe, 'because he would not be a-cited and called by the law', and at Upottery Joan Sweetland was equally determined in her refusal to attend the court to which she had been summoned. At Swimbridge William Budd 'could not agree' with his parish priest about his 'penance-doing'. And William Gooding of Whitchurch, though compelled to perform a public penance for adultery in the market-place at Tavistock, nevertheless ignored the command of the ecclesiastical court to avoid the company of his concubine and blithely continued in the adulterous liaison.[94]

More contemptuous still were the people of Tiverton. One of their number, John King, was excommunicated in *circa* 1562 for his 'incontumacy and evil life'. Yet King, 'being so stout and disobedient, would in no wise obey', reported his parish priest to the bishop's chancellor. 'But came at Evensong or Evening Prayer, and would not void for anything that I could say; but gave railing words, until the constables sent for him and commanded him out of the church.' 'So little reverence', lamented the priest, 'he gave to the spiritual laws.' The anxious cleric urged the chancellor to have King punished: 'for his fault is great, by report of his neighbours; and his disobedience is worse, as he doth take the law to be of no force'. 'Wherefore', he added revealingly, 'if due punishment should miss upon him, to the example of others, it were in vain for us in Tiverton to declare and excommunicate any. The people are so stout, and careth so little what they do and how evil they live, when they will laugh out the matter and say, "It is but a money matter." So little they regard it.' In 1531 excommunication had evoked fear; now it was often treated with derision.[95]

A less overt but equally dangerous challenge to ecclesiastical discipline was being mounted by the citizens of Exeter. In the early years of Elizabeth's reign their mayors began to assume responsibility for the detection and punishment of incontinence within the city – a function which had traditionally belonged to the spiritual authorities. 'By which your indirect dealing', complained the ecclesiastical commissioners to the mayor in 1570, 'you do, not a little, prejudice and derogate the queen's majesty's ecclesiastical laws.' Nor was this the only indication of an increasingly assertive attitude among the citizens. A long-standing dispute with the cathedral canons, concerning jurisdiction in the cathedral close, had in 1547 erupted into a violent

---

[94] CCB 778, sub 30 November 1533; CCB 855, fols. 115v–16, 186, 191–1v, 210v, 375, 376v; C 1 892/17–18; STAC 2/32/28; Pill 1968, p. 51.
[95] CCB 779, letter at back of volume, *c.* 1562.

brawl. And in 1560, when the Bishop of Exeter procured a commission of the peace, the citizens resolutely barred him from their guildhall and thus forced him to withdraw. The resistance was headed by Robert Midwinter. It was therefore not without reason that the bishop, when writing to the Mayor of Exeter in 1561, referred to 'all [the] old matters which heretofore hath bred choler and stomach between us'.[96]

A final approximate index of attitudes is provided by the level of violence to which clerics might be subjected. The evidence would suggest that on the eve of the Reformation this was relatively low: the alleged attack upon a 'clerk' at St Teath in 1527[97] was an exceptional occurrence. Again – as was indicated, for example, by a royal proclamation of 1547[98] – it was in the Reformation decades that the level appears to have most markedly risen.

Threatening behaviour was increasingly reported. In as early as *circa* 1530, at Marystow, the vicar was physically intimidated by five men. These, he complained, 'daily do threaten and menace [him]; whereby [he] is in daily fear and dread to go and come to his parish church, to do and say his divine services'. In 1534, at St Cleer, a chaplain similarly protested against his terrorization by a number of 'misruled persons', who 'daily do menace and threaten [him]'. 'Whereby', he added, 'he is in dread of his life, and dare not to tarry and dwell in the said country.' At Launceston, in 1538, another chaplain was threatened with death by a group of some 20 men; they declared openly that 'they will have a limb or an arm of him'. In 1540, at Bridestow, the parson was terrorized by several laymen with 'fearful words', and in *circa* 1546, at Paul, the vicar was threatened by his own parishioners. In Mary's reign the vicar of Halberton fled from his cure after less than 18 months, 'fearing of his life'. Richard Berry – who had already killed one man – had begun to threaten him with 'many vile words'. William Harris, when rebuked by the vicar of Marldon in 1558, responded by challenging the priest to '[ex]change a four or five blows'; and an equally pugnacious reaction was evoked from Oliver Bennett when, in 1562, he was cited by the vicar of Spreyton to appear at Exeter before the Archdeacon's Court. Bennett, it was reported, 'did thrust the vicar into the breast with his fist, and bade him come out into the churchyard; and said that the vicar should go out, and he would fight with him'.[99]

A number of clerics were irreverently manhandled. In 1541 the vicar

---

[96] CCB 41, p. 51; Harleian 352, fols. 64v–5; Hooker, Commonplace Book, fol. 353; *Exeter Records*, p. 46.
[97] STAC 2/22/376.
[98] *TRP*, 1, p. 407.
[99] STAC 2/15/316; 21/163; 25/310; 30/104; 31/178; CCB 855, fols. 287–7v, 366–6v; CCB 855A, fols. 222, 234–4v.

of Awliscombe was kidnapped by Edward Sewell, John Pring, and other of his own parishioners: they imprisoned him forcibly in the house of John Mitchell. In 1556, at St Keyne, parishioners broke into the parsonage at night and unceremoniously hauled the parson from his bed. They also pulled out the woman who, before the official annulment of clerical marriages, had been his wife. Parson and wife were then fastened into the stocks at Duloe, in which ignominious position they were compelled to remain until the following midday. Another priest was forced to sit in the stocks at Silverton in 1557; his humiliation, which was inflicted by William Furse, lasted from six or seven o'clock in the morning until one in the afternoon. Even less respectful of the cloth were the bailiffs William More and Richard Purnell when, in 1568, they attempted to arrest the vicar of St Cleer in his parish church. They pulled him down by his arms and coat, and tore the gown from his back. Only the intervention of his wife and two sons prevented them from dragging him out of the church by his legs.[100]

Several assaults were evidently intended to cause discomfort, pain, or even injury. The treatment meted out in 1560 to the vicar of North Tawton was comparatively mild. John Leathener first insulted him – 'I pray you, get you out of my company, for I cannot abide you!' – and then flung his ale into the cleric's face. Other attacks were more serious. At St Cleer in 1534 the terrorized chaplain was reportedly beaten up by some 20 men, and a group of similar size was said to have attacked the chaplain at Launceston in 1538. Sometimes fists were used. William Furse, quarrelling angrily with a priest at Silverton in 1557, 'by chance hit him upon the nose, and it gushed out with blood'. Thereupon the priest 'was drunk, and fell down'. Another priest, attacked by William Harris at Paignton in 1558, received 'a blow with his fist, between the shoulder and head'.[101]

Weapons, however, might also be employed. When, in 1557, the vicar of Morebath attempted to collect an unpaid tithe from one of his parishioners, he encountered violent resistance. After 'multiplying words', priest and layman 'went by the ears together, and were both down', and as they wrestled together on the ground the vicar was cut by his opponent's sword. In 1558 Thomas Jewett, determined to prevent the vicar of Burrington from passing through his land, first aimed a blow at the priest with his staff and then hurled a stone, catching the vicar between the shoulders. 'And thereupon the said vicar departed home to the vicarage, and tarried in the said ground no longer.' When subsequently testifying in the Consistory Court, the battered priest 'brought in a great stone, which he affirmed to be the stone that Jewett aforenamed threw at him'. A similar treatment

---

[100] STAC 2/19/341; CCB 855, fols. 36v, 190v; CCB 856, fols. 297–7v.
[101] STAC 2/15/316; 30/104; CCB 855, fols. 190v, 366–6v, 470–0v.

was accorded to the vicar of Exminster when, in this same year, he attempted to admonish Thomas Langmead for chastising a servant. 'What hast thou, priest, to do withal?', exploded Langmead. 'In a fury', he lashed at the priest with a stick and inflicted two stripes upon his back. In this year also an equally injudicious attempt to discipline an errant layman brought similar violence upon the vicar of Colebrooke. The vicar was confronted by John Ball, and was asked to explain why he had laid a charge against him of marital misconduct. Ball then began to attack the unfortunate cleric with a stick, and only the intervention of a third party prevented a serious assault.[102]

On occasion the violence was positively homicidal. In 1529, in one north Devon parish, the priest refused to bury a parishioner unless first granted a cow as his mortuary. According to local report, the enraged parishioners thereupon forced their priest into the open grave and proceeded to bury him alive. By 1549, certainly, at least some laymen were eager to kill priests. After the south-western rebellion the vicar of St Thomas' was hanged from his own church tower by Bernard Duffield. Hooker noted that Duffield, a servant of Lord Russell, was 'nothing slack to follow his commission'. Indeed he inflicted the maximum humiliation upon the priest by dressing him in his mass-vestments, and suspending a holy-water bucket, sprinkler, sacring bell, beads and other accoutrements about him as he dangled in chains. 'There he, with the same about him, remained a long time.' Between 1551 and 1553, moreover, there were attempts to murder the Bishop of Exeter himself. The culprits' identities are not recorded, but the incidents occurred at Bodmin and Totnes.[103]

The trend should not be exaggerated. On the eve of the Reformation, reverence for clerics had been by no means total; nor was it wholly eradicated in the subsequent decades. Some sources, particularly legal records, inevitably emphasize discords rather than harmonies in the relationship between people and priests. These qualifications made, an examination of the verbal, financial and behavioural evidence would seem to indicate a marked diminution of respect for the clergy in the Reformation years. The vicar of Gulval must have spoken for many of his clerical colleagues when, in 1553–5, he lamented 'the unquiet time which lately hath grown'. It had witnessed, he complained, 'the disturbance of divers parsons and vicars'.[104]

---

[102] CCB 855, fols. 275–5v, 356–6v, 361–1v, 369v–70.
[103] Prince 1701, pp. 181–2; 'Description of Exeter', p. 68; Hooker, Commonplace Book, fol. 350.
[104] C 1 1378/19–21.

7

Summation of Part One

How, in brief, did the people of the South-West respond to the challenge of the Reformation?

The region has conventionally been stereotyped as remote, conservative and change-resistant. The available evidence, however, would indicate that the decline of popular support for the traditional activities and institutions was in reality both more sudden and more drastic than has usually been assumed. Until *circa* 1530 the overall level of this support would appear to have remained high. By 1547, nevertheless, it had already started to diminish, and in Edward's reign, in most places, it experienced a devastating collapse. Even in the favourable conditions of Mary's reign its recovery was no more than partial, and after the accession of Elizabeth it again slumped. By the 1560s, only a limited minority of the region's inhabitants could still be described as verbally, financially or actively supportive of the old religion.

The decline of popular Catholicism would seem in general to have proceeded more rapidly in the east of the region than in the west. It is possibly significant that bequests to specifically traditionalist activities and institutions appear in 43% of the Cornish wills in the years 1520–69, as against 35% of the Devonian.[1] Certainly it was in Cornwall that insurrection was plotted in 1537, that serious rioting occurred in 1548, and that the rebellion originated in 1549, whereas in this last crisis it was Devon that seems to have provided the bulk of the region's active loyalists. Yet the contrast should not be exaggerated. Devon also contained traditionalists, as was apparent in 1549. Cornwall, on the other hand, produced a number of loyalists in 1548–9, as well as some overt anti-Catholics like Sampson Jackman and Agnes Priest. In addition a variety of impieties – such as the exploitation of churches, the defrauding of clerics, and the theft of sacramental apparatus – were committed in Cornwall as well as in Devon: John

---

[1] Specifically traditionalist activities and institutions include vestments, altar plate, sacrament lights, intercessions, images, rood-lofts, beads, monks, friars and religious guilds.

145

Jelly of Davidstow affords a conspicuous example. In both counties, above all, the predominant reaction to assaults upon the old religion was usually acquiescence rather than resistance.

In general the decline of Catholic commitment would seem to have proceeded more swiftly among townsmen than among their rural counterparts. Many of the most virulent anti-Catholics lived in Exeter, Axminster, Totnes and other towns. In 1548 most of the rioters came from modest-sized communities like St Keverne, and were husbandmen, yeomen or mariners; many of the loyalists came from Launceston, Plymouth and Stratton. In 1549 the rebellion appears to have drawn recruits primarily from rural parishes like Sampford Courtenay, whereas the loyalist bastions were Exeter, Plymouth, Totnes and other towns. Again, however, the distinction should not be overdrawn. Most towns, including Exeter and Plymouth, contained traditionalist factions, and some, including Bodmin and Torrington, produced rebels in 1549. On the other hand, rural parishes contributed a number of loyalists in 1548–9, and proved capable of producing anti-Catholics like Kenton's Martin Alley and Whitchurch's William Gooding.[2] They saw an increasingly cynical treatment of clerics, of church goods, and of intercessory endowments; and they seem in most cases to have complied with official instructions for the cessation of masses and the removal of altars, images, and other Catholic apparatus. In rural as well as urban communities, moreover, bequests to traditionalist activities and institutions appear in approximately 80% of the wills in the years 1520–44, but in only approximately 20% of those in the years 1545–69. In both town and countryside the decline was unmistakable.

Even less clearly defined were distinctions of age and of gender. It appears inherently probable that the young were quicker than their elders to abandon the traditional religion. Certainly many anti-Catholics, like Philip Nichols, were relatively young, and many Catholics, like the Clyst St Mary woman who continued to use prayer-beads in 1549, were old.[3] In a number of families, such as the Trottes of Cullompton, the traditionalist piety of parents was manifestly not emulated by their children. Nevertheless the young might occasionally remain Catholic, as did the children of Agnes Priest in Mary's reign. But of greatest significance is the fact that, in the course of the Reformation decades, even the older age groups would seem in general to have moved decisively away from traditional Catholicism. This shift is

---

[2] As an illustration of the limitations of sociological interpretation, it may be noted that both traditionalists and non-traditionalists were to be found among (a) shoemakers (e.g. Maunder of Sampford Courtenay, Philip Gammon); (b) merchants (e.g. John Wolcott, John Budleigh); (c) clothiers (e.g. Richard Taylor, the Exeter shearmen); (d) mariners (e.g. the St Keverne mariners in 1548, the Exmouth mariners in 1549); (e) yeomen (e.g. John Chapel, John Helier); and (f) husbandmen (e.g. Richard Rawe, John Warren).

[3] For Nichols' self-description as 'young', see *Copy of a Letter*, p. 36.

unquestionably evident among testators, who were usually of above-average age. It is also of note that both Thomas Bennett and Agnes Priest, at the time of their anti-Catholic outbursts, were more than 50 years old.[4]

Were women in general more conservative than men? Thomas Cranmer, denouncing the south-western rebels in 1549, criticized 'fond [i.e. foolish] women, which commonly follow superstition rather than true religion'.[5] Females of this type undoubtedly existed: they included the rioters at St Nicholas' Priory in 1536, the Clyst St Mary bead-user in 1549, and the wives who donated a manual to Morebath church in Mary's reign. On the other hand, many of the identifiable traditionalists – like Smith, Staplehead and Wolcott at Exeter – were in fact men; and in 1548–9 the rioters and rebels were of course predominantly male. Among the anti-Catholics, moreover, were a number of women like Joan Alley, Agnes Priest and the wife of Thomas Bennett. And although female wills in the years 1520–69 are relatively few, it may be significant that they in fact contain a somewhat lower proportion of bequests to traditionalist purposes than do their male equivalents.

For the average inhabitant of the South-West – whether Devonian or Cornish, urban or rural, young or old, male or female – the Reformation unquestionably entailed a dramatic decline of support for traditional religion. John Hooker observed that the pre-Reformation era had been characterized by 'the blind devotion of the people'. Richard Carew agreed that it had been a time when 'devotion ... exceeded knowledge'. Both men, in Elizabeth's reign, had no doubt that this age of 'devotion' was decisively past.

---

[4] For Bennett and Priest, see *Acts and Monuments*, II, pp. 1040, 2052.
[5] *EHD*, p. 378.

Part Two

EXPLANATION

8

Spiritual motivations: Lutheranism, Calvinism and other faiths

That the period 1530–70 witnessed a devastating erosion of popular Catholicism would seem to be established beyond reasonable doubt. Yet the causal factors behind this phenomenon remain far from self-evident. With what justification may it be attributed to an upsurge of enthusiasm for an alternative brand of Christianity?

The verbal evidence unquestionably indicates that, in a number of cases, abandonment of traditional Catholicism was the result of positive conversion to Protestant beliefs. The most crucial of these beliefs concerned the location of religious authority and the means of human salvation. The former was held by Protestants to reside ultimately in the Bible rather than in the institutional Church. The latter they asserted to be solely by faith in the atoning work of Christ, and not by meritorious actions, participation in sacraments, or the intercession of saints.

The distinctively Protestant attitude towards the Bible was expressed with particular vigour by Philip Nichols of Totnes in the years 1547–9. Not only did this young layman study it personally in his native tongue – 'I follow the English translators', he records, 'whose learning I cannot correct' – he in fact revered it as the living voice of God himself. 'Being read unto the people', he believed, 'to instruction and edifying of the congregation, [it] is the word of God; yea, Christ, the bread of life, which came from Heaven, so that who so eateth thereof shall live ever.' In consequence he regarded it as the final authority for Christians, 'alone sufficient to teach us the true worship of God, faith in his promises, and, in all good works, to walk the way to everlasting life', and he explicitly agreed with Luther that it – rather than the Church – constituted the 'touchstone' by which all doctrine should be assessed. 'I say plainly', he insisted, 'that to deny the scripture – the prophets and apostles whose prophecies are written in the Bible – to be a sufficient doctrine and instruction necessary for our salvation; or to say that it ought not to be the touchstone and trial of all other doctrines, above all other doctrines of any other men, above their laws, decrees, and customs or ceremonies, beside this book: whether it be

151

of men or angels, it is not only heresy but also a devilish and damnable doctrine.'[1]

This Protestant concept of biblical authority undoubtedly underlay Nichols' hostility to traditional Catholicism. Whereas, for example, he commended the Prayerbook of 1549 for its biblical content, he condemned the abrogated Latin service as having 'little scripture in it, saving here and there a patch; and the rest partly out of some friar's bosom, a piece out of some monk's cloister, another portion out of some book of false, feigned Lives and Miracles'. The traditional intercessions for the dead he similarly dismissed as without biblical foundation: 'Christ speaketh not any one word of Purgatory – no, nor any place of all the scriptures, from the first word of *Genesis* to the last of St John's *Revelation.*' 'As for matins-mumblers and mass-mongers, with *diriges* and trentals, with such superstitious prayers: the scripture speaketh not of them.' And it was largely on such grounds that he attacked the cult of images. 'All the scriptures', he declared, 'cry out upon [images], even from the beginning of the Old Testament to the latter end of the New.' 'If ye shall read the scriptures', he assured the south-western rebels, 'ye shall find almost no leaf void of some warning to beware of worshipping images, nor void of God's threatening for that most grievous wickedness.'[2]

Nor was Nichols the only layman whose anti-Catholicism is attributable to a Protestant biblicism. At Exeter, in 1531, the established Church was denounced by Thomas Bennett for claiming that the word of the pope was as authoritative as the word of God. Bennett's anti-papal attitudes would indeed seem to have sprung largely from a personal study of the biblical prophecies, which led him to identify the pope with the Antichrist, the whore of Babylon, and other predicted enemies of the truth. A similar conviction regarding the authority of scripture is also discernible behind the anti-Catholicism of Philip Gammon at Axminster in 1535–6 and of John Bougin at Totnes in 1548. Gammon proclaimed, for example, 'that it was written in the Gospels that, if a man were not disposed to fast nor abstain, he might choose: for he was bound by no means to fast, but at his pleasure'. Bougin, in the will which he wrote 'with my own hand', bequeathed his soul to God and his body to Christian burial, 'abolishing all feig[ned] ceremonies contrary to holy scripture, which is God's word and commandment'. 'For so is my belief', he explained, 'as the very word of God doth teach me, written in the Bi[ble].'[3]

Equally biblicist was Agnes Priest of Boyton in the reign of Mary. 'Albeit she was of such simplicity and without learning', says Foxe, 'yet you could

[1] *Copy of a Letter*, esp. pp. 3, 14–27, 42–4, 55–6.
[2] Royal 18 B XI, fols. 21–6; *Godly New Story*, p. 47; *Copy of a Letter*, pp. 49–51.
[3] *Acts and Monuments*, II, pp. 1037–40; STAC 2/2/267; Murray, 3, John Bougin, 1548.

declare no place of scripture but she would tell you the chapter. Yea, she would recite to you the names of all the books of the Bible.' It was largely this enthusiasm for the scriptures that impelled her not only to reject the restored Catholic practices but also openly to controvert the traditionalist clergy. Auricular confession, for example, she denounced as contrary to scripture – which (she pointed out) says 'Who can number his sins?' She informed a craftsman whom she found restoring images in Exeter Cathedral that he was a 'whore-hunter': 'for', she explained to him, 'doth not God say, "You go a-whoring after strange gods, figures of your own making"?' She was even emboldened by her confidence in scripture to debate sacramental theology with the Bishop of Exeter. Her biblicism, moreover, was shared by many of the townsmen of South Molton. In 1562, following the departure of their minister, William Ramsey, to a new pastorate at Chard, these evidently fervent Protestants urged him to send them a letter containing 'some comfortable places of the scriptures'. His reply to their 'godly request' was a lengthy epistle, 'drawn out of the lively and most pure veins of the divine scriptures, as well Old as New Testament'.[4]

A Protestant attitude towards the Bible was in most cases accompanied by a Protestant concept of salvation. At Exeter in 1531 Thomas Bennett reportedly declared the true Church to exist 'where the true faith and confidence in Christ's death and passion, and his only merits and deservings, are extolled, and our own depressed'. This fundamental soteriological conviction apparently led him to regard the eucharist as essentially commemorative rather than miraculous: it was to be celebrated 'in remembrance of [Christ's] blessed passion and only sacrifice upon the cross, once for all'. For the same reason he rejected intercession for the souls in 'feigned Purgatory', and vigorously repudiated the offering of prayers to the saints. 'Christ', he explained to supporters of saint veneration, 'is our only advocate, mediator, and patron before God his Father, making intercession for us.' 'It is God only upon whose name we must call. And we have no other advocate unto him but only Jesus Christ, who died for us and now sitteth at the right hand of the Father to be an advocate for us; and by him must we offer and make our prayers to God, if we will have them to take place and to be heard.'[5]

The repudiation of purgatorial beliefs by Philip Nichols was similarly a logical consequence of his Protestant soteriology. 'As touching Purgatory', he asserted, '... the blood of our Lord and Saviour Jesus Christ is as able to wash away, to cleanse, to remit and to cover all the sins of as many as live and die in his faith as he was (by the same faith) to purge and wash all our sins clean away at our baptism – before we had reason or

---

[4] *Acts and Monuments*, II, pp. 2049–52; Lansdowne 377, fol. 8v.
[5] *Acts and Monuments*, II, pp. 1037–40.

knowledge in our own selves to seek or take refuge [in] his mercy, or to make any claim to his most bitter passion.' 'The souls of them that die in the state of grace – that is, in the true faith of our Lord Jesus Christ – are sure to be glorified in Heaven, together with their bodies at the general resurrection. And in the mean time, they sleep in Abraham's lap (saith scripture) in rest and peace, in hope and expectation of the joys to come.' And since, argued Nichols, the wicked and unbelieving proceed immediately to Hell, a purgatorial 'third place' is altogether unneeded. One might equally claim a fourth place for the Devil, he mocked: if souls be refused entry into Heaven until purged of their wickedness, may not they be debarred from Hell until purged of their virtue? This confidence in the doctrine of justification by faith alone in fact underpinned Nichols' hostility to the entire sacramental structure of traditional Catholicism. The communion he regarded as essentially a spiritual reception of Christ in remembrance of his death. In consequence the sacrament was not to be superstitiously reserved or venerated, but should be received by the laity frequently and in both kinds. Services, moreover, should be conducted in English, so that laymen could intelligently participate.[6]

Convictions of this type were also expressed by Agnes Priest in the reign of Mary. Behind her rejection of trentals, *diriges*, soul-masses and purchased prayers there again lay a resolute confidence in the sufficiency of Christ's atonement, for, she declared, 'God's Son hath, by his passion, purged all'. And again this led logically to the belief that the eucharist was non-miraculous. 'Christ', she reportedly asserted, 'did command it to be eaten and drunken in remembrance of his most blessed passion, our redemption'; it remained 'nothing but very bread and wine'. When the Bishop of Exeter quoted to her the words spoken by Christ over the bread and the wine, she replied bluntly that 'he meant that it is his body and blood not carnally but sacramentally'. Christ, she insisted, is in Heaven, and is not to be found on this earth in bread; his sacrifice on Calvary was complete, and requires no sacramental repetition.[7]

That distinctively Protestant beliefs were beginning to be expressed orally or in writing by at least some members of the non-gentle laity in the period 1530–70 is thus beyond dispute. At the same time, however, there can be equally little doubt that such assertions of commitment to the new religion remained comparatively uncommon. In the great majority of recorded cases, in fact, a verbal, financial or behavioural declension from traditional Catholicism was not accompanied by any expression of Protestant conviction. Markedly more typical than Agnes Priest were Martin Alley, William Gooding

---

[6] Royal 18 B XI, fols. 11–17v, 22–4, 25–6.
[7] *Acts and Monuments*, II, pp. 2049–52.

or Christopher Sampford, none of whom seems ever to have justified his unmistakable hostility to the old religion by an appeal to the Bible or by a declaration of solifidian belief.[8] When testifying in court, certainly, defendants charged with such offences sought usually to deny the accusation – as did the three alleged disdainers of the rood at Swimbridge who appeared before the Consistory Court in 1557[9] – or to offer some form of excuse, as was attempted by Roger Gill and Thomas Perry of Axminster before the same court in 1556. Gill admitted weeks of absence from the restored Catholic services but claimed that he had been sick. Perry, facing a similar charge, explained that he was an ostler at a local inn, and thus was often commanded by his master to attend the guests at service-time. 'But when they have no guests', he assured the court, 'then [he] goeth to the church, and goeth in procession, and doth all other things as becometh a Christian man to do.'[10]

That the overt expression of Protestant convictions remained relatively rare is confirmed by a study of the wills. The characteristically Protestant preamble to a will not only omits the traditional bequest of the testator's soul to Our Lady or to the saints, but also declares his confidence in its salvation by the atoning work of Christ. Terminology of this type is conspicuously absent from all of the 30 wills with recorded formulae in the years 1520–9, and appears in at most 2 of the 30 in the years 1530–9. In 1536 the Cornishman William Nanfan expressed his belief that God would grant, 'after this present and miserable life, eternal life to all faithful souls in the joy everlasting' – a statement which possibly implies a denial of Purgatory – while in 1538 John Forde of Ashburton commended his soul 'to Almighty God and to his infinite mercy, trusting that by the merits of his passion [I am] to have the fruition of his Godhead in Heaven'. The Protestantism of even these two testators is highly doubtful: Forde in fact arranged prayers and masses for his soul in friaries and in 20 local churches.[11] Protestant phraseology, moreover, is found in only 3 of the 37 wills with formulae in the years 1540–9. Two of these three testators, namely Nicholas Wise in 1540 and Richard Colwill in 1547, may not have been permanently resident in the South-West: Wise, though associated with Sidenham and Bodmin, was buried at Shoreditch, and Colwill owned land both in Devon and elsewhere. Within the sample, therefore, the only certain resident of the region to express an unambiguously Protestant commitment before 1550 was John Bougin of Totnes. In 1548 he arranged psalms at his burial, instead

[8] See above, pp. 28–9, 31, 40, 43, 78–9, 98, 102–3, 128, 130, 139, 141, 146; below, pp. 175, 213, 216.
[9] See above, pp. 62, 79–80.
[10] CCB 855, fols. 49, 63; see also above, p. 43.
[11] PROB 11 26, fol. 79v; 27, fol. 4v.

of 'ceremonies contrary to holy scripture', and, in an implicit repudiation of purgatorial belief, he specified that these were to be recited 'in the honour of God, and with thanksgiving that it hath so pleased him to call me to his mercy and grace'.[12]

Of the 18 wills with recorded formulae from January 1550 to July 1553, a neutral commendation of the soul to God is found in 11; that made in 1551 by a husbandman of Alvington, Roger Birdwood, provides an example. A twelfth, made by John Hart of Axminster in 1552, fails even to bequeath the soul. A Protestant confidence in the sufficiency of Christ's atonement is expressed in the remaining six, which were made by John Bond of Crediton and John Harris of Stowford in 1550, by Philip Mayhew of Exeter in 1551, by John Anthony of Dartmouth and John Hurst of Exeter in 1552, and by William Amadas of Plymouth in 1553. Bond commended himself 'to Almighty God and to his Son Jesu Christ, by whose blood and passion I verily trust to be saved', while Mayhew entrusted himself to 'my Lord God, my only saviour and redeemer'. Anthony, a merchant, bequeathed his soul to God, 'believing that by the merits of Christ's passion [I am] to have remission of all my sins, and to be one of the same number that are elected to be with him in everlasting glory'. Hurst, another merchant, committed himself to 'Almighty God, my maker, who hath bought me with his precious blood; whereupon my faith and hope is that I shall inherit the kingdom of Heaven'. Amadas, in June 1553, commended himself to Christ, 'in whom and by whom is all my whole trust of clean remission and forgiveness of my sins'.[13]

The commitment of William Amadas to the new religion is beyond doubt, but in the five other cases it is less certain that a solifidian formula reflects an internalized personal conviction rather than a dutiful conformity to the official norms. A degree of conformism is suggested by the rapidity with which such terminology ceased to appear after the death of Edward VI: it is found in at most 4 of the 32 wills with formulae in the years 1553–9. In 1554 the Devonian Henry Reynold required burial 'according unto God's holy word', and in 1558 John Lane of Broadhembury declared himself to be 'perfect in mind and, trusting in Jesu, safe in soul'. The former appears to have rejected funereal intercessions as unscriptural, and the latter to have been assured of his salvation through Christ. Both Reynold and Lane, nevertheless, required the disposal of their goods 'for the wealth of my soul' or 'for my soul'; therefore the only unambiguously Protestant wills from this period were those made by John Drake of Exeter in 1554 and Griffith Ameredith, also of that city, in 1557. Drake – a merchant, who

---

[12] PROB 11 28, fol. 149; F44 Alen, Richard Colwill, 1547; Murray, 3, John Bougin, 1548.
[13] PROB 11 33, fol. 155; 34, fols. 154v, 225; 35, fols. 169, 212; 36, fol. 20v; 44, fol. 274; 42A, Roger Birdwood, 1551. For Amadas, see also below, p. 248.

had actively resisted the rebellion of 1549 – proclaimed his 'faithful trust and hope in the infinite goodness of Almighty God, my maker and redeemer', and his expectation of eternal life 'after my departing out of this wretched and transitory life'. Ameredith, a draper, committed himself to God, 'trusting to be saved by the shedding of Christ's blood, and in all the merits of his passion'.[14]

Even after the restoration of Protestant government under Elizabeth I such terminology was far from common: it appears in no more than 4 of the 30 wills with formulae in the years 1560–9. In 1560 William Lake, a merchant of Plymouth, described himself as a 'most miserable sinner', and appealed to God 'that the merits of thy Son Jesus Christ may be a full redemption and satisfaction for the trespasses that I have done or committed since I came into this wretched world, so that my most wretched soul may be saved amongst thy saints'. In 1562 Joan Lake of Plymouth – possibly his widow – expressed a similar confidence in her salvation 'by no other means' than the passion of Christ. In this year also a yeoman of Combe Pyne, John Helier, declared that he expected to receive, through the merits of Christ's passion and resurrection, 'the fruition of his Godhead in Heaven'. And in 1566 Robert Ebsworthy of Bridestow bequeathed 'my soul to God, and my body to the earth, and my sin to the Devil; desiring God, for Christ's sake, to forgive them'. Phraseology of this type is nevertheless absent from the 26 other wills in the sample. Most, like those made by Elizabeth Davey, a widow of St Austell, in 1564, and John Rewe, a yeoman of Culmstock, in 1566, merely included a neutral commendation of the soul to God. Although other possible indications of Protestantism occasionally appear – in 1560 John Hawkins of Axminster described his executors, William Mallock and Walter Bowden, as 'my well-beloved friends in Christ' – the wills would thus indicate that overt declarations of belief in the new religion were still comparatively few.[15]

The impression conveyed by the verbal evidence is therefore that a positive commitment to Protestantism, though increasingly discernible among members of the non-gentle laity in the Reformation decades, nevertheless remained limited to a relatively small proportion of the regional population. To what extent is this impression substantiated by the evidence of financial activity?

In the reign of Edward VI, and again in the early years of Elizabeth I, the expenditure of south-western parishes upon the apparatus of Protestant

[14] PROB 11 37, fols. 144, 178; 41, fol. 243; 42A, John Lane, 1558. For Drake, see also above, pp. 36–7. For Ameredith, see Hooker, Commonplace Book, fol. 352.
[15] PROB 11 44, fol. 269v; 45, fol. 60v; 46, fols. 128v, 258v; 47, fol. 143; 48, fol. 459v; 49, fol. 233.

worship was generally dutiful and conformist but seldom enthusiastic: it seems rarely to have exceeded the minimum required by the law. Prayerbooks and psalters for the new services were acquired with relative promptitude by most of the parishes with extant accounts, firstly in 1549–53[16] and again in 1559–60.[17] Thus Woodbury, to cite but one example, bought its Communion Book in 1549 and two psalters in 1549–50; these were accompanied by 'four books of prick-song, to sing at the communion'. In 1552 the parishioners paid 4s 8d for 'a new Communion Book, when he was altered'. This, the second Edwardian Prayerbook, was carried to the village from Exeter. Finally, and with equally prompt obedience, the Elizabethan Prayerbook and two psalters were purchased by the parishioners in 1559. Other requisites of the Protestantized liturgy were similarly bought. Under both Edward and Elizabeth, in order to facilitate a congregational communion in both kinds, 'bread and wine for the parish' became everywhere a regular item of parochial expenditure.[18] Under both monarchs, moreover, the wooden tables necessary for the Protestant communion service seem generally to have been acquired; in 1550–1, for example, they were erected at Exeter Holy Trinity, Ashburton, Chagford, Woodbury and elsewhere.[19] These were provided with appropriate cloths,[20] and with kneeling mats[21] or benches[22] for the use of communicants. Occasionally, as at Exeter St John's Bow in 1569–70, a chancel was apparently reseated in order to accommodate the new service.[23] Early-Elizabethan parishes also provided

---

[16] CWA Woodbury, 1549–50, 1552. See also CWA Antony, 1553; CWA Ashburton, 1553; CWA Camborne, 1552; CWA Coldridge, 1553; CWA Crediton, 1552; CWA Dartmouth, 1552; CWA Exeter HT, 1552; CWA Exeter SJB, 1552; CWA Exeter SMM, fol. 12; CWA Exeter SMS, 1552; CWA Morebath, 1553; Additional 32243, HCWA Stratton, 1553; and *Tavistock Records*, p. 23.

[17] CWA Woodbury, 1559. See also CWA Antony, 1559; CWA Ashburton, 1560; CWA Braunton, 1559; CWA Camborne, 1560; CWA Chagford, 1560; CWA Coldridge, 1560; CWA Crediton, 1559; CWA Dartington, 1559; CWA Exeter SJB, 1559; CWA Exeter SMM, fol. 16; CWA Exeter SMS, 1559; CWA Exeter SP, 1560; CWA Kilmington, 1559; ? CWA Molland, 1559; CWA Morebath, 1559; CWA S. Tawton, 1559; CWA Winkleigh, 1560; Additional 32243, HCWA Stratton, 1559; and *Barnstaple Records*, I, pp. 212–13.

[18] E.g. CWA Woodbury, 1552–3; CWA Kilmington, 1560.

[19] For Edwardian tables, see CWA Ashburton, 1551; CWA Chagford, 1551; CWA Exeter HT, 1550; and CWA Woodbury, 1550. That most Exeter churches erected communion tables under Edward VI is indicated by *Inventories, Exeter*. For the official decree concerning tables in November 1550, see ER XV, fols. 119v–20. For Elizabethan tables, see CWA Chagford, 1560; CWA Coldridge, 1560; CWA Exeter SMS, 1559; CWA Molland, 1559; CWA S. Tawton, 1559; CWA Winkleigh, 1560; CWA Woodbury, 1559; Additional 32243, HCWA Stratton, 1559; *Barnstaple Records*, I, p. 213; and DRO 1660 A 12.

[20] E.g. CWA Coldridge, 1551; and CWA St Breock, fol. 16. For Brixham, Culmstock and Holcombe Burnell, see Pevsner 1952B, pp. 64, 98, 180.

[21] E.g. CWA Woodbury, 1553; and CWA Exeter SJB, 1568.

[22] E.g. CWA Crediton, 1552; and CWA Exeter SP, 1569.

[23] CWA Exeter SJB, 1570. See also possibly CWA Exeter SMS, 1567.

their clergy with desks[24] from which to read it, and with surplices[25] in which to officiate.

Yet the investment was rarely impressive. The surplices purchased by Stratton in 1562–3, by Crediton in 1566 and by Morebath in 1566–7 cost them no more than 15s, 10s and 10s respectively. At Exeter Holy Trinity, only 20d was devoted in Edward's reign to the construction of the communion table; and at Woodbury the equivalent expenditure amounted to a mere 6d. At the beginning of Elizabeth's reign 13s was expended upon the requisite table by Barnstaple, 5s 8d by Coldridge, and 3s by Stratton. At Woodbury in 1559 the parishioners invested precisely 4d, with which they purchased a 'plank to lie before the high altar'. Equally makeshift was the structure at Crediton, where, it was recorded in 1559, a broken Easter sepulchre 'serveth now for the holy communion table'. Although several Elizabethan communion tables, often finely carved, are still to be seen within the region's churches, not one is firmly datable to before 1570. It may also have been in these years that, as an economy measure, redundant Catholic copes were refashioned into the communion-table cloths surviving at Brixham, Culmstock and Holcombe Burnell.

The accounts and inventories show in addition that, with possible exceptions like the plain chalice of 1551 to be found at Totnes, few of the parishes invested in plate for the Protestant liturgy in Edward's reign, and that the larger communion cups designed to facilitate the reception of the wine by the lay congregation remained virtually unknown. At Exeter St Sidwell's, where the chalice had been stolen, communicants were thus compelled to drink from a redundant Catholic pyx.[26] Even between 1559 and 1570 the new type of cup appears to have been purchased only by the wealthiest of parochial communities, as at Exeter St Mary Major, Barnstaple, Bodmin and Stratton, and at Stratton the necessary £3 19s was not expended until 1569–70. Most parishes, like Woodbury in 1566–7 or Crediton in 1568, merely employed an old and intrinsically unsuitable Catholic chalice.[27] That it was only in the 1570s that the new vessels were commonly acquired is attested not only by the inventories and accounts but also by the surviving Elizabethan examples, of which the majority – made usually by the Exeter silversmith Jones or the Barnstaple craftsmen Cotton and Matthew – are

---

[24] E.g. CWA Ashburton, 1567; CWA Chagford, 1564; CWA Chudleigh, 1562; CWA Coldridge, 1560; CWA Dartington, 1565; CWA Molland, 1560; CWA S. Tawton, 1565; CWA Winkleigh, 1563; and CWA Woodbury, 1570. See also Cox 1915, pp. 197–9.

[25] E.g. Additional 32243, HCWA Stratton, 1563; CWA Crediton, 1566; and CWA Morebath, 1567.

[26] Pevsner 1952B, p. 297; *Inventories, Exeter*, p. 75.

[27] CWA Crediton, 1568; CWA Exeter SMM, fol. 16; CWA Woodbury, 1567; Additional 32243, HCWA Stratton, 1570; *Barnstaple Records*, I, p. 200; *Inventories, Cornwall*, p. 32.

dated by their inscriptions to this decade.[28] And if the expenditure of parishes upon the apparatus of Protestant worship was in general unenthusiastic, donations by individuals for this purpose were conspicuous by their absence: they appear in none of the Edwardian or early-Elizabethan wills.

Generally unspectacular too was the level of investment in Protestant preaching. Sponsors were to be found mainly among the corporations and substantial inhabitants of the towns, as at Ashburton in 1548–9, at Barnstaple in 1552 and 1560–2, at Crediton in 1551, 1552 and 1561–9, at Dartmouth in 1570, at Plymouth from as early as 1541 and again in 1547, 1549–50 and 1553, at South Molton in *circa* 1560, and at Totnes in 1548. In some cases – as at Totnes, where in 1548 John Bougin invested £6 on a series of 12 sermons – a programme of preaching was thus financed. Usually, however, the preaching was occasional rather than sustained, and the expenditure correspondingly modest. Thus 16s was invested by the churchwardens of Ashburton in 1548–9, 6s 8d by the corporation at Barnstaple in 1552, and 6s 8d and 5s by the corporation at Crediton in 1569. Only rarely, moreover, was the preaching of the new religion sponsored by a rural parish, as at South Tawton and Woodbury in 1564–5. The wardens of the former rewarded their preacher with 5s, while those of the latter provided a dinner.[29]

The expenditure of parishes upon Protestant or Protestant-approved literature was seldom more enthusiastic. Under Henry VIII, Edward VI and Elizabeth I, official instructions concerning the purchase of English Bibles and of Erasmus' paraphrases of the New Testament seem generally to have been obeyed. This obedience, nevertheless, was sometimes delayed; and expenditure on Protestant books that were not specifically required by the law remained almost unknown. A rare exception was provided by the parishioners of South Tawton, who in 1560–1 acquired a copy of Calvin's *Institutes*.[30] Investment by individuals remained similarly uncommon. Personal copies of the English Bible were owned by at least one inhabitant of Axminster in 1535–6, by Alice Bennett of Broadclyst in 1567, and by John Judde of Stratton in 1570. The most conspicuous exception to the prevailing indifference was provided by a merchant from Exeter, John

[28] E.g. CWA Chagford, 1574; CWA Chudleigh, 1573; CWA Crediton, 1577; CWA Exeter SJB, 1573; CWA Exeter SP, 1572; CWA Kilmington, 1576; ? CWA Morebath, 1571; and CWA Woodbury, 1572. See also Pevsner 1952B, p. 31. For Archbishop Parker's regulations concerning communion, see *Documents of Church History*, p. 471.

[29] CWA Ashburton, 1549; CWA Crediton, 1551–2, 1561, 1565, 1567–9; CWA S. Tawton, 1565; CWA Woodbury, 1565; *Barnstaple Records*, II, pp. 99, 126; CR Dartmouth, Receivers' Accounts, 1570; *Plymouth Records*, pp. 114, 117; PROB 11 44, fol. 274; Murray, 3, John Bougin, 1548; Lansdowne 377, fols. 8v–11; Thompson 1934–5, pp. 352–5. See also below, pp. 244–51.

[30] See below, pp. 190–2. For South Tawton, see CWA S. Tawton, 1561.

Budleigh. In December 1558 he financed the establishment of a printing-press in the city of Geneva, and appointed Rowland Hall to supervise the publication of the celebrated Geneva Bible. After his return to England in 1559 he settled in London, where he subsequently obtained a patent to print this quintessentially Protestant version of the scriptures.[31]

The financial evidence would thus confirm the impression that Protestant commitment, though undoubtedly beginning to appear among the non-gentle laity, was before 1570 confined to a comparatively small percentage of the south-western population. By the standard of parochial and individual investment in the old religion on the eve of the Reformation, expenditure on the new religion in the subsequent decades was but seldom more than mediocre.

The final type of evidence requiring examination is that of behaviour. That Protestantism was indeed beginning to secure a measure of positive support at the middle and lower-middle levels of lay society is again indicated by the increasing evidence – found under the non-Protestant as well as Protestant regimes – of an active popular participation in the meetings, prayer sessions, Bible-readings, services and other practices of the reformed religion. It was at Exeter that this phenomenon was most conspicuous. Here, in the years immediately preceding 1531, the schoolmaster Thomas Bennett was already engaged in 'conferences' with 'such as he could learn and understand to be favourers of the gospel and zealous of God's true religion'. 'Of such', it is reported, 'he would be inquisitive, and most desirous to join himself unto them'. In addition to Bennett himself this embryonic Protestant group appears to have included his wife and son – the latter of whom set up heretical bills on his father's behalf – as well as an unspecified number of 'friends'; amongst these were 'a shearman or two', who were suspected of possessing heretical literature. Before the end of Henry's reign, moreover, its numbers would seem to have risen. In 1537 the new and fervently Protestant Dean of Exeter, Simon Heynes, evidently regarded the citizens as promising candidates for conversion to the new religion: 'I like the people of this town very well', he declared, and contrasted them favourably with the conservative local clergy. By 1543, certainly, 'sundry persons' at Exeter were said to have been converted to the dean's heretical views.[32]

By 1549, furthermore, a significant number of the citizens had 'wholly [applied] themselves to the reformed religion and to the king's proceedings, and endeavoured themselves to obey and follow the same'. Among them were three merchants, namely John Budleigh, John Midwinter and John Periam; Periam, for example, was reportedly 'very zealous in the true religion

---

[31] STAC 2/2/267–72, 287; 29/111; CCB 855B, sub 28 February 1566/7; Additional 32243, HCWA Stratton, 1570; Garrett 1966, pp. 92–4.
[32] *Acts and Monuments*, II, pp. 1037–40; *LP*, XII(2), 557; *APC*, I, pp. 97, 150–1.

of the gospel'. These Protestant convictions must largely explain the willingness of both Budleigh and Periam to finance the suppression of the south-
western rebellion in 1549. Even in the difficult circumstances of Mary's
reign this group provided the city with a mayor, John Midwinter, with
several of the mayoral officers, and with a chamberlain, John Hooker. In
1554 it was reported that 'the Mayor of Exeter and his brethren' were
'of several religions'. Apparently also associated with the group were John
and William Kede. Described by Foxe as 'not only brethren in the flesh
but also in the truth', and as sons of the similarly Protestant Robert Kede,
these visited Agnes Priest of Boyton during her imprisonment for heresy
at Exeter in 1558.[33] And after the accession of Elizabeth, Protestant activity
in the city inevitably increased. The mayor in 1559, Robert Midwinter,
appears to have followed his brother John in supporting the new religion.
By December 1559, certainly, a number of the citizens were meeting each
day in the quire of Exeter Cathedral and, to the chagrin of the cathedral
clergy, were persistently singing English psalms. These 'godly doings of the
people' – who included several women as well as John Periam and Richard
Prestwood – were subsequently upheld by the royal visitors and by Archbishop Parker himself. In the early years of the reign, moreover, the new
morning services in the cathedral reportedly attracted a 'great resort of the
people'.[34]

Activity evidently Protestant in character is also discernible in other of
the urban communities. At Plymouth, between 1535 and 1537, a number
of the townsmen not only informed against religious traditionalists to
Thomas Cromwell, but also corresponded with the apparently Protestant
'curate' of St Margaret-in-Lothbury in London: he informed them of the
progress of the Reformation in the capital, and saluted them with 'greeting
and good health in our Lord Jesu Christ'. In 1535–6 one of this 'confederate
band' of Plymouthians was in fact denounced as a 'naughty heretic knave'.
They included William Ashridge, John Eliot, William Hawkins and James
Horsewell; most of these were merchants, and the latter three were mayors
of the town between 1535 and 1539. Protestantism would thus appear to
have motivated the active co-operation of William Hawkins in the dissolution of Plymouth's religious houses and the suppression of its traditional
image cults. It explains also the resolution with which he led the town's
resistance to the rebellion of 1549.[35]

---

[33] 'Description of Exeter', pp. 41, 55; Hooker, Commonplace Book, fols. 350, 351, 353,
357; Prince 1701, pp. 75, 387–8; SP 11/2/15; *Acts and Monuments*, II, p. 2051.
[34] Hooker, Commonplace Book, fols. 352–3; CAB 3552, fols. 140, 145–8. For Budleigh,
Periam and the 1549 rebellion, see above, p. 37.
[35] *LP*, VIII, 87, 676; X, 52, 462; XI, 166; XII (1), 152–3; XII (2), 480; XIX (2), 340. For
Hawkins, see above, pp. 26, 37, 67, 75, 117, 125.

Nor were Exeter and Plymouth altogether unique. At Axminster, in 1535–6, several 'friends and adherents' of the shoemaker Philip Gammon were said to be similarly 'suspect of heresy'. Among these were Robert Gammon – presumably a relative – and John Matthew.[36] At Chagford, by 1549, a tinner named Kingwell was reportedly 'earnest in the reformed religion'. This active commitment undoubtedly motivated his opposition to the rebellion of that year.[37] By Mary's reign, moreover, a Protestant group would seem to have operated in or around Launceston. This was apparently described by Agnes Priest in 1558 as a part of 'the true Church', which she held to exist wherever three or four were gathered in God's name; 'to that Church will I go', she declared, 'as long as I live'. It may have organized its own communion services, book-readings and sermons.[38]

At South Molton, certainly, there existed by 1562 an organized group of committed Protestants. This was described by their former pastor, William Ramsey, as 'the faithful congregation, which is in Christ Jesu, of South Molton'. Among the members to whom Ramsey sent greetings in his epistle were Robert Capp, Thomas Hunt, William Tucker and 'all them which are or hath been your mayors, constables, bailiffs or other officers, with all your burgesses, merchants, victuallers, artificers and labourers, which are in the Lord and promoters of the kingdom of God and Christ'. Nor were these Protestants alone in north Devon. Ramsey instructed that his epistle be read also to 'the congregations dispersed here and there abroad'.[39]

Other behaviour, particularly in Elizabeth's reign, would suggest that even in rural communities a positively supportive attitude towards the new religion was occasionally beginning to emerge. In 1560, for example, William Saward of Stoke-in-Teignhead apparently accused his vicar in the Consistory Court of refusing to administer the communion 'according unto the order of the Book of Common Prayer'. In 1562 the vicar of Rockbeare was accused of neglect in performance of the new services by four of his parishioners, namely John Cruchard, the yeoman John Holmere, Christopher Philmore and John Vicary. In 1569 the vicar of Ilsington was similarly accused by his parishioners of neglect in the administration of the communion.[40]

That active Protestant commitment was increasing in the Reformation decades is thus again evident. Again, nevertheless, there can be little doubt that this commitment remained limited to a relatively small percentage of the regional population. It is revealing, for example, that throughout this period the entire south-western peninsula produced no more than two

---

[36] STAC 2/2/267; 29/111.
[37] 'Description of Exeter', p. 66.
[38] *Acts and Monuments*, II, p. 2050.
[39] Lansdowne 377, esp. fols. 8v–9, 26v–8.
[40] CCB 855, fol. 430v; CCB 855A, fols. 215–17; CCB 856, fols. 319–19v, 320v.

martyrs for the Protestant faith. These, predictably, were Thomas Bennett and Agnes Priest: the former perished at the stake at Livery Dole, outside Exeter, in January 1532, while the latter was burned in Southernhay, outside the same city, in November 1558.[41] The region witnessed nothing remotely comparable to the holocausts of the South-East. Even more striking is the fact that, with these two exceptions, not one prosecution of a non-gentle layman on an explicit charge of adherence to the new religion would appear to be recorded for the South-West in the *Acts and Monuments* of John Foxe, in the writings of John Hooker, in the state papers, in the act-books and deposition-books of the Consistory Court, or in the registers of the Bishops of Exeter. The sources, it is true, are incomplete: thus it is only from evidence presented in Star Chamber that the heresy charge brought against Philip Gammon before the bishop's commissary is now known.[42] Nevertheless the evidence indicates that under Henry VIII and Mary the number of individuals prepared openly to flout the laws against Protestantism was never high.

Significant too was the general unwillingness of south-western people to actively resist the overtly anti-Protestant campaigns of the Marian regime. In January 1554 a number of local gentlemen, headed by the Carews, attempted to raise the region in support of the rebellion initiated in Kent by Sir Thomas Wyatt. The movement – which was led by Protestants, and which was at least partly pro-Protestant in its objectives – conspicuously failed to attract more than minimal support from the people of the South-West. Among the few exceptions were Peter Willis of Totnes and possibly John Budleigh, Nicholas Hilliard and Peter Hilliard of Exeter. The £50 owed to the queen in March 1554 by 'Peter Willis, of Totnes in the county of Devon, merchant apothecary', was probably a fine for his involvement in the insurrection. The citizens of Exeter nevertheless shut their gates against the rebels, who were reportedly opposed also by the townsmen of Totnes and by the inhabitants of the surrounding countryside. 'The commons of Devonshire', observed Sir John St Leger, 'are assuredly the queen's; and the city of Exeter also.' In consequence the collapse of the south-western revolt was both rapid and ignominious.[43]

Similarly indicative of the relative scarcity of Protestant commitment is the fact that less than 20 members of the region's non-gentle laity appear to have fled into continental exile in the reign of Mary. Of these the most important was the Exeter merchant John Budleigh. His son Thomas was later to record that 'my father, in the time of Queen Mary being noted

[41] *Acts and Monuments*, II, pp. 1037–40, 2049–52.
[42] STAC 2/2/267–72, 287; 23/273; 29/111.
[43] SP 11/2/11–16, 18, 26; 3/5, 10; Garrett 1966, pp. 92–4, 183, 337; Rowse 1941, pp. 305–7. See also Loades 1965; and Clark 1977, pp. 87–98.

and known to be an enemy to popery, was so cruelly threatened and so narrowly observed by those that maliced his religion that – for the safeguard of himself and my mother, who was wholly affected as my father – he knew no way so secure as to fly into Germany'. The Budleighs found refuge at Wesel and Frankfurt before settling in Geneva, where in 1557 they were received into membership of the Protestant congregation led by John Knox. By this date the Budleigh household included not only John, his wife, and their son Thomas, but also their daughter, their infant sons Miles and Zachary, and John's brother Nicholas, and to these must be added John's merchant apprentices, John Boggens and Richard Vivian, as well as his maidservant Eleanor. John himself was subsequently elected to be a senior of the congregation. Exeter may have provided two other exiles, namely Peter and Nicholas Hilliard. The former was at Calais by 1555, while the latter – perhaps his brother, and possibly the Exonian later to achieve fame as a painter of miniatures – became a member of the Knoxian congregation at Geneva in 1557. The town of Totnes contributed a woman named Eleanor, who was in Geneva by 1558, as well as the 'merchant apothecary' Peter Willis and his wife. Willis had reached the city of Calvin by 1556; in 1557 he was admitted to residence, and in 1558 was elected to be a deacon of the congregation. Apparently from Totnes also, though originally born at Ilfracombe, was the fervently Protestant exile Philip Nichols. By 1557 he was living, with his wife, at Aarau. In addition there were a few exiles associated with Devon whose status and place of origin remain obscure. It is nevertheless patent that exile for the Protestant faith was a course adopted by no more than an arithmetically insignificant percentage of the regional population.[44]

Even passive resistance to the Marian campaign against Protestant practices would seem not to have been extensive. Certainly the majority of parishes in the years 1553–8 appear to have obediently removed or even destroyed the Protestant liturgical apparatus acquired between 1549 and 1553. The early-Elizabethan expenditure on communion tables would suggest that Edwardian tables had frequently suffered destruction in the reign of Mary.[45] And although some of the Edwardian service-books were apparently consigned to storage – as at St Breock, where 'two psalters in English' and a 'Communion Book' remained in 1557 – others were certainly surrendered to the authorities in response to the official instructions of 1555. The parishioners of Dartmouth, for example, delivered their Communion Book into confiscation at Totnes in 1554–5.[46]

[44] Prince 1701, p. 75; Garrett 1966, pp. 72, 92–4, 183, 236–7, 318, 337; see also pp. 119, 203, 210.
[45] See above, pp. 158–9.
[46] *TRP*, II, pp. 57–60; CWA St Breock, fol. 3v; CWA Dartmouth, 1555.

Nicodemism?

Under both Edward and Elizabeth the majority of south-western people seem dutifully to have attended the officially sanctioned Protestant services in their parish churches. In 1551, for example, in a wedding service at Butterleigh, the bride and groom conformably received the communion 'as the manner was then'. Shortly after the Elizabethan reimposition of Protestantism, moreover, Sir John Chichester could rejoice that in Devon 'the service in the church is well received and done for the most part of the shire'.[47] Under both regimes, nevertheless, it is evident that regular attendance was by no means universal. In 1551 the Bishop of Exeter and his clergy were instructed by the Council to 'persuade the people to resort more unto the Common Prayer than they have done',[48] and in Elizabeth's reign the problem recurred.

In 1560, at Exeter, the aldermen were instructed to ascertain whether apprentices and journeymen were in fact attending church. In 1563 it was reported that John Parker of Luppitt 'hath been at no church almost these twelve months'. In 1567, at Stoke Gabriel, Edward Sweetland was accused of non-attendance during Lent and at Easter; he admitted being 'absent some time, this last Lent, from his parish church'. Similar omissions were confessed by Mary Sweetland in this year. In 1568, at Egloshayle, four men named Hamleigh, Rowe, Soby and Tregarthen were accused of missing services and of neglecting the communion. At Launceston in the same year there were said to be recalcitrants who 'do not come to church to serve God, not in long time'. Another absentee was John Clogg of Morchard Bishop. In 1569 he attempted to assure the Consistory Court that, as a thatcher, he had neither house nor master, 'but goeth about unto work by the day's work, and doth keep his Sabbath day at the end of the week where as he doth end his work' – which might be with Mr Bury at Chulmleigh, with Mr Flear at St Thomas' near Exeter, or in one of the neighbouring parishes. Clogg's vicar, however, was unconvinced, and demanded that 'the penalty of the statute' be imposed upon him. It was also in 1569 that William Lyle of Bishopsteignton was charged with non-attendance, and that services were said to be missed by several of the parishioners at Ilsington. And at Launceston in 1570 it was reported of John Stowe that 'he doth not repair unto the church on the Sabbath day, as (by the statute in that behalf provided) he ought to do'.

If the Mr Flear visited by John Clogg was the gentleman of that name who in 1564 was reputed to be a Catholic, it is possible that the thatcher was absconding from his parish church in order to hear clandestine masses

[47] CCB 855, fol. 224; SP 12/6/17.
[48] ER XV, fols. 121–1v. See also *Documents of Church History*, pp. 369–72.

in the houses of traditionalist gentry. In the majority of cases, however, absence from the Protestant services would appear to have been motivated by essentially negative considerations – by indolence, by indifference, or even by irreligion – rather than by a positive enthusiasm for the Catholic faith. At Luppitt in 1563, for example, the absenteeism of John Parker was the result not of traditionalist piety but of a violent irreligion: 'he hath almost killed his wife divers and sundry times', it was reported, '... and regardeth neither God nor man'. Others neglected the new services in order to evade their arrest for debt, as at Launceston in 1568, or to engage in work or in some other secular occupation, as at Egloshayle in the same year. Hamleigh, Rowe and Tregarthen admitted absences upon 'just cause' and on account of 'very urgent business' or 'very lawful business'. Several absented themselves in order to indulge in sport or recreation. Edward Sweet-land, at Stoke Gabriel in 1567, allegedly played bowls and football instead of attending church. Mary Sweetland, in the same year, confessed that during the services she had 'some time been at the Ale, and some time at the dance'. In 1569, at service-time, William Lyle of Bishopsteignton allegedly played tunes upon his rebec; he was a minstrel. Also at this date, at service-time, a number of the parishioners of Ilsington reportedly assembled to enjoy a game of cards.[49]

In not one of these cases does a Catholic motivation for non-attendance appear to have been asserted by a defendant, alleged by an informant, or even suspected by a court. It is again evident that although popular devotion to the old religion had been largely destroyed, it had by no means always been replaced by an enthusiasm for the new. It was not only the relatively small number of intractable Catholics who failed to accord Protestantism their whole-hearted support, it was also – and in greater numbers – the neutral, the uncommitted, and the religiously indifferent.

Even when the new services were attended they were not always treated with respect. In 1568, at St Cleer, the communion table itself appears to have been violently profaned by William More and Richard Purnell. In the previous year a woman of Stoke Gabriel, being instructed by her vicar to reconcile herself before receiving communion, retorted contemptuously that 'she should answer for her sins herself'. Equally disrespectful were the young parishioners of Morchard Bishop who, after attending a service of Evening Prayer in 1567, engaged in boisterous horseplay in a local wood. One of them, Roger Rowland, mockingly parodied the Protestant commu-nion service by distributing to his companions a pocketful of raisins, and

---

[49] *Exeter Records*, pp. 24, 315; CCB 856, fols. 15–16, 202–3v, 311–11v, 319v, 321, 370–3v; Peter 1885, pp. 203–4. For Flear, see *Original Letters*, p. 70.

Mixed responses

by adding the words: 'Take and eat this in the remembrance of me.' There is little doubt that this incident is again to be attributed to irreverence rather than to Catholicism. When subsequently examined by the Consistory Court, the miscreants meekly acknowledged that 'the communion now used in the church' was indeed 'a holy and blessed sacrament, to put us in remembrance that Christ died for us'. One of Rowland's companions, Robert Back, testified that he 'did speak it merrily, and in no hurt', and another, John More, added that 'they all be heartily sorry for their doings'.[50]

While the attitude of most south-western people towards the new religion remained unenthusiastic, the proportion of them actively hostile to it would seem to have progressively diminished. Before about 1550, such hostility was not uncommon. In 1531–2, at Exeter, the Protestantism of Thomas Bennett evoked a fierce antagonism from some – though by no means all – of his fellow-townsmen, and in 1535–7, at Plymouth, the enemies of James Horsewell denounced him as a heretic and secured his temporary banishment from the town. At Axminster, in 1535–6, some of the neighbours of Philip Gammon – including Thomas Hoare, John Massey, Richard Osborne and John Sampford – not only physically threatened him but also caused him to be charged with heresy before the bishop's commissary and in the Hundred Court. They decried his 'erronious and heretical opinions' as 'odious to God and man'. In 1549 Protestants were abused by some Exeter citizens, while at Chagford the outspoken Protestantism of Kingwell the tinner earned him the 'great hatred and malice' of his neighbours. Moreover, the articles of the south-western rebels this year not only ridiculed the new service as a 'Christmas game', but also demanded the execution of those who refused to worship the reserved sacrament: 'we will have them die like heretics against the holy Catholic faith'.[51]

Nor were the victims of popular anti-Protestantism to be found solely among the non-gentle laity. In 1549 gentlemen like Walter Raleigh Esquire and Sir Peter Carew were hated and even attacked by rebels on account of their zeal for the new religion,[52] and a similar hostility was sometimes directed against clerics known or believed to be its devotees. Simon Heynes, Exeter's dean from 1537, was for this reason 'marvellous hated and maligned at', and the parson of Sampford Peverell was in 1539 denounced as a heretic by William Cater of Tiverton. Between 1547 and 1549 the vicar of St Stephen's-by-Saltash attributed an attack upon his vicarage by John Debble, Robert Smith and Thomas Spore to the fact that he had 'ever favoured,

---

[50]   CCB 855B, sub 7 February 1566/7; CCB 856, fols. 15v–16, 297–7v.
[51]   *Acts and Monuments*, II, pp. 1037–40; *LP*, X, 52; XII (1), 153; STAC 2/2/267–72, 287; 23/273; 29/111; 'Description of Exeter', pp. 44–6, 66; Royal 18 B XI, fols. 12, 22.
[52]   'Description of Exeter', esp. pp. 31–3.

maintained and supported the king's majesty's godly and just proceedings in matters of religion, ever furthering the same to the uttermost of his power'. The three laymen, he lamented, regarded his Protestantism with 'disdain'.[53]

On the other hand, the fact that most of the known Protestants in the Henrician South-West seem not to have been delivered to the courts by their neighbours might mean that even before 1550 an active hostility to the new religion was becoming confined to a minority of the regional population. After 1550, certainly, it appears to have substantially declined. Coverdale, the overtly Protestant Bishop of Exeter between 1551 and 1553, was reportedly 'hated of the adversaries of the gospel'. In Mary's reign the unpopularity of the vicar of Alvington may have been due in part to his religious proclivities – 'I think that you be Mr Coverdale's man', he was told by the hostile Fairweather of Malborough – while the incumbents of Jacobstowe and St Keyne were resented by their parishioners on account of their marriages under the Edwardian regime. In 1554 the yeoman John Chapel complained bitterly that the parson of St Teath 'was married, and had a woman'; 'never continued resident within the same parish, but was a common preacher and an unquiet person'; 'passed from place to place, never resident upon the said benefice, nor never kept hospitality there'. The minister of Protestantism by no means always won popular favour. On the other hand, he seems but rarely to have been delivered to the persecuting courts by his parishioners. Not one of the region's resident Protestant clergy was burned at the stake between 1555 and 1558.[54]

An active hostility to lay supporters of the new religion was similarly becoming less common. William Smith, Mayor of Exeter in 1553, reportedly proved himself in Mary's reign to be 'an enemy to all such as were known or suspected to be true professors of the gospel'. In collusion with traditionalist clerics he thus devoted himself to the 'troubling, vexing and persecuting of godly men', and in particular of John Budleigh and John Periam. Boyton's Agnes Priest, on account of her Protestantism, was 'rebuked' and 'troubled' by her husband and children, and eventually accused of heresy by her neighbours.[55] Again, however, the fact that of all the known Protestants in the Marian South-West only Agnes was consigned to a heretic's death would undoubtedly suggest that implacable hostility to the new faith was in decline. More typical now than the persecutor William Smith was his fellow-Exonian Walter Staplehead, mayor of the city in 1556. In spite of his conservative sympathies – he was, says Hooker, 'over-much blinded in popery' – Staplehead treated his Protestant neighbours with a tolerance that would have

---

[53] Hooker, Commonplace Book, fol. 344; SP 1/154/181–2; C 1 1273/55–6.
[54] 'Synopsis Chorographical', p. 107; CCB 855, fols. 36v, 39v, 49v–50, 70v; C 1 1347/16–18.
[55] Hooker, Commonplace Book, fol. 350; *Acts and Monuments*, II, pp. 2049–52.

enraged the rebels of 1549, 'and did, both friend[li]ly and lovingly, bear with them and wink at them'.[56]

What conclusions can be constructed from the evidence surveyed? That only a decreasing minority of south-western people were actively resistant to the new religion would seem to be established. Under both Edward and Elizabeth the great majority of men and women appear to have submitted dutifully to the forms imposed by law. At the same time, however, an examination of the evidence in its various forms can leave little doubt that in the Reformation decades no more than a relatively small percentage of the regional population could plausibly be described as convinced and committed adherents of the Protestant faith. An external conformity was by no means invariably – or even usually – the consequence of an internal religious conversion.

This conclusion is confirmed by contemporary observations. In 1531, after a decade of Protestant penetration into the realm, Thomas Bennett could still reportedly lament that in the South-West 'the people of Christ knoweth no gospel well near but the pope's gospel'. A Protestant minister who had been in Exeter during Bennett's residence there would later recall that, with one or two exceptions, 'there was few or none ... that knew anything of God's matters'. Progress thereafter was in some places notable but in general restricted. At the beginning of Edward's reign the inhabitants of two of the largest towns in Cornwall, Bodmin and Falmouth, could still be described by the chantry commissioners as spiritually 'very ignorant'. Philip Nichols, at Totnes in the years 1547–9, remained acutely aware that he belonged to a small minority. Indeed he admitted that, among the 'great audience' attending the controversial sermon by Dr Chrispin at Marldon in 1547, he alone appeared to be offended by the canon's attack upon Protestant doctrine. Even in Exeter, according to Hooker, Protestants were still outnumbered in 1549.[57]

In 1551, in a missive to the Bishop of Exeter, the Council interpreted the plague then raging as a divine judgement upon popular indifference to the new religion: 'We cannot but lament the people's wickedness, through the which the wrath of God hath been thus marvellously provoked. For, the more we study for to instruct them in the knowledge of God and his most holy word, that consequently they might follow and observe his laws and precepts, so much the more busy is the wicked spirit to alienate their hearts from all godliness.'[58] A decade later, Protestants remained conscious of a diabolically inspired aversion to their form of 'godliness'. In 1562

---

[56] Hooker, Commonplace Book, fol. 351.
[57] *Acts and Monuments*, II, pp. 1038–9; *Copy of a Letter*, pp. 31–2; 'Description of Exeter', p. 41. For Bodmin and Falmouth, see below, p. 254.
[58] ER XV, fols. 121–1v.

William Ramsey urged his converts at South Molton to pray for the salvation of 'all such as are holden yet in the chains of ignorance of God and Christ, and Antichristical superstition, by the crafty delusion of the prince of darkness and god of this wicked world'.[59]

Only to a limited extent, therefore, can acquiescence or co-operation in the destruction of the old religion be explained as the consequence of authentic conversion to the new. By 1570, Catholic devotion had been largely suppressed, but in most individuals and communities it had yet to be replaced by a positive commitment to the Protestant alternative. More usually it was replaced by conformism, passivity, or even indifference. While the elimination of traditionalist piety had been executed with substantial success, the substitution of a variant form of Christianity was proving to be a process both logically distinct and chronologically more protracted.

[59] Lansdowne 377, fols. 27v–8.

took time for folk to change

9

Non-spiritual motivations: politics, economics and other forces

Before 1570, no more than a restricted minority of south-western people experienced a spiritual conversion to the Protestant faith. In order to understand responses to the assault upon traditional religion, it is therefore imperative to examine carefully the range of essentially non-spiritual impulses by which these responses might also be conditioned.

By no means the least powerful of these impulses was the Tudor Englishman's sense of obligation to established authorities. Among the most frequently reiterated axioms of political thought were the divine approbation of the government, the moral duty of obedience, and the consequent sinfulness of resistance. Though couched in the language of theology, such beliefs transcended religious divisions and were asserted by Protestant, Catholic and neutral alike. 'In the Bible', the south-western rebels were told by Philip Nichols in 1549, 'ye should have learned that princes and magistrates are the ministers of God, and therefore thoroughly to be obeyed; and that no man ought to speak evil of them, much less to resist them or arise against them.' 'God's most holy word', he assured them, 'pronounceth a plain sentence of eternal damnation upon all such as be seditious rebels against their kings or magistrates.' In 1562 the Protestants of South Molton were similarly reminded (by William Ramsey) of their compelling duty to obey their rulers.[1]

Nor was this sense of obligation confined to Protestants. When the opposition of Exeter's mayor and aldermen to the rebellion of 1549 was subsequently analysed by John Hooker – who, it should be noted, must have been personally acquainted with many of them – he observed that the chief reasons behind their loyalism included 'their duty to God' and 'their obedience to the king'. He also represented them as denouncing supporters of the insurrection as 'enemies and rebels against God, their king, and [their] country', and as remembering that they 'had sworn their fidelity and allegiance to their king and prince'. These considerations, says Hooker,

---

[1] Royal 18 B XI, esp. fols. 3–5, 35, 37v; Lansdowne 377, fol. 20.

outweighed the fact that as a group they were 'not yet fully resolved and satisfied in religion'; indeed 'some – and the chiefest of them – did like and were well-affected to the Romish religion'. Among the common people of Exeter, moreover, personal preferences in religion would seem usually to have been subordinated to a similar sense of duty towards the prince and the magistrate. 'The most part of the citizens', recalls Hooker, 'were of [the rebels'] opinions, and of the like affections in religion'; yet only a minority proved willing to conspire in their support. Throughout the siege, Exonians in general remained 'dutiful and obedient'.[2]

The prevalence of this sense of duty is confirmed by contemporary observations. In 1536 Dr Tregonwell was impressed by the degree of 'conformity' to be found even amongst the Cornish, and by their readiness to obey the royal authority. 'Conformable' was the term employed by Sir William Godolphin to describe the Cornish in 1537, and also by the royal commissioners to describe the Devonians in 1553. In 1569 the justices reported a 'conformable order' in Cornwall and a 'dutiful obedience' in Devon.[3] The value thus placed by Tudor society upon duty, obedience and conformity to the established authorities will undoubtedly help to explain why the south-western people, though but rarely converted to Protestantism, nevertheless tended in most cases to acquiesce in, or even to co-operate with, the official campaigns against their traditional religion. It will help to explain also the reluctance of Protestants to resist the Marian campaign against their own religion.

If the assault upon Catholic practices and institutions was facilitated by the Tudor Englishman's sense of obligation to authority, it seems to have been further assisted by another important component of his psyche: xenophobia. Although foreigners of all races had long been the object of his suspicion, fear or hatred, the marriage between Queen Mary and King Philip ensured that it was the Spanish against whom these emotions would be most powerfully directed. In 1554 it was reported that 'there was a great rumour in all parties of [Devon] that if the King of Spain should land there, that it should be a great destruction to the country'. The propagation of 'shameful rumours', and the utterance of 'slanderous' and 'seditious' words, were among the accusations against the Devonian Robert Glamfield in 1556. In 1557, at Dartmouth, there occurred a 'fray between the Spaniards and Englishmen', and in 1558 Spaniards were allegedly 'evil-intreated by the inhabitants of Plymouth'. This xenophobic reaction to the Spanish intruders undoubtedly helped to alienate a number of south-western people from the religious policies of the regime with which the foreigners were so closely identified. In 1554 the queen complained to Sir Hugh Pollard and other

---

[2] 'Description of Exeter', esp. pp. 37–8, 42, 52.
[3] SP 1/106/134; 12/60/27, 39; *LP*, XII (1), 1127; Stowe 141, fol. 67.

Devonians that anti-Spanish rumours were being circulated by 'lewd and ill-disposed persons' – some of whom, she protested, in fact sought 'the hindrance of the true Catholic religion and divine service now (by the goodness of God) restored'. Certainly the hostility to Catholicism expressed by Sampson Jackman and John Cowlyn of Stoke Climsland in December 1553 would appear to have been induced or increased by a crude xenophobia. 'Outlandish men', they feared, 'will come upon our heads; for there be some at Plymouth already.' Nor did the connection between anti-Spanish and anti-Catholic sentiments cease with Mary's death; indeed it was to prove an increasingly powerful factor in the reign of her half-sister. When, in 1569, plate and treasure bound for Spain were detained from ships at Saltash and Fowey by the Plymouthian William Hawkins, the seizure was justified on the grounds that the booty had been collected by order of the pope for use against Protestants.[4]

While xenophobia might help to turn men against the old religion, it was inevitably insufficient to transform them into intelligent adherents of the new. Sometimes, indeed, it may have deterred them from embracing the doctrinal systems originating in Germany and Switzerland. This would explain, for example, the anxiety of Philip Nichols to minimize his intellectual debt to the German Reformation. 'I am none of Luther's disciples', he insisted; 'for I know not Luther.'[5] Racial sentiment, in the form of Celtic antipathy to the language and culture of the Anglo-Saxon, may also help to explain the particular reluctance of the Cornish to espouse the new religion. Certainly it contributed to their initial distaste for the English-language services of the Protestant Prayerbooks. 'We Cornishmen', proclaimed the rebels in 1549, 'whereof certain of us understand no English, utterly refuse this new English.'[6]

A sense of duty towards the established authorities, and an equally ingrained antagonism towards foreigners, together provide a partial explanation for the acquiescent or co-operative responses of most men and women to the assault upon the Catholic religion. These, nevertheless, were by no means the only non-spiritual impulses by which their responses might be conditioned. The English, asserted the Venetian ambassador in 1557, 'will accommodate themselves to any religious persuasion, but most readily to one that promises to minister to licentiousness and profit'.[7] Evidence from the South-West would suggest that this assessment, though exaggerated, was by no means totally devoid of truth.

Opposition to the traditional jurisdiction of the Church, for example,

[4] SP 11/2/2, 5, 15; 12/49/1; *APC*, V, p. 290; VI, pp. 179, 303.
[5] *Copy of a Letter*, p. 13.
[6] Royal 18 B XI, fol. 22.
[7] *Readings in European History*, II, pp. 150–1.

would seem to have been inspired less often by a belief in the theology of Luther or Calvin than by a desire to evade the moral – and in particular the sexual – restraints imposed upon the laity by the clergy and its courts. Verbal outbursts, lawsuits, evasions, assaults and other expressions of antagonism to ecclesiastical authority were not infrequently provoked by the layman's resentment of clerical efforts to reprove or to punish his acts of 'licentiousness'. It was the attempt of a Church court to penalize his fornication that impelled John Star of Shute, in Mary's reign, to physically attack its summoner. In the same reign a charge of marital misconduct drove John Ball to assault the vicar of Colebrooke, while an attempted rebuke for mistreating a servant aroused Thomas Langmead to attack the vicar of Exminster. Langmead's angry retort – 'What hast thou, priest, to do withal?' – may indeed be regarded as epitomizing the hostility of the layman to clerical interference in his personal affairs. On occasion, moreover, a neglect of Catholic services was apparently due to a preference for 'licentious' activity. One Sunday afternoon in 1558 was spent by Alice Watts of Ottery St Mary in committing fornication with a man named Wynsham, 'when all his household was gone to evensong'.[8]

Unspiritual impulses of this type not only motivated opposition to the traditional religion, they must also have served to limit enthusiasm for the Protestant alternative. The adulterous propensities of Whitchurch's William Gooding, for example, brought him into conflict not only with the conservative ecclesiastical authorities in Mary's reign but also with the Protestant Bishop Coverdale under Edward. Absence from Protestant services, moreover, was not infrequently motivated by a wholly unspiritual preference for sports or recreations: these included bowls, football, drinking, dancing, music-making and cards. A typical case was that of Mary Sweetland, who in 1567 neglected her parish church in order to enjoy 'the Ale' and 'the dance'.[9]

If the Venetian ambassador was at least partly justified in asserting the motivatory significance of 'licentiousness', he would appear to have been equally perceptive in stressing the importance of 'profit'. The south-western evidence suggests that in many cases a powerful incentive to withdraw support from traditional activities and institutions was provided not by spiritual conviction but by material interest.

There can be little doubt that the decline of investment in ritual apparatus, intercessions, images, churches, guilds and clergy, and the increase of sales, appropriations and thefts, should be attributed far more often to essentially economic considerations than to any expansion of Protestant belief. A typical

---

[8] CCB 855, fols. 186, 361–1v, 369v–70, 377v.
[9] CCB 855, fols. 115v–16, 150v–1v; CCB 856, fols. 15v–16.

case occurred between 1533 and 1538, when the feoffees of John Cockmathew refused to provide image lights in St Austell church. It is revealing
that their impiety was attributed by the wardens not to heretical tendencies
but simply to 'their great covetous minds'. Similarly materialistic motives
must usually be ascribed to despoilers of ritual equipment, like John Jelly
of Davidstow; to expropriators of intercessory endowments, like Richard
Drewe of Exeter; to embezzlers of church money, like John Weare of Halberton; to withholders of tithes, like William Morecombe of Hatherleigh; and
to defrauders of clerics, like Richard Clace and German Pike of Shillingford.
Offenders were frequently denounced by their victims as covetous or self-
seeking; almost never were they described as heretics.[10]

What is true of individuals is true also of parochial communities. The
Edwardian inventories, for example, reveal that whereas proceeds from the
sale of church goods had but rarely been expended upon Bibles, sermons
or other Protestant purposes, they had often been diverted to purely utilitar-
ian ends. Water conduits had thus been constructed at Kingswear; quays
or harbours built at Torre and Budleigh, and bridges maintained at Looe
and Tavistock. At Exeter the excavation of a canal was thus financed: Hooker
records that 'the most part of the parish churches of this city gave some
portion of their plate and jewels'. At St Gluvias the £20 raised by the sale
of church goods was intended to rebuild the market-house at Penryn. At
Liskeard, Looe, St Cleer, St Neot and Warleggan, profits were 'converted
to the use of the said parishioners'.[11]

Material advantage will help to explain not only the erosion of financial
commitment to traditional Catholicism but also the active co-operation of
many people in its destruction. To inform against opponents of the official
Reformation might prove a profitable enterprise. When, in 1539, information provided by John Northbrook resulted in the execution of an allegedly traditionalist gentleman, he was rewarded by the grant of the
gentleman's house. This (according to Hooker) he had consciously sought.[12]
Even more lucrative might be the military support of a reforming regime
against its conservative opponents. After the suppression of the 1549 revolt,
Lord Russell rewarded his supporters with the lands, goods and ransoms
of his prisoners. The loyalist mayor and aldermen of Exeter were granted
the manor of Exe Island. Many, moreover, were certainly attracted to service
in the loyalist cause by the prospect of pay. In Exeter the parish of Allhallows
sold a chalice 'to pay soldiers' wages when the city was besieged'. In east

[10] C 1 728/23; 781/26; 1061/30; 1138/88; STAC 3/2/20; CCB 855, fols. 375, 376v.
[11] E 117 1/48–52B; 2/7, esp. fols. 2v, 4v, 10–11; SP 15/3/29; Hooker, Commonplace Book,
      fol. 347.
[12] Hooker, Commonplace Book, fol. 344.

Devon, similarly, Russell employed 'a mass of money' to recruit 'a great number of men'. And wages might be augmented by plunder. After their victory at Fenny Bridges, for example, 'the soldiers and serving-men gave themselves all to the spoil'. The expectation of material reward would therefore appear to have been markedly more important than Protestant conviction in inducing support for the anti-Catholic regime.[13]

A force as potent as the hope of economic gain was the fear of economic deprivation. Among the factors motivating the loyalism of Exeter in 1549 was the manifest propensity of the rebels to engage in plunder. The mayor and aldermen, says Hooker, anticipated 'the perils which might in such a cause ensue'.[14] Equally frightening to the wealthier citizens was the rebel demand for a confiscation of 'the half-part of the abbey lands and chantry lands in every man's possession': in May, ex-monastic property had been purchased by the Chamber and 32 individuals. Nor were they alone in their fear. 'I believe there be few in the realm', observed the anonymous gentleman of Devon, 'but it will make them smart to forego [their] abbey and chantry lands.' In subsequent years, and particularly in the reign of Mary, economic considerations of this type undoubtedly served to limit enthusiasm for a restoration of the traditional religion. The anti-Catholic attitude of the merchant John Periam, though primarily the consequence of his Protestant beliefs, cannot have been totally unconnected with his purchase in 1549 of bells, lead, stone and timber from the dissolved college at Glasney.[15] Further down the social scale, moreover, the fear of economic deprivation was by no means unimportant as a motive force. The prospect of dismissal and unemployment must largely explain, for example, the tendency of servants, apprentices and employees to conform at least outwardly to the religion of their masters. In particular it will help to explain the active opposition of many 'serving-men' – such as Foxe, the servant of Sir Hugh Pollard – to the Catholic rebellion of 1549.[16]

Economic fears must also have deterred potential dissidents from an overt resistance to the anti-Catholic regimes. The price of opposition to a reforming government was publicly demonstrated by the fines, ransoms and confiscations inflicted upon the defeated insurgents in 1549. John Furse of Crediton, for example, 'was then given, body and goods, like a rebel'; 'that trouble cost him seven score pounds'.[17] Under Elizabeth, moreover, even non-violent recusancy was liable to substantial financial penalties. In 1559 the Act

---

[13] 'Description of Exeter', pp. 53–5, 65; Rose-Troup 1913, pp. 505, 507.
[14] 'Description of Exeter', p. 38.
[15] Royal 18 B XI, fol. 33v; Rose-Troup 1913, p. 491; Rowse 1941, p. 298; see also above, pp. 122–3.
[16] 'Description of Exeter', pp. 30–1; see also below, p. 222.
[17] 'Description of Exeter', p. 65; Rose-Troup 1913, pp. 381–3.

of Uniformity imposed a fine of 12d upon each failure to attend the new services, and the prospect of 'the penalty of the statute' must help to explain the subsequent outward conformity of the majority of south-western people.[18]

While essentially economic fears thus induced active co-operation and deterred active resistance, their most powerful impact was inevitably upon financial behaviour. As the Reformation progressed, the layman's expenditure upon traditional activities and institutions was increasingly discouraged by the erosion of his confidence in them as secure repositories for his investment.

This confidence was probably beginning to decline by as early as 1535–6, when the government was already perceived locally to be hostile to traditional religion. At Axminster, indeed, the enemies of Philip Gammon now feared that 'the king and his council be of the same sect that he is'.[19] From 1536, moreover, the region witnessed an officially sanctioned assault upon its long-established religious houses, culminating in the despoliation of their churches and the plunder of their ritual treasures. At Plymouth, to cite but one example, the townspeople saw the confiscation of vestments, plate, chalices and other equipment from their Carmelite friary in 1538.[20] This campaign seems not only to have deterred investment in the surviving houses during their final years – by the spring of 1538 it was widely rumoured in Devon, 'both among great estates and low', that a total dissolution was now imminent[21] – but also to have aroused a widespread apprehension that the next victims of the governmental assault would be the parish churches. 'Before my coming into this country', Dr Tregonwell informed Cromwell from Cornwall in as early as the autumn of 1536, 'it was by some light persons reported that I should come hither with the king's grace's authority – by your lordship's occasion and commandment – to take away the crosses, chalices and other jewels of the churches'.[22] Fears of this nature must largely explain the decline of investment in the fabrics and furnishings of parish churches from the 1530s on, and also the increasing willingness of parochial communities to sell their apparently vulnerable ritual apparatus. The decision of the parishioners of Davidstow to sell their best chalice in about 1545 was certainly induced by a belief that royal commissioners were about to confiscate one chalice from every church that owned three, and to remove 'such other jewels of churches as they listed to take'.[23]

[18] *Documents of Church History*, pp. 458–67. For the 'penalty of the statute', see above, p. 166.
[19] STAC 2/23/273.
[20] *LP*, XIII (2), 381.
[21] SP 1/132/3–4.
[22] SP 1/106/134.
[23] STAC 3/2/20.

The Edwardian government, writing to the Bishop of Exeter in 1547, placed the blame for the recent spate of selling upon 'vain bruits' of this type;[24] but these can only have been multiplied by the activities of its own commissioners. It was in 1547, in the hundred of Penwith, that William Body created the impression that an official seizure of church goods was about to occur.[25] Any remaining confidence appears to have been largely destroyed by the subsequent official confiscations – a series of shocks from which it was never, even in Mary's reign, to recover.[26]

Similarly corrosive of investors' confidence in the future of traditional practices and institutions was the increasingly hostile official attitude towards the customary intercessions. In as early as 1529 stipends for masses on behalf of the dead were restricted by statute, and the total suppression of religious houses between 1536 and 1539 threw further doubt upon governmental commitment to the intercessory practices which had constituted their primary *raison d'être*. Even more disturbing were the statute which, in 1545, threatened to confiscate the property of chantry foundations, and the consequent activities within the region of 'the king's visitors for the church's lands', whom the churchwardens of Woodbury, for example, were obliged to meet in 1545–6. The expectations of an imminent dissolution, thus aroused, inevitably discouraged new investment and accelerated the conversion of existing endowments to more secular ends. At Davidstow, in *circa* 1545, the parishioners were impelled by such a fear to sell the oxen with which they had maintained a chantry priest, 'lest they be taken ... for the king'. From 1547, moreover, official hostility was increasingly apparent, and the climate of uncertainty thus created is evident in the request of Peter Amis of Lanlivery in July 1547 for a trental, 'if it may be'. The final blow to investors' confidence, from which its recovery in Mary's reign was only very partial, was delivered by the Edwardian dissolutions.[27]

Apprehensions of this type, initiated by government policies and pronouncements and often magnified by local rumour, must help to explain also the increasing reluctance of communities and individuals to invest in apparatus for other traditional activities, such as roods, rood-lofts and saint figures, or in other traditional institutions, such as the local religious guilds. The decline of financial support for images, for example, seems to have been primarily a pragmatic reaction to the officially sanctioned iconoclasm, and when, shortly after the injunctions of 1538, the parishioners of Rewe

---

[24] ER XV, fol. 115v.
[25] Harleian 352, fols. 65v–6v.
[26] See above, pp. 38–9.
[27] Cook 1954, pp. 261–2; Woodward 1966, pp. 171–2; CWA Woodbury, 1546; STAC 3/2/20; PROB 11 32, fol. 15v. For dissolutions, see above, pp. 38, 110–11.

attempted to appropriate the image gifts in their church, they were most probably intending to anticipate an official seizure of such oblations.[28]

If financial commitment to the old religion was undermined by this series of confidence-reducing developments, it may also have been eroded by the increasingly insistent demands made by essentially non-religious causes upon the available wealth of lay society. There would appear to be a substantial measure of validity in the argument that as the sixteenth century progressed, resources customarily bestowed upon religious activities and institutions were increasingly required for military or naval operations and – above all – for the relief of the poor.

In several cases the sale of ritual apparatus was certainly necessitated by the war against France in 1543–6. When, in 1543–4, church treasures worth more than £41 were sold by the townsmen of Plymouth, the proceeds were used by them to purchase gunpowder, bows and arrows for their town's defence. Similar considerations prompted the sale of silver chalices and other sacramental equipment at Dartmouth in 1544–5: the £16 2s 3d thus raised was intended 'for gunpowder, and for the gunners' wages'. At approximately this time the purchase of guns and gunpowder at Kingswear and East Budleigh 'for the defence of the country', and the equipment of a bulwark at Salcombe, were also financed by the sale or pawning of ritual equipment. And it was in obedience to an alleged commission to raise money for the French wars that chalices and other plate were surrendered by the parishioners of Halberton in 1546.[29]

The traditional pattern of expenditure by parish churches was also modified on occasion by the demands of war. In the closing years of Henry VIII's reign, parochial contributions to 'the king's grace's business' ranged from approximately £1 at Chagford and £3–4 at Camborne and Modbury to £7–8 at Stratton and Dartmouth and more than £25 at Ashburton.[30] The reigns of Mary and Elizabeth, moreover, saw a modest but constant outlay by south-western parishes upon soldiers, arms and armour: Braunton, for example, spent 29s 9d on soldiers in 1557–8, £3 10s in 1562–3 and 26s 8d in 1568–9.[31] Further expenditure was necessitated by military operations against the internal disturbances of 1548–9, ritual apparatus being

---

[28] C 1 924/9–10; see also above, pp. 67–8.

[29] *Plymouth Records*, p. 113; CWA Dartmouth, 1545; E 117 2/7, fols. 4v–5, 11; C 1 1138/93–4.

[30] CWA Ashburton, 1544; CWA Camborne, 1543, 1546; CWA Chagford, 1545–6; CWA Dartmouth, 1547; CWA Modbury, 1545; Additional 32244, SWA Stratton, 1544, 1546.

[31] CWA Braunton, 1558, 1563, 1569. See also, for example, CWA Antony, 1559; CWA Camborne, 1557; CWA Dartington, 1557; CWA Exeter SP, 1570; CWA Molland, 1557; and Additional 32244, SWA Stratton, 1558.

sold or pawned for these purposes not only in Exeter but also at Ashburton, Boconnoc, East Newlyn, Lanteglos and Polruan, Modbury, Morval, St Veep and Tavistock.[32]

Markedly more insistent was the pressure exerted upon the available economic resources by the demands of poor-relief. The expansion of population, inflation of prices and relative depression of wages, together with short-term events like the 'dearth' of 1549, combined to create problems of poverty that contemporaries regarded with rising alarm.[33] Not only for reasons of disinterested philanthropy, but also – and particularly after the disturbances of 1549 – as a pragmatic preventative against riot and disorder, the more substantial sectors of lay society increasingly channelled their surplus wealth towards the poor.

The percentage of south-western testators making bequests to the poor rose from 20% in the years 1520–9 to 28% in the years 1530–9. After dropping to 19% in the years 1540–6 it increased to 32% between 1547 and 1549 and to 47% between 1550 and 1553. In the years 1553–9 the percentage was 32% and in the years 1560–9 43%. At first, charity of this nature was frequently associated with intercession. In 1529, for example, John Greenway of Tiverton bequeathed £20 and a dinner to the poor men, women and children attending his funeral 'to pray for my soul and all Christian souls', and in 1540 William Rich of Ermington donated 6s 8d to the poor at his burial, 3s 4d to those at his 'month's day' and a further 3s 4d to those at his anniversary. Increasingly, however, charity was divorced from intercession, and indeed became a rival to the traditional religious benefactions. In 1564, for example, the Cullompton merchant John Cole left 40s to the poor but only 4d to his church. In 1565 Robert Eliot of Morchard Bishop bequeathed a half-bushel of rye to each poor householder in his parish and £4 to its poor-box, while in 1567 Robert Pyne of Axminster donated 40s to the poor; neither offered a penny to a church, a cleric, or any other religious cause.[34]

In a similar manner the resources of parochial communities were increasingly consumed by poor-relief. The churchwardens' accounts show that this trend began in the latter years of Henry VIII, accelerated under Edward VI, and continued into the reigns of both Mary and Elizabeth. In 1550–1, to cite but one instance, the parishioners of Ashburton contributed £5 'to the poor people for one whole year', and a further £5 on the Sunday before

---

[32] See above, pp. 37, 76.
[33] See above, pp. 10–11.
[34] PROB 11 24, fol. 10; 28, fol. 182v; 47, fol. 142v; 48, fol. 491v; 49, fol. 13v.

St Barnabas' Day.[35] Regular poor-rates, and poor-wardens to enforce them, had been instituted at Chagford by 1551, at South Tawton by 1558, at Exeter by 1560, at Ashbury and Stoke Gabriel by 1567, and at Morchard Bishop and Rewe by 1569.[36] At Rewe, in 1569, only one of the Ales still wholly benefited the church; the other raised money for artillery, for soldiers and for the poor.[37] Charity might also be financed by the sale of church goods. This occurred at Exeter under Edward VI, when several churches sold plate 'for the relief of the poor in the commotion time', and at Plymouth and St Breock in the early years of Elizabeth's reign.[38]

Poverty might help to explain also the decline of support for Catholicism at the lower levels of lay society. It possibly underlay thefts of church property, resistance to the financial demands of the clergy, and reluctance to invest in traditional practices and institutions. It may have induced the preference – demonstrated, for example, by Thomas Perry of Axminster and John Smith of Landkey in the reign of Mary – for gainful employment instead of attendance at the Catholic services: Pirry served guests at an inn, while Smith apparently wound yarn.[39] On occasion the neglect of traditional observances was certainly the result of financial inability. When brought before the Mayor of Exeter for violating the Lenten fast in 1556, an inhabitant of the city confessed that his poverty had compelled him to make a soup from forbidden scraps of bacon. 'The mayor', records Hooker, 'perceiving the state of the man and his necessity, did bid him afterwards to be better advised, and to do no more so; and so did dismiss him.' The impulse here was not – as had initially been suspected – a heretical conviction: it was material necessity.[40]

A number of essentially economic considerations thus tended to undermine the layman's support for traditional religion. At the same time, these were certainly insufficient in themselves to transform him into a convinced adherent of Protestantism, and may indeed have deterred him from it. Under Mary, overt commitment to the new faith carried the risk of heavy fines (as was discovered by Peter Willis of Totnes) or of even more expensive exile abroad (as was the fate of the Exeter Budleighs).[41] Under Edward

[35] CWA Ashburton, 1551. See also, for example, CWA Antony, 1546, 1549, 1551, 1553, 1559; CWA Ashburton, 1544, 1554; CWA Camborne, 1557; CWA Chagford, 1558; CWA Dartmouth, 1547; CWA Exeter SMS, 1552; CWA Modbury, 1548; CWA Molland, 1559; CWA Morebath, 1549; CWA Woodbury, 1548; Additional 32243, HCWA Stratton, 1547; and Additional 32244, SWA Stratton, 1558.
[36] CWA Chagford, 1551; CWA S. Tawton, 1558; MacCaffrey 1958, p. 111; CCB 856, fols. 15–15v, 26, 311v, 351v–2.
[37] CCB 856, fol. 392.
[38] Rose-Troup 1913, pp. 503–7; *Plymouth Records*, pp. 232–3; CWA St Breock, fol. 16.
[39] CCB 855, fols. 63, 214v; see also above, p. 43.
[40] Hooker, Commonplace Book, fol. 351.
[41] See above, pp. 164–5.

and Elizabeth, moreover, simple financial considerations may well have contributed to the reluctance of individuals and communities to invest in Protestant books, in Protestant sermons, or in the tables, cups and other
apparatus required by the Protestant liturgies. Economics weakened
devotion to the old religion, but by no means necessarily stimulated enthusiasm for the new.

Attempts to explain men's responses to the Reformation in terms of their
material interests can nevertheless be no more than partly valid. They fail,
for example, to account for the apparent non-resistance of individuals and
groups whose economic interests were in reality damaged rather than
enhanced by the campaigns against the old religion. These included craftsmen
like John Dawe of Lawhitton and John Pares of North Lew, whose incomes
were largely dependent upon rood-loft construction;[42] lessees of parsonages
like Roger Wallace and George Rolle, whose revenues were boosted by
offerings to images at Rewe and Pilton;[43] and even small farmers like 'the
people of the country' around St Day, who sold provisions to the pilgrims
visiting their figure of the Trinity.[44] In such cases alternative inducements
to acquiescence must be sought.

One such inducement was possibly the fear of social isolation. The punishment of excommunication, when imposed upon a layman by an ecclesiastical
court, prohibited him from meeting with his fellow-parishioners in the parish
church. It thus excluded him from the social centre of his local community.
It also barred him from serving on a jury, from appearing as a witness,
and even from bringing a legal action to recover debts. As a deterrent against
resistance to the official religious policies it might therefore prove by no
means ineffectual. In Elizabeth's reign, for example, it appears to have been
the shock of their excommunication by the ecclesiastical authorities that
impelled a number of hitherto hesitant parochial communities to demolish
their prohibited rood-lofts. This is observable between 1562 and 1565 at
South Tawton and Stratton, and probably also at Dartington and Kilmington. At South Tawton the Four Men were excommunicated in 1562–3
'because the rood-loft was up': and in the same year the offending structure
was duly removed. At Stratton the loft was pulled down after the appearance
of John Marres and John Judde before the Bishop of Exeter 'for the rood-loft',
and after the excommunication of the entire parish. At Cornwood in 1562
it was the leading inhabitants who were excommunicated 'for not obeying
their ordinary's commandment in plucking down of their rood-loft'. On
the day following the pronouncement of this punishment the parishioners
assembled in their church to remove the illegal structure. 'Forasmuch as

[42] See above, pp. 52, 64.
[43] See above, pp. 66–7.
[44] Henderson 1923–4, p. 196; see also above, p. 54.

we be excommunicate for not plucking down of the rood-loft', they were exhorted by Robert Hill, 'let us agree together and have it down, that we may be like Christian men again of holy time.'[45]

By the 1560s, nevertheless, the fear of excommunication had become far from universal; many, like the people of Tiverton, regarded it now as 'but a money matter'.[46] More persistently potent in deterring opposition to the Reformation were the physical punishments inflicted upon dissidents by the temporal authorities. In 1557 the Venetian ambassador noted the tendency of the English to conform to the religion of their monarch, 'not from any inward moral impulse but because they fear to incur his displeasure',[47] and evidence from the South-West would again suggest that his observation was by no means totally inaccurate.

It is difficult, for example, to evade the conclusion that the acquiescence of most south-western people in the Henrician Reformation is at least partly attributable to the manifest determination of the regime to arrest, interrogate, pillory, enstock, imprison and even execute the opponents of its religious policies. At Plymouth in 1533, for instance, dissidents were 'committed to ward for a time, and punished by pillory and stocks'. In order to maximize their public impact these painful and humiliating punishments were performed in market-places on market-days. They were organized by Sir Piers Edgcumbe, acting upon letters received from Thomas Cromwell. The Council of the West, instituted in 1539, was similarly instructed to punish dissidents 'extremely, for [the purpose of] example': its devices were to include pillorying and ear-cropping. And punishment could be capital as well as corporal. In 1537, for example, the fisherman of St Keverne who attempted to defend the abrogated saints' days seems subsequently to have been hanged in chains at Helston. In 1538 a Plymouth man was executed for treason, while at Exeter William Jordan paid for his treasonable words by being hanged and quartered. It is not difficult to understand why John Davey of Exeter St Sidwell's, when accused of treason in this year, elected to flee from the county.[48]

As the government acknowledged in an instruction to the justices of Cornwall in *circa* 1537, repressive measures of these types compelled even those people inwardly sympathetic to the old religion to 'do show outward, for avoiding of danger of the law'. Official orders to the Council of the West in 1539 similarly noted the tendency of Catholic sympathizers to conform

---

[45] Hill 1969, pp. 343–69; CWA Dartington, *c*. 1563; CWA Kilmington, 1562, 1565; CWA S. Tawton, 1563; Additional 32243, HCWA Stratton, 1563–5; Additional 32244, SWA Stratton, 1564–5; CCB 779, sub 15 May 1562.
[46] See above, p. 141.
[47] *Readings in European History*, II, pp. 150–1.
[48] SP 1/80/193; Titus B 1, fols. 172–9; *LP*, XII (1), 685, 1127; XIII (1), 416, 453, 580.

outwardly to the Reformation – not 'with the heart' but 'with the tongue only, for a form'.[49] Some men, moreover, were induced by the prospect of such punishments not only to acquiesce but even actively to co-operate. In 1536, during the riot in defence of images at St Nicholas' Priory, the mayor and aldermen of Exeter were patently more anxious to appease the royal visitors than to preserve the sacred figures. Hooker observes revealingly that the mayor was 'very loth the visitors should be advertised of any such disorders'. Similar fears might lead a man to inform against his neighbour. The accusation levelled against a local gentleman by John Northbrook and Adam Wilcox at Exeter in 1539 sprang in part from their apprehension that, after their discussion with him of the current religio-political 'prophecies', he might in fact report them to the authorities as traitors. 'Wherefore', they allegedly argued, 'let us prevent him and play sure, and go to Mr Mayor, and first accuse him; and so shall we save ourselves.' The gentleman, in consequence, was executed, while his accusers evaded punishment.[50]

If fears of this nature were thus already prevalent in the reign of Henry VIII, they can only have been intensified in the Edwardian years by the retribution inflicted by the regime upon the rioters of western Cornwall in 1548 and upon the rebels from both Cornwall and Devon in 1549. The disturbance at Helston in 1548 was followed by hangings and quarterings, which, in order to impress the local population, were conducted at Launceston and Plymouth as well as in London. At Plymouth a 'traitor of Cornwall' was hanged and quartered, and one of his quarters dispatched to Tavistock for exhibition.[51] Even more terrifying was the vengeance wrought upon the rebels of 1549. A high proportion of the insurgents was slaughtered in the field by the loyalist forces. Some 300 were reportedly killed at Fenny Bridges, and 1,000 at Clyst St Mary. On Clyst Heath 'they were all overthrown, and few or none left alive': 'great was the slaughter and cruel was the fight'. Further killings occurred at Sampford Courtenay. A total of about 4,000 rebels were said to have been slain, some of these being summarily executed after their surrender. Having suppressed the insurrection, Lord Russell organized numerous executions in Exeter and in the surrounding countryside; then he marched westwards through Devon and into Cornwall, causing 'execution to be done upon a great many'. Suspected ringleaders were his primary targets. The operation initiated by Russell was completed by Sir Anthony Kingston, whose brutality – even by the standards of the sixteenth century – was conspicuous. Amongst those who died on the gallows were Nicholas Bowyer, the deputy mayor of Bodmin; the servant of a Bodmin miller; John Payne, the mayor, or port-reeve, of St Ives; and William Mayow

[49] Stowe 142, fol. 14; Titus B 1, fol. 176.
[50] Hooker, Commonplace Book, fols. 343–4; SP 1/102/33.
[51] Rose-Troup 1913, pp. 89–92.

of St Columb Major.[52] The government's conscious purpose in organizing this gruesome and invariably public punishment of the rebels was – as Russell was reminded by Protector Somerset himself – 'that their example should be terror this great while to all the country, and not to attempt such kind of rebellion again'.[53] The impact of this policy of 'terror' upon the region is impressively attested by its failure to mount a rebellion or even a significant riot in defence of the old religion in the subsequent two decades. Even in the 1560s the 'commotion' of 1549 remained a vivid memory in the minds of south-western men and women.[54]

The fear of punishment not only induced acquiescence in the assault upon Catholicism, it seems also to have restricted overt commitment to the Protestant alternative. In the reign of Henry VIII, potential converts must have been deterred not only by the possibility of banishment from their local communities – a punishment threatened against Philip Gammon of Axminster and apparently inflicted upon James Horsewell of Plymouth[55] – but also by the ultimate prospect of imprisonment and death at the stake. Thomas Bennett was incarcerated in the bishop's prison and 'kept in stocks and strong iron, with as much favour as a dog should find'; then he was consigned to the flames.[56] Particularly terrifying was the Act of Six Articles, which, in 1539, imposed the death penalty upon open denials of Catholic sacramental doctrine:[57] it was hated by Philip Nichols for its 'extreme bloodiness'. In 'our west parts', observed Nichols in 1547, Protestants had hitherto faced 'huge rocks and wild seas'.[58] The dangers returned in Mary's reign – 'those tyrannical days', in the view of an Exeter Protestant, 'when fire and faggot carried the sway'. Several laymen, including John Budleigh and John Periam, reportedly encountered persecution, though the supreme penalty was paid only by Agnes Priest. Her execution, like Bennett's, was deliberately performed in public, and was witnessed by 'innumerable people'.[59] Under both Henry and Mary, therefore, profession of the new religion remained a potentially hazardous venture. It was said of one Devonian Protestant, Robert Kede, that he 'all his life suffered nothing but trouble for the gospel'.[60]

The sense of obligation to authority, xenophobia, the urge for moral or sexual self-determination, the hope of material gain, the fear of material loss, the pressure of secular financial demands, the dread of social isolation,

---

[52] 'Description of Exeter', pp. 55–70; Rose-Troup 1913, pp. 306–12; Rowse 1941, pp. 285–6.
[53] *Prayerbook of 1549*, p. 54.
[54] E.g. CCB 855B, sub 2 April 1565.
[55] STAC 2/29/111; *LP*, XII (1), 153.
[56] *Acts and Monuments*, II, pp. 1037–40.
[57] *Documents of Church History*, pp. 303–19.
[58] Royal 18 B XI, fol. 10v; *Copy of a Letter*, p. 1.
[59] Hooker, Commonplace Book, fols. 350–1; *Acts and Monuments*, II, p. 2052.
[60] *Acts and Monuments*, II, p. 2051.

of corporal punishment or of death – a remarkably wide range of essentially non-spiritual considerations may have served to induce an acquiescent or even co-operative response to the assault upon traditional religion. At the same time these factors were in themselves insufficient to create an intelligent commitment to the Protestant faith, and indeed must frequently have operated as deterrents against it. Together they help to explain why, for the average man and woman, the Reformation was less a transition from one form of religious commitment to another than a descent from a relatively high level of devotion into conformism, inactivity, and even disinterest.

10

Mediate influences: literature, drama and art

Of the types of mediate influence available to the sixteenth-century propagator of religion, potentially among the most effective in the battle for men's minds was the written word. It is therefore significant that in the South-West the utilization of this medium by religious traditionalists would seem never to have been extensive. Evidence of the dissemination of Catholic books, pamphlets or even bills is in fact relatively scarce. At Exeter, it is true, 'seditious bills' supporting the opponents of iconoclasm were posted in 1536; a paper implying that Henry VIII was 'cursed of God's mouth' was discussed by some of the citizens in 1539; and 'most slanderous and seditious bills' were 'affixed to doors and scattered in the streets' in 1547. Thereafter such activity apparently subsided, though bills maintaining the doctrine of transubstantiation and denying the identification of the pope with Antichrist were erected in the city by a doctor in as late as 1561. One of the very few cases of this type to be reported from outside Exeter occurred at Alphington, where, in 1567, books written on the continent by the exiled Thomas Harding – and presumably smuggled thence into the South-West – were read by Thomas Stephens. Stephens, moreover, commended these works to Simon Hamlyn as 'good and Catholic', 'did praise them above all measure', and indeed read one of them aloud to John Alderhead and John Helmer. His wife also invited Mary Harris to their home in order to 'hear a book read, which did intreat of holy bread and holy water'. This illicit activity seems not to have won the general approbation of the parish. Mary Harris apparently declined to participate, and according to one of the five parishioners who eventually testified against him in the Consistory Court, Stephens had to hide the identity of his copy of Harding while reading it in church by covering it with his cloak.[1]

The apparent rarity of such attempts to propagate Catholicism through the medium of the written word provides another reason for the limited

---

[1] SP 1/102/33; Hooker, Commonplace Book, fols. 344, 354; *APC*, II, pp. 538–9; CCB 856, fols. 143v–6.

ability of Catholicism to withstand the assaults to which it was subjected in the Reformation decades. In particular it helps to explain its failure to remain a potent subterranean force while under official disapprobation. But to what extent is the restricted growth of Protestant commitment in the same decades to be attributed to a similar underutilization of this important medium?

Protestants were undoubtedly more strongly committed than Catholics to the dissemination of relatively inexpensive religious literature. At Exeter in 1549 they were indeed derided by their traditionalist enemies as 'two-penny book men'. In the same city, in 1531, the houses of Thomas Bennett and of certain shearmen had been searched by the authorities for heretical bills and books, and it had been by posting bills upon the doors of the cathedral that Bennett had attempted to publicize his Protestant convictions. 'I put up the bills', he reportedly told the Exeter clergy, 'that many should read and hear what abominable blasphemers ye are.' By 1547 Philip Nichols of Totnes had read 'godly and learned treatises', and by 1549 he had himself written three pieces of religious propaganda, of which two – *The Copy of a Letter* and *A Godly New Story* – had been published. By 1558 Protestant literature appears to have been employed by a group existing in or near Launceston: in that year Agnes Priest admitted that her knowledge of the new religion had been acquired in part from 'godly books, which I have heard read'.[2] In some towns, moreover, the faith of Protestants was sustained by a correspondence with fellow-believers in other parts. At Plymouth, in the years 1535–7, the Protestant merchants thus received news and fraternal greetings from a cleric in London, and at South Molton, in 1562, it was by means of a lengthy epistle that the 'faithful congregation' was exhorted by its former pastor to persevere in its Protestant commitment. This epistle was to be read not only to the South Molton congregation but also to those 'dispersed here and there abroad'.[3]

Outside such towns, on the other hand, evidence of the dissemination of Protestant writings is markedly less frequent. Eleven tracts, together worth 24s, were owned by the parson of St Teath – an enthusiastic propagator of the new religion – in 1554. The parish of South Tawton purchased a copy of Calvin's *Institutes* for 12s in 1560–1, and 'a book of my lord Jewel's' – presumably the bishop's *Apologia* in defence of the reformed Church of England – had reached the parish of Alphington by 1567.[4] In both town and country, moreover, wills, inventories, accounts and other sources would suggest that Protestant propaganda of this type was seldom in practice

[2] 'Description of Exeter', p. 46; *Acts and Monuments*, II, pp. 1037–40, 2050; Royal 18 B XI, fol. 11v.
[3] *LP*, X, 462; Lansdowne 377, fols. 8v–28.
[4] C 1 1347/16–18; CWA S. Tawton, 1561; CCB 856, fol. 146.

accessible to more than a minority of the local population. Nor should it be assumed that even when accessible it was invariably effective in winning men's minds. It was regarded with contempt by conservatives at Exeter in 1549, and evidently viewed with suspicion by the yeoman who stole the parson of St Teath's tracts in 1554. The reading of Bishop Jewel's book by Thomas Stephens of Alphington similarly failed to convert him to the Protestant cause.[5]

Even more important to Protestants than the dissemination of such writings was the popularization of Bible-reading. It is therefore significant that of the 398 wills made by south-western laypeople in the period 1520–69, not one records the possession of a Bible, and that other sources contain no more than occasional evidence of personal ownership. Among the small number of recorded exceptions were the Latin New Testament owned by Thomas Bennett at Exeter in 1531, the English New Testaments owned by at least one inhabitant of Axminster in 1535–6 and by Alice Bennett of Broadclyst in 1567, and the apparently complete English Bible owned by John Judde of Stratton in 1570. Alice Bennett, for example, possessed 'a book of the New Testament, in fair print, after Tyndale's translation'. It is probably not coincidental that three of these four cases come from towns. Even at Exeter, nevertheless, inventories suggest that Bibles remained uncommon in the citizens' homes until the last generation of the sixteenth century.[6]

For the average layman, in consequence, access to the Bible depended upon its availability within his parish church. It is evident from the wardens' accounts and inventories, however, that before 1538 the possession of this book by a parochial community was virtually unknown. In theory the situation was rectified in 1538, when every parish church was officially enjoined to purchase a Bible in English and to display it for public consultation.[7] By 1540 copies had been acquired by Exeter St Petrock's, by the towns of Chagford and Dartmouth, and by the rural parishes of Iddesleigh, Morebath and Woodbury. At Morebath, for instance, 'the church book called the Bible' was carried from Exeter and displayed on a cord within the church.[8] On the other hand, no expenditure of this nature had yet been recorded by accounts or inventories for St John's Bow and St Mary Steps at Exeter, for Ashburton, Bodmin, Camborne, Stratton and Tavistock, or

---

[5] 'Description of Exeter', p. 46; C 1 1347/16–18; CCB 856, fols. 143v–6.
[6] *Acts and Monuments*, II, p. 1038; STAC 2/29/111; CCB 855B, sub 28 February 1566/7; Additional 32243, HCWA Stratton, 1570; MacCaffrey 1958, p. 271.
[7] ER XV, fol. 76.
[8] CWA Chagford, 1540; CWA Dartmouth, 1539; CWA Exeter SP, 1540; CWA Iddesleigh, 1539; CWA Morebath, 1538; CWA Woodbury, 1539.

for rural Antony and South Tawton,[9] and when allowance has been made for documentary incompleteness, an extensive reluctance to invest seems probable. At Ashburton, Camborne, Stratton and elsewhere, compliance appears eventually to have been induced by a royal proclamation of 1541, which imposed financial penalties for further delay. Thus at Stratton – where, in 1540, the apparitor had been compelled to 'sue for the books' – a Bible was finally purchased in 1541.[10] The chain for its display, nevertheless, arrived only in 1542 – in which year also a chain was eventually acquired at Iddesleigh, and a chain with a 'desk to lay the Bible on' was bought at Woodbury.[11] These dilatory responses to the injunction of 1538 would suggest that local enthusiasm for the vernacular scriptures was far from overwhelming.

In 1547 all parishes were instructed by the Edwardian regime to exhibit not only a Bible but also a translation of Erasmus' *Paraphrases* of the Gospels.[12] Some responded by purchasing a new Bible[13] or display desk;[14] most showed little eagerness to supplement their Henrician expenditure upon such items. The *Paraphrases* seem usually to have been acquired by 1549, as at Holy Trinity, St John's Bow, St Mary Major and St Petrock's in Exeter, at Ashburton and Stratton, and at Antony, Morebath and Woodbury. At Stratton, for example, the stockwardens in 1547–8 paid their vicar 6s 'for half-part of a book called *Erasmus*'.[15] On the other hand, only a few of the recorded parishes appear to have followed official directives by painting biblical texts upon the rood-lofts or interior walls of their churches. The exceptions – Exeter Holy Trinity, Exeter St Olave's, Ashburton, Dartmouth – were all urban.[16]

Significant also was the apparently general reluctance of parochial

9 CWA Antony; CWA Ashburton; CWA Camborne; CWA Exeter SJB; CWA Exeter SMS; CWA S. Tawton; Additional 32243, HCWA Stratton; Additional 32244, SWA Stratton; *Bodmin Register*, pp. 38–42; *Tavistock Records*, pp. 16–19.
10 *LP*, XVI, 803: CWA Ashburton, 1541; CWA Camborne, 1543; Additional 32243, HCWA Stratton, 1541–2; Additional 32244, SWA Stratton, 1540.
11 Additional 32243, HCWA Stratton, 1542; CWA Iddesleigh, 1542; CWA Woodbury, 1542. For the purchase of new copies, see CWA Chagford, 1542; CWA Iddesleigh, 1542; and CWA Morebath, 1542–3.
12 *TRP*, I, pp. 395–6.
13 CWA Exeter HT, 1548; CWA Exeter JSB, 1548, 1550; CWA Exeter SMM, fol. 11; CWA Woodbury, 1547.
14 CWA Exeter HT, 1548; CWA Woodbury, 1548.
15 CWA Antony, 1549; CWA Ashburton 1549; CWA Exeter HT, 1548; CWA Exeter SJB, 1549; CWA Exeter SMM, fol. 11; CWA Exeter SP, 1549; CWA Morebath, 1549; CWA Woodbury, 1548; Additional 32244, SWA Stratton, 1548. For subsequent purchases of Bibles and *Paraphrases*, see, for example, CWA Antony, 1553; and CWA Dartmouth, 1553. Bibles and *Paraphrases* seem usually to have been omitted from the official Edwardian inventories of church goods (e.g. *Inventories, Exeter*).
16 Bond and Camm 1909, I, p. 101; *Inventories, Exeter*, p. 62; CWA Ashburton, 1551, 1554; CWA Dartmouth, 1554; CWA Exeter HT, 1549.

communities to resist the Marian campaign against vernacular scripture. Bibles and *Paraphrases* seem usually to have been removed from public display. Although some evaded confiscation – 'a Bible and two *Paraphrases* in English' remained at St Breock in as late as 1557[17] – the early-Elizabethan expenditure upon new copies of these books would suggest that their sur-render to the Marian authorities had in fact been frequent. At Morebath, certainly, the two prohibited volumes were despatched to Exeter in 1555, and at Dartmouth, in the same year, the books were delivered into confisca-tion at Totnes.[18] Even the painted scriptural texts were now attacked. At Ashburton, in 1553–4, the wardens paid for 'striking out of the scripture upon the rood-loft', and at Dartmouth, in this same year, a man received 2s 'for blotting out of the Ten Commandments'.[19]

Only after the accession of Elizabeth did repression cease. In 1559–60 the exhibition of English Bibles and *Paraphrases* was restored not only in the nave of Exeter Cathedral – where they were accessible to laymen – but also, in response to the official instructions, in most of the parish churches with extant accounts. At Exeter St Petrock's, for instance, a reading-desk was removed from the chancel and placed 'in the body of the church, to set the Bible on'.[20] Some of the copies apparently survived from Henrician or Edwardian times,[21] though the 'mending' or rebinding sometimes necess-ary – as at Stratton, Kilmington and South Tawton – might indicate that they had suffered neglect or damage in Mary's reign.[22] Others, as at Exeter St Petrock's, Exeter St John's Bow and Dartington, appear to have been retrieved from confiscation: St John's Bow simply paid 2d 'for fetching home of the *Paraphrases*'.[23] At Crediton and Morebath, and possibly at Antony, Braunton, Molland and elsewhere, copies had to be newly purchased. Thus at Morebath both 'the Bible' and 'Erasmus' were once more acquired, while at Braunton a man was paid 20s 'to buy books and other stuff at Bristol fair'.[24] In many parishes further copies would be added during the subse-quent decade.[25]

---

[17] CWA St Breock, fol. 3v. For other possible survivals of Bibles, see below, p. 192.
[18] CWA Dartmouth, 1555; CWA Morebath, 1555. For early-Elizabethan expenditure, see below, p. 192.
[19] CWA Ashburton, 1554; CWA Dartmouth, 1554.
[20] CAB 3552, fol. 138; *TRP*, II, p. 119; CWA Exeter SP, 1560. See also *Barnstaple Records*, I, p. 213; and CWA Coldridge, 1560.
[21] CWA Chagford; CWA Exeter SJB; CWA Exeter SMS; CWA Exeter SP; CWA Kilmington; CWA S. Tawton; CWA Woodbury; Additional 32243, HCWA Stratton. See also possibly CWA Ashburton; and CWA Coldridge.
[22] CWA Kilmington, 1559; CWA S. Tawton, 1560; Additional 32243, HCWA Stratton, 1560.
[23] CWA Dartington, 1559; CWA Exeter SJB, 1559; CWA Exeter SP, 1560.
[24] CWA Antony, 1559–60; CWA Braunton, 1559; CWA Crediton, 1559; CWA Molland, 1559; CWA Morebath, 1559. See also CWA Exeter SMM, fol. 16.
[25] E.g. CWA Ashburton, 1569; CWA Exeter SJB, 1565; CWA Exeter SP, 1563; Additional 32244, SWA Stratton, 1564.

Between 1560 and 1563 copies of the Ten Commandments appear to have been exhibited by most of the parish churches. At Molland, for instance, the wardens paid for 'setting up of the Ten Commandments' on tablets, while at Woodbury a frame was bought for the 'book of the Commandments'.[26] Painted texts, however, were slower to arrive. Exeter St Petrock's invested £3 6s 8d in 'new writing of the scriptures about the church' in 1562–3, while Crediton spent 12d on 'writing of the sentences' in 1563, and 16s on 'painting [of] the scriptures' in 1565. The Commandments seem not to have been painted until about 1565–6 at South Tawton, 1567–8 at Ashburton, Braunton, Dartington and Morebath, 1568–9 at Molland and possibly Winkleigh, and 1569–70 at Exeter St Mary Steps, Coldridge and Woodbury. Thus at Woodbury it was in as late as 1569–70 that a painter received 10s 'for painting the queen's arms and the Ten Commandments in the church'. Some parishes were even more dilatory: Chudleigh would be censured for its 'lack of the Ten Commandments' in as late as 1579.[27]

Not only, then, was scripture rarely owned by the individual layman; before the 1560s its availability to him in his parish church was intermittent, and even its display in the form of the painted text remained uncommon. It is therefore not surprising that evidence for its actual study at the middle and lower levels of lay society is relatively sparse. It was certainly read by Thomas Bennett at Exeter until 1531, by 'certain persons', including Philip Gammon, at Axminster in 1535–6, by Philip Nichols at Totnes in 1547–9 and by Alice Bennett at Broadclyst in 1567. 'The time which he had to spare from teaching', says Foxe of Thomas Bennett, 'he gave wholly to his private study in the scriptures', and Alice Bennett, explaining her reading of Tyndale's New Testament, testified that during the services in her parish church she 'doth most commonly use her book in godly prayer'.[28] The teachings of the Bible seem also to have been known to other laypeople, including John Bougin of Totnes in 1548, Agnes Priest of Boyton in 1558, and the congregation at South Molton in 1562, but whether this knowledge was derived from personal study rather than from clerical preaching or

---

[26] CWA Ashburton, 1562; CWA Crediton, 1561; CWA Dartington, c. 1563; CWA Exeter SJB, 1561; CWA Exeter SMS, 1561; CWA Exeter SP, 1561; ? CWA Kilmington, 1562; CWA Molland, 1561; CWA S. Tawton, 1561; CWA Winkleigh, 1563; CWA Woodbury, 1561; Additional 32243, HCWA Stratton, 1561; *Tavistock Records*, p. 26.

[27] CWA Ashburton, 1568; CWA Braunton, 1568; CWA Chudleigh, 1579; CWA Coldridge, 1570; CWA Crediton, 1563, 1565; CWA Dartington, 1568; CWA Exeter SMS, 1570; CWA Exeter SP, 1563; CWA Molland, 1569; CWA Morebath, 1568; CWA S. Tawton, 1566?; ? CWA Winkleigh, 1569; CWA Woodbury, 1570. See also *Documents of Church History*, p. 471.

[28] *Acts and Monuments*, II, p. 1037; STAC 2/29/111; *Copy of a Letter*, pp. 41–2; CCB 855B, sub 28 February 1566/7.

teaching remains unclear. Agnes Priest, for example, frequently quoted scripture but certainly never read it for herself.[29]

In 1531 Thomas Bennett reportedly acknowledged that most of his contemporaries 'know not the scriptures'. 'Alas', agreed Philip Nichols in 1548, 'what case were we in, when we knew not what was the Old Testament, nor what was the New. The Bible was an unknown thing within these twenty year here in England.' It is significant that the oaths taken by mayors and other officials at Dartmouth in the reign of Henry VIII were sworn not upon a Bible but upon a 'holy mass-book'. Even in the reign of Edward VI, moreover, the continuing scarcity of Bible study at the popular level was bitterly lamented by Protestants like Nichols of Totnes. And in as late as 1567, the reaction of Alice Bennett's vicar to her Bible-reading – he assumed that she was a Catholic perusing prohibited literature – would suggest that it remained a far from usual activity in the parishes of the South-West.[30] Some laymen, particularly before 1550, indeed regarded the practice with considerable suspicion. At Axminster in 1535–6 it was explicitly on account of Philip Gammon's association with the scripture-reading group that the understeward of the hundred, Richard Drake, threatened him with banishment, reviled him as a heretic, and even attacked him with a sword. A similar attitude was expressed by the south-western rebels in 1549: 'We will have the Bible, and all books of scripture in English, to be called in again; for we be informed that otherwise the clergy shall not of long time confound the heretics.'[31]

As conservatives thus acknowledged, Protestant conviction was not infrequently the fruit of Bible study. 'The more he did grow and increase in the knowledge of God and his holy word', reports Foxe of Thomas Bennett, 'the more he did mislike and abhor the corrupt state of religion then used.' Bible study was similarly an important factor initiating or sustaining the faith of individuals like Philip Gammon and Philip Nichols. Nichols may well have been thinking of his own conversion when in 1549 he declared that 'the public knowledge of the Bible and holy scriptures hath confounded [the priests'] trumpery, and hath opened to the eyes of the world all their deceitful doctrine'.[32] Conversely, the restricted expansion of Protestant commitment at the popular level must be attributed in no small measure to the relative scarcity of such study. 'For want of true knowledge' of the Ten Commandments, admitted even the conservative Bishop of Exeter in

[29] Murray, 3, John Bougin, 1548; *Acts and Monuments*, II, pp. 2049–52; Lansdowne 377, fol. 8v. For Priest's illiteracy, see *Acts and Monuments*, II, p. 2051.
[30] *Acts and Monuments*, II, p. 1039; *Godly New Story*, pp. 57–8; *Dartmouth*, pp. 187–92; *Copy of a Letter*, pp. 44–5, 49–40; Royal 18 B XI, fols. 28–8v; CCB 855B, sub 28 February 1566/7.
[31] STAC 2/29/111; Royal 18 B XI, fol. 27.
[32] *Acts and Monuments*, II, p. 1037; STAC 2/29/111; Royal 18 B XI, fol. 28.

1538, 'many of the unlearned people of the diocese have been blinded, following their own superstitious fancies and omitting to do the works of mercy and other acts commanded in holy scripture.' The connection between biblical ignorance and spiritual blindness was even more apparent to Thomas Bennett and Philip Nichols. 'Alas', sighed Nichols, 'how was it possible that we should be obedient unto the voice of our Lord God, and walk in his ways, when we knew them not, nor could we tell what they meant.' He told the south-western rebels that their ignorance of the scriptures had kept them 'in such blindness and gross ignorance that ye know not what pertaineth to your souls' health or damnation'.[33]

It is thus evident that while the utilization of the written word by Catholic propagandists was generally infrequent, the exploitation of this medium by their Protestant counterparts was seldom more than partially effective. How are these failures to be explained?

Potential readers of either type of literature must sometimes have been deterred by governmental prohibition. An Act of 1543, for example, sought to suppress Bible-reading among the middle and lower ranks of lay society; and the unauthorized reading of scripture was again officially forbidden in 1555. Printers faced similar deterrents: thus the production of Catholic books was obstructed by the official prohibition of unlicensed printing in 1559.[34] A more important factor, however, was probably the dissuasive activity of the local clergy. The reading of traditionalist literature was inevitably condemned by Protestant ministers: the public denunciation by the vicar at Broadclyst in 1567 was doubtless not untypical.[35] Traditionalist clerics, on the other hand, persistently dissuaded laymen from the study of Protestant publications in general and of English Bibles in particular. In 1526, for example, archiepiscopal instructions to the Bishop of Exeter ordered the confiscation not only of books by Tyndale and the continental reformers but also of vernacular translations of the New Testament, and in 1535, in a sermon allegedly sponsored by the same bishop at Sturminster Newton, the audience was warned against reading the New Testament in English. 'They knew not what "the Bible" meant', said Philip Nichols of the pre-Reformation clergy. 'They were not acquainted with the New Testament'; indeed, he jibed, 'some of them thought it should be heresy because it was called the "New" Testament!' By their hostility to the vernacular Bible they had barred laymen from access to Christ himself: 'His doctrine, with all the scriptures, had they locked from us, so that none of us durst look upon it in the tongue that we understood; so that we could have but

---

[33] *LP*, XIII (1), 1106; *Acts and Monuments*, II, p. 1039; *Godly New Story*, pp. 66–7; Royal 18 B XI, fol. 28.
[34] *Reformation in England*, p. 115; *TRP*, II, pp. 53–4, 128–9.
[35] CCB 855B, sub 28 February 1566/7. For this vicar (Richard Holland), see below, p. 249.

small hope through comfort of the scriptures.' In 1531 the clergy at Exeter were similarly criticized by Thomas Bennett for their deliberate suppression of 'the word'. 'Ye bear such a goodwill to it', he sarcastically told them, 'that ye keep it close, that no man may read it but yourselves.'[36]

Although priests were instructed by the injunctions of 1538 to encourage the reading and hearing of the English Bible, Philip Nichols could complain in as late as 1547 that often in practice 'they withdraw all men from reading and hearing it as much as they can'. The words of scripture, he exclaimed, are the words of life: 'but what life can they be unto us if they be kept from us, so that we know them not? Did Moses hide them away, and say they would "make men heretics"?' Two years later, according to Nichols, Bible-reading was still discouraged by traditionalist priests. 'This blindness', he told the laymen in the rebel forces, 'have they hitherto kept you in by shutting up the scripture from you... If they might likewise have the scriptures plucked out of all Englishmen's hands, indeed it would be easy for them to reign as they lust.'[37]

In the subsequent two decades, as the clergy's traditionalism declined,[38] its overt hostility to lay Bible-reading seems markedly to have abated. In Mary's reign, nevertheless, a conservative cleric like Gregory Bassett could still declare contemptuously of Agnes Priest that 'she was out of her wit, and talked of the scripture as a dog rangeth far off from his master when he walketh in the fields'.[39] Before 1570, moreover, clerics who actively encouraged their people to read the scriptures would appear to have been relatively few. Among the exceptions was William Ramsey, who in 1562 exhorted his former congregation at South Molton to reject human traditions and to arm itself with scriptural doctrine – 'whereby ye may resist all papistical superstition and idolatry'.[40]

An additional obstacle to the dissemination of religious literature, whether Catholic or Protestant, was not infrequently its cost. The 'two-penny book' apparently used by Protestants at Exeter in 1549 must have been widely affordable, but tracts like those owned by the parson of St Teath in 1554, and books like that purchased at South Tawton in 1560–1, were too expensive for the average layman. The former cost an average of more than 2s each, while the price of the latter was 12s. Similarly the price of a printed Bible – 13s 4d at Morebath in 1538, for example, and 20s at Crediton in 1559 – effectively removed the option of personal ownership from the

---

[36] *LP*, IV, 2607; X, 1140; *Godly New Story*, pp. 65–7; *Acts and Monuments*, II, p. 1039.
[37] ER XV, fol. 76; *Copy of a Letter*, pp. 44–5, 49–50; Royal 18 B XI, fol. 28.
[38] See below, pp. 229–31.
[39] *Acts and Monuments*, II, p. 2051.
[40] Lansdowne 377, fols. 11v–12.

reach of the common man or woman; not even a relatively inexpensive version was to be printed in England before 1575. Financial considerations of this nature may have contributed also to the reluctance of parochial communities to purchase their copies of the requisite books. In 1549 Morebath had to pledge its best cope of crimson velvet in order to buy the *Paraphrases*.[41]

In Cornwall, and particularly in its western parishes, a further barrier was presented by the linguistic factor. To the Cornish-speaking population, literature written in English was certainly alien and possibly – as the Cornish rebels maintained in 1549 – incomprehensible.[42] But probably the most fundamental reason for the limited effectiveness of the written word as a medium of religious propaganda, either Catholic or Protestant, was the persistence of widespread illiteracy.

That the general level of literacy had been rising for several generations before the Reformation is indicated by the increasing use of inscriptions – frequently in English – upon memorials, brasses, glass and other furnishings of the parish churches.[43] By the sixteenth century, nevertheless, it appears to have been markedly higher in the towns – particularly among the commercial and professional groups, for whom it was occupationally imperative as well as financially attainable – than in most of the rural communities. At Exeter, certainly, a substantial number of literates is suggested not only by the existence of citizens able to write, like the merchant Thomas Bond in 1501, or possessed of books or bills, like the schoolmaster Bennett and the unnamed shearmen in 1531, but also by the relative frequency with which both Catholics and Protestants posted bills; Bennett, indeed, reportedly assumed that 'many' would thus 'read and hear'. By 1553, in fact, the city contained a sufficiently large reading public to sustain a 'bookseller', by name John Gropall.[44] Other probable or certain urban literates included the shoemaker Philip Gammon and his associates at Axminster, the people who read to Agnes Priest at or near Launceston, at least some of the merchants at Plymouth, John Judde at Stratton, and Philip Nichols and John Bougin at Totnes.[45]

Even in the towns, however, literacy was far from universal. When, at Dartmouth in 1511, John Rowe received a written bond, he was unable to read it; in consequence he was compelled to take it to a priest, 'and

---

[41] 'Description of Exeter', p. 46; C 1 1347/16–18; CWA Crediton, 1559; CWA Morebath, 1538, 1549; CWA S. Tawton, 1561; Hill 1969, p. 49.

[42] Royal 18 B XI, fol. 22. See also Rowse 1941, pp. 22–3.

[43] For, for example, Tiverton (1517) and Cullompton (1526), see above, pp. 90–1.

[44] PROB 11 13, fol. 198v; 37, fol. 73v; *Acts and Monuments*, II, pp. 1037–40. For bill-posting, see above, pp. 188–9.

[45] See above, pp. 189–90, 193.

heard him read'.[46] In rural environments, moreover, evidence of this attainment is markedly less common. The exceptions included William Mayor, who at Throwleigh in 1556 was able to read out the wardens' accounts to the assembled parishioners, as well as Thomas Stephens at Alphington and Alice Bennett at Broadclyst in 1567.[47] Agnes Priest of Boyton was certainly illiterate, and John Alderhead, John Helmer and Mary Harris of Alphington were apparently able only to 'hear a book read' and not to read it for themselves. In some rural parishes, furthermore, the fact that the writing of wardens' accounts was delegated to a priest, as at Morebath, or to a literate person hired for the purpose, as at Woodbury, could mean that the wardens themselves were unequal to the task. It is therefore not surprising that the laymen in the rebel army in 1549 – who appear to have been recruited predominantly, though not exclusively, from the countryside rather than from the towns – were described by Philip Nichols as 'simple, unlettered folks'.[48]

The geography of literacy is attributable primarily to the superiority of most towns in terms of financial resources and, in consequence, of educational facilities. Thus at Exeter, in 1537, Tristram Hengescott was able to provide for his son to be 'guided and kept to the school to his learning', and to receive 'learning in writing and reading'. The cost of education helps also to explain the higher level of literacy among the more substantial members of the non-gentle laity, particularly merchants, than among their socioeconomic inferiors and the poor, and, in combination with contemporary attitudes to gender roles, it explains why the attainment was so markedly more common among men than among women. With occasional exceptions like Alice Bennett, the majority of known literates were male.[49]

That reading remained a far from universal activity in the South-West is confirmed not only by the 398 wills – of which not one records the possession of a book – but also by the retarded development of local printing. The region's first press was not established until *circa* 1525, when a monk of Tavistock Abbey printed a translation of Boethius' *Consolation of Philosophy*. After the dissolution of the abbey in 1539, its press appears to have fallen silent; and it is doubtful whether another book was printed within the region before the seventeenth century. This explains why, in 1547–8, the tracts written by Philip Nichols of Totnes had to be published in distant London. It probably meant also that John Gropall, Exeter's bookseller in

---

[46] CR Dartmouth, Proceedings of Mayor's Court, sub 14 April 1511.
[47] CCB 855, fol. 43v; CCB 855B, sub 28 February 1566/7; CCB 856, fols. 143v–6.
[48] *Acts and Monuments*, II, p. 2051; CCB 856, fols. 143v–6; CWA Morebath; CWA Woodbury, 1554; Royal 18 B XI, fol. 20. For literacy in general, see Cressy 1980.
[49] See below, pp. 235–6. For Hengescott, see PROB 11 26, fol. 91v.

1553, was dependent for his wares upon imports from the capital; the executor of his will was a bookseller in London.[50]

The evidence thus leaves little doubt that for a substantial number – and probably the great majority – of the south-western people, the reading of literature in general, and of religious literature in particular, was seldom a practicable option; only when read aloud by a member of the literate elite did it temporarily become an intelligible medium of instruction. This fundamental fact of sixteenth-century life will in part explain the concentration of popular Protestantism in towns rather than in rural areas, at the middle rather than at the lowest levels of lay society, and among men rather than among women. It will also explain why religious propagandists, when attempting to convey their convictions to the population at large, were compelled to employ a variety of alternative and non-literary modes of communication.

Among these latter was the performance of drama. The potential of this medium as a vehicle of religious instruction is impressively attested by the four plays that have survived from the pre-Reformation South-West. The *Origo Mundi, Passio Domini Nostri* and *Resurrexio* – which together constituted a trilogy, acted on three consecutive days, known as the *Ordinalia* – vividly represented the biblical story from the creation of the world to the ascension of Christ. The fourth play, *Beunans Meriasek*, celebrated the life and miracles of St Meriasek of Camborne; it was probably performed annually, on his feast day. The *Ordinalia* is datable to the late-fourteenth or fifteenth century, and the *Beunans*, according to the manuscript, to as late as 1504. All four works appear to have been composed by members of the clergy, the author of the *Beunans* being 'Dominus Hadton', and their geographical provenance is indicated by their language – which is Cornish – as well as by their allusions to Cornwall's topography.[51]

The popularity of such plays is demonstrated by the sizeable earthen ampitheatres that were constructed for their performance in the open air. Examples remain at St Just-in-Penwith and Perranzabuloe, the latter of which boasts a spectator capacity of approximately 2,000; audiences must have been attracted from throughout the surrounding countryside.[52] Further evidence of the importance of religious drama is afforded by an inventory for Bodmin and by the warden's accounts for Ashburton. In 1539 the parish of Bodmin retained the equipment for its passion play: this included costumes

---

[50] Hoskins 1954, p. 281; Finberg 1951, pp. 290–3; *Copy of a Letter*; *Godly New Story*; PROB 11 37, fol. 73v.

[51] The *Origo Mundi, Passio Domini Nostri* and *Resurrexio* are translated in *Ancient Cornish Drama*; references are to the line-numbering of this edition. For their date, see Fowler 1961. *Beunans Meriasek* is translated in *Beunans Meriasek*; references are to the line-numbering of this edition.

[52] *Survey of Cornwall*, p. 192.

for Christ himself as well as for the 'tormentors' in the crucifixion scene.[53] In Devon, similarly, an extensive collection of costumes, visors, wigs and other properties for the 'players' was owned by the parishioners of Ashburton. New tunics and headcrests for their performances were added in 1528–9; costumes were newly painted, and golden skins purchased, in 1534–5; a wig was acquired in 1536–7, and gloves in 1537–8. Among the characters appearing in this Ashburton play, which evidently focused on the Gospel stories, were God, Christ, King Herod, and a number of devils, but also featured was a local saint, the celebrated Rumon of Tavistock. It was acted annually, at the feast of Corpus Christi, and the organization of a special 'players' Ale' to coincide with the performances would suggest that the audiences were again substantial.[54]

The primary function of such drama was undoubtedly the inculcation of religious beliefs. A variety of devices, it is true, was employed to render it more readily palatable to its audiences: the *Ordinalia* included comic interludes as well as evidently spectacular effects like earthquakes, eclipses, and even a parting of the Red Sea. Nevertheless the didactic element was inescapable. The dramatic action was interrupted by overt assertions of dogma: 'Father and Son and Holy Ghost, / Three persons and one substance, / That is the true faith, / As holy Church teaches us.' In one scene of the *Beunans*, St Meriasek was depicted explaining the doctrine of the Virgin birth. As sunlight passes through glass, he assured a scornful pagan, so Christ miraculously entered his mother's womb. Later the pagan was shown questioning the necessity of Christ's death, thus enabling the saint to expound the doctrine of the atonement in reply: 'Through the sin of Adam our father / He and his lineage were damned, / But the Godhead wished / Again that he should be redeemed / To salvation. / The Son was conceived / And took manhood, / For that the Godhead could not / Suffer passion.' At such points the actor representing St Meriasek became little more than the mouthpiece through which the clerical author of the play conveyed his convictions.[55]

The religious instruction thus transmitted to lay audiences was invariably traditionalist in content. The *Beunans*, based on a written life of the Camborne saint, was unambiguously hagiographical and heavily permeated by miracle. It also featured the legend of Pope Silvester and the Emperor Constantine. Equally obnoxious to Protestants would be the *Ordinalia*, which, while based ostensibly on the Bible, in fact also contained a number of episodes devoid of scriptural warrant. The *Resurrexio*, for example, depicted scripturally recorded events like the guarding of Christ's tomb, the experience

[53] *Bodmin Register*, pp. 38–42.
[54] CWA Ashburton, esp. 1529, 1535, 1537–8.
[55] *Beunans Meriasek*, esp. 844–58, 874–90, 1317–20.

of the three Marys, the encounter on the Emmaus road, the disbelief of Thomas and the ascension of Christ. Interwoven with these, however, were scenes representing the imprisonment and miraculous release of Joseph of Arimathea and Nicodemus, the harrowing of Hell, the greeting of the Virgin Mary by the risen Christ, the healing of the emperor by St Veronica, the miracle of the robe, and the death of Pontius Pilate. Biblical history was thus combined inextricably with subsequent tradition and legend.[56]

Each play was designed not only to extend the religious knowledge of its spectators but also to reinforce their religious commitment. This latter purpose was implicit throughout the *Ordinalia*, but was particularly evident in its emotive portrayal of the sufferings, death and eventual triumph of Christ. It became explicit when the actor playing Nicodemus addressed an appeal directly to the audience: 'You go, reflect on his passion / Every man in his heart / And keep it steadfast and true. / It was not for himself / He suffered it certainly / But for love of mankind. / Show love to him / With thy heart worship him / Do, day and night: / When thou be passed from the world, / With Christ be thou dwelling, / Within his court.' Similarly the purposes underlying the *Beunans* were affective as well as cognitive. It visibly demonstrated to its spectators the power and compassion of their local saint, not only as a spiritual intercessor but also as a healer of physical and mental infirmities: Meriasek was seen curing the sick, maimed, leprous, blind, deaf, crippled, demon-possessed and insane. In one scene he was depicted at Camborne itself, founding his church and establishing his miracle-working holy well. 'Grievance and disease of the season,' he promised, '/ If a loyal Christian have it / And remembers me in this place, / Jesus, Lord, dear heart / His grievance will assuage. / Likewise the water of the fountain / For a man insane certainly / I pray that it be a salve / To bring him again to his sense.' The saint was also shown arranging his own feast day – the first Friday in June – and promising reward to all who would observe it. Finally the essential message of the play was overtly stated: 'Whoever trust in him / And loyally pray to him / Jesu has granted to them / Their desire readily.'[57]

The popularity of traditional Catholicism in the pre-Reformation South-West must therefore be attributed in some part to the influence exerted by the plays. The effectiveness of the *Beunans Meriasek*, for example, is suggested by the continuing cult of Meriasek at Camborne: one of the local guilds was indeed dedicated to him.[58] Again, the glazier who in *circa* 1500 produced the Creation window at St Neot – or, more probably, the donor

---

[56] *Beunans Meriasek*; *Ancient Cornish Drama, Resurrexio.*
[57] *Ancient Cornish Drama, Passio Domini Nostri*, esp. 3223–34; *Beunans Meriasek*, esp. 1000–8, 4302–9, 4553–6.
[58] See above, p. 107.

who dictated its content – appears to have been strongly influenced by the
Origo Mundi: even the treatment of the legend of the Holy Rood in this
play is reproduced in the glass.[59] Conversely, the decline of popular Catholicism in the Reformation decades must have been in part due to official
assaults upon the traditional drama.

Some of the Cornish plays were still performed in Elizabeth's reign, and
in 1566 the parish of Bodmin retained its costumes for Jesus, his tormentors
and the devils.[60] It is improbable, however, that scenes considered superstitious by the Protestant authorities can long have evaded their censorship,
and it is in fact evident that some of the region's traditional religious drama
was totally suppressed. Particularly well documented is the situation at Ashburton. Rattlebags and devils' heads for the customary play were purchased
here in 1542–3, gloves in 1545–6, and gowns in 1547–8 – in which year
the players were still paid for their performance at the feast of Corpus Christi.
After 1548, however, expenditure of this nature was conspicuously absent
from the accounts, and failed to reappear until after the death of Edward
VI, in 1553–4. During the reign of Mary, costumes for the actors were
repainted or replaced – gloves, for example, were acquired for 'him that
played God Almighty' in 1555–6, and for 'him that played Christ' in 1558–9
– while wine was provided for the actor who represented St Rumon of
Tavistock in 1555–6. After 1559–60, nevertheless, such expenditure again
ceased: henceforth the formerly important Ashburton play appears to have
been effectively and permanently suppressed.[61]

While Protestants thus seem to have been largely successful in destroying
the drama as a medium of Catholic propaganda, they signally failed to
exploit its potential for the dissemination of their own religion. 'Players'
performed frequently in churches and other public places in the Edwardian
and early-Elizabethan periods, but there is no indication that their performances were ever overtly Protestant in character. Most, like those of the 'inter-
lude-players of St Dennis' at St Breock in 1567, were probably in fact non-
dogmatic and designed essentially to entertain.[62] This failure of the Protestants may be attributed largely to their innate suspicion of the performing
arts, and to the difficulties inherent in the presentation of their rigidly

[59]   Rushforth 1927B, pp. 154–9.
[60]   *Survey of Cornwall*, p. 192; *Inventories, Cornwall*, p. 32.
[61]   CWA Ashburton, esp. 1543, 1546, 1548, 1554, 1556, 1559–60.
[62]   CWA St Breock, fol. 19. For 1547–53, see CWA Antony, 1549; CWA Camborne, 1550;
       CWA Dartmouth, 1553; *Barnstaple Records*, II, p. 98; and *Plymouth Records*, p. 117.
       For 1559–70, see CWA Ashburton, 1564; CWA Braunton, 1566; CWA Chudleigh, 1569;
       CWA Winkleigh, 1569; *Barnstaple Records*, II, p. 143; *Plymouth Records*, pp. 117, 120;
       and *Tavistock Records*, p. 26. For apparently similar groups under Henry VIII and Mary,
       see, for example, CWA Ashburton, 1535, etc.; CWA Camborne, 1540; CWA Morebath,
       1532; Additional 32243, HCWA Stratton, 1538–9; *Barnstaple Records*, II, p. 117; and
       Plymouth Records, p. 114.

monotheistic and solifidian doctrines in a dramatic form; it must also have been due in part to the regional scarcity of Protestant clergy capable of organizing activities of this type.[63] It provides another partial explanation for the relative superficiality of the region's Protestantization in the Reformation decades.

The attendance of the average layman at religious plays was probably restricted to a small number of occasions within the year. A more persistent influence upon his consciousness was that exerted by the various types of art to be viewed weekly or even daily within his parish church.

The utilization of such art as a medium of religious propaganda in the pre-Reformation South-West is impressively demonstrated by the surviving sculptures, roof-bosses, bench-ends, murals, screen-paintings and stained glass.[64] These are predominantly the products of the late-fifteenth and early-sixteenth centuries. Their period of origin is most usually indicated by a stylistic feature – such as the late-Perpendicular tracery of a painted screen, as at Plymtree, or the careful delineation of a face in glass, as at Doddiscombsleigh – or by a detail of costume or armour, such as the fashion of *circa* 1500 in the window depicting St George at St Neot. Greater precision is sometimes provided by a heraldic device like the double rose of Henry VII, as on a bench-end at Frithelstock, or the pomegranate of Katherine of Aragon, as on the rood-screens at Blackawton and Bridford. Not infrequently there is an inscription. Bench-ends at Monkleigh, Coldridge, Altarnun and Hartland are thus datable to 1508, 1511, 1525 and 1530; screens at Marwood and Bradninch to *circa* 1520 and 1528; sculpture at Woodleigh to *circa* 1527; glass at Broadwood Kelly to 1523, and at St Neot to 1523, 1528 and 1529. It is evident that on the eve of the Henrician Reformation, religious art continued to be produced in considerable quantity.

Though doubtless imported on occasion from outside the South-West, it seems more usually to have been the work of local craftsmen. Early-Tudor Exeter boasted a school of woodcarvers, and possibly also a school of sculptors.[65] The finance was provided by the parishioners as a body or by particular groups, families or individuals. At Chagford the wardens invested more than £10 in 'pageants' in 1513–14, while at North Petherwin their counterparts paid £3 and other sizeable sums to a glazier in *circa* 1520. At Bodmin, in 1507–8, the £12 paid to two craftsmen 'for the painting of four histories in the rood-loft' was contributed in part by the local guilds, and, according to their inscriptions, the three stained-glass windows erected at St Neot between 1523 and 1529 were donated by the parish's wives, young men

[63] See below, pp. 231–2.
[64] For specialist works, see note 4 to Chapter 1.
[65] Bond and Camm 1909, I, pp. 139–40; II, p. 280; Cave 1948, p. 20; Rushforth 1927A, pp. 29–31.

and young women. While the iconographical details may have been supplied by the parish priest, in most cases the subject matter was probably selected by the donors themselves. Several of the saints represented in glass at St Neot, for example, appear to have been the patrons of the donors depicted below them: thus St John is shown in the window erected by John Motton, and St Katherine in that financed by Katherine Burlas.[66]

The religion propagated by church art was invariably traditionalist in character. The murals at Breage, for instance, portray not only Christ but also St Christopher, St Thomas Becket, and the Cornish St Corentin; and another local cult figure, Morwenna, appears in a painting at Morwenstow. The screen-paintings of 1528 at Bradninch combine biblical prophets and apostles, and biblical events like the fall of man, the annunciation and the crucifixion, with figures from post-biblical history and legend; these include Christopher, Francis, George, Giles and Sebastian as well as the four doctors of the Latin Church – Ambrose, Augustine, Gregory and Jerome – and even the celebrated Sibylline oracles. The screen at Ashton similarly juxta-poses New Testament characters and later saints, the latter including not only major figures like Antony, George, Katherine, Margaret, Sebastian, Sitha, Thomas of Canterbury and Ursula but also the locally venerated Sid-well of Exeter. Bench-ends may, as at Launcells, represent episodes from the ministry, passion and exaltation of Christ, but saints are more frequent: a single end at Combeinteignhead shows George and his dragon, Agnes and her lamb, Hubert with his bow, and Genesius in his jester's costume.

The combination of scripture with tradition is particularly observable in the glass of *circa* 1480–1530 at St Neot. Its representation of the Genesis story – from creation to flood – intrudes not only the shooting of Cain by Lamech, but also the sowing of apple pips in the mouth of the dead Adam; from these, according to legend, will spring the tree for Christ's cross. Also portrayed in the St Neot glass, alongside figures from the New Testament, are apocryphal subjects like the daughters of St Anne and the coronation of Our Lady; international celebrities like George – whose exploits and martyrdom fill an entire window – as well as Barbara, Christo-pher, Gregory, Katherine and Leonard; and local saints such as Clere, Ger-man, Mancus, Mabena and Meubred. One window, dated 1528, is devoted to St Neot himself. After portraying his abdication of the throne and his adoption of the religious life, it depicts his piety and miracles: he saves a hind from a hunter, is supernaturally supplied with fish in his holy well, and is provided with deer to replace his stolen cattle. Finally he is seen

---

[66] CWA Chagford, 1514; CWA N. Petherwin, fol. 43v; BA Bodmin, Receivers' accounts, 1508; Rushforth 1927B, pp. 150–90.

at Rome, kneeling to receive a blessing from the pope himself. The legend was rooted in its local environment: Neot's well stood within the parish, and the horn given to him by the hunter was preserved in the priory at Bodmin.[67]

Art, like drama, was designed not only to convey knowledge but also to reinforce commitment. Many examples – such as the 'Neot' window itself – were patently intended to stimulate the confidence of viewers in the powers of a particular saint. Amongst representations designed to heighten devotion to Christ were those portraying his sufferings, as in the mural at Breage, or depicting either his five wounds or the instruments of his passion, as in the glass at Sidmouth, on a boss at Payhembury, or on the bench-ends of Kilkhampton, Poughill and many other south-western churches. That representations of this type exerted a powerful influence upon men's minds is suggested by the protest of Otto Corbin at Exeter in 1515: 'I will never worship and believe in the five wounds of Christ till I have married the fifth wife.'[68] Other motifs were intended to induce fear and repentance: they included the Weighing of Souls, a warning of the ultimate judgement, as in a mural at Poundstock.

If, on the eve of the Reformation, traditionalist religion was propagated by art forms of this nature, its erosion during the Reformation decades must be in some measure attributable to the decline of their utilization as media of religious influence.

Of the wall-painting and stained glass extant in the region's churches, none is datable to the period 1530–70: at St Neot, significantly, the latest date inscribed on the glass is 1529.[69] With possible or probable exceptions on stylistic grounds, as at Gidleigh, Ilsington, Lustleigh, Mawnan, Ugborough and elsewhere, or with an inscribed date, such as the 1547 at East Allington,[70] screen-work seems similarly to have been in decline. Only bench-ends continued to be produced in substantial quantity. Stylistic evidence for a date in this period – particularly the introduction of Renaissance forms, absent at Hartland in 1530 and at North Lew in 1537, but appearing at Dowland in 1546[71] – is found on ends at Abbotsham, Broadwood Widger, Gorran, High Bickington, Lapford, Lifton, Littleham, Morwenstow, Mullion, Newton St Petrock, St Levan, St Minver, Sheviock, Sutcombe and Stockleigh Pomeroy, and on the bench-front at Warkleigh. In addition the date 1537 is inscribed at East Budleigh and North Lew, and the date 1546

---

[67] Rushforth 1927B, pp. 150–90. Neot's well survives. For his horn, see above, p. 56.
[68] ER XIII, fols. 179v–81.
[69] Rushforth 1927B, pp. 150–90.
[70] Pevsner 1952B, p. 125.
[71] Pevsner 1952B, pp. 27–8.

at Dowland and Lewannick.[72] The documentary sources, moreover, would suggest that while expenditure on church art continued after 1530 – Ashburton, for example, invested 50s 4d in alabaster pageants between 1536 and 1538[73] – it probably declined before 1547 and virtually ceased between 1547 and 1553. Nor did it regain its pre-Reformation levels in Mary's reign. The pictures acquired at Ashburton and South Tawton cost 13s 4d and 20s 8d, and the cloth-painting purchased at Camborne 19s.[74] In parishes like Exeter St Petrock's and Stratton, furthermore, the Marian accounts record no attempts to repaint the murals obliterated in the previous reign.[75] Under Elizabeth, finally, expenditure again slumped.

Not only did the Reformation decades thus witness a drastic reduction in the quantity of art produced for parish churches, they also saw an important change in its essential nature. The bench-ends datable to this period by considerations of style, and those inscribed with the dates 1537 and 1546 at East Budleigh, North Lew, Dowland and Lewannick, together demonstrate an unmistakable tendency to replace traditionalist representations with secular motifs. Saints, passion instruments and the five wounds were increasingly displaced by tracery, foliage, arabesques, grotesques, medallioned profiles, initials and heraldry. At East Budleigh, for example, the entire set of 63 ends carved in 1537 is (apart from angels) totally destitute of religious figures or emblems.[76] Other art forms experienced a similar transformation. True, non-biblical saints appear on bas-relief panels at Mullion and on the screen at Ugborough, and the five wounds on the pulpit at Lanherne. If, as is possibly indicated by stylistic details, these are mid-Tudor, they are most probably Marian. On the other hand the screen at Throwleigh – erected in 1544 but now removed – was painted with scriptural subjects, and that at Lustleigh, which may be mid-Tudor, depicts biblical prophets and apostles.[77] Possibly from these decades too are the screen-paintings at Marwood, Sutcombe and Swimbridge, where the traditional saints are replaced by foliage or early-Renaissance decoration.[78] At Morwenstow, where the screen would be completed in as late as 1575, its motifs were exclusively secular: they included doves, foxes, oak leaves and vines.[79] Overtly traditionalist elements are also absent from the possibly mid-Tudor

[72] Pevsner 1952A, pp. 81, 129; Pevsner 1952B, p. 125; Cox 1916, p. 67.
[73] CWA Ashburton, 1537–8.
[74] CWA Ashburton, 1558; CWA Camborne, 1557; CWA S. Tawton, 1557.
[75] CWA Exeter SP; Additional 32243, HCWA Stratton; Additional 32244, SWA Stratton. For Edwardian obliteration, see below, pp. 207–8.
[76] Pevsner 1952B, pp. 27–8; Cox 1916, p. 78.
[77] Bond and Camm 1909, II, pp. 228, 330, 353, 388, 392.
[78] Pevsner 1952A, pp. 121, 147–9.
[79] Bond and Camm 1909, II, p. 391.

5 All Saints', East Budleigh. Bench-ends of 1537 in the nave. The ends illustrate the increasing importance of congregational seating; they also show the beginnings of a trend away from carved saints and other traditional religious motifs.

pulpits at East Allington and St Ives, and from the sculptures of *circa* 1546 on the tower at Cullompton.[80]

The trend is confirmed by the documentation. Even the pictures bought at Ashburton and South Tawton in Mary's reign portrayed a biblical figure.[81] The glass purchased by Dartmouth church in 1541–2 was uncoloured, and the glass erected in the church at Tavistock in 1566–7 showed not saints or martyrs, nor even scenes from the life of Christ, but the arms of Queen Elizabeth and of the Earl of Bedford.[82] The queen's arms were also painted in Woodbury church in 1569–70.[83]

This decline in the production of Catholic art was accompanied – and doubtless accelerated – by an assault upon the existing works. In 1538

[80] Bond and Camm 1909, II, p. 287; Cox 1915, pp. 51, 56, 60–1; Pevsner 1952B, p. 96; Moger, 22, John Hill, 1546.
[81] CWA Ashburton, 1558; CWA S. Tawton, 1557. In both cases this was the apostle Andrew.
[82] CWA Dartmouth, 1542; *Tavistock Records*, p. 29.
[83] CWA Woodbury, 1570.

representations of Thomas Becket were condemned by Henry VIII, and a general eradication of 'superstitious' pictures, paintings and glass was ordered by Edward VI in 1547 and by Elizabeth in 1559.[84] A consequent obliteration of traditionalist murals is not infrequently indicated by the accounts. The walls of parish churches were washed or white-limed at Exeter Holy Trinity and Exeter St John's Bow in 1547–8, at Exeter St Petrock's, Antony and probably Stratton in 1548–9, at Exeter Holy Trinity (again) and Ashburton in 1549–50, and at Stratton (again?) in 1551. At Exeter St Petrock's, for instance, the wardens paid for 'washing away of images, and for white-liming of the same'. At Stratton, where two barrels of lime had been delivered in 1548, the wardens in 1551 paid 2s 6d 'for four bushels of lime, and carriage home of it', and a further 4s 4d 'for white-liming of the church'.[85] Further washing and white-liming followed Elizabeth's accession, as at Dartington in 1558–9, at Ashburton in 1559–60, at Kilmington in 1560–2, at Woodbury and possibly Barnstaple in 1564–5, at South Tawton in about 1565–6 and at Chagford in 1567. Thus at Ashburton the wardens paid 6s 8d 'for washing the images in the church and the church house', and at Dartington their counterparts bestowed 16d upon Robert Edward 'for two days' labour, mending of the walls and whiting of the aisles and chancel'.[86]

Free-standing pictures were also attacked. 'Two pictures, of the north side and south side', were apparently removed at Stratton in 1548. Some of the deposed icons – like the crucifixion at Exeter St Lawrence's and Our Lady and St John at Dartington – were evidently consigned to storage; occasional Marian expenditure upon their 'mending' suggests damage or neglect. Others were lost to the parish by sale. Pictures were sold at Stratton – to Richard Core, for 2s 8d – in 1549, a 'plaster' at Exeter St Petrock's in 1550–1, and painted cloths at Ashburton between 1550 and 1552.[87] In 1559, moreover, public burnings of Catholic art were organized by the Elizabethan visitors. At St Mary Steps, eight 'pictures' were removed from the church; they were then 'burned, by the commandment of the Queen's Majesty's visitors, in the visitation in the churchyard of Exeter'. At the same time, at Crediton, two 'pictures of Our Lady' were consigned to the flames. Destruction was accompanied by sale. Camborne, for example,

---

[84] *TRP*, I, pp. 275–6, 401; II, p. 123.
[85] CWA Antony, 1549; CWA Ashburton, 1550; CWA Exeter HT, 1548, 1550: CWA Exeter SJB, 1548; CWA Exeter SP, 1549; Additional 32243, HCWA Stratton, 1548, 1551.
[86] CWA Ashburton, 1560; CWA Chagford, 1567; CWA Dartington, 1559; CWA Kilmington, 1562; CWA S. Tawton, 1566?; CWA Woodbury, 1565; *Barnstaple Records*, I, p. 211.
[87] CWA Ashburton, 1551–2; CWA Dartington, 1554; CWA Exeter SP, 1551; Additional 32243, HCWA Stratton, 1548; Additional 32244, SWA Stratton, 1549; *Inventories, Exeter*, p. 38. For mending, see CWA Dartington, 1554.

would sell a 'painted cloth' (for 4s 8d) in 1561–2; it was probably that purchased (for 19s) in 1556–7.[88]

Less clearly documented is the assault upon stained glass. Certainly at Halberton, in 1553, glass was ripped from the windows of the parish church by impious laymen. Similar damage in Edward's reign is possibly indicated by expenditure upon the glazing of church windows between 1547 and 1553, as at Exeter St Mary Steps, Bodmin, Camborne, Dartmouth and Stratton,[89] and upon their repair between 1553 and 1558, as at Exeter St Petrock's, Crediton, Dartmouth, Stratton, Antony, Coldridge, Dartington, Morebath and South Tawton.[90] More glazing followed Elizabeth's accession, as at Exeter St John's Bow, Ashburton, Camborne, Stratton, Tavistock, Braunton and St Breock. Thus at St Breock, in 1565, a glazier received 40s 'for mending the windows', while at Stratton, in 1567, 22s 6d was paid for 'new glass', and 13s for mending the church windows.[91] Although expenditure of this type does not necessarily prove deliberate glass-breaking, it is probable that the replacement glass was usually non-traditionalist – as at Tavistock in 1566–7 – or even uncoloured.

That the Edwardian and early-Elizabethan destruction was by no means total is demonstrated by the examples of Catholic art still to be seen on the walls, windows, tombs, benches, bosses and screens of south-western churches. On the other hand it must be remembered that the survivals represent no more than a fraction of the art to be found in the region on the eve of the Reformation. It is also significant that the two art forms of greatest importance as instructional media – wall-painting and stained glass – are particularly uncommon today. The extensive glass at Doddiscombsleigh and St Neot is highly exceptional; it cannot be coincidental that both parishes are remote. Murals are similarly rare and seem usually to have been hidden by whitewash until their recovery in the nineteenth or twentieth centuries; this was the fate of the figures at Breage, Linkinhorne and St Thomas-by-Launceston.[92] It is also revealing that whereas the Cornish saint Mawes was, in Leland's time, 'painted as a schoolmaster',[93] no paintings of him appear to have survived. In most cases it was the smaller, less visible and consequently less instructionally effective types of medieval art that were

[88] CWA Camborne, 1557, 1562; CWA Exeter SMS, 1559; DRO 1660 A 12.
[89] STAC 4/8/47; CWA Bodmin, 1552; CWA Camborne, 1550, 1552; CWA Dartmouth, 1553; CWA Exeter SMS, 1552; Additional 32243, HCWA Stratton, 1549, 1553.
[90] CWA Antony, 1554; CWA Coldridge, 1555; CWA Crediton, 1554; CWA Dartington, 1556; CWA Dartmouth, 1554; CWA Exeter SP, 1558; CWA Morebath, 1556; CWA S. Tawton, 1554; Additional 32244, SWA Stratton, 1557.
[91] CWA Ashburton, 1561; CWA Braunton, 1559; CWA Camborne, 1561; CWA Exeter SJB, 1562; CWA St Breock, fol. 14; Additional 32243, HCWA Stratton, 1559, 1567; *Tavistock Records*, p. 29.
[92] Peter 1885, p. 359; Pevsner and Radcliffe 1970, p. 103.
[93] *Leland*, I, p. 200.

permitted to remain – hence their comparatively numerous appearances on bench-ends, the lower panels of screens, roof-bosses and the upper stages of towers. Even in these locations, signs of assault are by no means uncommon. On the rood-screen at Kenn, for instance, a Trinity and an Annunciation have been mutilated, and on the chantry screen at Paignton the sculpted figures of Our Lady and other saints have been decapitated. Traditionalist subjects, like the Virgin at North Molton, occasionally remain on towers, but more frequent are conspicuously empty figure niches, as at Chittlehampton, Lapford, South Molton and elsewhere.

While such visible examples of destruction can rarely be dated by inspection, the documentary evidence of deliberate assault during the Reformation decades would indicate that in many cases they are most plausibly attributable to this period. On occasion, moreover, the dating is relatively firm. Not only on the panels of the rood-loft at Atherington, but also on the rood-screens at Chivelstone, East Allington and South Pool, the original saint figures would appear to have been obliterated and replaced by non-religious motifs in the reign of Elizabeth.[94] By this time the suppression of traditionalist art, though by no means complete, had already been substantially achieved.

[94] Bond and Camm 1909, I, p. 92; II, p. 347; Pevsner 1952A, plate 19; Pevsner 1952B, pp. 78, 125, 267.

11

Immediate influences: example, action and oral communication

The religious attitudes of the layman were shaped not only by his exposure to mediate influences, particularly literature, drama and art, but also by his experience of direct contact with a wide variety of individuals and social groups.

In many cases a powerful influence was undoubtedly exerted by his family in general and by his parents in particular. Several members of one family might be simultaneously active in the religious life of their parish: examples include the Noseworthies at Chagford and the Rumbelows at Morebath. Familial influences are discernible also among the Catholic extremists in 1548–9. In 1548 the Cornish rioters included John and William Kilter, both of Constantine; Alan and Richard Rawe, of Gwennap and St Keverne; John Tribo the elder and John Tribo the younger, both of St Keverne; and James and John Tregena, the former of St Keverne. The power of parental training was evident also among the traditionalists at Exeter in 1549: Hooker sneered that these rejected 'any other religion than that as they were first nozzled [i.e. suckled] in'. The rebels of this year indeed demanded a return to the religious practices of 'our forefathers'.[1]

At the same time, however, anti-Catholic attitudes might also be propagated by means of the family. Protestant parents, including Thomas Bennett, John Budleigh, Robert Kede, Philip Nichols, and their respective wives, seem frequently to have successfully transmitted their religious convictions to their offspring. Bennett's son posted heretical bills; Budleigh's son Thomas grew up to be hostile to 'popery'; and the two sons of Kede, John and William, similarly espoused the faith of their father. The sons of Nichols were also imbued with their father's religion: one would become an Exeter canon, and another a Puritan minister in Kent. Further familial influence is indicated by the shared Protestantism of Philip and Robert Gammon, of Nicholas and Peter Hilliard, and of John and Robert Midwinter. The Gammons were

---

[1] CWA Chagford; CWA Morebath; Rose-Troup 1913, pp. 85, 90–1; 'Description of Exeter', p. 42; Royal 18 B XI, fols. 7v, 25.

both suspected of heresy; the Hilliards were both Marian exiles; and the Midwinters, who were brothers, were 'both of one complexion' in religion. In addition it is very possible that John Boggens, the merchant apprentice exiled to Geneva, was related to the Protestant merchant of virtually identical name at Totnes. Certainly the Budleigh brothers, John and Nicholas, were companions-in-exile in the city of Calvin.[2]

Examples of this type attest the often crucial importance of the family in the formation and maintenance of religious attitudes. Its influence, nevertheless, was by no means irresistible. The drastic decline of devotion to the traditional religion in the period 1530–70 must indeed represent the failure of virtually an entire generation to reproduce the levels of piety attained by its parents. The oligarchy at Exeter, though 'nozzled in the Romish religion', refused to defend it from the Edwardian onslaught in 1549,[3] and such declensions from parental example and training were increasingly common. At Holsworthy, where land had been donated by Thomas Newcourt to maintain a chantry priest, it was apparently reappropriated between 1538 and 1544 by his heir, John Newcourt.[4] At Cullompton, where the inmates of John Trotte's almshouse had prayed for the soul of its founder since its establishment in *circa* 1523, the almshouse was dissolved in *circa* 1544 by Trotte's own sons.[5] Robert Hooker of Exeter was a religious conservative, whose will in 1534 ordered trentals from the friars, but his son John was to become a fervent Protestant.[6] Another Exeter conservative was William Hurst, who contributed to the rood-loft at St Petrock's between 1555 and 1557; nevertheless his daughter married an apparent Protestant, John Drake.[7] Thomas Dowrish of Crediton supported the Catholic rebellion of 1549, but another member of his family, possibly his son, helped to organize Protestant preaching in the town in the 1560s.[8] At Stratton the Juddes had been traditionalists, and in 1534 had provided a warden for the store of Our Lady. By 1570, however, John Judde was the owner of an English Bible.[9]

Parental and familial devotion to the old religion was thus increasingly abandoned. Philip Nichols indeed insisted that, as Christ had rejected the traditions of the elders and fathers in his day, so now the traditions inherited

[2] *Acts and Monuments*, II, pp. 1038, 2051; Prince 1701, p. 75; Garrett 1966, pp. 92–4, 183, 236–7; STAC 2/2/267; Hooker, Commonplace Book, fol. 353. For Bougin of Totnes, see above, pp. 152, 155–6.
[3] 'Description of Exeter', pp. 42–6.
[4] C 1 976/32–3; 1042/7–9.
[5] *Certificates, Devon*, p. xxi.
[6] PROB 11 26, fol. 76; Prince 1701, pp. 387–8.
[7] CWA Exeter SP, 1556–7; PROB 11 37, fol. 144.
[8] Rose-Troup 1913, p. 355; CWA Crediton, 1569.
[9] Additional 32244, SWA Stratton, 1534; Additional 32243, HCWA Stratton, 1570.

from 'our forefathers' should be overthrown.[10] At the same time, however, it was not impossible for the influence of Protestant parents or families to be resisted. Agnes Priest, for example, failed to convert her children to the new religion.[11] Brothers, moreover, might choose divergent paths. The rebellion of 1549 was supported by one of the Drewe family but opposed by his brother, who in fact subsequently surrendered him to Lord Russell.[12]

Important also might be the influence exerted upon each other by marriage partners. A mutual consolidation in Catholicism appears to have been achieved in the reign of Henry VIII by John and Joan Greenway at Tiverton,[13] John Simon and his wife at Exeter,[14] and John and Joan Tackle at Honiton:[15] the Greenways, for example, appear together in sculpture before an assumption of Our Lady. Wives accompanied their husbands in the rebellion of 1549,[16] and in 1567 the traditionalist activities of Thomas Stephens at Alphington were abetted by his wife.[17] The anti-Catholic equivalents of such couples included the Alleys of Kenton,[18] the Bennetts[19] and Budleighs of Exeter,[20] the Nichols' of Totnes[21] and possibly the Lakes of Plymouth.[22] Thus the wife of Thomas Bennett 'was contented to bear the cross with him', and provided sustenance for him in prison. Conversely, 'when she lamented he comforted her, and gave her many good and godly exhortations'. The wives of Philip Nichols and John Budleigh shared their husbands' exile for the Protestant cause, and both Martin and Joan Alley were suspected of contempt for Catholic sacraments.

Such instances reflect not only the importance of the marriage bond in Tudor society but also the dominance of husbands over wives. It is significant, for example, that Agnes Priest failed to convert her husband to her new-found Protestant faith. 'When I would have him to leave idolatry and to worship God in Heaven', she lamented, 'he would not hear me; but he, with his children, rebuked me and troubled me.' On the other hand, he equally failed to regain her for the old religion.[23] Nor was she the only wife capable of independent action: at Exeter in 1536 the female opponents

---

[10] *Copy of a Letter*, pp. 19–21, 58–9.
[11] *Acts and Monuments*, II, p. 2050.
[12] *Prayerbook of 1549*, p. 53; Rose-Troup 1913, p. 288n.
[13] PROB 11 24, fol. 10; 27, fol. 226v; see also above, p. 91.
[14] PROB 11 22, fol. 8.
[15] PROB 11 23, fol. 71; see also above, p. 89.
[16] 'Description of Exeter', p. 38.
[17] CCB 856, fols. 143v–6.
[18] CCB 855, fols. 111v, 174v–5.
[19] *Acts and Monuments*, II, pp. 1039–40.
[20] Prince 1701, p. 75; Garrett 1966, pp. 92–4.
[21] Garrett 1966, pp. 236–7.
[22] PROB 11 45, fol. 60v; 46, fol. 258v.
[23] *Acts and Monuments*, II, p. 2050.

of iconoclasm explicitly denied that they had been encouraged to riot by their husbands.[24]

Sometimes as persuasive as the parent, relative or marriage partner was the neighbour. At Sampford Courtenay in 1549 resistance to the new Prayer-book appears to have been initiated by a small group of laymen; their defiance was then emulated by their fellow-parishioners, and subsequently copied by the inhabitants of neighbouring communities. Thomas Stephens and his wife attempted to exert a similarly traditionalist influence upon their neighbours at Alphington in 1567.[25] Protestantism might equally be disseminated by such means. At Exeter, until 1531, Thomas Bennett engaged in 'conferences' of a religious nature with neighbours whom he considered sympathetic. At Axminster, in 1535–6, Philip Gammon was reportedly 'always glad to teach and reason [about his religious views] to divers persons at divers sundry times'. For this reason, conservatives feared that 'erroneous and heretical opinions' were now 'like to increase daily and grow in the said town, to the utter destruction of the same'. At Chagford, in 1549, Kingwell the tinner was both a 'sharp inveigher' against the old religion and an 'earnest defender' of the new. Similarly Agnes Priest, in Mary's reign, 'never ceased to utter her mind, as well as she durst'. Even during her detention at Exeter, 'divers [people] had delight to talk with her; and ever she continued talking of the sacrament of the altar'. At South Molton, according to William Ramsey, the Protestants propagated their faith by their personal example to their neighbours. 'The sweet smell of your godly living and unfeigned faith', he told them in 1562, 'coupled with sincere love among yourselves, [has been] spread abroad everywhere; by means whereof, ye are become the example of godliness out-through all the coasts round about you.'[26]

Again, nevertheless, the influence could be resisted. It was neighbours who testified in court against the Catholic Thomas Stephens, and neighbours who instigated proceedings for heresy against Philip Gammon and Agnes Priest. Kingwell of Chagford similarly failed to convince his traditionalist neighbours to accept the new religion. They, for their part, 'used all the devices they could to recover him to their opinions, sometimes [with] fair words, sometimes with threatenings, and sometimes with imprisonments', but they 'could not reclaim him to their disposition'. Not even the strongest forms of neighbourhood pressure proved automatically effective.[27]

---

[24] SP 1/102/33.
[25] 'Description of Exeter', pp. 26–7; CCB 856, fols. 143v–6.
[26] *Acts and Monuments*, II, pp. 1037, 2050; STAC 2/2/272; 29/111; 'Description of Exeter', p. 66; Lansdowne 377, fol. 11.
[27] CCB 856, fols. 143v–6; STAC 2/2/267–72; 23/273; 29/111; *Acts and Monuments*, II, p. 2050; 'Description of Exeter', p. 66.

A significant influence upon the religion of the layman might also be exerted by his employer. Economically substantial Catholics undoubtedly encouraged traditionalist practices among their employees. In 1554, for example, the Exeter alderman John Tuckfield bequeathed 5s to his servant Roger Robinson 'to pray for me', and he donated money on the same condition to another servant, to his apprentice and to each of his 'maidens'.[28] Among Tuckfield's Protestant equivalents was John Budleigh: in Mary's reign he took with him into exile not only his wife, children and brother but also a number of his servants and apprentices, including his maidservant Eleanor and his 'merchant apprentices' John Boggens and Richard Vivian. The extended household, with its patriarchal structure, might thus function as an effective propagator or reinforcer of religion. An anti-Catholic influence seems also to have been exerted upon his employees by an innkeeper at Axminster in 1556: he allegedly commanded his ostlers to wait upon his guests rather than to attend the restored traditionalist services.[29]

The holders of local office were likewise in potentially influential positions over their fellow-laymen. Churchwardens, if Catholic, could certainly provide a lead by purchasing traditionalist apparatus, suppressing Protestant literature, or initiating legal action against the religiously negligent and dissident. Their accounts nevertheless leave little doubt that in the majority of cases wardens were unwilling to resist an official decree, and the predominantly conformist and acquiescent response of parochial communities to the assault upon traditional religion must be attributed in no small part to the example thus provided by their elected representatives. Without the co-operation of these crucial officials it is indeed difficult to conceive how the Reformation could have been effectively implemented. Some wardens, moreover, as at St Michael Penkevil between 1529 and 1532, at Ashbury in 1566–7 and at Rewe in 1569, were conspicuously impious in their attitudes to parish churches.[30] A similarly negative example was sometimes provided by members of parish councils, as at Halberton between 1544 and 1547 or at Spreyton in 1562.[31]

Another influential office was that of constable. At Axminster in 1535–6 it was the constable, John Sampford, who headed the traditionalists, and in Cornwall during the rebellion of 1549 it was (according to Carew) 'the constables' command and example' that 'drew many of the not-worst-meaning people into that extremest breach of duty'.[32] More often, nevertheless, the constables appear to have conformed to the government's religious

---

[28] PROB 11 39, fol. 203.
[29] Garrett 1966, pp. 72, 92–4, 318; CCB 855, fol. 63.
[30] C 1 623/12; CCB 856, fols. 25v–6, 351v–3.
[31] C 1 1138/88; CCB 855A, fols. 222, 234–4v.
[32] STAC 2/29/111; *Prayerbook of 1549*, p. 42; Rowse 1941, p. 98.

policies. They co-operated, for example, in the compilation of church inventories for the Edwardian regime, as at Germoe in 1549. On occasion, moreover, they took the lead in the denunciation of priests, as at St Breock in 1542 and at Paul in *circa* 1546, or in the embezzlement of church property, as at Davidstow in *circa* 1545.[33] Impiety of this nature might also be displayed by bailiffs of hundreds, most notoriously by Christopher Sampford at Halberton.[34]

The influence exerted upon townsmen by their oligarchies was sometimes traditionalist. In 1549, for example, the rebels included the mayors of Bodmin and Torrington, and at Exeter, in Mary's reign, the old religion was supported by mayors like William Smith and Walter Staplehead as well as by aldermen like John Blackaller and William Hurst.[35] Again, however, the predominant direction of influence was undoubtedly towards conformity. Thus at Exeter, during the Henrician Reformation, the mayors and aldermen played a vital role in the dissolution of religious houses, in the suppression of opposition, and in the interrogation of suspected dissidents: a notable example was the quelling of the riot at St Nicholas' Priory. In 1549 it was largely the authority exercised by the mayor and aldermen – who '[did] their best endeavour to keep their own citizens in peace and quietness' – that prevented the majority of Exonians from actively assisting the rebellion. In 1552, and again in 1559, the mayor co-operated in the official confiscation of church goods.[36] At Plymouth, mayors and aldermen co-operated in the Henrician campaigns against religious houses and image cults,[37] and at Lostwithiel it was on the orders of their mayor that the townsmen defaced St George's chapel in 1549.[38] Oligarchies might also provide their social inferiors with a 'perilous example' of tithe refusal, as at Helston in *circa* 1540, or of goods detention, as at Exeter in 1555.[39]

It would thus appear that the influence exerted by non-gentle laymen in local office – whether churchwardens, vestrymen, constables, bailiffs, mayors or aldermen – was not only extensive in effect but also predominantly conformist or even anti-traditionalist in character; it will further help to explain the acquiescence of the population at large in the Henrician, Edwardian and Elizabethan Reformations. Only in a minority of cases, particularly in towns, was this influence positively Protestant. Supporters of the new religion were to be found in the oligarchies at Exeter, Plymouth and else-

[33] SP 15/3/31; STAC 2/31/11, 178; 3/2/20.
[34] C 1 1138/93–4; STAC 4/8/47.
[35] Royal 18 B XI, fol. 37; Hooker, Commonplace Book, fols. 350–1; SP 11/2/15.
[36] Hooker, Commonplace Book, fols. 343–4, 349; SP 1/102/33; *LP*, XIII (1), 453; XIII (2), 354; 'Description of Exeter', p. 42; CWA S. Tawton, 1559.
[37] *LP*, XIII (2), 381, 389; *Plymouth Records*, p. 110.
[38] E 315 122/15–28.
[39] C 1 1020/4–9; *APC*, V, pp. 112–13.

where, and at South Molton the 'promoters of the kingdom of God and Christ' included mayors, constables and bailiffs.[40] Again, however, it is evident that the influence of such officials was never totally effectual. In 1536 and 1549 the religious policies of Exeter's mayors and aldermen were resisted by minority groups within the city. When Alderman Blackaller attempted to quell the rioters at St Nicholas' Priory, their leader Elizabeth Glandfield reportedly 'gave him a blow and sent him packing'.[41]

The peninsularity of the South-West and the underdevelopment of road transport together ensured that contact with the inhabitants of other regions was generally infrequent. In consequence the influence exerted upon the people of Devon and Cornwall by traditionalist laymen from other counties would seem seldom to have been substantial. An exception was provided by the rising in defence of saints' days that was planned by Carpisack and Treglosack of St Keverne in 1537; this they allegedly conceived while on an expedition to sell fish at Southampton, near which town they were chided by two men for their failure to rise in support of the 'Northern men'.[42] On the other hand, neither in 1536–7 nor in 1569 is there any evidence that rebellious traditionalists in the North of England ever attempted to foment a supportive insurrection in the South-West.[43] Co-ordination of this nature was virtually precluded by the facts of geography.

Contact with Protestants from other regions was by no means unknown. Two of Exeter's leading Protestant merchants, John Budleigh and John Periam, were connected commercially not only with Bristol – where the new religion had early taken root – but also with London, where its greatest strength lay. Among Budleigh's associates in the capital was another Marian exile, the merchant Hugh Offley. In 1559, moreover, Periam and other Protestant Exonians were actively supported in their attempt to restore 'godly' worship in the cathedral by a number of visitors from London. These were evidently merchants, who had travelled to Exeter in order to attend a fair.[44] Other south-western Protestants with London connections included the mercantile group at Plymouth,[45] Philip Nichols of Totnes,[46] and possibly Nicholas Wise of Sidenham and Bodmin.[47] Nichols, for example, had his anti-Catholic tracts published in the capital by John Day and William Seres.

40 See above, pp. 162–3.
41 Hooker, Commonplace Book, fol. 343; 'Description of Exeter', pp. 42–6.
42 SP 1/118/247–8.
43 Dodds 1915; Sharp 1975.
44 'Description of Exeter', p. 55; MacCaffrey 1958, pp. 80, 253; Garrett 1966, pp. 92–4, 240; Hooker, Commonplace Book, fol. 352; CAB 3552, fols. 140, 145–8. For Bristol, see also Powell 1972. For London, see, for example, *Acts and Monuments*; and Garrett 1966.
45 LP, X, 462.
46 *Copy of a Letter; Godly New Story.*
47 PROB 11 28, fol. 149.

It may also be significant that a leading role in the attack on the vicar of Townstall's glebe land, and in the robbery of Townstall parish church, was played by the Londoner Nicholas Adams.[48] At the same time, however, contact with the metropolis by no means always resulted in conversion to the new religion. The Tiverton merchant John Greenway, who was actually in London when he died, remained a Catholic;[49] so, in most respects, did the Exeter merchant William Hurst, who similarly traded in the capital.[50] Traditionalist apparatus and service-books might indeed be purchased in London by the representatives of south-western parishes: in Henry's reign Morebath thus acquired a banner of St George, and Dartmouth a mass-book and processional.[51]

In addition to these English connections there was a measure of contact with other nations. Of these the Welsh, Irish, Breton, French and Spanish were predominantly conservative in their influence. The Tiverton clothier John Ap Price, who had doubtless immigrated from Wales, was one of the few Marian testators to invoke the Virgin and saints and to order a place on a bede-roll and masses for his soul.[52] Another Tivertonian Catholic, John Greenway, was connected by the wool trade with Ireland, and either trade or fishing brought many Irishmen to Cornwall: one of them donated four yards of kersey to Stratton church in 1539, 'to be set upon the bede-roll'.[53] A Frenchman donated a cross to the church at Camborne in 1543.[54] Bretons, moreover, not only helped to erect the region's rood-lofts, as at North Petherwin in *circa* 1520, and welcomed its pilgrims to their shrines, like that at Lantregar in 1537, they also supported its traditionalist insurrections in 1548–9. Among the rioters at Helston in 1548 were Laurence Breton, alias Franke, and Michael Vian Breton, and in 1549 the rebels' chief gunner, the 'alien' John Hammon, may well have been a Breton too.[55]

Nevertheless the influence transmitted by such contacts was by no means invariably traditionalist. In 1549 the anti-rebel forces in the South-West included 1,000 Welshmen under Sir William Herbert, and the will made in 1557 by Griffith Ameredith, a Welsh-born citizen of Exeter, would suggest that he was in fact a Protestant.[56] Bretons, moreover, actively supported the iconoclasm at Exeter in 1536. It is also significant that when Simon

[48] STAC 3/3/81; E 117 2/7, fol. 12.
[49] PROB 11 24, fol. 10.
[50] MacCaffrey 1958, pp. 80, 253.
[51] CWA Morebath, 1539; CWA Dartmouth, 1542.
[52] PROB 11 41, fol. 253v.
[53] Prince 1701, pp. 324–5; *Leland*, I, p. 179; Additional 32243, HCWA Stratton, 1539.
[54] CWA Camborne, 1543.
[55] *Leland*, I, p. 179; CWA N. Petherwin, fols. 36v, 43, 49v; *LP*, XII (2), 301, 1325; Rose-Troup 1913, p. 85; 'Description of Exeter', p. 33; Cornwall 1977, pp. 79, 104.
[56] 'Description of Exeter', p. 64; PROB 11 41, fol. 243; Hooker, Commonplace Book, fol. 352.

Wheeler, a shipowner from Torre, made his will in the Breton port of Brest in 1556, he used a traditional formula but made no bequests to religious purposes: contact with Catholic Europe did not always result in Catholic commitment.[57] From Mary's reign, indeed, contact with the Spanish was more likely to result in violent antagonism than in conversion to their religion.[58]

The geographical location of the South-West ensured that its intercourse with the Protestant-dominated areas of Europe was in general less frequent. Before 1570, certainly, its trade with the Netherlands and with the Baltic states was minimal.[59] A Fleming helped to defend Exeter from the rebels in 1549;[60] on the other hand, the 'Dutchman' who repaired the images in Exeter Cathedral in 1558 can scarcely have been a committed Protestant.[61] Movement from the South-West to the continent was also limited. Although the Protestantism of Exeter's John Hooker owed much to his sojourn at Strasburg in Edward's reign,[62] his experience was altogether uncommon, and even in Mary's reign only a small number of the region's non-gentle laity sought refuge from persecution in either Germany or Switzerland.[63] Nor did these necessarily carry back to the South-West the doctrines of the continental Reformation. The Totnes merchant Peter Willis appears to have been trading in Devon again by 1565, but the household of John Budleigh, after its return to England in 1559, settled not in Exeter but in London.[64]

Parents, relatives, marriage partners, neighbours, employers, officials, individuals from other regions or from other countries – the religious attitudes of the average man might be shaped by his contact with a wide variety of members of the non-gentle laity. Equally significant, nevertheless, might be the influence exerted upon him by the few hundred families within the region who constituted its dominant elite. As its major landlords and employers, as its justices, sheriffs and members of parliament, and as its most highly educated and articulate social group, the gentry of the South-West inevitably exercised a considerable degree of control over the middle and lower sectors of the regional society. In religion, as in secular affairs, the influence of this elite was always substantial.

Until the 1530s the direction of this influence was predominantly traditionalist. Both the construction and the furnishing of the region's parish

---

[57] Hooker, Commonplace Book, fol. 343; SP 1/102/33; PROB 11 39, fol. 415v.
[58] See above, pp. 173–4. See also, for example, *LP*, XV, 426.
[59] MacCaffrey 1958, pp. 151, 167.
[60] See above, pp. 36–7.
[61] *Acts and Monuments*, II, p. 2051. The term implies a German rather than a Netherlander.
[62] Prince 1701, pp. 387–8.
[63] See above, pp. 164–5.
[64] Garrett 1966, pp. 92–4, 337; Prince 1701, pp. 75–82.

churches were actively forwarded by its gentry. Among the various coats-of-arms displayed on the church at Launceston – which was rebuilt between 1511 and 1524 – are those of its chief patrons, the Trecarrels; major patronage of this type was also exercised by the Bonvilles at Ottery St Mary, by the Gilberts at Marldon, by the Kirkhams at Ashcombe, and by scores of other gentle or noble families throughout the pre-Reformation South-West. The churches at Bovey Tracey, Sampford Peverell and Uplowman were largely reconstructed in *circa* 1500 by the Beauforts. The arms of donors are frequent in glass, as at Doddiscombsleigh, and on bench-ends, as at Golant: in the former parish they commemorate the Chudleighs and Dodscombes, and in the latter the Colquites. At Coldridge, according to an inscription, the benches were donated in 1511 by Sir John Evans.[65] Gentlemen might also involve themselves in the organization of parochial religion. At Stratton John Chamond Esquire served as a warden of the High Cross guild in 1518, and helped to arrange the contract for the new rood-loft in 1531.[66]

Inevitably the piety of the gentry was never universal. Between 1517 and 1520 the churches at Blackawton, Powderham and Rattery were robbed by James Courtenay, Thomas Gibbes and William Gibbes;[67] in *circa* 1523 the efforts of the parishioners of Probus to rebuild their church were deliberately obstructed by Nicholas Carminow;[68] and in 1527 the mob that demolished the Abbot of Tavistock's weir was assembled by William Harris, John Kelly and Henry Trecarrel.[69] In general, nevertheless, the example provided by this class for its social inferiors was undoubtedly supportive of traditional religion.

It is therefore significant that in the Reformation decades no more than a relatively small proportion of this class seems ever to have actively resisted the official anti-traditionalist campaigns. In 1548, for example, the riot at Helston was supported by few or no gentry.[70] In the rebellion of 1549, according to Hooker, 'the obstinacy of the people' was reinforced by some of 'the best', 'who did both favour their cause and secretly encouraged them therein', and certainly those gentlemen who joined the revolt were often followed by their servants, as was Humphrey Arundell Esquire by Thomas Leigh of Week St Mary. On the other hand it is equally certain that neither in Devon nor in Cornwall was the insurrection ever joined by more than

---

[65] Pevsner 1952A, pp. 75, 157; Pevsner 1952B, pp. 40, 121, 203, 221, 255; Pevsner and Radcliffe 1970, pp. 74, 97.

[66] Additional 32243, HCWA Stratton, 1518; *Blanchminster's Charity*, pp. 91–4. See also Additional 32244, SWA Stratton, 1534.

[67] STAC 2/21/158; *LP*, XIII (2), 21.

[68] STAC 2/17/209.

[69] STAC 2/30/115.

[70] Rose-Troup 1913, pp. 74–96.

a tiny percentage of the gentry: the Protector was exaggerating only slightly when he reckoned the total at 'not past two or three'. Militant Catholics like Arundell, Bury, Coffin, Pomeroy and Winslade in fact proved altogether unrepresentative of their social class.[71] Even non-violent resistance to the official Reformation seems not to have been extensive. In 1564 the Bishop of Exeter's list of prominent Catholics within his diocese included names like Arundell, Kirkham, Roscarrock and Tregian, but the total number – approximately 15 – again represented no more than a small minority of the several hundred gentle families within the South-West.[72] And with only three exceptions – an Arundell, a Courtenay and a Godolphin – the justices of both counties subscribed dutifully to the Act of Uniformity in 1569, promising to attend their parish churches, to participate in the common prayer, and even to receive the Protestant communion.[73]

Not only did the gentry thus fail as a group to lead resistance to the Reformation; in numerous instances it indeed co-operated actively in its implementation. In the reign of Henry VIII, for example, suspected dissidents were examined and punished by gentlemen like Sir Thomas Dennis, Sir Piers Edgcumbe, Sir William Godolphin and the brothers Pollard. Thus Dennis interrogated the rioters at St Nicholas' Priory in 1536. It was Hugh and Richard Pollard who apparently executed the iconoclasm at Pilton in 1537, and Godolphin who prevented the rising in defence of saints' days at St Keverne in the same year.[74] Dennis, Edgcumbe, Godolphin and Sir Hugh Pollard also served, under the presidency of Lord Russell, in the Council of the West. At its institution this body was explicitly instructed to 'give straight charge and commandment to the people to conform themselves' to the new laws, and particularly to those against the pope – 'whose abuses they shall so beat into their heads by continual inculcation as they may smell and perceive the same'.[75]

In Edward's reign official policies like the suppression of chantries and the confiscation of church goods were similarly implemented by the local gentry. The chantry commissioners for Devon, for example, were Sir Roger Bluett, Robert Cary, Anthony Harvey, George Haydon, Sir Hugh Pollard and John Prideaux. Thus it was by command of his master, Anthony Harvey, that a servant attempted to collect dues belonging to the dissolved guild of St Lawrence at Ashburton in 1548. The church inventories were compiled

---

[71] 'Life of Carew', p. lxxxvi; Rose-Troup 1913, esp. p. 355; 'Description of Exeter', p. 37. For the influence of Pomeroy, see *Prayerbook of 1549*, p. 49. For the possible role of the Courtenays, see Youings 1979.
[72] *Original Letters*, pp. 67–70.
[73] SP 12/60/27, 39.
[74] *LP*, VI, 503; XII (1), 1000, 1127; XIII (1), 416; SP 1/80/193; 102/33; E 315 126/16–17.
[75] Rowse 1941, p. 241; Titus B 1, fols. 172–9.

under the supervision of gentlemen like Richard Chamond Esquire, John Godolphin, Sir Richard Grenville, John Killigrew and John Reskymmer in Cornwall in 1549, and Sir Gawen Carew, Sir Peter Carew, Anthony Harvey and Thomas Hatch in Devon in 1553.[76] In 1547, moreover, it was Sir William Godolphin who pacified the 'tumultuous assembly' in defence of church goods in the hundred of Penwith,[77] and in 1548 it was 'the gentlemen of the country', including Sir Richard Edgcumbe, who organized the suppression of the riot in defence of images at Helston.[78]

Most significantly of all, the rebellion of 1549 was opposed, defeated and subsequently punished by members of several of the region's most important gentle families; the names included Bluett, Carew, Champernowne, Chichester, Courtenay, Dennis, Grenville, Pollard, Raleigh, Russell and Yarde. Of these the most active were Lord Russell and Sir Gawen and Sir Peter Carew. Not only did gentlemen thus provide their inferiors with a public example of loyalism, they also thus induced a virtually automatic opposition to the revolt among their numerous dependants. 'Serving-men', observed the anonymous gentleman of Devon, 'be commonly brought up in such civility that hardly they be made traitors; it is a common proverb that "trust serving-man, trust gentleman".' Serving-men accompanied their masters not only on the abortive expeditions of pacification to Sampford Courtenay and Clyst St Mary, but also into the fierce fighting at Crediton, Fenny Bridges and elsewhere. At Crediton, for example, it was a servant of Sir Hugh Pollard who set fire to the rebel-held barn. Kingwell, the anti-rebel tinner from Chagford, was a servant of the loyalist Mr Charles of Tavistock, and the Exmouth mariners who rescued Walter Raleigh Esquire from the insurgents were very possibly his employees. After the revolt's suppression, the Council accordingly instructed Russell to convey its gratitude to the gentlemen, soldiers and serving-men 'who have so valiantly acquitted themselves in the service of his majesty'.[79]

Under Elizabeth, as under Henry and Edward, the official religious policies were implemented by local gentlemen. In 1559, for instance, several were to be found among the commissioners who organized the assault upon altars, images and other traditionalist apparatus; they included Sir Peter Carew, Sir Arthur Champernowne and Sir John Chichester.[80] In all three reigns,

---

[76] STAC 3/2/14; E 117 1/48–52B; 2/7; SP 15/3/29–46.
[77] Harleian 352, fol. 65v.
[78] *Plymouth Records*, pp. 16, 115.
[79] 'Description of Exeter', esp. pp. 27–34, 55–7, 66; *Prayerbook of 1549*, p. 65; *Survey of Cornwall*, pp. 265, 292, 380; Rose-Troup 1913; Garrett 1966, pp. 118–19. For the gentleman of Devon, see Rose-Troup 1913, p. 488. For Raleigh's ship-owning, see SP 11/3/10.
[80] CAB 3552, fol. 137.

therefore, the gentry played a crucial role in the imposition of the Reformation upon the south-western people.

Not only did this elite generally acquiesce in, or co-operate with, official campaigns against the old religion. In an increasing number of cases it engaged in semi-official or unofficial activities of a conspicuously anti-traditionalist type. Popular confidence in the future of Catholic practices was undermined by the spectacle of gentlemen demolishing crosses or seizing ritual apparatus, as was done in Edward's reign by Sir Roger Bluett and Walter Raleigh Esquire at Exeter, and Sir John Chichester, John Parker Esquire and others at Barnstaple;[81] encouraging the breaking of the Lenten fast, as did Mr Charles of Tavistock at about the same time;[82] or leading opposition to the use of holy water, as did a Trelawney at Menheniot in the reign of Mary.[83] In particular the confidence of men and women in intercessions was eroded by the example of their social superiors. In as early as 1529–32 gentlemen detained deeds from a guild of the Trinity at Exeter, appropriated an annuity that had maintained a chantry priest at Tretherf, and dissolved a stipendiary post at Thornbury. Property at St Winnow, granted by William Casely Esquire to maintain prayers and an obit, was reclaimed by his heirs in *circa* 1537. At Colyford, from 1537, Robert Stowford Esquire refused to pay a chantry priest more than half of his customary income. Another gentleman, John Kellow, laid claim to land at Lansallos that had allegedly maintained obits. More chantries were privately dissolved by the Carminows at St Michael Penkevil in 1542 and by other gentle families at Colebrooke and Halberton in *circa* 1545.[84]

Another gentleman, Mr Gibbes, apparently shielded from punishment the desecrator of a cross at Silverton in Mary's reign. It may not be coincidental that one of the despoilers of images at Rewe in 1538, John Richards, had been associated with William Gibbes Esquire.[85] Others took the lead in the expropriation of income belonging to parish churches and chapels. Among the offenders were Gilbert Becket Esquire at Pelynt in 1530, John Mallet Esquire at St Giles-in-the-Wood in 1543–5, and Edward Knolles at Littlehempston in *circa* 1570.[86] And others, on the eve of the dissolutions, appear to have encouraged anti-monastic behaviour among their inferiors. The men who attacked the Prior of Bodmin's servant at Padstow sometime between 1533 and 1538 were led by a Carminow. The Bodmin townsmen who at about this time raided their prior's weir were supported by an

---

[81] Rose-Troup 1913, pp. 505–7; *Barnstaple Records*, I, pp. 198–9.
[82] CCB 855, fol. 5v.
[83] CCB 855, fols. 127v–8v.
[84] C 1 601/1; 631/4, 1228/63; *Certificates, Devon*, pp. xxi–xxii, 25; *Certificates, Cornwall*, pp. 28, 53–4; Henderson 1923–4, p. 389.
[85] SP 11/2/15; C 1 924/9–10; 1121/12–14.
[86] STAC 2/21/94; C 1 1378/39; C 3 202/65.

Arundell. And in *circa* 1536 it was through John Holbeam Esquire that the inhabitants of Torre presented their bitter petition against the abbot.[87]

Even more evident was the influence of gentlemen upon popular attitudes to the secular clergy. From 1534, when the trend was initiated by Sir Thomas Dennis, they were appropriating advowsons from the Bishop of Exeter.[88] From 1542, moreover, they were ruthlessly acquiring favourable leases on, or even outright possession of, the lands of the bishop and of the dean and chapter. By 1551, when its annual income had thus been reduced from approximately £1,600 to about £500, one of the wealthiest English sees had been transformed into one of the poorest. The beneficiaries of this pillage included the Carews, Dennises, Killigrews and Russells.[89] Lesser clerics were similarly subjected to financial exploitation. In 1540 an Arundell was charged by the vicar of Hartland with a forcible expulsion from land at Morwenstow and Poundstock, and by the 1550s behaviour of this type was no longer uncommon. Philip Dennis, for example, blackmailed the parson of North Lew. Walter Hele detained rent from the vicar of Cornwood; Anthony Amory occupied the rectory at High Bickington; John Plemin stole glebe land from the vicar of Gulval; and the vicarage and glebe at Bovey Tracey were seized from the vicar by John Southcott Esquire and his son.[90] In Edward's reign certain gentlemen were described by the vicar of St Neot as 'devilish', and devoid of 'the fear of God and all Christian charity'. Because he had testified against them in a legal case they had allegedly threatened him with death.[91] In Mary's reign one of the cathedral clergy at Exeter complained about local gentlemen 'who never did the Church good, nor peradventure intend'.[92]

Some, in addition, proved conspicuously unwilling to defend the clergy from lay hostility. In 1534, at St Cleer, an assaulted chaplain failed totally to secure protection from the local justices. His assailants, he lamented, were 'so greatly friended, favoured and supported by men of authority and power in that country, and their said misdemeanours there so maintained'. In Edward's reign, when the plundered parson of Bittadon appealed to the gentry for redress, they 'rather mocked [him] than caused him to have any restitution'. He described his plunderers as 'belonging to certain gentlemen', who shielded them from the law. It is also revealing that when, in Mary's reign, the anti-clerical, and indeed anti-Catholic, Cornishmen Cowlyn and Jackman were reported by Sir John Arundell to the Bodmin sessions, his

[87] STAC 2/21/96; 29/55; Rowse 1941, p. 176.
[88] CAB 3551, fol. 118 etc.; *LP*, XIV (2), 177.
[89] CAB 3551, fol. 147 etc.; 3552, fols. 50v–1; Rowse 1941, pp. 143–4, 292–5. See also Pill 1963.
[90] STAC 2/30/4; C 1 1325/35; 1341/77–9; 1378/19–21; 1381/68; 1386/17.
[91] C 1 1201/15–16.
[92] CAB 3552, fol. 118v.

traditionalist zeal seems not to have been shared by the justices, 'who, not-withstanding [the evidence against them], at the said sessions bailed the said Jackman and Cowlyn'. Arundell was thus compelled to complain to the Council itself.[93]

In some cases, indeed, popular antagonism to clerics was actively encour-aged by gentlemen. In 1529 it was Sir William Coffin of Portledge who allegedly ordered a group of mortuary-resisting parishioners to bury their priest alive. The raid on Bridestow parsonage in 1540 was directed by Peter Courtenay Esquire, while the attack on the vicar of Hartland's timber rights in this year was the responsibility of Bartholomew Fortescue Esquire. In 1551 it was a justice of the peace, Mr Tremayne, who publicly announced to the parishioners of Lamerton that henceforth they need pay only three offerings to their vicar. A witness records that Tremayne 'loved not Sir Harry Hawkins, then vicar of Lamerton'. In Mary's reign the priest-assault-ing parishioners of St Keyne were led by a justice of the peace; the Stokenham men who withheld rent from their vicar, by John Halse Esquire; the des-poilers of the vicarage at St Just, by a Godolphin. And in 1568, at Honiton Clyst, the conspiracy to discredit a cathedral canon seems ultimately to have been organized by the Yardes of Treasuresbeare.[94]

Throughout the Reformation decades, it is true, a number of gentlemen remained supportive of traditional practices or institutions. Between 1538 and 1544, for example, the property rights of a guild at South Petherwin were defended by Richard Tremayne Esquire. Thomas Arundell Esquire donated vestments to Stratton church in 1540 and contributed to the rebuild-ing of its chancel in 1544–5. A justice of the peace, John Saintclair, attempted to prevent the confiscation of guild property at Ashburton in 1548. In Mary's reign a chasuble, banner and corporas case were bequeathed to Woodbury church by Edward Ford; another gentleman served as warden of St Brannoc's store at Braunton; and two more, Humphrey Stephens and William Wyke, sought to protect from financial exploitation the church at North Lew.[95] Such men, nevertheless, were increasingly uncommon. The evidence leaves little doubt that in general the assault upon Catholicism was substantially facilitated by the acquiescence or co-operation of the region's dominant social group.

The motives inducing these gentry responses were inevitably complex. One factor – expressed, for example, by the Devon gentleman in his tirade against the rebels of 1549 – was the ineradicable sixteenth-century sense

[93] STAC 2/30/104; C 1 1369/11–20; SP 11/2/2.
[94] Prince 1701, pp. 181–2; STAC 2/21/163; 32/4; C 1 1389/68–71; 1467/41; CCB 855, fols. 36v, 50v–1v, 53; CCB 856, fols. 271–3v.
[95] C 1 959/35–7; 1482/97; STAC 3/2/14; CWA Braunton, 1555; CWA Woodbury, 1554; Additional 32243, HCWA Stratton, 1540; Additional 32244, SWA Stratton, 1545.

of obligation to established authority.[96] Another was physical fear: the
hanging, drawing and quartering of rebel gentry after 1549 must have constituted a sobering deterrent to further resistance.[97] But arguably more important than either of these factors were considerations of material interest.
Certainly the general failure of the south-western gentry to support the
1549 revolt is attributable largely to its investment in the confiscated lands
of religious houses and chantry foundations – the partial return of which
was explicitly demanded by the rebel articles. 'If I should fight with those
traitors', exclaimed the gentleman of Devon, 'I would, for every two strokes
to be stricken for treason, strike one to keep my lands: the which I bought
too surely to deliver it at a papist's appointment.' The greatest recipient
of such lands in the South-West was in fact the commander of the loyalist
forces, Lord Russell.[98] Support for anti-traditionalist regimes might also
have been induced by the expectation of material reward. Godolphin, pacifier
of the St Keverne conspiracy in 1537, was rewarded by a grateful government
with lucrative office. After the 1549 rebellion the estates of Arundell, Bury
and Winslade were granted to the Carews and William Gibbes Esquire;
Russell himself received land worth some £300 per annum.[99]

In a number of cases the gentry were motivated at least in part by Protestant
convictions. In *circa* 1530 William Strode of Newenham was imprisoned
at Exeter on suspicion of heresy. He certainly corresponded with Thomas
Bennett. In 1535–6 Axminster's Philip Gammon was protected against
heresy charges by his own master, Sir William Carew of Mohun's Ottery:
the latter was described as 'the great bearer, aider, helper and maintainer
of the said Philip Gammon in his affairs'. But it was Carew's son, Sir Peter,
whom Hooker would laud as 'an earnest promoter of God's true religion',
'a great favourer of all Protestants', and a patron 'most godly affected to
all good and godly men'. In 1547 Philip Nichols indeed attributed the survival
of the region's nascent Protestant minority to the protection afforded by
Sir Peter: 'Praised may the name of God be therefore, that so provideth
for young sucklings: which else should be overwhelmed before they were
weaned from their milk.' Carew was patron to both Hooker and Nichols;
the latter described him as his 'singular good master'. In addition he was
associated with the apparently Protestant Griffith Ameredith, and he was
related by marriage to the certainly Protestant John Budleigh. In 1548–9
half of the cost of Ashburton's *Paraphrases* was contributed by a gentleman,
George Young, and during the 1549 rebellion a number of the local gentry

[96] Rose-Troup 1913, pp. 486–8, 492.
[97] 'Description of Exeter', p. 70.
[98] Royal 18 B XI, fol. 33v; Rose-Troup 1913, pp. 491–2; Rowse 1941, pp. 296–8.
[99] 'Description of Exeter', p. 65; Rose-Troup 1913, pp. 380–1; Rowse 1941, pp. 231, 290.

– including William Hellions and Walter Raleigh Esquire, as well as Sir Peter Carew – were regarded as heretics by the Catholic insurgents. Raleigh's wife was described by Foxe as a 'worthy gentlewoman ... of a good and godly opinion'. She visited Agnes Priest in prison and engaged her in religious discussion. Another gentry family of Protestant inclination were the Tremaynes, and it can scarcely be coincidental that their dependants included Peter Willis, merchant of Totnes and Marian exile. In and around South Molton, similarly, the Protestants were led by gentlemen. In 1562 these included Sir John Chichester as well as a Courtenay, a Fortescue, a Parker and a Pollard.[100]

At least some of the south-western gentry were thus active in the propagation of the new religion. Their commitment – itself attributable to factors such as literacy, education and possibly contact with London – helps to explain the emergence and survival of Protestantism at the popular level. At the same time, it is evident that enthusiasts of this type remained uncommon. Hooker in fact lamented that in 1549 the South-West was 'not stored' with 'well-persuaded magistrates'. He suspected that even among the justices who attempted to quell the insurrection, some 'did not like the alteration [of religion]'. In 1547 Philip Nichols was similarly dismayed that, of the 'men of worship' attending Dr Chrispin's anti-Protestant sermon at Marldon, not one was prepared to refute it. It is also significant that with only a small number of exceptions – including Carew, Gibbes and apparently Raleigh – the region's gentry failed to support the partially Protestant rebellion of 1554. Several, including Sir Thomas Dennis, indeed opposed it. Nor do the several hundred members of this social group appear to have contributed more than about 21 individuals to the Protestant exodus from Marian England. Among them were three Carews, three Killigrews and three Tremaynes, as well as two Courtenays, a Chichester, a Godolphin and a Russell. In as late as 1564, moreover, a number of the justices of Devon and Cornwall appear to have been religiously neutral or conformist rather than committedly Protestant. These, reported Bishop Alley, 'are not so earnest to maintain the ecclesiastical policy as they are wished to be'. If the existence of sympathetic gentlemen will partly explain the emergence of popular Protestantism, their relative scarcity before the 1560s provides a further reason for its generally retarded development.[101]

At the same time, it cannot be assumed that the gentry's influence upon

---

[100] *Acts and Monuments*, II, pp. 1037, 2051; STAC 2/29/111; 'Life of Carew', p. cxiv; *Copy of a Letter*, dedication, pp. 1–2; CWA Ashburton, 1549; 'Description of Exeter', pp. 31–3, 66–7; Lansdowne 377, fols. 26v–7v; MacCaffrey 1958, p. 212; Garrett 1966, pp. 104–8, 337; Roberts 1962–4, pp. 295–6.
[101] 'Description of Exeter', pp. 26, 28; *Copy of a Letter*, pp. 31–2; SP 11/2/11–16; 3/10; 'Life of Carew', p. lxxxix; Garrett 1966, pp. 70, 104–8, 118–21, 130–2, 162, 205–7, 209, 228–9, 272–3, 275–7, 281–2, 287, 309–11; *Original Letters*, p. 69.

its inferiors was invariably effectual. In 1549, at Sampford Courtenay, Crediton and Clyst St Mary, parishioners refused to be dissuaded by gentlemen from resisting the new religion. When 'earnestly reproved' by William Hellions, the rebels imprisoned and then murdered him. At the other end of the ideological spectrum, at Exeter in 1532 Thomas Bennett ignored the two gentlemen who 'willed him to revoke his errors'. Unmoved by their 'fair promises and goodly words', and then by their 'rough threatenings', he died at the stake without recanting. Equally obdurate was Agnes Priest, when urged to recant by 'the gentlemen of the country'.[102]

Of the many and varied forms of influence that shaped popular attitudes the most crucially important were probably those exerted by the religious professionals – the monks, friars and secular clergy. This corps of several hundred men was in potentially influential contact not only with individual layfolk, in informal conversation or in the rite of confession, but also with lay groups, particularly of children, in an educational context, and with lay congregations, in church services and especially in sermons. These contacts allowed them to play a uniquely powerful role in the formation of public opinion.

Until the 1530s the religious attitudes conveyed to laymen by contact with these professionals were almost invariably traditionalist. In 1531, at Exeter, the clergy were dismissed by Thomas Bennett as 'blind guides': he believed that they were leading the people 'headlong to everlasting damnation'. The friars in particular he condemned as 'superstitious', complaining of their influence over laymen in the act of confession. Monks of St Nicholas' Priory at this date were similarly reported to be 'superstitious'. In 1534 some of the region's religious were said to have sworn their obedience to the king 'with an evil will', and in 1539 its monks would be denounced by Sir Richard Grenville as 'devourers of God's word', and 'sprays to the Devil's Bishop of Rome'. Traditionalist also at the beginning of the Henrician Reformation were Bishop Veysey, most of the cathedral canons and virtually all of the parochial clergy. Foxe claims that when Bennett's heretical declaration appeared on the cathedral doors 'the bishop and all his doctors were as hot as coals, and enkindled as though they had been stung with a sort of wasps'. Many of the region's priests, moreover, were in 1536 reportedly unwilling to propagate the official injunctions and articles. 'The priests of this country are a strange kind', observed the new and fervently Protestant Dean of Exeter in 1537. 'Very few of them', he feared, were 'well-persuaded'. A similar evaluation of the pre-Reformation clergy was made by Philip Nichols: 'They thought [faith] to be too little to bring them to Heaven;

[102] 'Description of Exeter', pp. 27–8, 30–1, 33–6, 66–7; Rose-Troup 1913, p. 127; *Acts and Monuments*, II, pp. 1040, 2051.

and therefore all the mass, matins, evensongs, *diriges*, holy bread, holy water, palms, ashes, with such other gear, should be a mean ... They held stoutly that "faith only" could not justify, neither could we by "faith only" be accepted into God's favour.' In brief, 'they knew not the gospel'. Typical of such clerics was Christopher Trychay, vicar of Morebath from 1520; he ended his early accounts with invocations of Our Lady or of saints.[103] The traditionalist influence thus exerted by the clergy must provide one of the most fundamental explanations for the strength of popular devotion to the old religion on the eve of the Reformation. In what measure was the decline of this devotion during the subsequent decades the result of a diminution of such influence?

Processes of change were undoubtedly initiated by the Henrician Reformation. Between 1536 and 1539 the region's monasteries were totally suppressed, and since no more than a minority of their inmates – such as the Bodmin monks who were instituted at Bodmin, Grade, Jacobstow, Morval, Padstow and St Breock – seem subsequently to have served as parish priests, the public influence of these conservatives was to a large extent eradicated.[104] Even more relevant to laymen was the government's increasing hostility to the predominantly traditionalist friars. In as early as 1533 the warden of Plymouth's Franciscans was examined by Sir Piers Edgcumbe and imprisoned in Launceston Castle. In 1534, on instruction from Thomas Cromwell, a pursuit of two friars observant was organized by the Sheriff of Devon. The offenders – who had urged people to remain loyal to the pope, criticized the king's remarriage and denounced recently authorized books, Hugh Latimer and other reformers – were eventually arrested in Cardiff. In 1537, again on Cromwell's orders, a friar at Exeter was arrested and delivered to the mayor, and in 1538 a Franciscan was imprisoned at Launceston on suspicion of treason. This latter year, moreover, witnessed the permanent suppression of every friary in the region. Again the episcopal registers would suggest that friars who secured benefices – like the Franciscan Gregory Bassett at Aylesbeare – were the exception rather than the rule.[105]

But of greatest long-term significance for the popular religion was the official campaign against traditionalist members of the secular clergy. In 1537 the papalist Reginald Pole was deprived of the deanery of Exeter. In 1533, at Plymouth, two priests were interrogated by Sir Piers Edgcumbe, while in 1536 a priest who had protested at Launceston against the taxation of stipendiaries was examined by Dr Tregonwell and reported to Cromwell.

---

[103] *Acts and Monuments*, II, pp. 1037–40; *LP*, VII, 869; XI, 954; XII (2), 557; XIV (1), 1338; *Godly New Story*, pp. 61–2; CWA Morebath.
[104] ER XIV, XV; Rowse 1941, p. 209.
[105] SP 1/80/193; *LP*, VII, 939; XII (2), 557; *Plymouth Records*, p. 109; ER XIV, XV.

In 1538 the supposedly seditious utterances of a priest at Week St Mary resulted in his appearance before Godolphin at the Bodmin sessions and in his imprisonment at Launceston. In this year also a Breton priest, who had attempted to spread disaffection in the South-West, was brought before Sir Thomas Dennis and committed to Exeter gaol; once more the incident was reported to Cromwell. A similar fate befell the two apparently clerical Spaniards who, after landing at Dartmouth in 1541, moved eastwards to Salisbury and spoke in favour of monasteries and the pope. By this date few of the region's own clergy dared openly to controvert the Henrician Reformation, and indeed not one appears to have refused the declaration against papal authority.[106]

Initiated under Henry VIII, the suppression of clerical traditionalism intensified during the Edwardian years. In 1548, for example, the St Keverne priest who had led the resistance to iconoclasm at Helston was arrested, conveyed to London and there executed. Other dissidents were imprisoned. But it was the rebellion of 1549 that resulted in the removal of the region's most intransigently conservative priests from their positions of public influence. The insurrection was attributed by the Council to 'the provocation only of certain popish priests'. A contemporary ballad agreed that 'Under confession, these priests do bind / The simple people, most earnest of all / On pain of damnation to follow their mind ... / To most rank treason they caused men to fall.' Such clerics inevitably provided prime targets for the victorious regime. Some, including the vicars of St Cleer and St Keverne, were attainted, and several – including the incumbents of Exeter St Thomas' and Pillaton, and probably those also of Gulval, Poundstock and St Neot – were publicly hanged. The vicar of St Thomas' – who had 'persuade[d] the people to the condemning of the reformed religion according to the king's proceedings' – was hanged in chains from his own church tower; there his body 'remained a long time'. The parson of North Lew, who subsequently admitted that he had performed mass in his parish church during the rebellion, was arrested as a traitor and threatened with a similar death. Others suffered imprisonment, or were forced to flee their cures: the parson of Bittadon later recalled that in order to avoid the imprisonment inflicted upon other priests, he had been 'enforced to hide himself for a season'. The number deprived of their benefices is unknown, but the frequency of institutions in the diocese during the months following the rebellion would suggest that it was by no means inconsiderable. In 1551, moreover, even the moderately conservative Bishop Veysey was deprived of his office, and replaced by the resolutely anti-traditionalist Miles Coverdale. It is therefore

[106] SP 1/80/193; 106/134; *LP*, VII, 1024–5, 1121, 1216; XIII (2), 267; XIV (1), 87; XVI, 1032, 1047. For Pole, see also Royal 18 B XI, fols. 32–3.

scarcely surprising that by the end of Edward's reign the number of clerics still willing to propagate the old religion appears to have been low.[107]

The Marian interlude brought temporary relief. In 1553 the see was restored briefly to the aged Veysey; then, in 1555, it was entrusted to the similarly conservative James Turberville. Other ecclesiastical offices were returned to Catholics.[108] Monks and friars, however, were never restored; and after the accession of Elizabeth the official repression revived. In 1559 her visitors ordered the expulsion from the cathedral of 'open enemies unto the word of God', and of 'talkers, mutterers and grudgers' against the religion newly established. By 1561 the traditionalists thus ousted from office included the dean, chancellor and several canons as well as Bishop Turberville himself; his replacement was the anti-Catholic William Alley. Of the parochial clergy the great majority would appear to have conformed, and the dissident minority was gradually silenced. In 1559 the vicar of Bodmin was ordered by the commissioners to make a public recantation in his parish church, and when, in 1561, an Exeter canon supported the doctrine of transubstantiation and denied that the pope was Antichrist, he was sent before the High Commission and compelled to recant. The irreconcilably Catholic were progressively removed from their benefices. In the first twelve years of the reign, incumbents were ejected or deprived – in most cases for Catholicism – in approximately 10% of the region's parishes.[109]

During the Reformation decades, in brief, the traditionalist influence exerted upon laymen by clerics was gradually reduced and eventually to a considerable extent suppressed. This important development will undoubtedly furnish another major explanation for the decline of popular devotion to the old religion. At the same time, the restricted growth of popular Protestantism must be attributed in substantial measure to the fact that no more than a relatively small percentage of the south-western clergy could yet be described as committed proponents of the reformed faith.

Enthusiasts unquestionably existed. They included Heynes, Coverdale and Alley at Exeter, as well as parochial clergy like Nicholas Daniel at St Teath, George Manning at Bovey Tracey and William Ramsey at South Molton.[110] Nor is there doubt that their influence over laymen could be considerable.

---

[107] Royal 18 B XI, fols. 3, 29, 37–7v; *Prayerbook of 1549*, pp. 15–19; 'Description of Exeter', pp. 65–8; C 1 1341/77–9; 1369/11–20; *Acts and Monuments*, II, p. 1305; *Cranmer*, II, pp. 502–3, 547; Rose-Troup 1913, pp. 91–2, 337, 497–502; Rowse 1941, pp. 253, 283–4; Cornwall 1977, p. 202.

[108] E.g. the chancellor Blaxton (*Acts and Monuments*, II, p. 2050).

[109] *Zurich Letters*, pp. 44–5; CAB 3552, fol. 138v; Hooker, Commonplace Book, fols. 353–4; Rowse 1941, p. 321; Field 1973, pp. 102–18; *Exeter Records*, p. 39; 'Synopsis Chorographical', p. 161; *CSPD*, VI, Addenda, Elizabeth, p. 45; SP 12/19/24.

[110] 'Life of Carew', p. cxiv; 'Description of Exeter', p. 190; C 1 1325/35; 1347/16–18; *Acts and Monuments*, II, p. 2051; Lansdowne 377.

When, in 1557, Griffith Ameredith of Exeter chose a Protestant formula for his will, he also made a bequest of 10s to the parson of St Petrock's, whom he described as 'my ghostly [i.e. spiritual] father'. This was William Herne, a supporter of the new religion in Edward's reign.[111] Clerical Protestantism, nevertheless, was by no means extensive. Even those who professed the new faith under Edward not infrequently conformed to the old under Mary: an example is in fact provided by William Herne himself.[112] Those who refused to submit – such as Coverdale and Manning – were usually deprived of their offices and benefices.[113] It is suggestive also that of the clerical exiles in Mary's reign, no more than two appear to have held livings or ecclesiastical offices within the South-West: these were Dr John Reynolds and Coverdale himself.[114] Similarly significant are the facts that only approximately 8% of the region's clergy would seem to have chosen the option of marriage in Edward's reign, and that this figure had risen only to approximately 17% by the time of Bishop Alley's report in 1561. Even these were by no means exclusively committed Protestants.[115]

It is therefore improbable that more than a small proportion of the south-western population will ever have received a favourable exposition of the Protestant gospel by means of contact with a member of the clergy. 'Where ye complain of the blindness and unwillingness of your curates to the setting forth of our proceedings', the rebels of Devon and Cornwall were told by Protector Somerset in 1549, 'we do not think your complaints much untrue in that behalf.'[116] In 1562, after the departure of William Ramsey, even the Protestants of South Molton found themselves 'destitute of a pastor to feed [their] souls with the wholesome food of God's word'. In the same year, at Rockbeare, the yeoman John Holmere reported that 'he never heard the vicar to move the parishioners to come unto the holy communion but once in a twelve months', and in 1568, at Egloshayle, a similar neglect of the Protestant communion was attributed by one of the inhabitants to the fact that 'their curate hath given them no instructions that they ought to receive it thrice a year'.[117]

The influence of the clergy was exerted by means of its contacts not only with individuals but also with groups. Of these the school group was potentially among the most important. In the South-West, on the eve of the official

[111] PROB 11 41, fol. 243; Hooker, Commonplace Book, fol. 350.
[112] Hooker, Commonplace Book, fol. 350.
[113] Hooker, Commonplace Book, fol. 350; C 1 1325/35.
[114] Garrett 1966, pp. 132–4, 270–1. For other clergy with south-western connections, see Garrett 1966, pp. 204–5, 308–9, 311–12, 325–7.
[115] Frere 1896, pp. 52–3; Alley Report; RBM 1928–9, I, pp. 38–41. The 1561 figure relates to Devon only.
[116] Rose-Troup 1913, p. 435.
[117] Lansdowne 377, fols. 8v, 21v; CCB 855A, fol. 215v; CCB 856, fol. 202.

Reformation, a number of schools were still organized and taught by both the regular and the secular clergy.[118] Tavistock Abbey, for example, boasted a school which dated from Saxon times, while Tywardreath Priory in its last years maintained a schoolmaster.[119] Exeter Cathedral maintained a grammar school, which in the 1520s was supervised by 'a very hard and a cruel master'.[120] The majority of schools, however, were associated with collegiate churches, as at Crediton, Ottery St Mary and Penryn, or with smaller chantry foundations, as at Ashburton, Barnstaple, Bodmin, Launceston, Marldon, Saltash, Truro and Week St Mary.[121] In addition a less formalized religious education would seem to have been provided by clerics in parish churches. It was presumably for this purpose that Creed sequences, for example, were painted on screens, as at Chudleigh and Kenton. Apostles, bearing articles of the Creed, were alternated with prophets, who carried corresponding predictions: thus Isaiah's 'Ecce virgo concipiet' was coupled with James' 'Qui conceptus est'.

The religious instruction conveyed to laymen through such channels was again predominantly traditionalist. At Week St Mary, for instance, the teacher-priest not only taught in the school, which stood near the parish church and which has in part survived, he also prayed for the soul of Dame Percival, its foundress. At Ashburton the teacher-priest was hired by the guild of St Lawrence, for the souls of whose members he was similarly required to intercede.

Again it was during the Henrician Reformation that traditionalist predominance began to diminish. Monastic education, as at Tavistock and Tywardreath, was abruptly suppressed in the years 1536–9. In 1538, moreover, Thomas Cromwell attempted to secure for his own nominee the mastership at Week St Mary, and by *circa* 1545 it had certainly been transferred to a non-conservative.[122] But the greatest damage was inflicted by the dissolution of colleges, guilds and other chantry foundations between 1545 and 1548. Some schools, as at Marldon, seem totally to have disappeared. Those refounded – as at Crediton in 1547, at Truro in 1549 and at Tavistock in 1551 – were now freed from the control of collegiate clergy, guild chaplains or chantry priests.[123] Nor was the damage more than partially repaired in Mary's reign. Tavistock boasted its own school house as well as its schoolmaster; on the other hand the schoolmaster at Stratton had to use the church

[118] The standard work is Orme 1976.
[119] Finberg 1951, pp. 274–5; Rowse 1941, pp. 168–9.
[120] 'Life of Carew', p. lxviii.
[121] *Certificates, Cornwall*, pp. 11–12, 29–31, 38–40, 46, 50–3; *Certificates, Devon*, pp. xiii, 64, 68–9; *Survey of Cornwall*, p. 282; Pevsner and Radcliffe 1970, p. 239.
[122] *LP*, XIII (1), 105; *Survey of Cornwall*, pp. 282–3; *Certificates, Cornwall*, p. 52.
[123] *Certificates, Cornwall*, pp. 32, 39, 46; *Certificates, Devon*, p. 69; *CPR*, I, pp. 43–5; Henderson 1923–4, p. 458; Hoskins 1954, p. 247.

house, while the parish priest at Kenton taught pupils in the church itself and even in his own chamber.[124] The extent to which this education was traditionalist remains unknown. From 1559, certainly, schoolmasters were officially prohibited from teaching any religion other than that 'now truly set forth by public authority',[125] and the system of licences subsequently employed by Bishop Alley must have ensured that overtly Catholic teachers were generally excluded from the region's schools.[126]

In what measure was this decline of traditionalist instruction accompanied by an expansion of its Protestant equivalent? In 1535–6 official decrees enjoined that children be taught the word of God and the royal supremacy as well as the Lord's Prayer, the Commandments and the Creed in their native tongue. Yet this constituted no more than a tentative step towards Protestant education: among the first clerics in the South-West to comply was in fact John Moreman, the essentially Catholic vicar of Menheniot. Moreover, the repetition of these decrees by Bishop Veysey in 1538 would suggest that their implementation had been by no means universal. One of the few committedly Protestant schoolmasters in the region before 1547 appears to have been William Cholwell at Week St Mary; he was praised by the chantry commissioners as 'a man well learned, and a great setter-forth of God's word'.[127]

Several of the schools refounded after the chantry dissolutions were undoubtedly Protestant in orientation. Thus at Crediton – where, in place of the teacher formerly provided by the collegiate church, a master was now appointed by the 'governors' of the parish church – the avowed purpose of the grammar school was the education of Devonian youth 'to the glory of the Church of England'. Elsewhere, as at Stratton in 1547–8, the character of the religious instruction imparted by Edwardian schools remains unclear.[128] In Mary's reign, certainly, the removal of Protestants from all teaching positions was officially decreed.[129] Only after the accession of Elizabeth does a comprehensive Protestantization of the educational processes appear to have been effected. The parochial clergy were now commanded to teach not only the Lord's Prayer, Creed and Commandments to their congregations, but also the new Catechism to their young. The

---

[124] *Tavistock Records*, pp. 22, 25; Additional 32243, HCWA Stratton, 1554–5; CCB 855, fol. 128v.

[125] *TRP*, II, pp. 126–7.

[126] See below, p. 235.

[127] *TRP*, I, p. 231; *Documents of Church History*, p. 272; 'Synopsis Chorographical', pp. 105–6; Prince 1701, pp. 387–8; ER XV, fol. 75; *Survey of Cornwall*, pp. 282–3; *Certificates, Cornwall*, p. 52.

[128] *CPR*, I, pp. 43–5; Additional 32243, HCWA Stratton, 1547–8.

[129] *TRP*, II, p. 38.

1560s, in addition, saw the rebuilding of the high school at Exeter, an achievement due largely to the Protestant John Hooker; the establishment of a grammar school at Plymouth, with a salaried teacher and its own school house; the continuing employment of schoolmasters at Crediton and Tavistock; and the issuing of teaching licences by Bishop Alley to men with suitable religious inclinations. Five such were licensed in 1568, and nine in 1569: they included Stephen Bell BA of Plymouth, John Eliot of Buckerell and Richard Martin of Chulmleigh.[130] By 1570, nevertheless, no more than a small minority of the region's adult population can yet have received an authentically Protestant education.

Educational developments will thus help to explain both the decline of the old religion and its retarded replacement by the new. Catholic schoolmasters had inevitably tended to produce Catholic scholars. One pupil of the chantry school at Barnstaple in *circa* 1530 had been Thomas Harding of Combe Martin; he became both an exile and an author in the Catholic cause. Protestant schools, on the other hand, must usually have produced Protestant pupils. According to a fellow-Protestant, Richard Carew, the pupils of William Cholwell at Week St Mary were 'virtuously trained up, in both kinds of divine and human learning', and at Bodmin, by 1548, a number of the scholars were avowed supporters of the new religion. Yet educational indoctrination was by no means irresistible. Among Harding's fellow-pupils in the Barnstaple chantry school was John Jewel of Berrynarbor, the future apologist for the reformed Church of England, and one pupil of the Catholic Dr Moreman was the future Protestant John Hooker. Nor was Protestant education invariably efficacious: at Bodmin in 1548 a number of the scholars continued to support the old religion.[131]

The extent to which education of any doctrinal hue was in practice available to the population at large must also be questioned. The school at Week St Mary was described by the chantry commissioners as 'a great comfort to all the country there, for that they that list may set their children to board there, and have them taught freely', and that at Ashburton was intended for 'the erudition of children, freely, for ever'. At Penryn the pupils were supposed to be 'poor men's children', and at Saltash children born within the borough. At Kenton the pupils taught by the priest in Mary's reign were local boys aged between six and eight. In addition, testators from below gentry level occasionally arranged an education for their off-

[130] *TRP*, II, pp. 119, 127; Hooker, Commonplace Book, fol. 354; *Plymouth Records*, pp. 50–1; CWA Crediton, 1561, 1569, etc; *Tavistock Records*, p. 29; CCB 41, pp. 17, 25–7, 29, 38, 42.
[131] Prince 1701, pp. 383f, 387–8, 418f; *Survey of Cornwall*, pp. 282–3, 293; 'Synopsis Chorographical', pp. 105–6.

spring. In 1537, for example, Tristram Hengescott of Exeter provided for his son to attend the local school until he attained the age of apprenticeship. In 1548 Exeter's Alderman Hunt arranged that his son would study in the grammar school before progressing to Oxford University; in 1560 William Cholditch of Cornwood, apparently a substantial farmer, ordered schooling for his son until he could read and write; and in 1566 arrangements for her son's education were made by the widow of the Exeter merchant Peter Lake.[132]

On the other hand provisions of this type occur in only a small percentage of the testatorial sample, and the existence of numerous illiterates – such as John Rowe of Dartmouth or Agnes Priest of Boyton[133] must indicate that even an elementary education was very far from universal. The chantry certificates in fact record provision for no more than a small proportion of the region's non-adult population. Schools were particularly rare in rural areas, but were also absent from communities like Gluvias, Helston or St Columb, with their 600–700 communicants, and even from Liskeard, with its 1,000.[134] Some of the schools, moreover, appear to have catered largely for the gentry rather than for inferior ranks. Week St Mary attracted 'the best gentlemen's sons of Devon and Cornwall', and the future Sir Peter Carew was educated at Exeter's grammar school.[135] Finally, most or all of the region's schools would appear to have excluded the female half of its population. In view of these facts it is not surprising that members of the educated minority – such as Bishop Veysey in 1538, or Philip Nichols in 1547 – should have referred to the laity at large as 'the ignorant people'.[136]

Even less accessible to the average man or woman was a higher education. Although from the 1560s on some parishes contributed modestly to the maintenance of poor scholars at Oxford, an educational experience of this nature was usually the privilege of the fortunate few: these included Thomas Bennett, John Hooker and the son of Exeter's Alderman Hunt. Women, again, were excluded. The restricted character of the region's contact with the universities – a fact attributable to social and economic considerations as well as to distance – further explains the slowness of its conversion to the new religion. It was at Cambridge, in the early 1520s, that Thomas Bennett had been influenced by the future martyr Thomas Bilney. Philip Nichols – who described himself as a young scholar, and who proved capable

---

[132] *Certificates, Cornwall*, pp. 11–12, 29–31, 38–40, 46, 50–3; *Certificates, Devon*, pp. xiii, 64, 68–9; CCB 855, fol. 128v; PROB 11 26, fol. 91v; 32, fol. 80; 48, fol. 440v; Moger, 6, William Cholditch, 1560.
[133] See above, pp. 197–8.
[134] *Certificates, Cornwall; Certificates, Devon*.
[135] *Survey of Cornwall*, pp. 282–3; 'Life of Carew', pp. lxvii–lxviii.
[136] EDCL 3498/88; *Copy of a Letter*, p. 11.

of citing Augustine, Jerome and Ambrose – may also have owed his Protestantism to a university education.[137]

By means of their contacts with individuals and with groups, the religious professionals undoubtedly exerted an often crucial influence upon popular religious opinion. The most potent of their instructional techniques, however, was probably the formal public sermon.

The importance, on the eve of the Reformation, of preaching is indicated by the number and quality of the later-medieval pulpits to be seen in the churches of Cornwall and Devon. That now at Witheridge was originally located in Exeter Cathedral; others may be found in towns, as at Bodmin, Camborne, Dartmouth, Kingsbridge, Launceston, North Molton, Padstow, Paignton, South Molton and Totnes, or in rural parishes, as at Antony, Bovey Tracey, Chittlehampton, Chivelstone, Coldridge, Dartington, Dittisham, Egloshayle, Halberton, Harberton, Holne, Ipplepen, Kenton, Laneast, Pilton, Pinhoe, Porthilly, Stoke Gabriel, Swimbridge and Torbryan. Constructed of either wood or stone, and often elaborately carved, these are usually sited in a prominent position immediately to the west of the rood-screen. They may be dated to the pre-Reformation generations by features of late-Perpendicular design, as at Dittisham; by image niches and sometimes, as at Bovey Tracey or Swimbridge, by saint figures; by emblems of the passion, as at Egloshayle; and occasionally by arms, like those of Oldham (Bishop of Exeter from 1504 to 1519) at Holne. That at Bodmin must date from 1491, when the town hired a carpenter to produce a pulpit on the pattern of that at Moretonhampstead, and that at Launceston is probably contemporary with the general rebuilding of 1511–24.[138] The virtual ubiquity of such structures on the eve of the Reformation is confirmed by the will of John Lane: in 1529 the Cullompton merchant donated money to no less than 100 neighbouring parish churches, 'to pray for me in their pulpits'.[139]

Similarly indicative of the importance of preaching was the installation of congregational seating, superseding the rush-covered floors utilized by the standing or kneeling congregations of earlier times; laymen increasingly expected substantial sermons. Thus when, in 1491, the townsmen of Bodmin commissioned their pulpit, they simultaneously ordered a set of benches; these were to be modelled on the examples at Plympton. At Ashburton the church was seated between 1510 and 1527, £11 being expended in

137 CWA Exeter SJB, 1565; CWA Ashburton, 1569; *Acts and Monuments*, II, p. 1037; Prince 1701, pp. 387–8; PROB 11 32, fol. 80; *Copy of a Letter*, pp. 36, 61f. For Bilney, see Dickens 1967A, pp. 117–20. For Cambridge, see Porter 1958.
138 For a general survey of pulpits, see Cox 1915. For Witheridge, see Cox 1915, p. 40. For Holne, see Pevsner 1952B, p. 181. For Bodmin, see *Bodmin Register*, p. 33. For Launceston, see Pevsner and Radcliffe 1970, pp. 96–7.
139 PROB 11 23, fol. 29.

6 St Thomas à Becket's, Bovey Tracey. Late-medieval stone pulpit in the nave. The elaborately sculpted and painted structure, with its saint figures in niches, demonstrates the already important role of preaching on the eve of the Reformation.

1513–14 alone, and seat rents featured in several sets of pre-Reformation accounts – as at Dartmouth, where seats were allocated to individual townsmen and their wives. Other documentary references confirm that most churches were in fact seated before the Reformation began. The chronology of this important development is also attested by the occasionally surviving later-medieval benches, bench-backs or bench-fronts, as at St Ives, Braunton and Frithelstock, and by the innumerable carved bench-ends to be found in churches throughout the region. Among the most complete sets are those at Altarnun, High Bickington, Kilkhampton, Launcells and Poughill; Altarnun alone boasts 79. An approximate date may be indicated by a stylistic feature, such as Perpendicular tracery; by a saint, passion emblem or other Catholic motif; or by a heraldic device, like the double rose of Henry VII at Frithelstock. Sometimes there are inscriptions, which indicate dates of 1508 at Monkleigh, 1511 at Coldridge, 1525 at Altarnun and originally at St Columb Minor, and 1530 at Hartland.[140]

Nor was preaching confined within churches. At Exeter, by 1523, sermons were delivered every Easter in the churchyard of St Mary Major; the requisite pulpit was attached to its charnel house. On St Petrock's Day, moreover, priests from Bodmin, Padstow and Little Petherick would assemble with their crosses and banners upon St Breage's Beacon; the celebrations included a sermon, doubtless in honour of St Petrock himself. Another outdoor sermon was delivered annually at East Newlyn. 'There was a chapel in the parish of St Newlyn in Cornwall', records Roscarrock, 'called "St Neighton's" of the saint to which it was dedicated. Which chapel had a yard belonging unto it, in which there were four stones on a little mount or hill at the north-west corner: where the crosses and relics of St Piran, St Crantock, St Cubert [and] St Newlyn were wont to be placed in the Rogation Week. At which time, they [i.e. the parishioners of Perranzabuloe, Crantock, Cubert and East Newlyn] used to meet there, and had a sermon made to the people.'[141]

In several cases – as on St Breage's Beacon or at East Newlyn – the sermons would seem to have been delivered by parish priests.[142] Lay audiences were also addressed by the Exeter canons, not only in the cathedral itself (particularly on Sundays) but also in parish churches. In 1528, for example, Canon Carsleigh preached at Topsham, while another doctor of divinity spoke at Dartmouth.[143] But the most active exponents of this

---

[140] For a general survey of benches, see Cox 1916. For Bodmin, see *Bodmin Register*, p. 33. These are now incorporated into choir stalls. For Ashburton, see CWA Ashburton, 1510–27. For Dartmouth, see CWA Dartmouth. For St Columb Minor, see Pevsner and Radcliffe 1970, p. 167. See also, for example, reference to a pew at Luxulyan for Nicholas Herle, his wife and his servants (STAC 2/32/53).

[141] Hooker, Commonplace Book, fol. 342; PROB 11 21, fol. 128; 'Lives of Saints', fols. 323v, 358v.

[142] 'Lives of Saints', fols. 323v, 358v.

[143] *Acts and Monuments*, II, p. 1038; CAB 3551, fol. 51; CR Dartmouth, Mayoral Accounts, 1528.

medium were the friars. In the years 1520–2 Bishop Veysey authorized Dominicans to preach in the Exeter churches, a Carmelite to preach throughout the diocese, and Franciscans 'ad predicandum, exponendum et seminandum verbum dei'. In 1524 the prior of the Exeter Dominicans preached at Columbjohn, while the warden of the Exeter Franciscans delivered a sermon on Good Friday. In 1531 the most influential preachers at Exeter included a Dominican and three Franciscans. A bench-end at Bodmin portrays a fox, in a pulpit, preaching to geese; it wears a friar's cowl.[144]

Religious instruction of this type was not only attended by members of the laity but also on occasion sponsored by them. At Dartmouth, in 1528, a preacher received payment for his efforts from the mayor, and at Exeter the sermons in St Mary Major churchyard were supported by a resident of this parish, John Bridgeman, when he drafted his will in 1523. 'For evermore', declared Bridgeman, 'I give 5s a year, out of my part of the house that Henry Leach dwelleth in, yearly to be paid unto the preacher that maketh the sermon on Easter Even yearly; and my cousin, the said Edward Bridgeman, shall pay the said 5s to the said preacher yearly.'[145]

When, in 1525, the schoolteacher Thomas Bennett began to reside at Exeter, he found himself by no means starved of sermonic instruction. On the contrary 'his greatest delight was to be at all sermons and preachings, whereof he was a diligent and an attentive hearer'. As, however, his Protestant tendencies increased, he came to regard the available preaching as essentially blasphemous,[146] and there can again be little doubt that the sermons to be heard at this date – not only in the city but also throughout the South-West – were indeed overwhelmingly traditionalist in their religious orientation. John Bridgeman, sponsor of the St Mary Major sermon, was certainly a conservative Catholic: he bequeathed money to his parish church, to a fraternity and to the Franciscans, and arranged obits, intercessory masses and prayers. Similarly Catholic at this time were Bishop Veysey – who not only preached personally, but also licensed preachers for the diocese – as well as most of the Exeter canons and the great majority of preaching parish priests. When, in 1531, Thomas Bennett posted his declaration upon the cathedral doors, 'order was taken that the doctors should in haste up to the pulpit every day, and confute this heresy'. Their objective, says Foxe, was 'to keep the people in their former blindness'. One of them denounced the declaration's author from the pulpit as a 'foul and abominable heretic' and invoked against him not only God but also Our Lady, St Peter, and the holy company of martyrs, confessors and virgins. Doubtless of a similar

---

[144] ER XV, fols. 3, 4v, 14–14v; *LP*, IV, 771; *Acts and Monuments*, II, p. 1038; Maclean 1870, p. 54.

[145] CR Dartmouth, Mayoral Accounts, 1528; PROB 11 21, fol. 128.

[146] *Acts and Monuments*, II, p. 1037; 'Synopsis Chorographical', p. 109.

hue were the sermons delivered by the priests on St Breage's Beacon and at East Newlyn; in both cases they were associated with local saint cults. But probably the most vigorously traditionalist of the orators were the friars. Of the four who preached at Exeter in 1531, three were dismissed by a contemporary Protestant as 'unlearned'. The fourth – a Franciscan named Gregory Bassett – was said to be 'learned more than they all, but as blind and superstitious as he which was most'. 'Ye spare not to make lying sermons to the people', the Exeter preachers were told by Thomas Bennett, 'to maintain your false traditions and foul gains'. When a Dominican protested that they preached the gospel daily, Bennett replied: 'What preaching of the gospel is that, when therewith ye extol superstitious things …?'[147]

During the subsequent decades of Reformation, the sermon retained its crucial importance as a mode of religious propagation. The continuing construction of pulpits is documented at Stratton between 1544 and 1547, at Exeter St Mary Steps, Exeter St Olave's and Camborne in Edward's reign, and at the cathedral and Exeter St Petrock's between 1560 and 1562. That erected by John Cholwill at Stratton between 1544 and 1547 cost some 33s 4d, and that by William Carter at St Mary Steps in 1551–2 only 12s, but the structure produced by Simon Knight for St Petrock's in 1561–2 cost almost £12.[148] Some extant pulpits are possibly datable to these decades by stylistic features, particularly by panels of early-Renaissance type: examples include those at East Allington, Landcross, Lanherne, St Ives, Stoke Rivers, Sutcombe and Welcombe.[149] This constructional activity may be attributable in part to an official decree which in 1547 ordered the installation of a pulpit in every church,[150] though that at Lanherne is more probably Marian. On occasion, moreover, a pulpit was relocated in a more prominent position. In 1560 'the pulpit next to the chancel' in Exeter Cathedral replaced 'the old pulpit in the body of the church'.[151] In addition, installation of the seating required by sermon-attending congregations is documented at Morebath in 1534, at Exeter Allhallows', Exeter St Petrock's and Tavistock under Edward VI, and at Braunton and Dartmouth under Mary. At Allhallows' the work was financed by a sale of church plate.[152] Stylistic evidence for a date in these decades is to be found on numerous extant bench-ends,

---

[147] PROB 11 21, fol. 128; *Acts and Monuments*, II, pp. 1037–9; 'Lives of Saints', fols. 323v, 358v.
[148] Additional 32243, HCWA Stratton, 1544, 1547; CWA Exeter SMS, 1552; *Inventories, Exeter*, p. 62; CWA Camborne, 1550; Hooker, Commonplace Book, fol. 353; CWA Exeter SP, 1562.
[149] For Lanherne, for example, see Bond and Camm 1909, II, 388, figure 125; and Cox 1915, p. 102.
[150] *TRP*, I, p. 401.
[151] Hooker, Commonplace Book, fol. 353. See also CWA Exeter SP, 1550.
[152] CWA Morebath, 1534; *Inventories, Exeter*, p. 11; CWA Exeter SP, 1551; *Tavistock Records*, p. 22; CWA Braunton, 1557; CWA Dartmouth, 1555.

and inscribed dates (1537 and 1546) at East Budleigh, North Lew, Dowland and Lewannick.[153]

Preaching thus remained a vitally important means of instruction, but to what extent did the instruction thereby imparted retain its customarily Catholic hue? An early and substantial blow to traditionalist control was the official campaign against friars. In 1538 the friar Alexander Barclay was discovered to be defending the old religion in both Cornwall and Devon; in Cornwall, for example, he had preached in honour of the Virgin Mary. In consequence he was interrogated at St Germans by a hostile gentleman, William Dynham, threatened with official retribution, and reported to Cromwell. This would seem to have persuaded him to conform thereafter. In the autumn of 1538, moreover, governmental suppression of the region's friaries effectively removed the Carmelites, Dominicans and Franciscans from its pulpits. Some of the most vigorous public advocates of the old religion were thus reduced to silence.[154]

Secular clerics – like the priest at Dartmouth in 1541–2, or the Exeter canons in their appropriated churches in 1545 – continued to preach throughout the reign. Most appear to have remained substantially conservative in doctrine, but strikingly few still dared to publicly defend the pope, the religious houses or the prohibited saint cults. A rare exception was the preacher in the cathedral close in 1534. The eyes of Christ's mystical body, he told his audience, were the clergy; its hands, the temporal authorities; its feet, the common people. But now, he declared, the body had become monstrous: 'for because, there as the eyes should stand, there standeth the hands; and thus all the other parts standeth out of order'. This critic of the royal supremacy was duly reported and committed to prison. There he begged for release, claiming that he had spoken 'with small advice and for lack of learning'. Submission was preferred to imprisonment and possible death; the great majority of preachers made a similar choice.[155]

Traditionalism was by no means wholly expelled from the pulpits. In 1547 Philip Nichols could still complain about clerics who 'never preach against [images], but rather defend them, to keep the unlearned in their blindness still'. After Edward's accession, nevertheless, the screw was increasingly tightened. In 1547 unlicensed preaching was prohibited. When, in March of this year, the cathedral canon Dr Chrispin preached at Marldon against the Protestant doctrine of scripture, he was reported to the royal visitors and subsequently committed to imprisonment in the Tower of London. A similar fate befell another conservative preacher, John Moreman.

[153] See above, pp. 205–6.
[154] *LP*, XIII (2), 596, 709.
[155] CWA Dartmouth, 1542; CAB 3552, fol. 40; *LP*, VII, 260. See also, for example, CWA Ashburton, 1540.

The damage thus inflicted upon traditionalist instruction was recognized by the rebels in 1549: they explicitly demanded the release of both Moreman and Chrispin, 'which hold our opinions', and urged that they be given livings 'to preach amongst us our Catholic faith'. The sanguinary suppression of the revolt not only ensured the failure of these demands, it seems also to have terrorized most of the surviving conservatives among the preaching clergy into an external conformity to the official religion. One of the few exceptions was the vicar of Ipplepen, who in 1552 was suspected of an 'unquiet sort of preaching'. He was reported, via the royal commissioners, to the Council – which, fearing 'the disturbance of true religion', ordered his examination. If found guilty, he was to make a public recantation wherever he had preached, and the local justices were to be consulted in order to determine his punishment.[156]

The reign of Mary seems never to have witnessed more than a partial revival of traditionalist preaching. The annual sermon at East Newlyn was temporarily restored 'in Queen Mary's time', when it was delivered by parson Crane. At Dartmouth, at the request of the conservative mayor Alan Savery, a preacher was paid 3s 4d in 1555, and at South Tawton the churchwardens rewarded a priest for his sermon in 1556–7. The accounts, wills and other documentary sources would nevertheless suggest that the number of Catholic preachers now operating in the region was substantially lower than the pre-Reformation level. Even at the cathedral itself, the chapter was informed in January 1557 that three preachers for Lent had 'at last' been found; these were a schoolmaster, Mr Dolbeare, and the vicar of Kenton.[157] One factor behind the scarcity was the increasing reluctance of laymen to seek ordination to the priesthood.[158] Another was the absence of any significant effort within the South-West to restore the friars, who had formerly provided many of the most powerful advocates of traditional Catholicism; among the conservatives at Exeter in 1558 was 'an old friar'.[159] The traditionalists' ranks had also been thinned by the passage of time: Chrispin had died in 1551, and in 1554 he was followed by both Moreman and Veysey.[160] It was the consequent shortage of Catholic preaching that in 1554 compelled the authorities to order the reading in churches of published homilies. Yet with occasional exceptions, including Morebath and possibly Molland, most

[156] *Copy of a Letter*, pp. 5–6, 33–4, 51; *TRP*, I, p. 396; 'Synopsis Chorographical', pp. 105–6; Royal 18 B XI, fol. 29; *Exeter Records*, p. 365.
[157] 'Lives of Saints', fol. 323v; CWA Dartmouth, 1555; CWA S. Tawton, 1557; CAB 3552, fol. 82. The 1555 account at Dartmouth, which was signed by Savery, also includes expenditure on Catholic apparatus and records the surrender of Protestant books.
[158] See above, p. 138.
[159] *Acts and Monuments*, II, p. 2051. This appears to have been Gregory Bassett.
[160] Rose-Troup 1913, pp. 107, 109.

of the parishes with extant accounts seem not even to have purchased a copy.[161]

In December 1558 unlicensed preaching was prohibited by the new Elizabethan regime. When, in the following spring, attempts to preach in the South-West 'without authority' were discovered, they were duly reported to the Council; the sheriffs of Devon and Cornwall were then ordered to confer with the local justices for their suppression, and the arrest of 'all such as shall so attempt to preach' was officially commanded. These measures were to prove substantially effective. At East Newlyn, for example, the customary traditionalist sermon certainly failed to survive into the new reign. Some of the Marian preachers, including those at the cathedral, were ejected from office; most, however, would again appear to have been pressurized into an external conformity. In 1560 Dr Gammon was discovered to be supporting 'articles of popery' in his sermons, and another cathedral preacher to be declaring that baptism and communion were necessary for salvation; both were duly compelled to make humiliating recantations of their error. By 1561, in consequence, overt advocacy of the old religion seems virtually to have been eradicated from the region's pulpits. The comprehensive report compiled in that year by Bishop Alley, after examining the condition of the diocese's several hundred clergy, found no more than three still daring to preach without official licence. These were John Donne at Clyst St Lawrence, Nicholas Mayhew at Whimple, and Christopher Trychay, the unmarried, non-graduate and indubitably conservative vicar of Morebath. They appear to have been the last, defiant preachers of traditional Catholicism, and it is improbable that their sermons will have long survived their exposure by the resolutely anti-Catholic bishop.[162]

The Reformation decades thus witnessed a progressive reduction – and eventually a virtual suppression – of traditionalist preaching within the South-West. To what extent was this crucial development accompanied by a corresponding upsurge in the preaching of the Protestant alternative?

From the 1530s on anti-papal sermons were increasingly frequent. In 1532 Canon Carsleigh of Exeter preached that if the pope could deliver souls from Purgatory, and yet required payment to do so, he deserved to be in Purgatory himself. By 1536 even Bishop Veysey was assuring Cromwell that, 'as to the setting forth of the abuses of the Bishop of Rome, I suppose no one has preached more freely than I'. In 1538, moreover, he ordered canons and parish priests to proclaim the royal supremacy, and certainly

---

[161] *TRP*, II, p. 38; CWA Morebath, 1556; CWA Molland, 1558.
[162] *TRP*, II, pp. 102, 120; *APC*, VII, pp. 65–6; 'Lives of Saints', fol. 323v; Hooker, Commonplace Book, fol. 353; Alley Report. References to the Alley Report may be found under place names. For the ejection of Marian preachers, see above, p. 231. For Trychay, see above, p. 229.

Canon Tregonwell, in his sermons, now attacked 'the corrupt state and arrogancy of the pope'. So did Simon Heynes, Dean of Exeter from 1537. Anti-papalism, nevertheless, was by no means necessarily accompanied by the propagation of a positively Protestant theology. Indeed in 1538, when Bishop Veysey ordered the appropriators of churches worth £20 per annum to provide quarterly sermons at their own expense, he also instructed the Exeter canons to base their sermons upon the non-Protestant *Institution of a Christian Man*, and he stressed that they were to avoid 'grafting or sowing in the heads of the ignorant people any dissension or varieties of opinions'. The sermons of Canon Tregonwell advanced no further theologically than to 'maintain Luther's doctrine in some points', and the preaching of another Henrician canon, Parkhouse, was dismissed by the Protestant John Hooker as providing his auditors with entertainment rather than edification.[163]

Of the relatively few authentically Protestant sermons to be heard in the Henrician South-West, the earliest were probably those delivered at Exeter by the redoubtable Hugh Latimer. In June 1534, after being sent to visit the city by Thomas Cromwell, he addressed audiences in the churchyard of the Franciscan friary and in St Mary Major parish church. The targets of his denunciation included not only 'popery' but also 'idolatry' and 'superstition'. After his departure, however, identifiable preachers of the new religion remained rare. Among them were John Cardmaker, an Exeter friar who had been converted by Latimer and who subsequently became the vicar of Branscombe; Simon Heynes, dean of the cathedral from 1537; and probably also the parsons of Sampford Peverell and Plymouth. In 1539 the parson of Sampford Peverell was criticized for preaching heresy, and from 1541 the parson of Plymouth – by order of the mayor, 'and other of the discretest of the said town and parish' – devoted himself on every Sunday, Monday, Wednesday and Friday to 'preaching of the word of God' to his parishioners. After Cromwell's execution in 1540, preachers of this type were potentially subject to official persecution. Dean Heynes, certainly, was now 'much maligned and envied at for his sincere and true preaching of the gospel, and by his adversaries sundry times accused and impeached for the same'. In 1543 his allegedly 'lewd and seditious preaching' resulted in his investigation by the Council and his imprisonment for almost four months; only the patronage of Sir Peter Carew protected him from worse.[164]

By 1547, in consequence, Protestant preaching had become accessible

---

[163] Hooker, Commonplace Book, fols. 342, 346, 349; *LP*, XI, 211; XIII (1), 75; ER XV, fols. 74v–5; EDCL 3498/88.

[164] *LP*, VII, 420; Hooker, Commonplace Book, fols. 342, 349; 'Life of Carew', p. cxiv; *APC*, I, pp. 97, 150–1; SP 1/154/181–2; Thompson 1934–5, pp. 352–5. See also *LP*, XVI, 578.

to no more than a small minority of south-western people. Nor was the situation rapidly rectified after Edward's accession. In Cornwall, indeed, his commissioners reported that licensed preachers were non-existent not only in sizeable settlements with 600–700 communicants – such as St Columb, Gluvias, Helston, Saltash and Truro – but also at Liskeard, with 1,000, and even at Bodmin, the largest market-town, with 2,000. There appears to have been a similar absence at Launceston, the shire town, and in the flourishing port of Falmouth. In response to this scarcity the commissioners proposed the installation of Protestant ministers at Bodmin, Falmouth, Launceston and Liskeard 'to preach and set forth the word of God to the people', but, with a probable exception at Launceston, the implementation of even this modest programme remains uncertain. One of the few certain achievements of the new regime was the despatch into the region of a single itinerant preacher, the 'very grave, godly and learned' Dr Tongue. He reportedly travelled 'throughout this whole diocese'. In September 1548, when 'sent to preach in Cornwall', he was paid £33 6s 8d by the Council, and he may also have been the preacher who spoke at Ashburton in 1548–9, receiving 16s from the churchwardens.[165]

Only in a limited number of cases were the deficiencies of governmental sponsorship effectively remedied by a local patron. One 'dear friend to all preachers' was Sir Peter Carew. He maintained his own preaching chaplain, not only 'to instruct his house and family' but also 'to preach elsewhere in the countries round about him', and he proved 'a patron to all godly preachers, in defence of whom he did oftentimes show himself both stout and hardy'. Philip Nichols applauded his efforts to make known the truth, to banish lies, to have the Lord truly worshipped and to root out idolatry. Somewhat lower in the social scale were the leading townsmen of Plymouth and John Bougin of Totnes. The Plymouthians sponsored sermons at the time of Edward's coronation and in 1549–50, when the Protestant Richard Howell preached. Bougin, in his will of 1548, arranged for a preacher in Totnes church to proclaim 'the true and sincere word of God … to the edifying of all Christian hearts'. He was apparently intended to preach 12 times, receiving 10s on each occasion.[166]

The wills and accounts would suggest that sponsorship of this type was far from common. In 1548 Philip Nichols indeed complained that whereas many of his contemporaries were purchasing prebends, benefices and church lands, few were in practice willing to bestow a substantial living upon

---

[165] *Certificates, Cornwall*, pp. 11, 16, 25–7, 29–32, 36, 38, 46, 50–1; *Acts and Monuments*, II, p. 2050; Hooker, Commonplace Book, fol. 348; *APC*, II, p. 220; CWA Ashburton, 1549.

[166] 'Life of Carew', p. cxiv; *Copy of a Letter*, pp. 1–4; *Plymouth Records*, pp. 114, 117; Murray, 3, John Bougin, 1548.

a preacher. Their excuse, he claimed, was that a preacher would only be corrupted by such wealth. John Hooker, recalling the situation in the South-West in 1549, similarly lamented the 'want' of 'learned preachers ... to teach and instruct the people'.[167] It was precisely this scarcity that compelled the regime to order the reading in church services of officially sanctioned homilies. Of the parishes with accounts, however, no more than a minority – including Exeter St John's Bow, Crediton, Woodbury and probably St Breock – would seem even to have purchased a copy of the homilies by the end of the reign.[168]

Only after the shock of the south-western rebellion – and after the displacement of Protector Somerset by the religiously more radical Earl of Warwick – does a substantial effort to improve the situation appear to have commenced. When in 1550 the Council determined to replace the traditional stone altars with wooden communion tables, it commanded Bishop Veysey to prepare the people for this transformation by means of sermons – not only in the cathedral but also in market-towns and other population centres. Thus, it was hoped, 'the weak conscience of others may be instructed' and 'this our pleasure the more quietly executed'. Nevertheless it was not until August 1551 – when the compliant but theologically conservative Veysey was eventually replaced by the reformer and Bible translator Miles Coverdale – that the diocese of Exeter for the first time experienced a bishop who was firmly committed to the preaching of the Protestant faith. Coverdale had arrived in the region in 1549, serving as chaplain to Russell's troops and preaching to them after their defeat of the rebels. Nor was the support accorded to him by the local clergy to be extensive. Mr Gregory and Dr Reynolds had been licensed to preach in the region since June 1549, and other Protestant preachers under the new bishop's direction included Mr Chudleigh, Nicholas Daniel, Richard Howell, George Ovie and Anthony Randall, but it was no more than a small number of men who in two years (1551–3) attempted the evangelization of the South-West.[169]

Their prime target – inevitably – was the densely populated and regionally dominant city of Exeter. Coverdale himself preached daily, with 'great and manifold [exertions] in the cause of the gospel'. His oratory was accessible to the citizens not only in their cathedral but also in the adjacent parish church of St Mary Major; in 1552 its three palls were regularly employed 'to cover the pulpit of the church at such time when my lord bishop, or

---

[167] *Godly New Story*, pp. 72–3; 'Description of Exeter', p. 26.
[168] *TRP*, I, pp. 402, 432–3; CWA Exeter SJB, 1547; CWA Crediton, 1551; CWA Woodbury, 1547, 1550; CWA St Breock, fol. 3v.
[169] ER XV, fols. 119v–20; XVII, fols. 18–18v; 'Description of Exeter', p. 58; *Prayerbook of 1549*, pp. 6–8. For Chudleigh, Daniel, Howell and Ovie, see below, p. 248.

any other worshipful preacher, shall preach there'.[170] Protestant sermons might also be heard in other towns. On at least one occasion Coverdale preached at Honiton. Sermons were organized at Crediton in 1551 and 1552; the speakers, who included Chudleigh and Howell, were rewarded by the urban authorities. At Barnstaple, in 1552, Ovie was paid 6s 8d by the corporation for his preaching on New Year's Day. And at Plymouth, in June 1553, William Amadas bequeathed 5s to his parson, 'desiring him (with a charitable devotion and an audible voice) to read unto his cure [i.e. his parishioners], three Sundays next following my death, the homily of the salvation of mankind by only Christ, our saviour from sin and death everlasting; divided into three parts, according to the king's majesty's order set forth in that behalf'. Amadas also arranged a dinner for the mayor and aldermen, at which the parson was to deliver 'some godly exhortation against the fear of death, and admonishment of their duties for the common wealth of their town'. The 'commoners' of Plymouth were similarly to be assembled, given drink, and then assailed by the parson with 'some godly exhortation of good works, and admonishment of their obedience to rulers and magistrates'.[171]

Rural communities may possibly have been visited on occasion by an itinerant evangelist like Nicholas Daniel, the parson of St Teath: Foxe describes him as 'a great doer and preacher sometime of the gospel, in the days of King Edward, in those parties of Cornwall and Devonshire'.[172] The wills, accounts and other sources would nevertheless imply that by the end of this reign the majority of the region's smaller towns, villages and hamlets had yet to hear regular sermons in support of the Protestant faith. Edward's death, moreover, brought the evangelization programme to a virtual halt. 'With his death', lamented Hooker, 'ended the preaching of [the] gospel and the true religion'. Protestant preachers were not totally silenced – it was in Mary's reign that William Ramsey began his ministry at South Molton – but, as Ramsey himself would later recall, this was for such preachers a 'perilous time'. Unlicensed preaching was prohibited. Several advocates of the new religion were removed from their offices, deprived of their benefices, or even compelled to take flight. George Manning, who was to preach Protestantism in Elizabeth's reign, now lost his benefice at Bovey Tracey. John Cardmaker was deprived of Branscombe; he was subsequently burned as a heretic at Smithfield. Coverdale himself was deprived of the see and forced into continental exile. There he was joined

---

[170] 'Synopsis Chorographical', p. 107; Hooker, Commonplace Book, fol 349; CWA Exeter SMM, fol. 13.
[171] CCB 855, fol. 48v; CWA Crediton, 1551–2; *Barnstaple Records*, II, p. 99; PROB 11 44, fol. 274.
[172] *Acts and Monuments*, II, p. 2051.

by another of the region's preachers, Dr Reynolds. Similarly exiled was Sir Peter Carew; thus was removed from the South-West its leading patron of Protestant preaching. Others were coerced into conformity. The Edwardian evangelist Nicholas Daniel, for example, now 'revolted from that which he preached before'. Daniel attributed this apostasy to his 'grievous imprisonments' and 'fear of persecution'; in particular he blamed 'cruel justices'. Accounts and wills confirm that Protestant preaching was generally suppressed. At Crediton, for example, the sermons inaugurated in Edward's reign were terminated after 1554.[173]

The preaching of the gospel, records Hooker, revived after Elizabeth's accession. In 1559 all preachers were officially instructed to proclaim the royal supremacy, to denounce traditionalist practices and to declare the word of God. In the early years of the reign, nevertheless, the scarcity of preachers both willing and able to fulfil this decree within the South-West remained painfully obvious to observers like the Earl of Bedford, Sir John Chichester and Philip Nichols. 'The lack is great of such good workmen in God's harvest', the Mayor of Exeter was reminded by Bedford in 1560, and in the same year Philip Nichols urged William Cecil to procure more preaching. William Alley, bishop from 1560, might be lauded by Hooker as a gifted man and a 'godly preacher', but few of his clergy were similarly equipped. According to the detailed report compiled by Alley in 1561, the entire diocese of approximately 600 parishes contained no more than about 28 licensed preachers. The cathedral boasted three, namely the dean Gregory Dodds, the treasurer (and Marian exile) Richard Tremayne, and Edward Riley; the city churches possessed none. Four were based in sizeable towns, at Cullompton, Fowey, Totnes and Truro, and the remainder at Bishop's Tawton, Blisland, Bovey Tracey, Bradford, Broadclyst, Chittlehampton, Clyst Hydon, Colan, Ermington, Holbeton, Instow, Lezant, Maker, Milton Damerel, Pillaton, St Minver, Sidbury, South Tawton, Stoke Rivers, Thorncombe and Washford. At Bovey Tracey, for example, the preacher was George Manning; at Chittlehampton, former home of the St Urith cult, Robert Bulpayne BA; and at Bradford, William Cavel MA – 'licentiatus predicat diligenter' was the recorded comment. Some, like William Ramsey at Washford, were non-resident; others, like John Service at South Tawton, preached only in their parish. The report leaves no doubt that the overwhelming majority of south-western parishes – perhaps 95% – still lacked a minister to preach the Protestant faith. Typical was the situation reported from the rural parish of Honeychurch: *Dominus Ricardus Downe, rector:*

---

[173] Hooker, Commonplace Book, fols. 349–50; Lansdowne 377, fol. 10; *TRP*, II, pp. 6–7; C 1 1325/35; ER XVI, fol. 100; Garrett 1966, pp. 132–4, 270–1; 'Life of Carew', p. xcii; *Acts and Monuments*, II, p. 2051; CWA Crediton.

non graduatus; presbyter non conjugatus nec concubinarius; satis doctus; residet; hospitalis; non predicat nullum aliud.[174]

The 1560s witnessed attempts to rectify this desperate scarcity. In 1560 the Earl of Bedford sent his own chaplain, Mr Huntingdon, to preach in the region, and requested the Mayor of Exeter to grant him assistance 'for the better setting-forth of God's truth and the queen's majesty's godly proceedings'. Another patron was the North Molton gentleman John Parker – 'a sure work and strong defence of God's word', William Ramsey called him in 1562, 'and lover of all true preachers'. Bishop Alley, for his part, not only organized 'prophesyings' – with prayers, sermons and mutual admonitions – for the spiritual edification of his clergy, he also licensed new preachers, such as Anthony Moreman in 1568, Nicholas Standen and Roger Sowden in 1569, and George Cotton and Roger Horwood (both of whom were MAs) in 1570.[175] Measures of this nature were to prove of crucial importance in the region's eventual Protestantization. By 1570, however, their impact upon the average layman was still patently limited.

The citizens of Exeter were relatively well provided. In 1559 the cathedral prebendaries had been ordered by the visitors to provide sermons on Sundays, while the dean was to arrange preachings at Christmas, Easter and Whitsun. Sermons were also delivered at the cathedral's morning services, to which there was (according to Hooker) a 'great resort of the people'. In 1570, for example, Canon Walton 'most godly did preach unto them, and gave them most godly exhortations'.[176] Other towns, however, were rarely as well served. Two preachers, of whom one was the Dean of Exeter, spoke at Barnstaple between 1560 and 1562, and two at Dartmouth in 1570; all received payment from the urban authorities. Crediton received visits from the bishop in 1565, 1567 and 1569 – during which he dined with the corporation and preached to the people – as well as from Mr Tremayne, Mr Cavel and other Protestants, who preached in 1561, 1567, 1568 and 1569. These sermons were sponsored by the corporation, whose leaders included Mr Dowrish and Mr Periam; in 1569, for example, they paid 5s and 6s 8d to two preachers. Only in 1570, nevertheless, would the preacher Mr Townsend begin to receive from the corporation a regular stipend of £5 per annum.[177] Accounts, wills and other sources would more-

---

[174] Hooker, Commonplace Book, fol. 352; *TRP*, II, pp. 118–19, 123; *Exeter Records*, pp. 41–2; SP 12/6/17; Rose-Troup 1913, p. 106n; 'Synopsis Chorographical', p. 161; 'Description of Exeter', p. 190; Alley Report. For Tremayne, see also Garrett 1966, pp. 311–12.

[175] *Exeter Records*, pp. 41–2; Lansdowne 377, fol. 27; McGrath 1967, p. 147; CCB 41, pp. 9, 21, 27, 44.

[176] CAB 3552, fol. 138; Hooker, Commonplace Book, fols. 352, 356.

[177] *Barnstaple Records*, II, pp. 99, 126; CR Dartmouth, Receivers' Accounts, 1570; CWA Crediton, 1561, 1565, 1567–70, etc.

over indicate that even in the towns such activity remained uncommon, while in the hundreds of rural parishes no more than an occasional visit from a licensed preacher could usually be expected. One such itinerant minister was George Manning of Bovey Tracey. In 1564–5 he preached at South Tawton, where the wardens paid him 5s, and at Woodbury, where he and his servant were rewarded with dinner; and in 1568–9 he preached in the Dartmoor village of Ilsington. In some places even this basic level of provision was not attained. At Stoke Climsland in 1566, for example, the vicar was accused of neglect in this respect; he claimed that he had 'done his diligence to have a sermon every month'.[178]

In the absence of regular preaching, congregational instruction in the Protestant faith must often have depended upon the minister's recitation, from the pulpit, of the official injunctions and homilies. In most of the parishes with accounts, copies of both publications were purchased in response to the order of 1559. In 1559–60 Coldridge, for instance, bought its book of injunctions and paid 16d for its book of homilies.[179] New copies were added in the following years, Woodbury, for example, acquiring another book of homilies for 4s in 1562–3,[180] and during the crisis of 1569–70 a number of parishes obtained special homilies 'On Rebellion'.[181] In practice, inevitably, the public recitation of these documents might be less than frequent. Between 1561 and 1565 one unnamed cleric reportedly neglected the reading of both the injunctions and the homilies, and in 1569 the vicar of Ilsington was said to read the injunctions 'very seldom', and the homilies – which should have been read every Sunday – at most once a year. A local man testified that homilies had been read 'not two times sithens that he was vicar'. And even when dutifully executed – as when the vicar of Stoke Climsland, during a local disturbance, read out the relevant homily 'On Obedience' – the recitation of a standard text can rarely have achieved the emotional impact of an evangelistic sermon.[182]

By 1570, in brief, the type of religious propaganda transmitted from south-

---

178 CWA S. Tawton, 1565; CWA Woodbury, 1565; CCB 855B, sub 19 January 1565/6; CCB 856, fol. 319.

179 *TRP*, II, pp. 118–19, 123, 132–3. For the purchase of homilies, see CWA Coldridge, 1559–60; CWA Crediton, 1559; CWA Exeter SJB, 1559; CWA Exeter SMM, fol. 16; CWA Morebath, 1559; and CWA S. Tawton, 1559. The absence of such expenditure from other churchwardens' accounts is possibly attributable to the survival of Edwardian homilies, as apparently at St Breock (CWA St Breock, fols. 3v, 16). For the purchase of injunctions, see, for example, CWA Antony, 1559; CWA Coldridge, 1560; CWA Dartington, 1559; CWA Exeter SJB, 1560; CWA Kilmington, 1560; CWA S. Tawton, 1559; Additional 32243, HCWA Stratton, 1559; and *Barnstaple Records*, I, p. 213.

180 CWA Woodbury, 1563.

181 E.g. CWA Coldridge, 1570; CWA Exeter SMS, 1571; ? CWA Exeter SP, 1570; ? Additional 32243, HCWA Stratton, 1570.

182 CCB 855A, loose sheet, charges v. unnamed cleric; CCB 855B, sub 19 January 1565/6; CCB 856, fols. 319–20.

western pulpits had unquestionably experienced a fundamental alteration. Traditionalist preaching – which in 1530 had reigned supreme – had been progressively reduced and eventually in most communities suppressed. Only in part, however, would it appear to have been effectively replaced by its Protestant equivalent. In consequence the total volume of preaching was probably substantially lower in the 1560s than it had been in the 1520s.[183] These crucial developments must together provide one of the most compelling explanations for the responses of south-western people to the sixteenth-century religious revolution. To a considerable extent they will explain, firstly, the vitality of popular Catholicism on the eve of the Reformation; secondly, its precipitous decline in the subsequent decades; and thirdly, the limited and retarded character of its replacement by an authentically Protestant piety.

The influence exerted upon the popular religion by traditionalist sermons was unmistakably apparent to Thomas Bennett. 'And when you preach', he reportedly told the conservatives at Exeter at 1531, 'God knoweth how you handle it: insomuch that the people of Christ knoweth no gospel well near but the pope's gospel. And so the blind lead the blind, and both fall into the pit. In the true gospel of Christ, confidence is none, but only in your popish traditions and fantastical inventions.' The potential impact of a Catholic sermon was also demonstrated by Canon Chrispin at Marldon in 1547. Philip Nichols admitted ruefully that Chrispin's oratory 'did deceive the ignorant people, which have little or no knowledge'; indeed he 'persuaded them all, for the most part, that nothing could be said to the contrary'. In 1549, moreover, a number of the people were thought to have been persuaded into rebellion by Mr Blaxton's preaching against 'the alteration of religion'. Conversely, therefore, the effective suppression of such preaching in the Reformation decades must have been substantially responsible for the drastic erosion of popular Catholicism. For this reason Philip Nichols supported the imprisonment of Dr Chrispin and Dr Moreman, and rejoiced that King Edward – like a father protecting his children – was thus shielding his south-western subjects from the harmful influence of traditionalism.[184]

Protestant preaching could prove similarly effective. In Edward's reign Philip Nichols indeed regarded the overthrow of papal darkness as a consequence of the preaching of the reformed faith: 'That gallant whore, trimmed with purple, hath been drunk with the blood of the saints; but the Lord hath shortened those days for his elected's sake, and hath destroyed this wicked [one] with the brightness of his coming, with the spirit of his mouth: for the gospel is preached.' Certainly the communities with significant

---

[183] See Cox 1915, pp. viii–ix, 82, 86.
[184] *Acts and Monuments*, II, p. 1039; *Copy of a Letter*, pp. 11, 31; *Prayerbook of 1549*, p. 18; Royal 18 B XI, fol. 29.

Protestant groups – Exeter, Plymouth, Totnes, Crediton, South Molton and several other towns – were usually those in which the new religion had been most vigorously preached. This factor alone will largely explain the predominantly urban character of popular Protestantism, and also its greater strength in Devon than in Cornwall.[185]

At Exeter, for instance, the Protestant faction in existence by 1549 must have included the 'sundry persons' who had reportedly been converted between 1537 and 1543 by the preaching of Dean Heynes. The newly acquired faith of the citizens was subsequently nurtured in the years 1551–3 by the sermons of Bishop Coverdale. Among the 'godly men' by whom these were attended was Thomas Prestwood; he was 'very zealous in religion, and greatly affected to the hearing of the preaching of the gospel; and very friendly to all good preachers, but specially unto Mr Coverdale'.[186] The conversion of Agnes Priest is also attributable primarily to the medium of preaching, to hear which she most probably travelled some six miles from her Boyton home to Launceston. 'I have upon the Sundays visited the sermons', she explained when subsequently asked where her instruction in Protestantism had been obtained, 'And there have I learned such things as are so fixed in my breast that death shall not separate them.'[187] At South Molton the Protestant group traced its genesis in Mary's reign to the preaching of William Ramsey. 'Since the first entrance that I had among you,' he later reminded its members, 'which was by preaching of the gospel, even in a perilous time, ye favoured me and the word of my preaching; and received it not as my doctrine, as it was not, but as the doctrine of the Holy Ghost, as it was indeed.' Ramsey rejoiced that the Moltonians had thus been 'delivered from their vain superstition, unto the true knowledge of Christ, by hearing and believing the gospel'.[188] Occasional converts may also have been won by itinerant preachers operating beyond the major population centres. Hooker suggests that the journey of Dr Tongue through the diocese in 1548 was not totally without fruit: 'he had a very sweet voice and an eloquent tongue, and did marvellously persuade the people'.[189]

If the existence of Protestant preaching in certain communities will largely explain their provision of converts to the new religion, it follows that the continuing scarcity of such preaching in most areas of the South-West will to a substantial extent explain the retarded development of popular Protestantism in the region as a whole. 'Through lack of preachers', lamented

---

[185] *Copy of a Letter*, p. 89. For Protestantism in Exeter, Plymouth, Totnes, Crediton and South Molton, see above, pp. 155–6, 161–5.

[186] *APC*, I, pp. 97, 150–1; 'Life of Carew', p. cxiv; Hooker, Commonplace Book, esp. fols. 348–9.

[187] *Acts and Monuments*, II, p. 2050.

[188] Lansdowne 377, fols. 9v–10v.

[189] Hooker, Commonplace Book, fol. 348.

the new regime in 1547, 'in many places of the king's realms and dominions the people continue in ignorance and blindness.' Thus at Falmouth, where the Edwardian commissioners noted the total absence of licensed preaching, they observed that in consequence 'the people thereabouts be very ignorant'. They were similarly struck by the absence of preaching at Bodmin: 'the Lord knows, the said two thousand people are very ignorant'. The rebels' hostility to the 1549 Prayerbook was attributed in part by Hooker to inadequate preaching; they acted, he thought, 'of ignorance'. Philip Nichols agreed that they were an 'ignorant multitude, not being well instructed', while the anonymous gentleman of Devon bewailed their 'ignorance, lacking teaching'. Not until well into Elizabeth's reign would the region experience a substantial assault upon this fundamental hindrance to its Protestantization.[190]

Preaching thus ranked among the most potent forms of influence; but even when practised it proved by no means invariably effective. Traditionalist sermons indeed evoked antipathy rather than devotion from individuals like Thomas Bennett, Philip Nichols and Agnes Priest. Bennett denounced them as false and superstitious, and Nichols vilified their exponents as 'biting serpents'. 'What profit riseth by you', the Marian preachers were asked by Agnes Priest, 'that teach nothing but lies for truth?' 'How save you souls, when you preach nothing but damnable lies, and destroy souls?'[191] On the other hand the preaching of the new religion could equally provoke antagonism. 'The parson of Sampford [Peverell] is a heretic', protested William Cater of Tiverton in 1539. 'Let him take good heed of his preaching, for the world will not prove as he thinketh it will.' 'He will be punished for his preaching.' In Edward's reign the future bishop William Alley, 'being an earnest preacher and much inveighing against false doctrine, was so despitefully dealt withal in the [cathedral] church that he durst not to adventure to come again into the pulpit'. In consequence the Carews 'guarded him and brought him to the pulpit sundry times, and there countenanced and supported him against all his adversaries'. 'God's word', observed Philip Nichols in 1547, 'is never spread abroad without contention, strife and much trouble.'[192]

Even when Protestant sermons were not overtly resisted, they were by no means automatically anointed with converting power. When, in June 1534, Hugh Latimer preached at Exeter in the Franciscans' churchyard, he was heard out by 'the people' in spite of a downpour of rain. According to Hooker, however, they listened merely 'for the good liking of the

---

[190] *TRP*, I, p. 402; *Certificates, Cornwall*, pp. 11, 16, 25–7, 29–32, 36, 38, 46, 50–1; 'Description of Exeter', pp. 26–7; Royal 18 B XI, fol. 21; Rose-Troup 1913, p. 485.
[191] *Acts and Monuments*, II, pp. 1039, 2051; *Copy of a Letter*, p. 5.
[192] SP 1/154/181–2; 'Life of Carew', p. cxiv; *Copy of a Letter*, p. 57.

eloquence of the man', 'for the novelty of the doctrine', or even 'for malice, to entrap him'; none seem to have experienced conversion. He attracted another large audience at St Mary Major, the church windows being deliberately smashed in order to let outsiders hear. Hooker says that 'the more he was heard, the more he was liked', but evidence of actual conversion among the citizens is again absent. Indeed, one of Latimer's auditors was Hooker's own father – who, when drafting his will in the following August, would nevertheless make the traditional bequests to the friars and to his parish church for trentals. Nor may it be assumed that even the frequent sermons of Bishop Coverdale were invariably effectual. In 1553, while he was preaching in the cathedral to the people of Exeter, the news arrived that Mary Tudor had been proclaimed as queen. With the exception of 'a few godly men', the entire congregation thereupon trooped out of the cathedral and left the bishop stranded in his pulpit. This spontaneous crowd reaction unquestionably indicates that even in Exeter, where Protestant preaching had largely been concentrated, it had as yet failed to secure more than an external and temporary conformity from the population at large.[193]

Nor was the recitation of a Protestant homily always received with respect. In 1566, at Dean Prior, John Foxe deliberately disrupted a homily by talking loudly to a child, and by ignoring the vicar's repeated commands to remove it. 'By reason of the noise of the said child', it was reported, 'the vicar was troubled and unquieted in the pulpit.'[194]

Instances of this nature provide salutory reminders that the influence of the religious professionals was never irresistible. In the Reformation decades, indeed, there is evidence of its substantial diminution.[195] When this important qualification has been made, it remains beyond doubt that the role of this body of men in the formation, consolidation or alteration of popular religious attitudes was frequently of paramount significance. By virtue of its contact with individuals, groups and congregations, it occupied a uniquely powerful position from which to condition the outlook of the laity.

For this reason it is imperative to analyse the factors which determined the outlook of the professionals themselves. How, firstly, is the decline of their traditionalist commitment to be explained? One factor was the elimination from their ranks, between 1536 and 1539, of the generally conservative monks and friars. The diminishing willingness of the remaining secular clergy to propagate traditional religion must be attributed in part to their conventional sense of obligation to established authorities, but also in part to their justified fear of the penal consequences of overt resistance. Punishments for clerical dissent were decreed by the Henrician, Edwardian and

[193] Hooker, Commonplace Book, fols. 342, 349; PROB 11 26, fol. 76.
[194] CCB 855B, sub 17 December 1566.
[195] See above, pp. 138–42.

Elizabethan regimes: thus life imprisonment was imposed by both the Edwardian and the Elizabethan Acts of Uniformity upon clerics who persistently refused to use the new Prayerbooks.[196] The punitive legislation, moreover, was locally enforced by gentlemen, like Carew, Dennis, Dynham, Edgcumbe, Godolphin or Russell, and was upheld also by laymen of lesser rank, such as Consen, Leigh and Shame, Andrew and Parrot, and Philip Nichols. The consequent arrests, imprisonments, interrogations, recantations, fines, deprivations, and even executions, not only effectively silenced the most overtly traditionalist priests, but also dissuaded their less heroic colleagues from the public propagation of the ancient religion.[197] Considerations of this nature must largely explain why a theological conservative like Christopher Trychay, vicar of Morebath from 1520 to 1573, in most respects conformed dutifully to every regime of the Reformation decades. They help similarly to explain why, in 1549, even the vicar of remote Sampford Courtenay obediently used the new Prayerbook on Whit Sunday, and was prepared to use it again on the following day – 'according', he told his parishioners, 'to the laws set forth'.[198]

Traditionalist zeal might also be eroded by material inducements. Dr Tregonwell – a loyal agent of Thomas Cromwell, particularly in the suppression of religious houses – was rewarded for his collaboration with lands, advowsons and annuities.[199] An additional factor was the reluctance of the south-western gentry to sponsor and mobilize traditionalist preachers; Catholic equivalents of the Carews and Russells would seem to have been virtually non-existent. But of even greater importance was the failure of Bishop Veysey to provide the traditionalist cause with decisive leadership. Veysey's career in royal service – which included a presidency of the Council of Wales – prepared him for a generally compliant role in the Henrician and Edwardian Reformations. Advanced in years, having been born in *circa* 1465, and frequently absent from his diocese, which he seems not even to have visited during the upheavals of 1547–51, he almost invariably preferred a dutiful conformity to an open resistance. After his death in October 1554, moreover, his successor was not consecrated for ten months. Nor does Bishop Turberville appear to have been particularly energetic in his efforts to restore the old religion: he did not even arrive in the diocese until six months after his consecration.[200]

Why, on the other hand, did no more than a minority of south-western

[196]   Dickens 1967A, pp. 304, 415.
[197]   See above, pp. 229–31, 242–4.
[198]   CWA Morebath; 'Description of Exeter', pp. 26–7. For other examples, see Rowse 1941, p. 155; and MacCaffrey 1958, p. 191.
[199]   Rowse 1941, pp. 187–93.
[200]   For an assessment of the diocesan administration of Veysey and Turberville, see Pill 1963. For Turberville's reluctance to burn Agnes Priest, see *Acts and Monuments*, II, p. 2050.

clergy become enthusiastic advocates of the Protestant alternative? One intermittent but powerful deterrent was official persecution, as was experienced by Simon Heynes under Henry VIII and by Nicholas Daniel under Mary. Shortly before 1531, for example, the Exeter preacher Gregory Bassett appears to have been dissuaded from his brief flirtation with Lutheranism by a period of harsh imprisonment at Bristol.[201] A second deterrent must have been the hostility directed against Protestant ministers not only by non-gentle laymen – such as John Chapel at St Teath in 1554[202] – but also by gentlemen and fellow-clerics. When Latimer preached at Exeter in 1534, a local gentleman named Thomas Carew reviled him as a 'heretic knave' and threatened to pull him from the pulpit by his ears.[203] Most of the friars similarly denounced Latimer's preaching as heretical, while the clergy of St Mary Major attempted to prevent him from even entering their pulpit. In 1535 a Barnstaple priest sought to silence an apparently pro-Reformation preacher, and from 1537 the ministry of Dean Heynes encountered substantial opposition from the Exeter canons.[204] Other hindrances to the emergence of a Protestant clergy included the theological conservatism of Bishops Veysey and Turberville – in 1551 the former was accused by the Council of a lack of diligence in promoting the Reformation[205] – and the relative scarcity of gentlemen who were prepared, like Carew and Russell, to finance and protect the preaching of the new religion.

But probably the most fundamental problem was one of education. When Dean Heynes observed in 1537 that 'very few' of the region's priests were 'well-persuaded', he also noted – as if in explanation – that very few were 'anything learned'. This relationship between the clergy's doctrinal conservatism and its lack of higher education was also noted by a minister at Exeter in 1531, and it was exemplified by the career of Morebath's non-graduate vicar, Christopher Trychay. University education did not always produce Protestants – Chrispin and Moreman had both been at Oxford – but it almost invariably provided some contact with Protestant ideas. This was particularly true of Cambridge, where, for example, Coverdale, Heynes and Latimer had studied. Yet it remained the privilege of a minority: the report compiled by Bishop Alley in 1561 would suggest that no more than approximately 20% of south-western clergy were graduates. This fact is itself attributable not only to the geographical remoteness of the peninsula from Oxford and Cambridge – Exeter lay about 150 miles from the former and about 230 from the latter – but also, as Philip Nichols realized, to the general

---

[201] *APC*, I, pp. 97, 150–1; *Acts and Monuments*, II, pp. 1039, 2051.
[202] C 1 1347/16–18.
[203] Hooker, Commonplace Book, fol. 342.
[204] Hooker, Commonplace Book, fol. 342; *LP*, VIII, 460; CAB 3552, fol. 14v.
[205] ER XV, fols. 121–1v; *Acts and Monuments*, II, p. 2050.

poverty of its livings. Few graduates can have been attracted to the region by the prospect of £10–20 per annum, and livings of this size could rarely have sustained ministers who were devoted to biblical study and preaching rather than engaged in agriculture or a comparably rewarding occupation. Poverty must also have prevented many of the parochial clergy from buying books, and thus from encountering the doctrines of the Reformation in a coherent literary form.[206]

A combination of factors thus ensured that in most parts of the South-West the cleric who was internally committed to the Protestant faith — and not merely externally acquiescent in its imposition — remained a comparatively unusual phenomenon. In consequence the occasions on which the layman received an enthusiastic and persuasive exposition of the new religion — either in personal conversation, through teaching, or from the pulpit — can but rarely have been more than infrequent.

[206] *LP*, XII (2), 557; *Acts and Monuments*, II, p. 1038; CWA Morebath; Rose-Troup 1913, pp. 104, 107; Porter 1958; Alley Report; RBM 1928–9, I, pp. 38–41 (figures for Devon only); *Godly New Story*, pp. 72–3; Dickens 1967A, p. 421; Rowse 1941, p. 160.

Summation of Part Two

How is the decline of popular Catholicism to be explained?

Only in part is the phenomenon attributable to an upsurge of alternative Christian convictions. The evidence suggests that before 1570 no more than a relatively small minority of south-western people were committed Protestants. Nor was their Protestantism wholly uniform. Episcopacy, for example, was accepted by Thomas Bennett but derided by Philip Gammon, while during their Genevan exile John Budleigh and Peter Willis participated as senior and deacon in a presbyterian form of organization. Infant baptism was supported by Philip Nichols but rejected by Philip Gammon. Agnes Priest was labelled by the ecclesiastical authorities as an 'Anabaptist', and Philip Gammon's alleged repudiation of Christ's virgin birth would certainly locate him outside the mainstream of Protestant belief.[1] For the majority of the region's inhabitants, in contrast, acquiescence or co-operation in the assault upon traditional religion was motivated by essentially non-spiritual considerations. Protestant conviction was less important than a sense of duty, xenophobia, a desire for moral freedom, financial calculation, or even physical fear.

The overall pattern again contained significant variations. In terms of geography, for instance, Protestant commitment was markedly more evident in Devon than in Cornwall. 'Devonshire', declared Philip Nichols in 1547, 'lacketh not some well-willers, at the least... that desire the glory of God and furtherance of his word.' Of the region's identifiable non-gentle lay Protestants, most were in fact Devonian; the exiles in this category, for example, were exclusively from Devon. On the other hand Cornwall produced occasional Protestants like Agnes Priest, and even in Devon the converts unquestionably remained a limited minority. In 1561 the Catholic Nicholas Sander reported that 'the most distant parts of the kingdom' –

---

[1] *Acts and Monuments*, II, pp. 1037–40, 2049–52; STAC 2/2/267–72, 287; 23/273; 29/111; Garrett 1966, pp. 92–4, 337; *Copy of a Letter*; *Godly New Story*; Royal 18 B XI.

amongst which he explicitly included Devon – were the 'most averse to heresy'.[2]

The majority of Protestants lived in urban communities. The most notable was Exeter; others included Axminster, Chagford, Crediton, Dartmouth, Plymouth, South Molton and Totnes. Many were merchants, such as John Anthony, William Ashridge, John Budleigh, John Drake, John Eliot, William Hawkins, James Horsewell, John Hurst, William Lake, John Midwinter, John Periam, Peter Willis, and certain merchants of South Molton. Also in their number, however, were the schoolmaster Bennett, the shoemaker Gammon, the tinner Kingwell and the draper Ameredith, as well as shearmen of Exeter and victuallers, artificers and labourers of South Molton. In 1547 Philip Nichols asserted that Protestantism was to be found in Devon 'as well among the poor creatures as the rich and worshipful', and undoubtedly it was beginning to reach the middle and lower-middle ranks of urban society. Again, nevertheless, the distinction was not absolute. Some Protestants lived in rural communities, such as Boyton, Bridestow, Broadclyst and Combe Pyne: Combe Pyne's John Helier, for example, was a yeoman. In both town and countryside, moreover, committed adherents of the new religion must usually have remained a minority – as even at Exeter under Edward VI.[3]

Most of the known Protestants were male. Yet once more there were exceptions, including Alice Bennett, Agnes Priest, Joan Lake and Eleanor of Totnes; the wives of Thomas Bennett, John Budleigh, Philip Nichols and Peter Willis; and the unnamed 'godly' women at Exeter in 1559. A number were relatively young. Philip Nichols in 1547 described himself as young, and of the Marian exiles John Boggens and Richard Vivian were of apprenticeship age, while Nicholas Hilliard joined Knox's congregation in 1557 at the age of 20. On the other hand by 1557 John Budleigh had fathered four children; by contemporary standards he was probably middle-aged. The Protestant testators were presumably in middle or old age, while at the time of their martyrdom both Thomas Bennett and Agnes Priest were over 50. Moreover, many of the young were neutral or indifferent. Of the Morchard Bishop parishioners who mocked Protestant services in 1567, Robert Back was 20, John More 23, and William Radford 24.[4]

Both Catholics and Protestants attributed their own religious outlook to divine revelation, and that of their opponents to satanic delusion. Thus Agnes Priest believed that 'the living God hath opened mine eyes', but dismissed traditionalist doctrine as 'devilish deceit'.[5] Whatever the validity

---

[2] *Copy of a Letter*, p. 5; Hughes 1950–4, III, p. 50. See also above, pp. 151–71.
[3] *Copy of a Letter*, p. 5. See also above, pp. 151–71.
[4] *Copy of a Letter*, p. 36; Garrett 1966, pp. 92–4, 183, 318; *Acts and Monuments*, II, pp. 1040, 2052; CCB 855B, sub 7 February 1566/7.
[5] *Acts and Monuments*, II, pp. 2050–1.

of such metaphysical interpretations, it is certainly possible to identify a wide range of human influences by which religious attitudes were shaped. These included mediate influences, in the form of literature, drama and art, and immediate influences, in the form of contact with other non-gentle laypeople and with members of the gentry and clergy. Until the 1530s the attitudes transmitted through these channels were overwhelmingly tradition-alist in character. Thereafter the propagation of Catholicism was reduced, and eventually to a considerable extent suppressed, but only in part was it replaced by its Protestant equivalent. In these developments must lie the most fundamental reasons for the strength of Catholicism before the Refor-mation, for its erosion in the period 1530–70, and for the limited extent of its replacement by commitment to the new religion.

Analysis of influences also helps to explain the geographical, sociological and gender variations in responses to the Reformation. The concentration of Protestant commitment in urban communities, for example, is to be attri-buted largely to the fact that both Protestant literature and Protestant preach-ing were usually more accessible to the townsman than to the inhabitant of a relatively small, poor and remote country parish. Considerations of this type similarly help explain in part the greater strength of the new religion in Devon than in Cornwall, among the middle and lower-middle social ranks rather than among the lowest, and among men rather than among women. The influences to which an individual was exposed did not automati-cally predetermine his religious choices, but they unavoidably established the parameters within which these choices would have to be made.

13

Perspective

One question remains. To what extent may the responses of south-western people to the Reformation be regarded as typical of those of the English people as a whole?

Comparison with other regions is hindered by the emphasis of most modern research upon the clergy and gentry rather than upon the mass of the population. It is further complicated by the differing sources and approaches employed by modern historians, and by the conflicting conclusions that these have sometimes produced. At one end of the spectrum, A. G. Dickens and G. R. Elton have argued that discontent with Catholicism increased markedly in later-medieval England; that Lollardy and anti-clericalism were widespread; and that (in consequence) Protestantism rapidly won support in the sixteenth century.[1] At the other end, C. Haigh and J. Scarisbrick have contended that Catholicism was still flourishing on the eve of the Reformation; that Lollardy and anti-clericalism remained relatively rare; and that (in consequence) the progress of Protestantism was both difficult and slow.[2] It is probable that only after many more local studies will a generally agreed picture of English responses to the Reformation eventually emerge. Nevertheless, a brief survey of the principal types of evidence – and in particular of those which are susceptible to some form of statistical analysis – would suggest that a number of general propositions may be plausibly essayed.

There are signs that, in several regions, the Reformation decades witnessed a rising volume of verbal outbursts by laymen against traditional religion and against priests.[3] But the most readily quantifiable type of verbal evidence is that provided by wills. These would indicate that the Catholic commitment of the English remained high until the Reformation, but declined markedly or even drastically thenceforth. In Kent, for example, the percentage of testators employing traditional formulae fell from over 90%

---

[1] Dickens 1967A; Elton 1977.
[2] Haigh 1987, esp. pp. 1–17, 19–33, 56–74, 176–208; Scarisbrick 1984.
[3] E.g. Haigh 1987, pp. 58, 72. Cf. Dickens 1959.

in the early 1530s to 72% in 1540, 52% in 1546, and 6% in 1552. After recovering to a peak of only about 40% in Mary's reign, it collapsed to 9% in 1560.[4] In Sussex and in the Midlands the decline was somewhat less rapid, but the overall pattern was not dissimilar.[5] In Northamptonshire the traditionalist percentage revived under Mary but slumped under Elizabeth, reaching 14% by 1566–9.[6] Even in remote Nottinghamshire and Yorkshire the figure had fallen from 89% in the late 1530s to 37% by 1550. Under Mary it recovered to 76%.[7] Catholic preambles were relatively slow to decline in York, but even here totalled only 24% by 1561–70.[8] In Hull, on the other hand, they plummeted under Edward, remained low under Mary, and after 1559 disappeared.[9] Albeit most rapid in the South-East, and somewhat slower in the North and West, the trend was everywhere substantially downward.

Once more the verbal evidence must be compared with the financial. Particularly revealing is the pattern of bequests. In London, for instance, the proportion of testators bequeathing to intercessions and religious houses declined only slightly between 1486 and 1525, but began to drop significantly from 1529–30.[10] In Sussex the percentage of wills containing intercessory endowments or other traditionalist bequests began to diminish in the last Henrician years, fell catastrophically under Edward, recovered only partially under Mary, and again collapsed after Elizabeth's accession.[11] Wills from the Midlands and from Somerset indicate high expenditure on Catholic activities and institutions until the 1530s, followed by decline under Henry, collapse under Edward, and no more than partial revival under Mary.[12] Bequests of this type declined under Henry VIII in the diocese of Lincoln, though less markedly in Lincolnshire than in Buckinghamshire or Huntingdonshire. Under Edward they collapsed.[13] Finally, an analysis of wills from ten geographically dispersed counties confirms that testatorial investment in religion experienced a drastic decline in the Reformation decades. This was fastest in London and Kent – where it began before 1530 but accelerated thereafter – and slowest in Yorkshire and Lancashire. It was

---

[4] Clark 1977, esp. pp. 58, 76.
[5] For Sussex, see Mayhew 1983. Midland wills have been analysed by my former pupil, Mr R. Harper, in a study which I hope will be published.
[6] Shiels 1979, pp. 15–18, 21–4.
[7] Dickens 1959, esp. pp. 171–2, 215–18, 220–1; Dickens 1967A, pp. 266–7.
[8] Palliser 1979, pp. 250–1.
[9] Cross 1979.
[10] Thomson 1965B.
[11] Mayhew 1983.
[12] For the Midlands, see note 5 above. See also Scarisbrick 1984, pp. 2–12. Somerset wills have been studied by my former pupil, Miss J. Bruton; her valuable analysis merits publication.
[13] Bowker 1981, esp. p. 177.

generally faster among merchants and artisans than among yeomen and husbandmen.[14]

Other types of financial evidence point in a similar direction. Chantries, for example, continued to be founded on the eve of the Reformation, though with greater enthusiasm in rural areas than in towns, and in the North and West than in the Midlands, South and East. In most areas, including even Yorkshire and Lancashire, the period 1530–48 nevertheless saw a marked decline in new foundations and an increase in private suppressions.[15] Similarly suggestive is the level of church-building by parochial communities. Sources both documentary and archaeological would indicate that until the 1530s this remained high in Middlesex, Kent, Suffolk, Norfolk, Cheshire, Yorkshire and elsewhere. Thereafter it everywhere fell, until by 1570 church-building had virtually ceased.[16] Noteworthy also is the sharply rising evidence of the sale or embezzlement of traditionalist apparatus – only some of which was ever returned under Mary[17] – and of resistance to tithes and other clerical dues.[18]

Nor is this all. A study of 198 sets of churchwardens' accounts throughout England has shown that although Catholicism continued to flourish in most parishes on the eve of the Reformation, the Henrician, Edwardian and Elizabethan orders against images, altars, intercessions, guilds and other traditional elements were generally obeyed with promptitude. It has also shown that although standard rites were usually restored under Mary, ornaments were mostly inexpensive, few images were bought, and many side altars and most guilds and intercessions did not return.[19] Other sources confirm that religious guilds, for example, were numerous and vital until the 1530s, but sometimes suffered falling recruitment or even dissolution in the late-Henrician years, were generally suppressed under Edward, and were only rarely revived in Mary's reign.[20] There are signs also of changing attitudes towards the clergy. The diocese of Chichester saw a deterioration of lay respect for church courts,[21] and many dioceses, including London, Lichfield, Hereford, Lincoln and York, experienced a drastic fall in the numbers of laymen seeking ordination.[22]

Visitation records would suggest that non-compliance with official orders

[14] Jordan 1959; Jordan 1960A; Jordan 1960B; Jordan 1961A; Jordan 1961B; Jordan 1962. For Lancashire bequests, see also Haigh 1975, pp. 69–70, 194.
[15] Kreider 1979, esp. pp. 78, 86–92, 154–60; Haigh 1975, pp. 71–2, 147.
[16] I intend to explore and document this point in a forthcoming article on the chronology of medieval church-building. See also Scarisbrick 1984, pp. 12–15.
[17] E.g. Scarisbrick 1984, pp. 93–6, 99–108.
[18] Bowker 1981, p. 87; Houlbrooke 1979, pp. 273–4.
[19] Hutton 1987.
[20] Scarisbrick 1984, pp. 19–39.
[21] Lander 1987.
[22] Haigh 1987, p. 71; Bowker 1981, pp. 125, 186; Hughes 1950–4, III, p. 53n.

existed but was rarely the norm. They suggest also that the destruction of Catholicism proceeded more rapidly in the South-East (Kent, Suffolk, Norfolk) than in the North (Lincolnshire, Yorkshire, Lancashire).[23] Similarly significant is the fact that the South-East mounted no substantial rebellion against the Henrician, Edwardian or Elizabethan Reformations.[24] In the North, the risings of 1536–7 attracted possibly 40,000 recruits, though their motives were far from exclusively religious.[25] Yet neither the revolution of 1547–53 nor the settlement of 1559 evoked serious northern resistance, and the Catholic rebellion of 1569 was joined by only 5,500, and was opposed by numerous loyalists from within the region.[26] And before 1570, even in Yorkshire and Lancashire, even non-violent Catholic recusancy was a very restricted phenomenon.[27] The evidence indicates that the most usual responses of the English people to the Reformation were co-operation or acquiescence rather than overt dissent.

The factors determining these responses are inevitably more difficult to evaluate. Nevertheless there is abundant evidence of the importance of essentially non-spiritual considerations, ranging from xenophobia and a sense of political obligation to economic interest and a fear of physical punishment.[28] In most areas of England, moreover, it would appear probable that responses to the Reformation were motivated more frequently by secular factors of this type than by an internal commitment to the Protestant faith.

It was in the South-East – where Lollardy had been relatively extensive[29] – that Protestant commitment was in general most strong. Protestant elements are discernible in the risings of 1549 and 1554 in Norfolk and Kent.[30] The Marian martyrdoms were largely concentrated in London, Essex and Kent, and to a lesser extent in Sussex, Suffolk and Norfolk; the martyrs were more frequently artisans than husbandmen.[31] The Marian exiles came far more often from the South-East than the North or West, and from the merchants and artisans than the yeomen and husbandmen.[32] Even in the South-East, nevertheless, the progress of Protestantism should not be over-

---

[23] Hutton 1987, pp. 127, 132, 135; *Harpsfield's Visitation*, I, II; Lincoln Visitation, pp. 389–413. For attempts to evade official orders, see, for example, Scarisbrick 1984, pp. 82–4.
[24] For the Tudor rebellions in general, see Fletcher 1973.
[25] Dodds 1915; Dickens 1967B; Davies 1968; James 1970. For other opposition to the Henrician Reformation, and its decline after 1537, see Elton 1972, esp. pp. 383–400.
[26] Sharp 1975; Reid 1906; James 1973.
[27] Dickens 1941; Aveling 1970, esp. pp. 165–9; Haigh 1975, esp. pp. 254–6, 259; Manning 1969, esp. pp. 45–6.
[28] Cf. Haigh 1987, pp. 11–17; Scarisbrick 1984, pp. 62, 81.
[29] Thomson 1965A; Davis 1983.
[30] For Norfolk, see Russell 1859; and Cornwall 1977. For Kent, see Loades 1965; and Clark 1977, pp. 87–98.
[31] Hughes 1950–4, II, pp. 259–64; Loades 1970, p. 12.
[32] Garrett 1966, pp. 32, 41, 67–349.

Perspective

estimated. In no year before 1560 were Protestant formulae employed by more than 10% of testators in Kent; they were most common in clothing districts and towns like Cranbrook, Maidstone and Sandwich.[33] In Sussex Protestant formulae or bequests – such as gifts financing the purchase of English Bibles or the preaching of Protestant sermons – increased under Edward, survived under Mary and revived under Elizabeth, but by 1559 they still appeared in only 14% of wills. They were most frequent in Hastings, Rye, Winchelsea and other towns.[34] Both in Kent and in Sussex by the beginning of Elizabeth's reign the majority of wills were religiously neutral.

Outside the South-East the new religion had even fewer apparent devotees. Except in Gloucestershire, Marian martyrdoms in the North and West were rare.[35] Protestant will formulae remained uncommon in Lincoln diocese until at least 1550, were used by at most 5% of testators in York diocese before 1558, and in as late as 1566–9 appeared in only 23% of wills from Northamptonshire. Despite exceptions like York, it was generally in and around towns like Halifax, Hull and Northampton that they were most frequent. By the 1560s, most wills in these regions would seem to have been religiously neutral.[36] Throughout England, moreover, churchwardens' accounts indicate that although most parishes conformed obediently to Protestant regimes, relatively few invested with enthusiasm in Protestant sermons or literature.[37] It thus appears probable that the destruction of Catholicism in the Reformation decades owed considerably less to the rise of Protestant convictions than to the motive power of essentially secular compulsions.

The final issue requiring further research is the relative importance of the various types of external influence that shaped the religious attitudes of the English people. In most regions, nevertheless, it would seem that the erosion of popular Catholicism is to be attributed substantially to two key factors. One was the predominantly compliant stance of the local clergy. This phenomenon is evident even in relatively remote areas like Lincolnshire and Yorkshire.[38] The other factor was the willingness of a majority of the gentry to acquiesce in, or even co-operate with, the official changes in religion. In 1564 fewer than one in three of English justices of the peace – and these chiefly in the North and West – were categorized by the bishops as unfavourable to the religion newly established; the rest were favourable

---

[33] Clark 1977, esp. pp. 58, 76, 102.
[34] Mayhew 1983. See also Manning 1969, esp. pp. xii–xiii.
[35] For Gloucestershire, see Powell 1969; and Powell 1972.
[36] Bowker 1981; Dickens 1959, esp. pp. 171–2, 215–18, 220–1; Dickens 1967A, pp. 266–7; Shiels 1979, pp. 15–18, 21–4; Cross 1979; Palliser 1979, pp. 250–1. See also Haigh 1975, esp. pp. 172–5, 185–6, 188, 202–3.
[37] Hutton 1987, pp. 124–5.
[38] Bowker 1987, pp. 75–93; Dickens 1959, esp. pp. 166–7, 181–2.

or neutral.[39] At the same time the importance of mediate influences should not be neglected. Traditionalist drama was censored: this happened even in distant York under Edward, and again under Elizabeth.[40] Traditionalist church art was frequently removed or destroyed. Wardens' accounts throughout England record the obliteration of murals and other works under Edward, and the assault was renewed after Elizabeth's accession.[41]

Similarly it appears to have been a combination of factors that in most regions retarded the advance of Protestantism. One was illiteracy; this generally constituted a greater barrier to the dissemination of heretical books and Bibles in the North and West than in the South-East, and in rural communities than in towns.[42] The North and West were further insulated against heresy by their geographical distance from London and from the Protestant areas of continental Europe. But arguably the most crucial factor was the deficiency of Protestant preachers. In general this was least serious in the comparatively wealthy and densely populated South-East, as in the dioceses of London and Rochester, but more severe elsewhere, as in the archdeaconries of Coventry and Leicester and the dioceses of Norwich, Peterborough, Winchester and York. The deficiency was usually most acute in rural areas. Since the new religion depended so often upon its dissemination by powerful and energetic preachers – like Ridley and many others in London, or John Melvin at Hastings, or John Rough at Hull – the scarcity of such men must to a considerable extent explain its restricted progress among the English people as a whole.[43]

In the present state of research, overconfident generalizations about England's responses to the Reformation remain injudicious. Nevertheless the evidence surveyed above would suggest that the south-western experience was by no means wholly untypical. In the South-East, it is true, there are signs of a partial weakening of Catholic enthusiasm before the Reformation; here the Dickens/Elton model has a measure of validity. Outside this region, however, devotion generally remained strong: in most parts of England it is the Haigh/Scarisbrick model that seems the more applicable. The evidence nevertheless indicates that traditionalist commitment collapsed dramatically in the Reformation decades, with only a partial and temporary recovery in Mary's reign. Though generally fastest in the South-East, the collapse eventually occurred in most regions of the realm. It seems probable that

---

[39] *Original Letters*, pp. 1–83; Trimble 1964, pp. 24–36.
[40] *York Records*, IV, p. 176; V, p. 100; VI, pp. 8, 134–5.
[41] Hutton 1987, p. 121; *English Church Furniture*, pp. 29–171; *Tudor Parish Documents*, pp. 31–2, 34, etc.
[42] For literacy and illiteracy, see Cressy 1980.
[43] Frere 1904, pp. 107–8; Houlbrooke 1979, pp. 202–3; Shiels 1979, p. 92. See also Hill 1969, pp. 31–77. For Melvin, see Mayhew 1983, pp. 50–1; for Rough, see Cross 1979, p. 273.

by 1570 no more than a relatively limited minority of the English people could have been meaningfully classified as committed Catholics. In this respect the evidence appears to contradict the Haigh/Scarisbrick emphasis upon the resilience and survival of the old religion. Against Dickens and Elton, on the other hand, it suggests that only a small percentage of the population could yet have been categorized as committed Protestants. These were generally more frequent in the South-East than elsewhere, and in towns than in rural communities.

In most regions of England, as in the South-West, the Reformation may thus have been less a transition from Catholicism to Protestantism than a decline from religious commitment into conformism or indifference. 'There are in England three religions', Bishop Bonner was told by Ralph Allerton in Mary's reign. 'The first is that which you hold; the second is clean contrary to the same; and the third is a neuter, being indifferent.'[44] 'Many', agreed Jewel at the beginning of Elizabeth's reign, 'will believe neither side, what-soever they allege. Bring they truth, bring they falsehood; teach they Christ, teach they Antichrist: they will believe neither, they have so hardened their hearts.'[45] Outside the Protestant and Catholic strongholds lay extensive areas of uncommitted territory. In these, throughout the subsequent decades, the rival forces would strive for mastery.

[44] Quoted in Alexander 1987, p. 167.
[45] Quoted in Hughes 1950–4, III, p. 58.

APPENDIX 1: MAPS

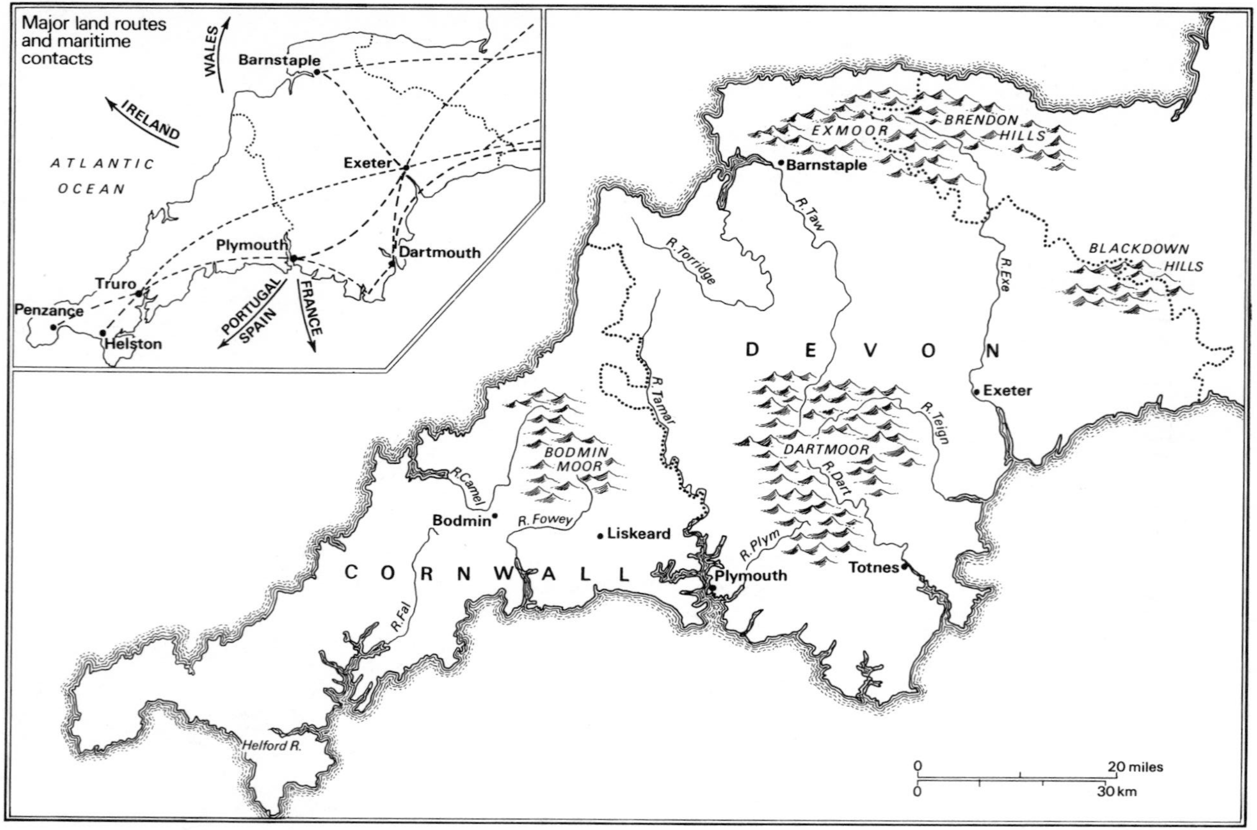

Map 1. The South-West

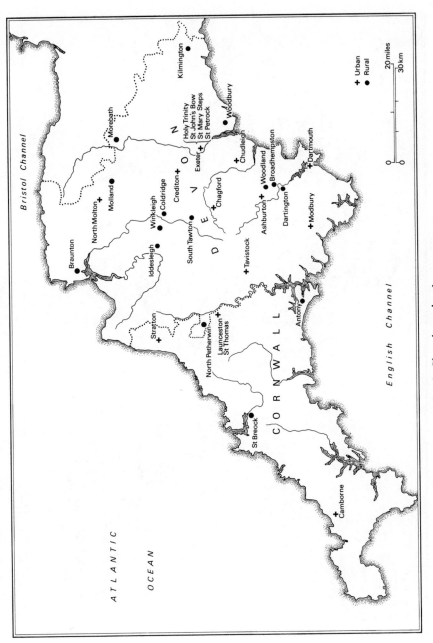

Map 2. Churchwardens' accounts

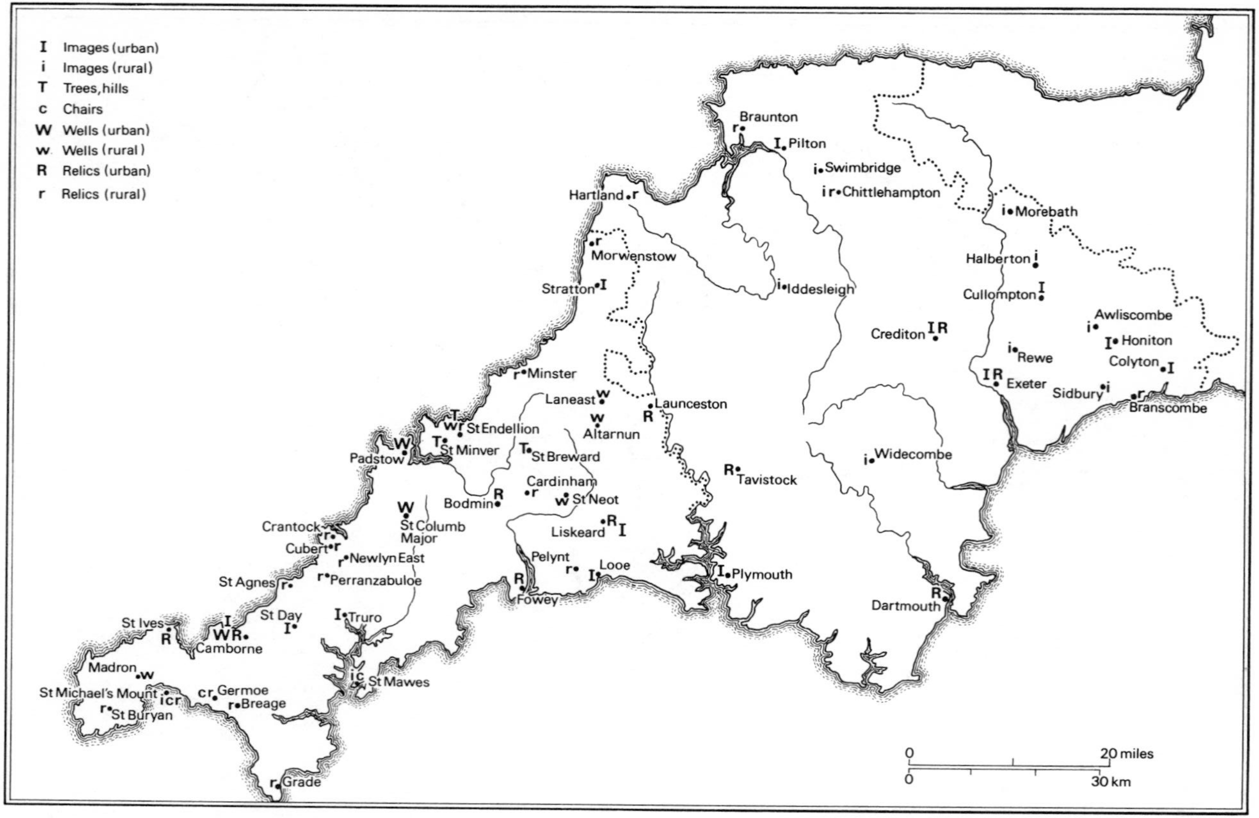

Awliscombe

I•Honiton

i• Colyton•I

r•Branscombe

i•Rewe

I•Morebath Halberton i•

Cullompton•I i•Exeter

I R Sidbury•i

Crediton I R

i•Swimbridge

i r•Chittlehampton

•Braunton

r• I•Pilton

i•Iddesleigh

i •Widecombe

R•
Dartmouth

R•Tavistock

R•
Hartland •r •Morwenstow •Launceston

Stratton•I W R

W•Minster Laneast •w R•
Altarnun I•Plymouth

r• W• R•St Neot

r•St Endellion •Cardinham Liskeard• R• I

T• •T•St Breward r• r• I•Looe

W r• •St Minver Pelynt r• R•
Padstow •Bodmin Fowey•

W•
St Columb Major

W•Newlyn East

Cuber• r•r•Perranzabuloe

Crantock r• I•Truro

St Agnes• •St Day I• I c• I c•St Mawes

I• •Germoe r•Grade

St Ives• W R• •Camborne c r• r•Breage

•Madron •w

St Michael's Mount• i c r•

r• r•St Burian

I Images (urban)
i Images (rural)
T Trees, hills
c Chairs
W Wells (urban)
w Wells (rural)
R Relics (urban)
r Relics (rural)

20 miles
30 km

Map 3. Cult objects

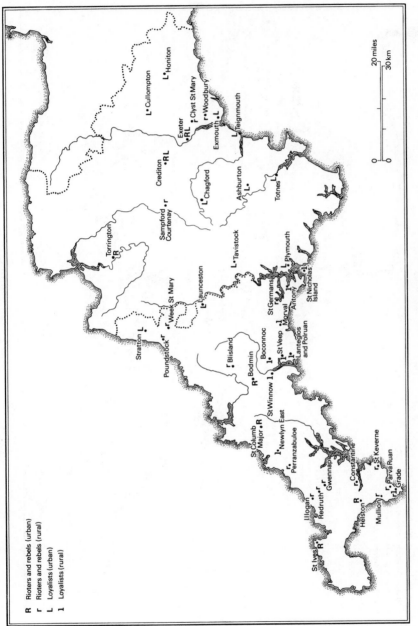

Map 4. Riot and rebellion, 1548–9

R   Rioters and rebels (urban)
r   Rioters and rebels (rural)
L   Loyalists (urban)
l   Loyalists (rural)

L• Cullompton
L• Honiton
Exeter L• Clyst St Mary
•RL r•Woodbury
Exmouth •L
Teignmouth L•
Crediton •RL
Chagford l•
Ashburton L•
Totnes •L
Sampford l•
Courtenay •r
Torrington
•R
L•Tavistock
Launceston
Week St Mary •l•
l•L
Plymouth
St Germans L•Morval L•
Stratton L• Antony •l
St Nicholas •l
Poundstock •r Island
St Veep •l
Bliisland r• Lanteglos
Boconnoc and Polruan l•
l•
Bodmin
R•
St Winnow l•
St Columb
Major •R
l•Newlyn East
Perranzabuloe
St Keverne
Gwennap• r•
Illogan r• Constantine r•
Redruth r• Parva Ruan
Helston •l r•
R Grade
St Ives Mullion l• l•
R•r•

0 20 miles
0 30 km

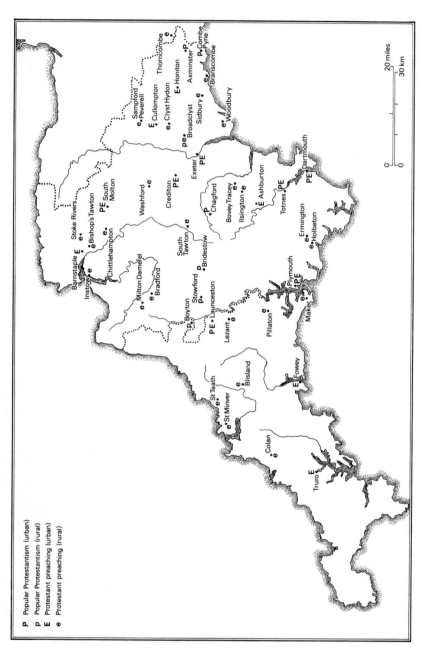

Map 5. Protestantism

P   Popular Protestantism (urban)
p   Popular Protestantism (rural)
E   Protestant preaching (urban)
e   Protestant preaching (rural)

Thorncombe
Sampford
•Peverell
E• Cullompton
Honiton
e• Clyst Hydon
E•
Axminster   P•Combe
•Pyne
Broadclyst
Sidbury e•   •Branscombe
pe•
e•Woodbury
Exeter
PE

Washford
•e
Crediton
PE•
Chagford
p•
Bovey Tracey
•e
Ilsington •e
E• Ashburton
Totnes •E
Dartmouth
PE•

Stoke Rivers•
e•   e•Bishop's Tawton
PE• South
•Molton
Barnstaple   E•
Instow• •e
•Chittlehampton
South
Tawton •e
•Bridestow
Ermington
•e
e•Holbeton

Milton Damerel
e•   •Bradford
Boyton
p• Stowford
Launceston
PE•   P•
Lezant   PE•
•e
Pillaton •e
Plymouth
•PE
Maker
e•

St Teath
•e
e•St Minver
Bisland
•e

Colan
•e

E• Fowey
E•

E
•Truro

20 miles
0
0
30 km

APPENDIX 2: GRAPHS

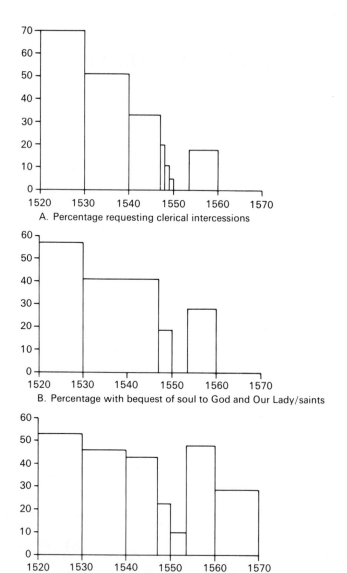

Graph 1. Wills (398 wills proved in the Prerogative Court of Canterbury and within the diocese of Exeter, 1520–69)

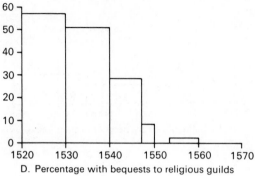

D. Percentage with bequests to religious guilds

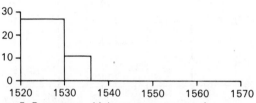

E. Percentage with bequests to monasteries

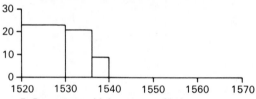

F. Percentage with bequests to friaries

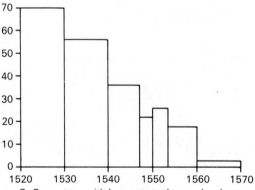

G. Percentage with bequests to the secular clergy

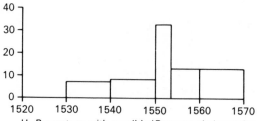

H. Percentage with possibly 'Protestant' phraseology

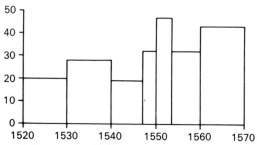

I. Percentage with bequests to the poor

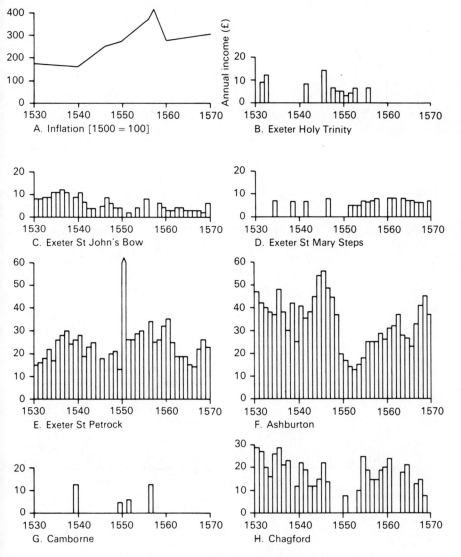

Graph 2. Churchwardens' accounts (A. from Phelps Brown and Hopkins 1956;
B–P. from churchwardens' accounts from 15 selected parishes, 1530–69)

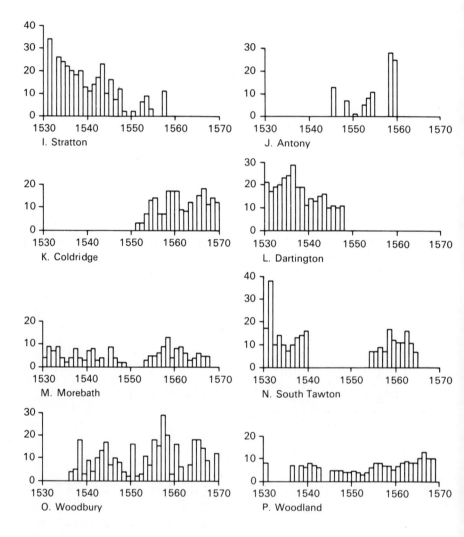

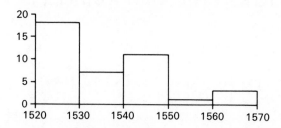

Graph 3. Datable church-building projects, 1520–69 (data from wills, episcopal registers, inscriptions, etc.)

BIBLIOGRAPHY AND ABBREVIATIONS

Unless otherwise indicated, the place of publication of books is London.

DEPOSITORIES

BL	British Library
CRO	Cornwall Record Office, Truro
CUL	Cambridge University Library
DCRSL	Devon and Cornwall Record Society Library, Exeter
DRO	Devon Record Office, Exeter
EDCL	Exeter Dean and Chapter Library
PRO	Public Record Office
TCCL	Trinity College, Cambridge, Library

PRIMARY SOURCES

Acts and Monuments	J. Foxe, *Acts and Monuments* ..., 2 vols., 1583
Additional 32243, HCWA Stratton	BL, Additional MS 32243, Stratton High Cross Wardens' Accounts
Additional 32244, SWA Stratton	BL, Additional MS 32244, Stratton Stockwardens' Accounts
Alley Report	DRO, Transcript 009/9, Bishop Alley, Report on Clergy
Ancient Cornish Drama	*The Ancient Cornish Drama*, ed. E. Norris, 2 vols., Oxford, 1859
APC	*Acts of the Privy Council of England*, ed. J. R. Dasent, 32 vols., 1890–1907
BA Bodmin	CRO, Borough Accounts, Bodmin
Barnstaple Records	*Reprint of the Barnstaple Records*, ed. J. R. Chanter and T. Wainwright, 2 vols., Barnstaple, 1900
Beunans Meriasek	*Beunans Meriasek: The Life of St Meriasek*, ed. W. Stokes, 1872
Blanchminster's Charity	*Records of the Charity Known as Blanchminster's Charity*, ed. R. W. Goulding, Louth, 1898
Bodmin Register	*The Bodmin Register*, 1827–38
C 1	PRO, Chancery, Early Chancery Proceedings
C 3	PRO, Chancery, Chancery Proceedings, Series II
C 82	PRO, Chancery, Warrants for the Great Seal, Series II

CAB	EDCL, Chapter Act Books, 3551, 3552
CCB	DRO, Consistory Court Books, 41, 775, 776, 777, 778, 779, 854 (I, II), 854A (I, II), 855, 855A, 855B, 856
Certificates, Cornwall	*The Chantry Certificates for Cornwall*, ed. L. S. Snell, Exeter 1953
Certificates, Devon	*The Chantry Certificates for Devon and the City of Exeter*, ed. L. S. Snell, Exeter, 1961
Copy of a Letter	BL, Reading Room 3932 A 28, P. Nichols, *The Copy of a Letter*, 1547
CPR	*Calendar of the Patent Rolls, Edward VI*, 6 vols., 1924–9
CR Dartmouth	DRO, Corporation Records, Dartmouth
Cranmer	*Memorials of Archbishop Cranmer*, ed. J. Strype, 3 vols., Oxford, 1848–54
CSPD	*Calendar of State Papers, Domestic, Edward VI–James I*, ed. R. Lemon and M. A. E. Green, 12 vols., 1856–72
CWA Antony	Churchwardens' Accounts, Antony (transcript in possession of Mr F. L. Harris)
CWA Ashburton	*Churchwardens' Accounts of Ashburton, 1479–1580*, ed. A. Hanham, Devon and Cornwall Record Society, Torquay, 1970
CWA Bodmin	CRO, Churchwardens' Accounts, Bodmin
CWA Braunton	DRO, Churchwardens' Accounts, Braunton
CWA Broadhempston	DRO, Churchwardens' Accounts, Broadhempston (transcript)
CWA Camborne	CRO, Churchwardens' Accounts, Camborne
CWA Chagford	DRO, Churchwardens' Accounts, Chagford
CWA Chudleigh	DRO, Churchwardens' Accounts, Chudleigh
CWA Coldridge	DRO, Churchwardens' Accounts, Coldridge
CWA Crediton	DRO, Churchwardens' Accounts, Crediton
CWA Dartington	DCRSL, Churchwardens' Accounts, Dartington (transcript)
CWA Dartmouth	DRO, Churchwardens' Accounts, Dartmouth
CWA Exeter HT	DRO, Churchwardens' Accounts, Exeter Holy Trinity
CWA Exeter SJB	DRO, Churchwardens' Accounts, Exeter St John's Bow
CWA Exeter SMM	DRO, Churchwardens' Accounts, Exeter St Mary Major
CWA Exeter SMS	DRO, Churchwardens' Accounts, Exeter St Mary Steps
CWA Exeter SP	DRO, Churchwardens' Accounts, Exeter St Petrock
CWA Iddesleigh	DRO, Churchwardens' Accounts, Iddesleigh
CWA Kilmington	*The Churchwardens' Accounts of Kilmington, 1555– 1608*, ed. R. Cornish, Exeter, 1901
CWA Launceston	CRO, Churchwardens' Accounts, St Thomas-by-Launceston
CWA Modbury	DRO, Churchwardens' Accounts, Modbury
CWA Molland	'Molland Accounts', ed. J. Phear, *Transactions of the Devonshire Association*, 35, 1903
CWA Morebath	*The Accounts of the Wardens of the Parish of Morebath, 1520–73*, ed. J. E. Binney, Exeter, 1904

CWA N. Molton	DRO, Churchwardens' Accounts, North Molton (transcript)
CWA N. Petherwin	CRO, Churchwardens' Accounts, North Petherwin
CWA St Breock	CRO, Churchwardens' Accounts, St Breock
CWA S. Tawton	DCRSL, Churchwardens' Accounts, South Tawton (transcript)
CWA Winkleigh	DCRSL, Churchwardens' Accounts, Winkleigh (transcript)
CWA Woodbury	DRO, Churchwardens' Accounts, Woodbury
CWA Woodland	DRO, Churchwardens' Accounts, Woodland (transcript)
Dartmouth	*Dartmouth*, I, ed. H. R. Watkin, Torquay, 1935
'Description of Exeter'	DRO, Book 52, J. Hooker, 'The Description of the City of Exeter'
Documents of Church History	*Documents Illustrative of English Church History*, ed. H. Gee and W. J. Hardy, 1896
DRO 745C	DRO, 745C, Burial Service
DRO 1660 A 12	DRO, 1660 A 12, Church Inventory, Crediton
DRO Misc. Roll 95	DRO, Miscellaneous Roll 95, Part of Gospel
E 117	PRO, Exchequer, King's Remembrancer, Church Goods
E 134	PRO, Exchequer, King's Remembrancer, Depositions
E 135	PRO, Exchequer, King's Remembrancer, Ecclesiastical Documents
E 178	PRO, Exchequer, King's Remembrancer, Special Commissions of Inquiry
E 315	PRO, Exchequer, Augmentations, Miscellaneous Books
EDCL 2864, 2920, 3498, 3508	EDCL, Miscellaneous Documents
EHD	*English Historical Documents*, V, ed. C. H. Williams, 1967
English Church Furniture	*English Church Furniture, Ornaments and Decorations at the Period of the Reformation*, ed. E. Peacock, 1866
ER	DRO, Episcopal Registers XIII–XIX, Bishops Oldham, Veysey, Coverdale, Turberville, Alley
Exeter Records	*Report on the Records of the City of Exeter*, Historical Manuscripts Commission, 1916
Glastonbury Commonplace Book	TCCL, 0/9/38, Monk of Glastonbury, Commonplace Book
Godly New Story	BL, Reading Room 4404 B 61, P. Nichols, *A Godly New Story*, 1548
Grey Friars Chronicle	*The Chronicle of the Grey Friars of London*, ed. J. F. Nichols, Camden Society 53, 1852
Harleian 352	BL, Harleian MS 352, Privy Council Letter Book
Harleian 2252	BL, Harleian MS 2252, J. Colyn, Miscellaneous Collections
Harpsfield's Visitation	*Archdeacon Harpsfield's Visitation, 1557*, ed. L. E. Whatmore, Catholic Record Society, 2 vols., 1950–1
Hooker, Commonplace Book	DRO, Book 51, J. Hooker, Commonplace Book
Inventories, Cornwall	*The Edwardian Inventories of Church Goods for*

	Cornwall, ed. L. S. Snell, Exeter, 1956
Inventories, Exeter	*The Edwardian Inventories for the City and County of Exeter*, ed. B. F. Cresswell, 1916
Lansdowne 377	BL, Lansdowne MS 377, W. Ramsey, 'Epistle to the Moltonians'
Leland	*The Itinerary of John Leland in or about the years 1535–1543*, ed. L. Toulmin Smith, 5 vols., 1964
'Life of Carew'	J. Hooker, 'Life of Sir Peter Carew', in J. S. Brewer and W. Bullen, eds., *Calendar of the Carew Manuscripts Preserved in the Archiepiscopal Library at Lambeth, 1515–1574*, 1867
Lincoln Visitation	Diocese of Lincoln, Visitation Returns, in J. Strype, *Ecclesiastical Memorials*, Oxford, 1822, III (2), pp. 389–413
'Lives of Saints'	CUL, Additional MS 3041, N. Roscarrock, 'Lives of the Saints'
LP	*Letters and Papers, Foreign and Domestic, of the Reign of Henry VIII*, ed. J. S. Brewer, J. Gairdner and R. H. Brodie, 23 vols. in 38, 1862–1932
Moger	DRO, Moger Abstracts of Wills, 47 vols.
Murray	DCRSL, Oswyn Murray Abstracts of Wills, 39 vols.
Original Letters	*A Collection of Original Letters from the Bishops to the Privy Council, 1564*, ed. M. Bateson, Camden Society NS 53, 1895
Plymouth Records	*Calendar of Plymouth Municipal Records*, ed. R. N. Worth, Plymouth, 1893
Prayerbook of 1549	*Troubles Connected with the Prayerbook of 1549*, ed. N. Pocock, Camden Society NS 37, 1884
Privy Council Proceedings	*Proceedings and Ordinances of the Privy Council*, ed. H. Nicolas, 7 vols., 1834–7
PROB 11	PRO, Prerogative Court of Canterbury, Registered Copy Wills
Readings in European History	*Readings in European History*, ed. J. H. Robinson, 2 vols., Boston, Mass., 1906
Reformation in England	*The Reformation in England*, ed. A. G. Dickens and D. Carr, 1967
REQ 2	PRO, Court of Requests, Proceedings
Royal 18 B XI	BL, Royal MS 18 B XI, P. Nichols, 'An Answer to the Articles'
SP 1, 10, 11, 12, 15	PRO, State Papers, Henry VIII, General Series; State Papers Domestic, Edward VI, Philip and Mary, Elizabeth I, Addenda Edward VI–James I
STAC 1, 2, 3, 4	PRO, Star Chamber, Proceedings, Henry VII, Henry VIII, Edward VI, Philip and Mary
Stowe 141, 142	BL, Stowe MSS 141, 142, State Letters
Survey of Cornwall	R. Carew, *Survey of Cornwall*, 1811
'Synopsis Chorographical'	DRO, H783, J. Hooker, 'Synopsis Chorographical'

Tavistock Records	*Calendar of Tavistock Parish Records*, ed. R. N. Worth, Tavistock, 1887
Titus B 1	BL, Cotton MS Titus B 1, Instructions to the Council in the West Parts
TRP	*Tudor Royal Proclamations*, ed. P. L. Hughes and J. F. Larkin, 2 vols., New Haven, Conn., 1964–9
Tudor Parish Documents	*Tudor Parish Documents of the Diocese of York*, ed. J. Purvis, Cambridge, 1948
Worcestre	*William Worcestre, Itineraries*, ed. J. H. Harvey, Oxford, 1969
York Records	*York Civil Records*, ed. A. Raine, 8 vols., Yorkshire Archaeological Society, Wakefield, 1939–53
Zurich Letters	*The Zurich Letters, 1558–1579*, ed. H. Robinson, 2 vols., Cambridge, 1842–5

SECONDARY SOURCES

Alexander, G., 1987. 'Bonner and the Marian Persecutions', in C. Haigh, ed., *The English Reformation Revised*, Cambridge
Anderson, M. D., 1955. *The Imagery of British Churches*
Aveling, J. C. H., 1970. *Catholic Recusancy in the City of York, 1558–1791*
Boggis, R. J. E., 1922. *History of the Diocese of Exeter*, Exeter
Bond, F., 1908. *Fonts and Font Covers*
1910. *Wood Carvings in English Churches*, 2 vols., Oxford
Bond, F. B. and B. Camm, 1909. *Roodscreens and Roodlofts*, 2 vols.
Bossy, J. A., 1976. *The English Catholic Community, 1570–1850*
Bowker, M., 1981. *The Henrician Reformation: The Diocese of Lincoln under John Longland, 1521–47*, Cambridge
1987. 'The Henrician Reformation and the Parish Clergy'. in C. Haigh. ed., *The English Reformation Revised*, Cambridge, 1987
Caiger-Smith, A., 1963. *English Medieval Mural Paintings*, Oxford
Cave, C., 1948. *Roof Bosses in Medieval Churches*, Cambridge
Chanter, J. F., 1914. 'St Urith of Chittlehampton', *Transactions of the Devonshire Association*, 46
Clark, P., 1977. *English Provincial Society from the Reformation to the Revolution: Religion, Politics and Society in Kent, 1500–1640*, Hassocks
Collinson, P., 1967. *The Elizabethan Puritan Movement*
Cook, G., 1954. *The English Medieval Parish Church*
Cornwall, J., 1977. *Revolt of the Peasantry, 1549*
Cox, J. C., 1913. *Churchwardens' Accounts*
1915. *Pulpits, Lecterns, and Organs in English Churches*, Oxford
1916. *Bench-ends in English Churches*, Oxford
Cox, J. C. and C. B. Ford, 1943–4. *The Parish Churches of England*
Crabbe, W. R., 1854. *Some Account of the Monumental Brasses of Devon*, Exeter
Cressy, D., 1980. *Literacy and the Social Order: Reading and Writing in Tudor and Stuart England*, Cambridge
Cross, C., 1976. *Church and People, 1450–1660*, Hassocks
1979. 'Parochial Structure and the Dissemination of Protestantism in sixteenth-century England', in D. Baker, ed., *Studies in Church History*, 16, Oxford

1982. 'The Development of Protestantism in Leeds and Hull, 1520–1640', *Northern History*, 18

Davies, C. S. L., 1968. 'The Pilgrimage of Grace Reconsidered', *Past and Present*, 41

Davis, J. F., 1983. *Heresy and Reformation in the South-East of England*

Dickens, A. G., 1941. 'The First Stages of Romanist Recusancy in Yorkshire', *Yorkshire Archaeological Journal*, 35

1957. *The Marian Reaction in the Diocese of York*

1959. *Lollards and Protestants in the Diocese of York, 1509–1558*

1967A. *The English Reformation*, 1967

1967B. 'Secular and Religious Motivation in the Pilgrimage of Grace', in G. J. Cuming, ed., *Studies in Church History*, 4, Leiden

Dodds, M. H. and R. Dodds, 1915. *The Pilgrimage of Grace and the Exeter Conspiracy*, Cambridge

Dunkin, E. H. W., 1882. *The Monumental Brasses of Cornwall*

Ellacombe, H. T., 1872. *The Church Bells of Devon*, Exeter

Elliott-Binns, L. E., 1955. *Medieval Cornwall*

Elton, G. R., 1972. *Policy and Police: The Enforcement of the Reformation in the Age of Thomas Cromwell*, Cambridge

1977. *Reform and Reformation: England 1509–58*

Farmer, D. H., 1978. *The Oxford Dictionary of Saints*, Oxford

Field, C. W., 1973. 'The Province of Canterbury and the Elizabethan Settlement of Religion', unpublished typescript, York Minster Library

Finberg, H. P. R., 1951. *Tavistock Abbey*, Cambridge

Fletcher, A. J., 1973. *Tudor Rebellions*

Fowler, D., 1961. 'The Date of the Cornish *Ordinalia*', *Medieval Studies*, 23

Frere, W. H., 1896. *The Marian Reaction in its Relation to the English Clergy*

1904. *The English Church in the Reign of Elizabeth and James I*

Garrett, C. H., 1966. *The Marian Exiles*, Cambridge

Gowers, I. W., 1970. 'Puritanism in the County of Devon between 1570 and 1641', unpublished MA dissertation, Exeter University

Haigh, C., 1975. *Reformation and Resistance in Tudor Lancashire*, Cambridge

1987. *The English Reformation Revised*, Cambridge

Heal, F. and R. O'Day, eds., 1977. *Church and Society in England: Henry VIII to James I*

Heath, P., 1969. *The English Parish Clergy on the Eve of the Reformation*

Henderson, C., 1923–4. *Ecclesiastical History of the 109 Western Parishes of Cornwall*, Truro

1925. *Cornish Church Guide*, Truro

1935. *Essays in Cornish History*, Oxford

Hill, C., 1969. *Society and Puritanism in Pre-revolutionary England*

Hoskins, W. G., 1954. *Devon*

Houlbrooke, R., 1979. *Church Courts and the People during the English Reformation, 1520–70*, Oxford

Hughes, P., 1950–4. *The Reformation in England*, 3 vols.

Hutton, R., 1987. 'The Local Impact of the Tudor Reformations', in C. Haigh, ed., *The English Reformation Revised*, Cambridge

James, M. E., 1970. 'Obedience and Dissent in Henrician England', *Past and Present*, 48

1973. 'The Concept of Order and the Northern Rising, 1569', *Past and Present*, 60

James, M. R., 1901–2. 'St Urith of Chittlehampton', *Cambridge Antiquarian Society Proceedings*

Jordan, W. K., 1959. *Philanthropy in England, 1480–1660*

   1960A. *The charities of London, 1480–1660*

   1960B. *The Forming of the Charitable Institutions of the West of England*, American Philosophical Society, NS 50

   1961A. *The Charities of Rural England, 1480–1660*

   1961B. *Social Institutions in Kent, 1480–1660*, Archaeologia Cantiana, 75

   1962. *The Social Institutions of Lancashire*, Chetham Society, Manchester

Kreider, A., 1979. *English Chantries: The Road to Dissolution*

Lander, S., 1987. 'Church Courts and the Reformation in the Diocese of Chichester, 1500–58', in C. Haigh, ed., *The English Reformation Revised*, Cambridge

Loades, D. M., 1965. *Two Tudor Conspiracies*, Cambridge

   1970. *The Oxford Martyrs*

MacCaffrey, W., 1958. *Exeter, 1540—1640*, Cambridge, Mass.

McGrath, P., 1967. *Papists and Puritans under Elizabeth I*

Maclean, J., 1870. *Parochial and Family History of the Parish and Borough of Bodmin*

Manning, R. B., 1969. *Religion and Society in Elizabethan Sussex*, Leicester

Mayhew, G. J., 1983. 'The Progress of the Reformation in East Sussex, 1530–1559: The Evidence from Wills', *Southern History*, 5

Maynard-Smith, H., 1963. *Pre-Reformation England*

Mozley J., 1940. *John Foxe and his Book*

Mumford, A., 1936. *Hugh Oldham, 1452–1519*

Nelson, P., 1913. *Ancient Painted Glass in England, 1170–1500*

Oliver, G., 1857. *Collections, Illustrating the History of the Catholic Religion*

   1861. *Lives of the Bishops of Exeter*

Orme, N., 1976. *Education in the West of England, 1066–1548*, Exeter

Owst, G., 1933. *Literature and Pulpit in Medieval England*, Cambridge

Oxley, J. E., 1965. *The Reformation in Essex*, Manchester

Palliser, D. M., 1971. *The Reformation in York*, York

   1979. *Tudor York*, Oxford

Peter, R. and O. Peter, 1885. *The Histories of Launceston and Dunheved*, Plymouth

Pevsner, N., 1952A. *The Buildings of England: North Devon*, Harmondsworth

   1952B. *The Buildings of England: South Devon*, Harmondsworth

Pevsner, N. and E. Radcliffe, 1970. *The Buildings of England: Cornwall*, Harmondsworth

Phelps Brown, E. H. and S. V. Hopkins, 1956. 'Seven Centuries of the Prices of Consumables', *Economica*, November

Phillips, J., 1973. *The Reformation of Images*, Berkeley

Pill, D. H., 1963. 'The Diocese of Exeter under Bishop Veysey', unpublished MA dissertation, Exeter University

   1968. 'Exeter Diocesan Courts in the Early Sixteenth Century', *Transactions of the Devonshire Association*, 100

Platt, C., 1981. *The Parish Churches of Medieval England*

Porter, H., 1958. *Reformation and Reaction in Tudor Cambridge*, Cambridge

Powell, K. G., 1969. 'The Beginnings of Protestantism in Gloucestershire', *Transactions of the Bristol and Gloucestershire Archaeological Society*, 90

   1972. *The Marian Martyrs and the Reformation in Bristol*, Bristol

Prince, J., 1701. *Worthies of Devon*, Exeter

Radford, U. M., 1949. 'The Wax Images Found in Exeter Cathedral', *The Antiquaries' Journal*, 29

'R.B.M.', 1928–9. 'Devon clergy in 1561', *Devon and Cornwall Notes and Queries*, 15

Reid, R., 1906. 'The Rebellion of the Earls, 1569', *Transactions of the Royal Historical Society*, 20

Risdon, T., 1811. *The Chorographical Description or Survey of the County of Devon*

Roberts, J., 1962–4. 'A Group of Elizabethan Puritans', *Devon and Cornwall Notes and Queries*, 29

Rogers, W., 1877. *The Ancient Sepulchral Effigies and Monumental and Memorial Sculpture of Devon*, Exeter

Rose-Troup, F., 1913. *The Western Rebellion of 1549*

Rowse, A. L., 1941. *Tudor Cornwall*
    1955. 'Nicholas Roscarrock and his Lives of the Saints', in J. H. Plumb, ed., *Studies in Social History*

Rushforth, G. M., 1927A. 'The Kirkham Monument in Paignton Church', *Exeter Diocesan Architectural and Archaeological Society Transactions*, 15
    1927B. 'The Windows of the Church of St Neot, Cornwall', *Exeter Diocesan Architectural and Archaeological Society Transactions*, 15

Russell, F. W., 1859. *Kett's Rebellion in Norfolk*

Scarisbrick, J., 1971. *Henry VIII*, Harmondsworth
    1984. *The Reformation and the English People*, Oxford

Scheurweghs, G., 1933—4. 'On an Answer to the Articles of the Rebels of Cornwall and Devonshire', *The British Museum Quarterly*, 8

Sharp, C., 1975. *The 1569 Rebellion*, Durham

Shiels, W. J., 1979. *The Puritans in the Diocese of Peterborough, 1558–1610*, Northamptonshire Record Society

Slader, J., 1968. *The Churches of Devon*, Newton Abbot

Smith, J. C. D., 1969. *Church Woodcarvings: A West Country Study*, Newton Abbot

Snell, L. S., 1967. *The Suppression of the Religious Foundations of Devon and Cornwall*, Marazion

Stabb, J., 1909—16. *Some Old Devon Churches*, 3 vols.

Thomas, K., 1971. *Religion and the Decline of Magic*

Thompson, C. H., 1934—5. 'Chantry Priests at Plymouth', *Devon and Cornwall Notes and Queries*, 18

Thomson, J. A. F., 1965A. *The Later Lollards, 1414–1520*
    1965B. 'Piety and Charity in Late-medieval London', *Journal of Ecclesiastical History*, 16

Trimble, W. R., 1964. *The Catholic Laity in Elizabethan England, 1558–1603*, Cambridge, Mass.

Westcote, T., 1845. *A View of Devonshire in 1630*, Exeter

Whiting, R., 1977. 'The Reformation in the South-West of England', unpublished PhD thesis, Exeter University
    1982. 'Abominable Idols: Images and Image-breaking under Henry VIII', *Journal of Ecclesiastical History*, 33
    1983. 'For the Health of my Soul: Prayers for the Dead in the Tudor South-West', *Southern History*, 5

Woodward, G. W. O., 1966. *The Dissolution of the Monasteries*

Youings, J. A., 1971. *The Dissolution of the Monasteries*
    1979. 'The South-Western Rebellion of 1549', *Southern History*, 1

INDEX

Creed, 31
Crewern, St, 59
Cromwell, Thomas, 1, 117, 123–4, 162, 184, 229–30, 233, 242, 244–5, 256
Cruwys Morchard, 87
Cubert, 58, 239
Cullompton, 9, 11, 19–20, 30, 37, 48–9, 53, 70, 86–7, 89–90, 93, 109, 120, 146, 181, 207, 212, 237, 249
Culmstock, 22, 157, 159
Cury, 94

Daniel, Nicholas, 231, 247–9, 257
Dartington, 5, 39, 42, 44, 69, 79–80, 82, 95, 112, 183, 192–3, 208–9, 237
Dartmouth, 5, 12, 17, 19, 22–3, 27, 40–1, 57, 65, 69, 73, 79, 89, 91–2, 95, 110, 114–15, 156, 160, 165, 173, 180, 190–2, 194, 197–8, 207, 209, 218, 230, 236–43, 250, 260
Davidstow, 28, 31, 146, 176, 178–9, 216
Dawe, John, 52, 183
Dawlish, 29, 130
Dean Prior, 103, 139, 255
Debble, John, 137, 168–9
Denbury, 33
Dennis family, 10, 12–13, 221–2, 224, 227, 230, 256
Derwa, St, 69
desks, 159, 191–2
Dinan, 59
Dittisham, 132–3, 137, 237
Doddiscombsleigh, 17–18, 138, 203, 209, 220
Dowland, 94, 205–6, 242
Down St Mary, 18, 33, 121, 133, 134
Dowrish family, 212, 250
Drake, John, 36, 156–7, 212, 260
drama, *see* plays
Drewe, Richard, 31, 176
Duffield, Bernard, 29, 144
Duloe, 29, 143
Dunkeswell, 119
Dynham family, 76, 242, 256

East Allington, 95, 205, 207, 210, 241
East Budleigh, 28, 180, 205, 206, 242
East Down, 26, 95
East Newlyn, 27, 58, 74, 76, 181, 239, 241, 243, 244
East Portlemouth, 90
Easter vigils, 2, 18, 33, 38, 41, 44
economic motivation, 175–83, 226, 256, 265
Edgcumbe family, 12, 184, 221–2, 229, 256
education, 198, 227–8, 232–7, 257–8
Egloshayle, 136, 166, 167, 232, 237

Elidius, St, 73
Eligius, St, 50, 51, 72, 78, 107, 110
Eliot, John, 117, 162, 260
Eliot, Robert, 100, 181
Ellis, John, 29, 100
Elwen, St, 59
employers, 215
Endellion, St, 55, 57, 59, 73
Engleborne, 122
Ennis family, 58, 92, 120, 121
episcopacy, 115, 126, 259
Erasmus, St, 49–50
Erasmus, *see Paraphrases* (Erasmus)
Ermington, 6, 32, 69, 181, 249
Essex, 265
excommunication, 126, 140–1, 183–4
Exeter, 4–5, 8–11, 13–14, 20, 23, 28, 31, 35–40, 42, 44–6, 59–60, 62, 70–1, 76, 80, 95, 105, 107, 114, 116–17, 119, 121–3, 125–6, 128–9, 131, 135, 139, 141–2, 146–7, 152–3, 156, 158–62, 164–6, 168–70, 172–3, 175–7, 181–2, 184–6, 188–90, 192–3, 196–8, 203–5, 211–19, 223, 226, 228–32, 235–6, 240–1, 243, 245, 247, 249–50, 252–7, 260
    Allhallows, 27, 93, 176, 241
    Cathedral, 10, 13, 18, 31, 48, 53, 56, 58–9, 61–2, 64, 66, 73–5, 78, 80, 113, 115, 126, 138–42, 153, 162, 189, 192, 208, 217, 219, 224–5, 228, 231, 233, 237, 239–45, 247, 249–50, 254–5, 257
    Holy Trinity, 5, 27, 40, 65, 68–9, 77, 92, 96, 99, 115, 158–9, 191, 208
    St David, 29
    St Edmund, 29, 103
    St George, 27
    St John's Bow, 5, 26–8, 40, 42, 45, 49–50, 65, 69, 77, 79, 95–6, 99, 103–4, 109, 112, 115, 158, 190–2, 208–9, 247
    St Kerrian, 27, 31, 93
    St Lawrence, 77, 208
    St Martin, 31, 102
    St Mary Arches, 27, 70, 77
    St Mary Major, 21–2, 28, 39, 44–5, 51, 79–80, 92, 159, 191, 239–40, 245, 247–8, 255, 257
    St Mary Steps, 5, 40, 44, 65, 68–9, 82, 92, 96, 99, 112, 115, 190, 193, 208–9, 241
    St Nicholas' Priory, 75, 118–20, 123, 125, 147, 185, 216–17, 221, 228
    St Olave, 27, 191, 241
    St Pancras, 27, 29
    St Petrock, 5, 20, 22, 25–7, 33, 40–3, 45, 65, 68–9, 77–81, 87, 96–7, 99, 112, 114, 119, 129, 190–3, 206, 208–9, 212, 232, 241